Footprint **Wales**

Rebecca Ford
1st edition

D0711538

"Brooded over by mist more often than swirled about by cloud, drizzled rather than storm-swept, on the western perimeter of Europe lies the damp, demanding and obsessively interesting country called by its own people Cymru and known to the rest of the world, if it is known at all, as Wales"

Jan Morris

Wales Highlights

See colour maps at back of book

❶ Cardiff
The cool Welsh capital is a must on any visit

❷ Museum of Welsh Life
Step back in time in this stunning outdoor museum

❸ Mumbles Mile
Dine out in this Victorian seaside resort, with its fine array of pubs and restaurants

❹ Gower Peninsula
Rightly famed for its great beaches

❺ Carreg Cennen Castle
Spectacular views at one of the most dramatic castles in Wales

❻ National Botanic Garden of Wales
Not just for the green-fingered. Rare plants, healing herbs and strangely shaped vegetables

❼ Dylan Thomas Boathouse in Laugharne
Inspirational home of the Welsh national poet

❽ Pembrokeshire Coast
Spectacular coastline traversed by an 87-mile path

❾ St David's Cathedral
The religous heart of Wales in a gloriously tranquil setting

Holyhead/Caergybi

Anglesey

Holy Island

Menai Bridge

Bangor

Caernarfon

Caernafon Bay

❶❶▲ Snowdon (1,085m)

Llŷn Peninsula

❶❷

Portmeirion

❶❶ Pwllheli

Harlech

Llanbedrog

❶❸

Bardsey Island

Barmouth

N

0 km   10
0 miles   10

Irish Sea

Aberystwyth

Aberaeron
New Quay

Cardigan/Aberteifi

Lampeter

Fishguard/Abergwaun

Newcastle Emlyn

Preseli Hills

Llandeilo

St Davids

Pembrokeshire Coast National Park

Carmarthen/Caerfyrddin

Ramsey Island

❾

Haverfordwest/Hwlddordd

❻

St Brides Bay

St Clears/Sanclêr

❼

❽ Milford Haven/Aberdaugleddau

Llanelli

Pembroke

Tenby/Dinbych-y-Psygod

Swansea Abertaw

❹ Gower

❸

⑩ Llŷn Peninsula
Wild, western finger etched with secret beaches

⑪ Snowdon
Take the mountain railway or walk to the top...

⑫ Portmeirion
Colourful, eccentric architecture in this dreamlike village

⑬ Harlech Castle
Impressive seaside setting for this ancient fortress

⑭ Centre for Alternative Technology
The cutting edge of green science

⑮ Red kite feeding
Close encounters of the feathered kind

⑯ Hay on Wye
This pretty little border town is the word capital of secondhand books

⑰ Brecon Beacons
Get outdoors and active in this rugged National Park

⑱ Big Pit
Travel deep into the heart of a Valleys' coal mine

⑲ Tintern Abbey
Romantic ruin that inspired poets and painters

⑳ Abergwseyn Pass
Explore the wild beauty of this stunning unspoilt landscape

Old meets new
Hemmed in by modern buildings, Swansea Castle is a visible reminder of Wales' turbulent history, with more castles per square mile than any other country in Western Europe.

A foot in the door

Wales is a deliciously complicated country – a Celtic cauldron where history and mythology, music and language, religion and radicalism, and gloom and good humour have simmered away for centuries, creating a distinctive cultural brew that has produced Merlin the magician and the Manic Street Preachers.

It's a culture that has proved remarkably durable: attempts to suppress it date back to Roman times and as recently as the 20th-century Welsh children were banned from speaking their own language. For hundreds of years, Wales has been dominated by it's larger, more powerful neighbour – England, yet both culture and language have managed to survive. Frequently overlooked by visitors to Britain, the country suffers from a remarkable level of international anonymity (the EU even managed to leave if off a recent map, sinking it under the Irish Sea). However, this has its advantages as any trip here offers a real sense of discovery.

Those that are aware of Wales tend to view it as a series of outdated stereotypes – a land of male voice choirs, coal blackened valleys, chilly chapels, insular attitudes, overcooked leeks and stovepipe hats. What they'll find is a rapidly changing country with a youthful, energetic capital, a vibrant culture, a clutch of contemporary hotels and trendy gastro pubs, and a buzzing range of high octane sports such as kite surfing, coasteering and mountain biking. The long standing inferiority complex is being replaced by an outward-looking confidence.

Of course some things don't change. The country's history is still evident in every castle and chapel; love of music, poetry – and beer is undiminished, and rugby is inspiring greater passions than it has for years. But while some grumble that they 'don't want to be cool' it looks like the new Cymru is well on its way.

6

1   *Life on the Brecon and Monmouthshire Canal is a world away from the fast pace of the city.* ▸▸ *See page 113.*

2   *The cantilever rock near the summit of Glyder Fach in Snowdonia is a favourite spot for photos and a cup of tea.* ▸▸ *See page 188.*

3   *Grey seals bask in the clear waters of Skomer Island in Pembrokeshire.* ▸▸ *See page 143.*

4   *Coasteering, a combination of rock climbing, scrambling and swimming, was invented in Wales.* ▸▸ *See page 48.*

5   *Make a pilgrimage to visit the shrine of St David in Britain's smallest city.* ▸▸ *See page 141.*

6   *One of the largest beaches on the Gower Peninsula, Rhossili Bay is popular for its surf, sand and sunsets.* ▸▸ *See page 120.*

7   *Meet the residents of Puffin island, near Anglesey, an excellent spot for bird-watching.* ▸▸ *See page 202.*

8   *The Great Barrier Reef it isn't, but the World Bog Snorkelling Championships is one of Wales' more eccentric festivals.* ▸▸ *See page 42.*

9   *Experience the romantic beauty of Tintern Abbey, the inspiration of poets, artists and winemakers.* ▸▸ *See page 101.*

10 *The colourful beach huts at Llanbedrog on the Llyn, also home to one of the best arts centres in the country.* ▸▸ *See page 205.*

11 *Cardiff Bay: the new Wales Millennium Centre looms behind the rosy Pierhead Building.* ▸▸ *See page 60.*

12 *Facing the Atlantic and with miles of unspoilt coast, Wales is popular with surfers.* ▸▸ *See page 49.*

Mountains and valleys
Just south of Beddgelert, the beautiful Aberglaslyn Pass makes for a dramatic approach to Snowdonia. Keep an eye on the weather, conditions can turn on a penny, even at low altitude.

Cool Cymru

For years Wales was always the poor Celtic relation in the British Isles. Ireland and Scotland were seen as cool, edgy countries with strong identities, romantic histories and thriving contemporary music, literature and arts scenes. Outsiders were always keen to grab a bit of reflected Celtic glory by claiming Scottish or Irish blood. Even Cornwall, though submerged into England, retained its romantic identity, and was the coastal playground of tanned surfers and the smart Chelsea set.

Wales, however, although it had a rich history, great scenery and a strong identity, just never seemed cool. The Welsh seemed to be acceptable targets for public insult and the country was always perceived as backward looking and rain sodden. It just wasn't sexy.

Now, at last, it's fighting back. In music it has produced performers such as Cerys Mathews, who fronted Catatonia, Charlotte Church, and Katherine Jenkins, the hot opera diva. There are young writers like Owen Sheers and actors like Ioan Gruffudd, Rhys Ifans and Catherine Zeta Jones. Surfers have discovered the stunning beaches, Cardiff has thrown off its industrial past and reinvented itself as a 21st-century capital, and the new Welsh Assembly building looks set to open on time and more or less within budget – something the Scottish Parliament didn't manage.

A nation divided

Wales, like England and Scotland, is no homogeneous whole. The most obvious divisions are between the north and the south. Not only is the landscape of the north more mountainous, rural and rugged than that of the softer, industrialized south, but the people tend to have more traditional attitudes and be more resistant to change. The greatest concentration of Welsh speakers are in the north west, around Anglesey and the Llŷn Peninsular, while Cardiff – which is more easily reached from England than much of north Wales – is often seen as anglicized and remote. There are also divisions on linguistic lines: the majority of Welsh people do not speak Welsh and some are still resistant to learning the language. And not surprisingly the east, which borders England and is green and pastoral, is very different to the Welsh-speaking coastal fringes of the west.

Compact charms

Wales may be small but it packs in an extraordinary variety of landscapes: rugged peaks in Snowdonia; moody mudflats on the Carmarthenshire coast; pretty villages in Glamorgan; mighty fortresses like Caernarfon and Harlech. The windswept Brecon Beacons offer adventurous outdoor activities, as do the picturesque coastlines of Pembrokeshire and the Gower, and the walking possibilities are endless. Then there are the lush green valleys, thundering waterfalls, isolated moorlands and bustling market towns – all this in a country that some people never even bother to visit.

Contents

Essentials

⁞ Footprint features

Planning your trip

Where to go

Wales might be a small country but there's a lot to see and do. The landscape encompasses everything from craggy mountains to isolated beaches; there are scores of cultural treasures including some magnificent medieval castles; and opportunities for activities range from coasteering to pony trekking. Allow yourself time to explore – not just because the slower pace of life is such a delightful feature of the country, but also because the mountain ranges make getting around a slow process, even though the roads are pretty good.

Away from the towns, exploring is easiest by car, as rural buses are infrequent and trains can be expensive and only cover the major routes. If you have sufficient time try to explore the lesser known corners; Wales' beauty lies in its wild countryside; finding a deserted sandy beach or a sleepy green valley is what it's all about.

One week

Cardiff, the capital, is the obvious place to start any trip to Wales and is easily reached by train from London, or by plane from some British regional airports. Once an industrial centre that grew rich on the coal trade, Cardiff's now one of the fastest developing cities in Britain and a thriving centre for the arts and culture in Wales. The shops are great, there's a good museum and art gallery and a wacky castle, and the glossy new Bay is crammed with waterfront bars and restaurants. From Cardiff you can travel north to the wilds of the Brecon Beacons National Park, a great place for those who like to get active; make a day trip to Hay-on-Wye to browse its famous bookshops; or go a short way along the coast to check out the surf on the Gower Peninsula. From there it's not far to sleepy Laugharne, a 'must see' spot for literature lovers as it was the home of Welsh poet Dylan Thomas. You'll have time, too, to head west to visit the undoubted jewel in the Welsh crown, the spectacular Pembrokeshire coast, home to St David's cathedral, soft sandy beaches and dramatic clifftops.

Two weeks

With two weeks to spare you can take in North Wales as well, with the striking scenery of the rugged Snowdonia National Park. You could easily fill your days here just walking or cycling, but make sure you don't miss places like the pretty village of Beddgelert, or some of the north's coastal treasures like Conwy or Caernarfon castles. You're close to the timeless Llŷn Peninsula, birthplace of the great Welsh statesman David Lloyd George, and also to the extraordinary village of Portmeirion which looks as if it was conceived in a colourful dream. You should make time for a trip on one of Wales' fine restored steam railways, too. If you're a history lover, take a trip over the Menai Bridge to Anglesey, the pastoral island that is crammed with Neolithic sites and which was the last outpost of the Druids.

One month

You can really explore Wales' hidden corners in a full month. Far to the north are sights like the grand old Victorian resort of Llandudno where Alice Liddell, immortalized by Lewis Carroll as *Alice in Wonderland*, used to holiday with her parents. You could also visit the tiny cathedral of St Asaph, rambling Bodelwyddan Castle, the ancient pilgrimage site of Holywell and the pretty town of Ruthin. Don't forget the unspoilt reaches of Mid Wales either, where you can watch red kites swooping down to feed, explore fine castles such as Powis, and go for long walks where you need never meet

another soul. If you head west you can explore the southern part of the Snowdonia
National Park and visit gorgeous Harlech with its dramatic castle and endless stretch of golden sand. You can come over all new-agey in Machynlleth, the green capital of Wales and the home of the Centre for Alternative Technology. A bit further south, along the coast, are pretty villages like Aberaeron and New Quay. Don't miss the chance to watch the wildlife on one of the many dolphin-watching trips.

A month will also give you time to see some of the most remote parts of Carmarthenshire, which offer a real taste of wild Wales, with crumbling castles, lush gardens, and history packed into every rock and stone. Then there's bustling Swansea, which has a new waterfront museum; the endearing and enduring resort of Tenby; the distinctive Valleys with their fascinating industrial heritage and, on the border with England, the picturesque ruins of Tintern Abbey.

When to go

The high season runs from April until October, when most attractions are open and summer festivities are organized in almost every town and village. Summer evenings are long, while in winter it can get dark as early as 1600. School holidays (most of July and August) are the busiest time of year, when the most popular tourist destinations, such as the Pembroke Coast, are really best avoided altogether. The best accommodation anywhere in the countryside must be booked well in advance for the summer months. Cardiff and other main cities don't really have a tourist season as such, which makes them an excellent alternative in the autumn and winter months (September to March). That said, many of Wales' seaside hotspots are also best appreciated once the weather's turned nasty or even in clear winter sunlight.

Climate

The Welsh temperate climate is notoriously unpredictable. Bright, sunny mornings can turn into a downpour in the time it takes to butter your toast. Predicting the weather is not an exact science and tables of statistics are most likely a waste of time. Very generally, the mountains receive more rain than the coast and October to January are the wettest months. Winters can be pretty harsh, especially in the mountains, making hiking conditions treacherous. May to September are the warmest months (in particular July and August), but you can expect rain at any time of the year, even in high summer. So, you'll need to come prepared, and remember the old hikers' adage that there's no such thing as bad weather, only inadequate clothing.

Tour operators

There are many companies offering general interest or special interest tours of Wales. Travel agents will have details, or you can check the small advertisements in the travel sections of newspapers, or contact the British Tourist Authority or the Welsh Tourist Board (see Finding out more, page 14) for a full list of operators.

General sightseeing tours

British Travel, T0800 3276097, www.british travel.com. Information on travel and accommodation throughout the UK.
Celtic Trails, T0800 9707585, www.walking wales.co.uk. Walking holidays with baggage transfer service.

Exodus Travels, T020 87723882, www.exodus.co.uk. London-based company offering a wide variety of specialist holidays.
Freedom Caravan Holiday Homes & Touring Parks, T0870 7403914, www.freedomhols.co.uk. Guide to caravanning and touring, with ratings and facilities for British parks.

Home at First, www.homeatfirst.com. Independent tours providing 'all the comfort of home'. Aimed at the over-50s.

Insight, T01475 741203, www.insight vacations.com. Escorted coach holidays.

Saga Holidays, T0800 300500, www.saga holidays.com. A British company with tours aimed at the mature traveller.

Shearings Holidays, T01942 244246, www.shearingsholidays.com. Coach or rail based holidays for the over-50s.

Wallace Arnold, T0113 2634234, www.wallacearnold.com. One of the pioneers of coach holiday travel. Branches all over the UK; also in Canada and Australia.

In the USA

Cross-Culture, 52 High Point Dr, Amherst MA01002-1224, T1-800 4911148, www.crosscultureinc.com. All-inclusive, small-group travel programs.

Especially Britain, T1-800-8690538, www.expresspages.com/e/especiallybritain. Independent fly-drive or rail tours, with a range of accommodation, including B&Bs and country houses.

Saga Holidays, 222 Berkeley St, Boston, MA 02116, www.sagaholidays.com. For the mature traveller.

In Australia and New Zealand

Adventure Specialists, 69 Liverpool St, Sydney, T02-92612927, www.total travel.com. Plenty of information and resources for booking your trip.

Adventure Travel Company, 164 Parnell Rd, Parnell, East Auckland, T09-3799755. New Zealand agents for Peregrine Adventures (below).

Peregrine Adventures, 258 Lonsdale St, Melbourne, T03-96638611, www.peregrine.net.au. Also has branches in Brisbane, Sydney, Adelaide and Perth.

Saga Holidays, 10-14 Paul St, Milsons Point, Sydney 2061, www.sagaholidays.com. For the mature traveller.

Backpackers and adventure tours

Many of these offer minibus tours with jump-on/jump-off services and activities.

Adventure Wales, T0845 3308584, www.adventure-wales.co.uk. Online directory of activity and adventure centres.

Bus Wales, T01446 774652, www.bus wales.co.uk. Tours for independent travellers all over the country.

Bushwakkers, T01874 636552, www.bush wakkers.co.uk. Adventure weekends, including canoeing, horse riding or fishing.

Contiki, www.contiki.com. Budget tours aimed at 18-35 year olds.

Dragon Backpacker Tours, T01874 658124, www.dragonbackpackertours.co.uk. Off the beaten track travel throughout Wales.

Haggis Tours, T0131 5579393, www.radical travel.com. Small group, guided tours throughout Wales.

Road Trip, T0845 2006791, www.road trip.co.uk. Variety of weekly tours from 5-9 days for around £130.

Shaggy Sheep, T01267 281202, www.shaggysheep.co.uk. Packaged tours for independent backpackers with weekend and jump-on/jump-off service.

www.uktrail.com A good resource for bus, walking, cycling and adventure tours, designed for budget and adventure travellers. The site also has information on accommodation.

Ecotourism

See also Volunteer work, p16, for eco-opportunities throughout Wales.

Countrywise, www.thingstodo.org.uk, www.foc.or.guk. David Bellamy promotes sustainable tourism in Wales. The website lists ideas for 'green' things to do.

Greenways Holidays, T01834 862109, www.holidays-in-wales.com. Specialists in the Pembrokeshire area and 'green' tourism.

Finding out more

A good way to find out more before your trip is to contact the **British Tourist Authority** (BTA), who represent the **Wales Tourist Board** (WTB) abroad. Their website, www.bta.org.uk or www.visitwales.com, is very useful as a first-stop directory for accommodation. Alternatively, you can write to the head office at Brunel House,

2 Fitzalan Road, Cardiff, CF24 4QZ. Both organizations provide a wealth of free literature and information such as maps, city guides, events calendars and accommodation brochures. Travellers with special needs should also contact their nearest BTA office (see below). For more detailed information on a particular area, contact the area tourist boards. **Tourist Information Centres** (TICs) exist in most Welsh towns and **National Park Information Centres** area good source of information for outdoor activities such as walking. Details are provided in the Ins and Outs section at the beginning of each area.

British Tourist Authorities overseas

Information can be obtained from the British Tourist Authority website, www.bta.org.uk, or from the offices listed below:
Australia Level 16, The Gateway, 1 Macquarie Pl, Circular Quay, Sydney NSW 2000, T02-93774400. **Belgium and Luxembourg** 306 Av Louise, 1050 Brussels, T2-6463510. **Canada** 111 Avenue Rd, Suite 450, Toronto, Ontario MR5 3J8, T416-9256326. **Denmark** Montergade 3, 1116 Copenhagen K, T33-339188. **France** Maison de la Grande-Bretagne, 19 Rue des Mathurins, 75009 Paris, T1-44515620. **Germany**, Austria and Switzerland Taunustrasse 52-60, 60329 Frankfurt, T69-2380711. **Ireland** 18/19 College Green, Dublin 2, T1-6708000. **Italy** Corso Vittorio Emanuele II No 337, 00186 Rome, T6-68806821. **Netherlands** Stadhouderskade 2 (5e), 1054 ES Amsterdam, T20-6855051. **New Zealand** 17th Floor, Fay Richwhite Building, 151 Queen St, Auckland 1, T09-3031446. **South Africa** Lancaster Gate, Hyde Park Lane, Hyde Park 2196, Johannesburg, T011-3250342. **USA** 7th Flr, 551 Fifth Av, New York, NY 10176-0799, T212-986-2200/ 1-800-GO-2-BRITAIN; 10880 Wilshire Blvd, Suite 570, Los Angeles, CA 90024, T310-4702782.

Useful websites

The official Welsh Tourist Board site and the various area tourist board sites have information on accommodation, transport and tourist sites as well as outdoor activities such as walking, skiing and fishing. Other useful websites include:

Travel and leisure
www.aboutbritain.com Useful links for accommodation and travel.
www.aboutwales.co.uk An encyclopaedia of information about Wales.

www.britannia.com A huge UK travel site. Click on 'Wales guide' for a massive selection of subjects plus links to various sites including newspapers.
www.bbc.co.uk The UK's most popular site with an excellent what's on guide.
www.data-wales.co.uk A wealth of facts and information on everything from festivals to pronunciation of Welsh names.
www.whatsonwhen.com Has a huge range of upcoming events around the world.
www.uktrail.com Provides comprehensive information on transport and hostels.
www.visitbritain.com Practical informative site with useful links and ideas.

Outdoors
See also, Sports and activities, p45.
www.ccw.gov.uk The Countryside Council for Wales provides information on nature reserves and walking and riding paths.
www.cycling.visitwales.com Excellent site for touring or mountain biking; even shows how steep the climbs are.
www.goodbeachguide.co.uk How to check your kid won't be bathing in sewage. Lists facilities and activities for over 400 recommended UK beaches. See also box, Blue Flag beaches, p48.
www.sustrains.org.uk Official site of the charity that coordinates the National Cycle Network. With a clickable, zoom-in map.
www.walkingworld.com Perhaps the best directory of British walks, although you have to pay to download their detailed maps.

History, politics and culture
www.cadw.wales.gov.uk See also p29. Historic environment agency, responsible for the protection of historic buildings, ancient monuments, historic parks and gardens, landscapes and underwater archaeology throughout Wales.
www.castlewales.com Information and links to over 400 castles throughout Wales.

www.homecomingwales.com/choirs
Information on Welsh choirs throughout the country. Also has general information and a section on tracing your Welsh family.
www.nationaltrust.co.uk Works to protect threatened coastline, countryside and buildings throughout the UK, improving public access and facilities.

Volunteer work
www.btcv.org.uk The British Trust for Conservation Volunteers provides volunteer opportunities, themed events and activities throughout the year.
www.cat.org.uk The Centre for Alternative Technology (see p158) relies on volunteers to keep the centre running.
www.rspb.org.uk The Royal Society for the Protection of Birds is a UK charity working to secure a healthy environment for birds and wildlife; volunteer opportunities.
www.wwoof.org Willing Workers on Organic Farms, volunteer opportunities for those interested in the organic movement.

Language

Wales is officially bilingual and as soon as you enter the country you will be aware of this, with road signs and place names appearing in both Welsh and English. *Cymraeg*, as the language is known in Welsh, is spoken by around 500,000 people and is closely related to other Celtic languages like Breton and Cornish. The language has its heartlands in the north and west, particularly in places like Anglesey, the Llŷn Peninsula, Caernarfon and parts of Cardiganshire and Carmarthenshire; you're less likely to hear it in the capital Cardiff or in towns and villages along the border. For many people it is their mother tongue and you will have plenty of opportunities to hear this ancient language (probably the oldest in Europe) spoken. The language has received plenty of support, unlike Cornish which has been shamefully neglected. There is a Welsh language television station S4C (Sianel Pedwar Cymru): established in 1982 it broadcasts for several hours in Welsh each day. Shows include the long running BBC Welsh soap *Pobol y Cwm* or 'People of the Valley', set in the fictional village of Cwmderi. The digital S4C2 channel shows the proceedings of the Welsh Assembly, and viewers can choose to watch in English or Welsh. Welsh language radio includes the BBC's Radio Cymru and a number of commercial stations such as Radio Ceredigion, which is bilingual. More information on the BBC services at www.bbc.co.uk/cymru.

Welsh language courses

There are several websites with information on summer courses and evening classes in Welsh, such as www.acen.co.uk and www.coleg. powys.ac.uk. There are also some online language sites, including www.cs.cf.ac.uk. Also try contacting:

Cardiff Language Academy, Oliver House, 16/17 High St, Cardiff, T02920 226047, www.cardifflanguageacademy.com.
Ceredigion Language Centre, T01545 572703, www.ceredigion.gov.uk.
Welsh Language Society, T01970 624501, www.cymdeithas.com. Based in Aberystwyth.

Disabled travellers

For travellers with disabilities, visiting Wales independently can be a difficult business. While most theatres, cinemas and modern tourist attractions are accessible to wheelchairs, accommodation can be more problematic. Most large, new hotels do have disabled suites, but many B&Bs, guesthouses and smaller hotels are not

● "I think my instinct will always be through the Welsh language... There will be English
● influences... but I think the language of my dreams will always be Welsh." Ioan Gruffudd, Cardiff-born actor, Mail on Sunday.

designed to cater for people with disabilities, so be sure to check first. Public transport is improving; newer buses have lower steps for easier access and some train services now accommodate wheelchair users in comfort. Taxis, as opposed to minicabs, all carry wheelchair ramps, and if a driver says he or she can't take a wheelchair, it's because they're too lazy to fetch the ramp.

Wheelchair users, and blind or partially sighted people are automatically given 30-50% discount on train fares, and those with other disabilities are eligible for the **Disabled Person's Railcard**, which costs £14 per year and gives a third off most tickets. There are no reductions on buses, however.

Contacts

If you are disabled you should contact the travel officer of your national support organization. They can provide literature or put you in touch with travel agents specializing in tours for the disabled.
Can Be Done, T020 89072400, www.can bedone.co.uk. A London-based tour operator that will arrange holidays for disabled visitors in a range of accommodation to suit individual requirements.
Disability Wales, T02920 887325, www.dwac.demon.co.uk. The national association of disability groups in Wales.
Holiday Care Service, 2nd floor, Imperial Building, Victoria Rd, Horley, Surrey RH6 7PZ, T01293 774535. Provides free lists of accessible accommodation.
Royal Association for Disability and Rehabilitation (RADAR), Unit 12, City Forum, 250 City Rd, London, EC1V 8AF, T020 72503222, www.radar.org.uk. A good source of advice and information, and produces an annual guide on travelling in the UK (£7.50 including p&p).
Royal National Institute for the Blind, T020 73881266, www.rnib.org.uk. Publishes a hotel guidebook for blind and partially sighted people. They also have maps for the blind of the main cities in Britain.

Gay and lesbian travellers

Wales is still an essentially rural part of Britain and, like other rural areas, is not as gay-friendly as cosmopolitan cities like London and Manchester. In 2000, the age of consent for homosexual males in Britain was reduced to 16, in line with that of heterosexuals, but more religious corners of the country disapproved. The gay scene in Wales is generally pretty quiet, if not non-existent in some parts, and open displays of affection would be unlikely to go down well in many places. Not surprisingly the capital, Cardiff, has the liveliest gay scene. In 1999, the first Mardi Gras lesbian and gay pride festival was held here and it is now an established feature of the city calendar, with dance, music, stalls and information. It takes place in September (see Festivals and events, page 42), www.cardiffmardigras.co.uk. Most of the gay venues in the city are focused on Charles Street in the city centre. The university towns such as Aberystwyth and Bangor also have small gay and lesbian scenes, as does the other main city in the south – Swansea.

Contacts

Useful support numbers and contacts are:
Cardiff T029 2034 0101; Rhyl T01745 337070 Swansea T01792 645325; Bridgend T01656 649990, www.thegylproject.co.uk; **Bangor Gayline**, T01248 363431, www.mesmac-north-wales.co.uk; and **Lesbian Line**, T01248 351263, www.lesbian-line-north-wales.org.uk.

There's also a useful general website – www.gaywales.co.uk; and a selection of websites listing gay events and venues: www.whatsonwhen.com; www.gaybritain.co.uk, www.gaytravel.co.uk, www.rainbow network.com and www.gaypride.co.uk.

Student travellers

There are various official youth/student ID cards available. The most useful is the **International Student ID Card** (ISIC). For a mere £6 the ISIC card gains you access to the exclusive world of student travel with a series of discounts, including most forms of local transport, up to 30% off international air fares, cheap or free admission to museums, theatres and other attractions, and cheap meals in some restaurants. There's also free or discounted internet access, and a website where you can check the latest student travel deals, www.usitworld.com. You'll also receive the ISIC handbook, which ensures you get the most out of services available. ISIC cards are available at student travel centres, such as **STA Travel** ① *86 Old Brompton Rd, London, SW7 3LH, T020 73616161, www.statravel.co.uk*; and **Trailfinders** ① *194 Kensington High St, London, W8 6FT, T020 79383939, www.trailfinders.co.uk*. US and Canadian citizens are also entitled to emergency medical coverage, and there's a 24-hour hotline to call in the event of medical, legal or financial emergencies.

If you're under 26 but not a student, you can apply for a **Federation of International Youth Travel Organisations** (FIYTO) card, or a **Euro 26 Card**, which give more or less the same discounts. If you're 25 or younger you can qualify for a **Go-25 Card**, which gives you the same benefits as an ISIC card. These discount cards are also issued by student travel agencies and hostelling organizations.

Studying in Wales

If you want to study in Wales you must first prove you can support and accommodate yourself without working and without recourse to public support. Your studies should take up at least 15 hours a week for a minimum of six months. Once you are studying, you are allowed to do 20 hours of casual work per week in the term time and you can work full-time during the holidays. In **North America** full-time students can obtain temporary work or study permits through the **Council of International Education Exchange** (CIEE) ① *205E 42nd St, New York, NY 10017, T212-8222600, www.ciee.org*. For more details, contact your nearest British embassy, consulate or high commission, or the **Foreign and Commonwealth Office in London**, T020 72701500.

Travel with children

Britain still lags some way behind southern Europe in its attitude towards young children and, unlike their Mediterranean counterparts, most British citizens are unlikely to feel better disposed towards foreign visitors travelling with kids. There are, however, lots of attractions geared to children, so finding something to keep the ankle-biters amused while the rain tips down outside shouldn't be a problem. The most frustrating aspect of travelling with kids in Britain is eating out. Some establishments are happy to help with high chairs and kids' menus, while others are downright unhelpful. In major towns and cities Italian restaurants are often more child-friendly. In more remote areas, however, most people are helpful and friendly. A very useful source of information is www.babygoes2.com.

Women travellers

Travelling in Britain is neither easier nor more difficult for women than it is for men. Generally speaking, people are friendly and courteous and lone women travellers shouldn't experience anything unpleasant. In the main cities and larger towns, take the usual precautions and avoid walking in quiet, unlit streets and parks at night.

Working in Wales

Citizens of **European Union** (EU) countries can live and work in Britain freely without a visa, but **non-EU residents** need a permit to work legally. This can be difficult to obtain without the backing of an established company or employer in the UK. Also, visitors from Commonwealth countries who are aged between 17 and 27 may apply for a working-holiday visa which permits them to stay in the UK for up to two years and work on a casual basis (ie non-career orientated). These certificates are only available from British embassies and consulates abroad and you must have proof of a valid return or onward ticket, as well as means of support during your stay. **Commonwealth** citizens with a parent or grandparent born in the UK can apply for a **Certificate of Entitlement to the Right of Abode**, allowing them to work in Britain.

Before you travel

Visas

Visa regulations are subject to change, so check with your local British embassy, high commission or consulate before leaving. Everyone needs a passport to enter. Citizens of Australia, Canada, New Zealand, South Africa or the USA do not need a visa and can stay for up to six months, providing they have a return ticket and sufficient funds to cover their stay. Citizens of most European countries do not need a visa and can stay for three months. Citizens of Albania, Bosnia, Bulgaria, Macedonia, Romania, Slovakia, Yugoslavia, all former Soviet republics (other than the Baltic states) and most other countries need a visa from the commission or consular office in the country of application.

❞ No vaccinations are required to enter the UK. See the Health section, page 50.

The **Foreign Office's** website, www.fco.gov.uk, provides details of British immigration and visa requirements. Also the **Immigration Advisory Service** (IAS) ① *County House, 190 Great Dover St, London SE1 4YB, T020 73576917, www.vois.org.uk*, offers free and confidential advice to anyone applying for entry clearance into the UK.

For **visa extensions** once in Britain, contact the **Home Office** ① *Immigration and Nationality Dept, Lunar House, Wellesley Rd, Croydon, London CR9, T020 86860688*, before your existing visa expires. Citizens of Australia, Canada, New Zealand, South Africa or the USA wishing to stay longer than six months will need an **Entry Clearance Certificate** from the British High Commission in their country. For more details, contact your nearest British embassy, consulate or high commission, or the **Foreign and Commonwealth Office** in London, T020 72701500.

Customs and duty free

There are various import restrictions, most of which should not affect the average tourist. It is difficult to bring pets into Britain, and tight quarantine restrictions apply (with some exemptions for dogs and cats travelling from Europe). For more information on bringing a pet, contact the **Department of Environment, Food and Rural Affairs** ① *Nobel House, 17 Smith Sq, London SW1P 3JR, T020 72386000, www.defra.gov.uk/animalh/quarantine*.

❞ For more information on British import regulations, contact HM Customs and Excise, Dorset House, Stamford St, London, SE1 9PJ, T020 79283344, www.hmce.gov.uk.

Visitors from EU countries do not have to make a declaration to customs on entry into the UK and do not have to pay tax or duty on goods bought in another EU country (as long as tax was included in the purchase price and the items are for the visitor's personal use). A customs officer is more likely to query their purpose if large quantities of alcohol or tobacco are brought in (more than 3,200 cigarettes, 3 kg of tobacco, 110 litres of beer, 10 litres of spirits, 90 litres of wine, 20 litres of fortified wine). Visitors from non-EU countries are allowed to import 200 cigarettes, or 250g of tobacco, 2 litres of wine, and 2 litres of fortified wine or 1 litre of spirits.

British embassies abroad

Australia High Commission: Commonwealth Av, Yarralumla, Canberra, ACT 2600, T02-6270 6666, www.uk.emb.gov.au.
Canada High Commission: 80 Elgin St, Ottawa, K1P 5K7, T613-2371530, www.britain-in-canada.org.
France 9 Av Hoche, 8e, Paris, T01-42663810, www.amb-grandebretagne.fr.
Germany Wilhelmstrasse 70-71, 10117 Berlin, T030-20457-0, www.britischebotschaft.de.

Ireland 29 Merrion Rd, Ballsbridge, Dublin 4, T01-2053700, www.britishembassy.ie.
Netherlands Koningslaan 44, 1075AE Amsterdam, T20-6764343, www.britain.nl.
New Zealand High Commission: 44 Hill St, Wellington, T04-4726049, www.britain.org.nz.
South Africa 91 Parliament St, Cape Town 8001, T21-4617220, www.britain.org.za.
USA 3100 Massachusetts Av NW, Washington DC 20008, T1-202-588 7800, www.britain-info.org. Also has regional consulates in 12 other cities.

What to take

Your main problem is going to be the weather, which is very unpredictable. You should therefore pack layered clothing and bring a lightweight waterproof jacket and warm sweater whatever the time of year. Light clothes are sufficient for the summer. You'll be able to find everything else you will need in most Welsh towns and certainly in Cardiff.

A sleeping bag is useful in hostels. A sleeping sheet with a pillow cover is needed for staying in **Youth Hostel Association** (YHA) hostels to save you the cost of having to hire one. A padlock can also be handy for locking your bag if it has to be stored in a hostel for any length of time. Other useful items include an alarm clock and an adapter plug for electrical appliances.

Insurance

Insurance is crucial if things go seriously wrong. A good insurance policy should cover you in case of theft, loss of possessions or money (often including cash), the cost of any medical and dental treatment, cancellation of flights, delays in travel arrangements, accidents, missed departures, lost baggage, lost passport, and personal liability and legal expenses. There's nearly always small print; some policies exclude 'dangerous activities' such as scuba diving, skiing, horse riding or even trekking. Older travellers should note that some companies won't cover people over 65 years old, or may charge high premiums. Not all policies cover ambulance, helicopter rescue or emergency flights home. Find out if your policy pays medical expenses direct to the hospital or doctor, or if you have to pay and then claim the money back later. If the latter applies, make sure you keep all records. Whatever your policy, if you have something stolen, make sure you get a copy of the police report, as you will need this to substantiate your claim.

Before shopping around for prices, check whether your credit card and home insurance companies offer overseas travel within your policy. If not, a good place to start is **STA Travel** at www.sta-travel.com. Travellers from North America can try **Travel Guard**, T1-800-8261300, www.noelgroup.com; **Access America**, T1-800-2848300; **Travel Insurance Services** (T1-800-9371387) and **Travel Assistance International**, T1-800-8212828. Travellers from Australia could try www.travelinsurance.com.au.

Money

Banks and bureaux de change

Branches of the main high street banks are found throughout the country and include: **Barclays, HSBC, Lloyds TSB** and **NatWest**. Bank opening hours are Monday to Friday from 0930 to 1600 or 1700. Some larger branches may open later on Thursdays and on Saturday mornings. Banks tend to offer similar exchange rates and are usually the best places to change money and cheques. Outside banking hours you'll have to use a bureau de change, which can be easily found at the airport, train stations and on the high street in larger cities. **Thomas Cook** and other major travel agents also operate bureaux de change with reasonable rates. Avoid changing money or cheques in hotels, as the rates are usually poor. Main post offices and branches of **Marks and Spencer** will change cash without commission.

Credit cards and ATMs

Most hotels, shops and restaurants accept the major credit cards (Access/MasterCard, Visa and American Express), though some places may charge for using them. Some smaller establishments such as B&Bs may only accept cash. Visa and Access/MasterCard holders can use all major high street banks (**Barclays, HSBC, Lloyds TSB, NatWest** and **Royal Bank of Scotland**). Amex card holders can use the **HSBC**, the **Royal Bank of Scotland** and any other bank or building society displaying the 'Link' symbol. The Cirrus symbol is accepted in most ATMs. Note that your bank may charge you for using a foreign ATM.

Travellers' cheques

The safest way to carry money is in travellers' cheques. These are available for a small commission from all major banks. **American Express (Amex), Visa** and **Thomas Cook** cheques are widely accepted and are the most commonly issued by banks. You'll normally have to pay commission again when you cash each cheque. This will usually be 1% or a flat rate. No commission is payable on Amex cheques cashed at Amex offices. Make sure you keep a record of the cheque numbers and the cheques you've cashed separate from the cheques themselves, so that you can get a full refund of all uncashed cheques should you lose them. It's best to bring sterling cheques to avoid changing currencies twice. Travellers' cheques are rarely accepted outside banks, so you'll need to cash them in advance and keep a good supply of ready cash.

Money transfers

If you need money urgently, the quickest way to have it sent to you is to have it wired to the nearest agent via **Western Union** (To800 833833) or **Moneygram** (To800 89718971). Charges are on a sliding scale, and it will cost proportionately less to wire out more money. Money can also be wired by **Thomas Cook** or **American Express**, though this may take a day or two, or transferred via a bank draft, but this can take up to a week.

Currency

The **British currency** is the pound sterling (**£**), divided into 100 pence (**p**). Coins come in denominations of 1p, 2p, 5p, 10p, 20p, 50p, £1 and £2. The main notes (bills) are £5, £10, £20 (£50 are not widely used and may be difficult to change).

Cost of travelling

Britain can be an expensive place to visit. In Wales, the minimum daily budget if you're staying in hostels or cheap B&Bs, cooking your own meals and doing minimal travelling will be around £30 per person per day. Those staying in more upmarket

B&Bs or guesthouses, eating out at pubs or modest restaurants and visiting tourist attractions can expect to pay around £60 per person per day. Single travellers will have to pay more than half the cost of a double room in most places and should budget on spending around 60% of what a couple would spend. In order to enjoy your trip to the full then you'll need at least £70 per day.

Taxes

Most goods in Britain are subject to a **Value Added Tax** (VAT) of 17.5%, with the exception of books and food. VAT is usually included in the price of goods. Visitors from non-EU countries can save money through the Retail Export Scheme, which allows a refund of VAT on goods that will be taken out of the country. Note that not all shops participate in the scheme and that VAT cannot be reclaimed on hotel bills or other services.

Getting there

If travelling long haul from outside of Europe it is usually cheapest to fly to an English city, usually London and travel overland to Wales from there. To south Wales the quickest route from Scotland, Ireland and Europe is by plane to Cardiff. To north Wales from Scotland or Ireland, or from England the cheapest way west is by coach or train. There are fast and frequent train services from London Paddington station and most other major cities.

Air

Cardiff has an international airport with flights from Scotland, Ireland and Europe. There are also daily flights from Amsterdam, from where it is possible to connect with airports all over the world. During the summer many charter flights fly direct to popular holiday destinations in Europe as well as to Toronto. Otherwise, the main point of entry will be one of the English airports. Competition means it is usually cheapest to fly to one of London's five airports. Heathrow is the largest and the busiest in the world; the other long-haul airport, Gatwick, is slightly smaller. London also has Stansted, Luton and the exclusive City Airport. Flights from North America arrive at Heathrow or Gatwick. Low-cost airlines generally fly into Gatwick, Stansted or Luton. Direct flights from Europe also arrive at Birmingham, Bristol, Liverpool and Manchester airports. Bristol Airport is most convenient for South Wales; Birmingham or Manchester Airports are good for Mid and North Wales.

Buying a ticket

There are a mind-boggling number of outlets for buying your plane ticket and finding the best deal can be a confusing business. **Fares** will depend on the season. Ticket prices are highest from around early June to mid-September, which is the tourist high season. Fares drop in the months either side of the peak season – mid-September to early November and mid-April to early June. They are cheapest in the low season, from November to April, although prices tend to rise sharply over Christmas and the New Year. It's also worth noting that flying at the weekend is usually more expensive.

One of the best ways of finding a good deal is to use the **internet**. There are a number of sites where you can check out prices and even book tickets. You can search in the travel sections of your web browser or try the sites of the discount travel companies and agents and the budget airlines listed in this section (see box page 23). Note that some low-cost operators are subject to rigid restrictions and need to be booked well in advance; check for hidden surcharges before booking.

⁞ Airlines and travel agents

The following airlines fly
direct to Cardiff Airport.
Air Wales T0870 7773131,
www.airwales.co.uk
BMI baby T0870 2642229,
www.bmibaby.com
KLM T08705 074074,
www.klm.com
Ryanair T0871 2460000
or T0871 2460016,
www.ryanair.com

Other websites
www.bestfares.com
www.cheapflights.com
www.deckchair.com
www.dialaflight.co.uk
www.expedia.com
www.ebookers.com
www.flycheap.com
www.flynowww.com
www.lastminute.com
www.opodo.com

Airport tax All tickets are subject to taxes (£10-20 depending on route), insurance charge (around £6) and passenger service charge, which varies according to airport. This adds up quickly – for economy-fare flights within the UK and from EU countries expect additions of £20-30. For inter-continental flights, this will rise to around £60-70.

Flights from the rest of the UK and Ireland

A small number of budget airlines fly daily to Cardiff International Airport from several British and Irish destinations. Prices on these flights can vary considerably, depending on the time and day of travel and how early you book your ticket. **Air Wales** fly from **Aberdeen, Dublin, Liverpool, Newcastle, Norwich** and **Plymouth**. BMI Baby fly from **Glasgow, Edinburgh, Belfast, Cork** and **Jersey**; and **Ryanair** fly from **Dublin**. Check the websites regularly to get the best deals (see box page 23).

Flights from continental Europe

In addition to regular flights operated by the major national carriers, the surge in **budget airline** routes means that you can fly from practically anywhere in Europe to anywhere in Britain at cheap rates. The budget airlines specialize in routes to provincial and smaller cities, and it's always worth checking what the onward transport arrangements are, since some airports are a long way from town. The flight consolidator www.opodo.com can often offer good rates, but it's worth noting that flight consolidators do not include budget airline fares – you'll have to search those out separately. Fares for a return ticket range from €15 to €300 on a scheduled flight. Budget airlines offer no frills: no meals, no reserved seating and baggage restrictions. However, you can sometimes travel for as little as €5. Check terms and airport location before booking: www.ryanair.com, www.flybe.com, www.easyjet.com, www.flybmi.com, www.virginexpress.com.

If you are flying direct to Cardiff **BMI Baby** fly from **Alicante, Faro, Geneva, Malaga, Palma, Paris, Prague**; and KLM fly from **Amsterdam** (AMS) three times daily .

Flights from North America

Direct flights between Cardiff and **Toronto** operate weekly during the summer with low cost operator **Zoom Airlines** (www.flyzoom.com), otherwise journeys may be made by travelling via **Amsterdam**, from where there are frequent flights direct to Cardiff, with a flight time of just one hour 25 minutes. Alternatively, there are regular non-stop flights to London from many US and Canadian cities, including **Atlanta, Boston, Calgary, Chicago, Dallas, Denver, Houston, Las Vegas, Los Angeles, Miami, Montreal, New York, Philadelphia, Phoenix, San Francisco, Seattle, Toronto, Vancouver** and **Washington DC**, and many more connections to other cities. Non-stop flights are also available from **New York** to Manchester and Birmingham.

Discount flight agents in North America

Air Brokers International, 323 Geary St, Suite 411, San Francisco, CA94102, T1-800-8833273, www.airbrokers.com. Specialist in RTW and Circle Pacific tickets.
Discount Airfares Worldwide On-Line, www.etn.nl/discount.htm.
STA Travel, 5900 Wiltshire Blvd, Suite 2110, Los Angeles, CA 90036, T1-800-7770112, www.sta-travel.com. Discount student/youth travel discount company.
Travel CUTS, 187 College St, Toronto, ON, M5T 1P7, T1-800-6672887, www.travelcuts.com. Specialist in student discount fares, IDs and other travel services.

For low-season Apex fares expect to pay US$200-450 from New York and other East Coast cities, and US$300-600 from the West Coast. Prices rise to around US$500-800 from New York and US$400-900 from the West Coast in the summer months. Low-season Apex fares from Toronto and Montreal cost around CAN$600-700, and from Vancouver around CAN$800-900, rising to $750-950 and $950-1150 during the summer.

Flights from Australia and New Zealand

The cheapest scheduled flights to London from Australia or New Zealand are via Asia with **Gulf Air, Royal Brunei** or **Thai Airways.** They charge from A$1,300-1,800 and involve a transfer en route. Flights via Africa start at around $2,000 and are yet more expensive via North America. The cheapest scheduled flights from New Zealand are with **Korean Air, Thai Airways** or **JAL,** all of whom fly via their home cities for around NZ$2,000- 2,300. The most direct route is via North America with **United Airlines,** via Chicago or Los Angeles. Fares range from around NZ$2,800 in low season to NZ$3,200 in high season. **Emirates** flies to Birmingham and Manchester from Sydney via Dubai, and Manchester is also served via Singapore on **Singapore Airlines**. Prices are slightly higher than flights to London.

Airline contact details

For airline offices in Cardiff, see p86.
Aer Lingus, T08450 844444, www.aerlingus.com.
Air Canada, T1-800 773000, www.aircanada.ca.
Air France, T08450 854444, www.airfrance.com.
Air Wales,T0870 7773131, www.airwales.com.
Alitalia, T0870 5448259, www.alitalia.com.
American Airlines, T1-800 4337300, www.americanairlines.com.
BMI, T0870, 6070555, www.flybmi.com.
British Airways, T0870 8509850, www.britishairways.com.
British European, T0870 5676676, www.flybe.com.
British Midland, T0870 6070555, www.flybmi.com.
Continental, T1-800 2310856, www.flycontinental.com.
Delta Airlines, T0800 414767, www.delta.com.
Easyjet, T0870 600000, www.easyjet.com.
Emirates, T0870 1286000, www.emirates.com.
Gulf Air, T0870 0000123, www.gulfair.com.
JAL, www.jal.com.
KLM, T0870 5074047, www.klm.com.
Korean Air, T1-800 4385000, www.koreanair.com.
Lufthansa, T08457 737747, www.lufthansa.com.
Qantas Airways, T0845 7747767, www.qantas.com.
Royal Brunei, www.bruneiair.com.
Ryanair, T0871 2460016, www.ryanair.com.
Singapore Airlines, T0870 6088886, www.singaporeair.com.
South African Airways, T020 73125000, www.flysaa.com.
Thai Airways, www.thaiair.com.
United Airlines, T0845 8444777, www.ual.com.
Virgin Atlantic, T01293 747747, www.virgin-atlantic.com.
Zoom Airlines, T1-866 3599666, www.flyzoom.com.

There are fast and frequent rail services to Cardiff from London, Bristol, Birmingham and most other major cities. From London, trains leave from Paddington station for South Wales or from Euston station for Mid or North Wales. Trains from Birmingham, Manchester and London also head to Mid Wales (Machynlleth, Llandudno or Welshpool) and North Wales (Holyhead, Bangor, Llandudno, Porthmadog and Pwllheli); it may be necessary to change more than once. Ticket pricing is complicated, but to get the best deal you should book in advance; travel on Fridays or during the rush hour (before 0900 weekdays) is generally more expensive. Compared to Europe, rail travel in Britain is overpriced and antiquated.

Enquiries and booking

National Rail Enquiries ① To8457 484950, www.nationalrail.co.uk, are quick and courteous with information on rail services and fares but not always accurate, so double check details and ask whether there are any cheaper fares. The website **www.qjump.co.uk** is a bit hit-and-miss but generally fast and efficient and shows you all the various options on any selected journey; while **www.thetrainline.co.uk** also has idiosyncrasies but shows prices clearly.

Fares

To describe the system of rail ticket pricing as complicated is a huge understatement and impossible to explain here. There are many and various discounted fares, but restrictions are often prohibitive, which explains the long queues and delays at ticket counters in railway stations. The cheapest ticket is an **Apex**, which must be booked at least two weeks in advance, though this is not available on all journeys. Next cheapest is an **Super Advanced** ticket which has to be booked before 1800 on the day before travelling, and again tickets are restricted in number. Other discount tickets include a **Saver Return**, which can be used on all trains, and a **Super Saver**, which costs slightly less but cannot be used on a Friday or during peak times. For example, a Saver Return ticket from London to Cardiff costs £50.80, while a Super Advanced ticket is £36 and an Apex is £24. All discount tickets should be bought as quickly as possible as they are often sold out weeks in advance, especially Apex and Super Apex tickets. The latter tickets guarantee seat reservations, but Saver and Super Saver tickets do not. These can be secured by paying an extra £1 when booking.

The cheapest return journeys are currently: from **London**: £42 to Cardiff (two hours); £55 to Aberystwyth (5½ hours); £61.50 to Bangor (3½ hours); from **Birmingham**: £37.50 to Cardiff (two hours) and £34.50 to Aberystwyth (three hours); from **Bristol**: £7.50 to Cardiff (45 minutes); and from **Newcastle**: £89 to Cardiff (7½ hours).

From continental Europe

All international connections pass through London. **Eurostar** ① To990 186186, www.eurostar.com, operate high-speed trains to London Waterloo from Paris (three hours) and Brussels (two hours 40 minutes) via Lille (two hours). Standard-class tickets to Paris and Brussels range from £70 for a weekend day return to £300 for a fully flexible mid-week return. There are substantial discounts for children (4-11 years) and for passengers who are under 26 years on the day of travel. It is worth keeping an eye open for special offers, especially in the low season. All other rail connections will involve some kind of ferry crossing (see below). For full details on rail services available, contact your national railway or **Rail Europe**, www.raileurope.com; they also provide information on routes, timetables, fares and discount passes.

Road

Bus/coach

Road links to Wales are good and this is the cheapest form of travel. The main operator between England and Wales is **National Express** ① T08705 808080, www.nationalexpress.com. Buses from London leave from Victoria station and travel via Bristol to South Wales (Newport, Cardiff, Swansea, Carmarthen and Pembroke Dock); via Birmingham and Shrewsbury to Mid Wales (Welshpool, Aberystwyth) or via Chester to North Wales (Wrexham, Llandudno, Bangor, Pwllheli and Holyhead). From the north of England, buses travel via Birmingham to South Wales, or via Manchester or Liverpool to North Wales, from where onward connections can be made.

Tickets can be bought at bus stations or from a number of agents throughout the country. **National Express** return fares from **London** start at around: £24.50 to Cardiff (3½ hours); £18.50 to Aberystwyth (7½ hours); £31.50 to Llandudno (eight hours). From **Bristol**, fares start at £7.50 to Cardiff (1 hour 15 mintues). From **Birmingham**, fares start at £22 to Cardiff (2 ½ hours) and £25.50 to Aberystwyth (four hours). From **Shrewsbury,** fares start at £18.50 to Aberystwyth (2½ hours). From **Chester** fares start at £10.50 to Llandudno (3½ hours). It's also worth trying **www.megabus.com** for cheaper, but slower, transport from London to Cardiff and Swansea.

Car

The most direct way to reach South Wales by car from London and southern and western England is on the **M4** motorway. The M4 crosses the Severn Estuary via the dramatic Severn Bridge (£4.50 per car, toll payable westbound only – you can leave Wales for free!). To North Wales, the **A55** expressway runs all the way from Chester to Holyhead following the coast; or from the Midlands, the **A5** through Llangollen. Mid Wales is best reached by the **A495** from Shrewsbury to Welshpool and then the **A458**; or the **A456** from Birmingham.

From continental Europe

If you're driving from continental Europe you can take the **Eurotunnel Shuttle Service** ① T0800 969992, www.eurotunnel.com, a freight train which runs 24 hours a day, 365 days a year, and takes you and your car from Calais to Folkestone in 35-45 minutes. Fares are per carload, regardless of the number of passengers, and range from £135 one way to £270 return depending on the time of year or how far in advance you book. For bookings, call T08705 353535. Foot passengers cannot cross on the Shuttle. You can also take a cross-channel ferry, see below.

Sea

From Ireland

There are direct ferry crossings from Ireland to Holyhead in North Wales and to Swansea, Fishguard and Pembroke Dock in the south. There are at least two sailings daily, apart from to Swansea which is served four times a week. There are more frequent sailings during summer. Fares vary considerably depending on the time of day, week and season. Check the websites for promotional offers; discounts are usually available for students and Hostelling International (HI) members.

Irish Ferries ① T0870 5171717, www.irishferries.com, run ferries from Dublin to Holyhead (5 daily, 3 hrs 15 mins) and Rosslare to Pembroke (2 daily, 3 hrs 45 mins). Prices cost from £15 each way for a foot passenger and from £83.50 each way with a car. Fast boats are also available.

Stena Line ① *T08704 006798, www.stenaline.ie*, run ferries from Dun Laoghaire and Dublin to Holyhead (2 daily, 1 hr 45 mins) and from Rosslare to Fishguard (2 daily, 3½ hrs). Fastboat services are also available; foot passengers are only permitted to travel on this service; fares start from £26 return, car £160 return.

Swansea-Cork Ferries ① *T01792 456116, www.swanseacorkferries.com*, run both car and foot passenger services to Swansea docks from mid-March to mid-January. They sail four times a week – more frequently in high season. Prices cost from £22 each way for foot passengers and from £119 with a car. The journey takes 10 hours.

From continental Europe

There are ferries to England from many European ports; the most useful for access to Wales are **Harwich** (served by boats from Denmark, Germany and the Netherlands); **Dover** (served by boats from Belgium and France); and **Portsmouth** (served by boats from France and Spain). **Poole, Portsmouth** and **Plymouth** are also served by boats from France. Prices vary enormously according to season, check prices for specific dates on one of the many online booking agent websites: **www.cheapferry.com**, **www.ferry-to-france.co.uk**, **www.ferrycrossings-uk.co.uk** or **www.ferrysavers.com**, or by contacting major route operators direct: **P&O Stena Line** ① *T0870 6000600, www.posl.com*, Spain, France, Irish Sea & North Sea routes; **Brittany Ferries** ① *T0990 360360, T33-299-828080 in France, T34-942-360611 in Spain, www.brittany ferries.com*, Spain and western France to south coast; **Fjord Line** ① *www.fjordline.com*, North Sea routes from Scandinavia. These also handle information on shipping.

Paddle steamers

During the summer months, the *Waverley* and the *Balmoral* paddle steamers travel from Penarth, Newport, Swansea and Porthcawl down the Bristol Channel to Ilfracombe in Devon and Minehead in Somerset. A one-way ticket costs around £15. This is a very pleasant and leisurely way to travel, however the cruises are cancelled during bad weather. Further information is available from **Waverley Excursions** ① *T0845 1304647, www.waverleyexcursions.co.uk*.

Touching down

Airport information

Most long-haul flights arrive in Britain via one of London's five airports: Heathrow, Gatwick, Stansted, City or Luton. There are also a number of long-haul flights to Manchester and Birmingham. Those arriving by budget airline at one of the other regional airports (Bristol, Cardiff or Liverpool) should check arrival information via the airline's website. For information on all UK airports, visit www.baa.co.uk. For details of onward connections to Wales, see Getting there, page 22.

Arriving at Cardiff

Cardiff International Airport (CWL) ① *Rhoose, near Barry, T01446 711111, www.cial.co.uk, www.cardiffairportonline.com*, Wales' small international airport, is 12 miles southwest of Cardiff's city centre and around a 30-40 minute taxi journey. The terminal's facilities include a few small bars selling drinks, snacks and teas and coffees, newsagents, a selection of duty free shops, and a children's play area. The airport is easily reached by car via the A4055, or taking the A4225 from the A48 or junction 33 off the M4. The **taxi** office is in the arrivals hall and taxis can be prebooked on To1446 710693, approximately £20-25 per journey. **Air Buses** operate between the city's central train and main bus station and the airport every 30 minutes, approximately costing £2.90 (Monday to Saturday from around 0650-1800, then every hour from 1936 and 2236 and on Sundays).

Arriving in London

Heathrow (LHR) ① *To870 0000123, www.baa.co.uk*, is about 20 miles west of London on the M4, just beyond the M25. Four terminals: **Terminal 1** for most domestic flights; **Terminal 2** for most European flights; **Terminals 3 and 4** for international flights. Journey time to central London by underground (the cheapest option) is about 50 minutes; by **Heathrow Express** train (To845 6001515) to Paddington about 15 minutes (£25 standard return). A taxi to central London will cost about £40 and takes an hour.

London Gatwick (LGW) ① *To870 0002468, www.baa.co.uk*, is 30 miles southwest of London on the M23, near Crawley. **Two terminals**: North and South. Journey time to central London by **Gatwick Express** (To845 8501530) to Victoria about 30 minutes (£21.50 standard return). A taxi to central London will cost about £75.

London City (LCY) ① *Royal Dock, To20 76460000, www.londoncityairport.com*, is six miles east of the City of London. There's a five-minute shuttle bus to Canning Town (£2.50) from where you can get the Jubilee Line or Docklands Light Railway into central London. A taxi to the centre will cost about £25.

London Luton (LTN) ① *To1582 405100, www.london-luton.co.uk*, is about 30 miles north of central London on the A1. A coach to Victoria takes one hour 30 minutes and costs £12 return. **City Thameslink** trains run throughout the day, cost £20.80 for a standard return and take 30 minutes. A taxi to central London costs around £55.

London Stansted (STN) ① *To870 000303, www.stanstedairport.net*, is also about 30 miles north of central London on the M11. **Stansted Express** trains to London Liverpool Street (standard return £24) depart frequently and take about 45 minutes. A taxi to central London will cost around £85.

Arriving at other UK airports

Bristol International Airport (BRS) ① *To870 1212747, www.bristolairport.co.uk*, eight miles south of the city centre, on the A38. One terminal with standard facilities. Taxi to Bristol city centre £16, or **Bristol International Flyer** coach link the airport with the railway station (Temple Meads) and the central bus station, £6 return, 30 minutes.

Birmingham International Airport (BHX) ① *To121 7675511, www.bhx.co.uk*, eight miles east of the city centre and has two terminals with standard facilities. A taxi to the centre costs around £12, or frequent trains run the 10-minute journey into the city centre. Connections to Wales can be made by rail or coach, with **National Express**, To8705 808080. There are no local bus services at night.

Liverpool John Lennon Airport (LPL) ① *To870 7508484, www.liverpooljohn lennonairport.com*, is seven miles southeast of the city in Speke. A regular bus runs to Liverpool city centre, from where connecting buses and trains can be taken.

Manchester International Airport (MAN) ① *To161 4893000, www.manchester airport.co.uk*, south of the city centre, at Junction 5 of the M56. Three terminals. Trains run from Manchester Piccadilly to North Wales. **National Express**, To8705 808080, runs from Terminals 1 and 2. A taxi into the city centre should cost around £15.

Touching down

Business hours 0900-1700.
Electricity The current in Britain is 240V AC. Plugs have three square pins and adapters are widely available.
Emergency services For police, fire and ambulance and, in certain areas, mountain rescue or coastguard, dial 999.
Laundry Most towns have coin-operated launderettes. the average cost for a wash and tumble dry is about £3. A service wash, where someone will do your washing for you, costs around £4-5. In more remote areas, you'll have to rely on hostel and campsite facilities.
Telephone To call Wales from overseas, dial 011 from USA and Canada, 0011 from Australia and

New Zealand, followed by 44, then the area code, minus the first zero, then the number. Useful numbers: operator T100, international operator T155; British Telecom directory enquiries T118 118.
Toilets Public toilets are found at most train and bus stations and motorway service stations. They may charge 20p, but are generally clean with disabled and baby-changing facilities. Those in town centres are often pretty grim.
Weights and measures Imperial and metric systems are both in use. Distances on roads are measured in miles and yards, and drinks poured in pints, but generally the metric system is used elsewhere.

Newcastle International Airport (NCL) ① *T0870 1221488, www.newcastleairport.com*, five miles north of the city. Metro trains run from the airport between 0545 and 2305, every 10 minutes, journey of 20 minutes to the city centre or the central train station; single fare £2.10. **National Express** coaches also run from the airport.

Tourist information

Tourist Information Centres (TICs)

Most cities and towns that you're likely to visit in Wales will have a local Tourist Information Centre (TIC), which can give you information on local attractions, restaurants and accommodation (including handling bookings – for a small fee) and help with visitors' enquiries, such as where to find an internet café. Many sell books, local guides, maps and souvenirs, and some have free street plans and leaflets describing local walks. In general, tourist offices tend to cater to those interested in taking tours or day trips, and are less useful if you're on a tight budget, in which case youth hostels can provide much the same information. See individual town information sections for lists of local TICs.

Museums, art galleries and stately homes

The **National Trust** ① *T0870 609 5380, www.nationaltrust.org.uk*, plays an active role in protecting and managing stately homes, gardens and the countryside of Wales and owns 133 miles of the Welsh coastline. If you're going to be visiting several sights during your stay, then it's worth taking annual membership or investing in a *National Trust Touring Pass*, available for seven or 14 days.

A similar organization is **CADW** ① www.cadw.wales.gov.uk, the historic environment agency responsible for protecting and conserving Wales' historic buildings, parks, monuments, gardens, landscapes and underwater archaeology. *CADW* (pronounced *cad-oo*) is a Welsh word meaning 'to keep'. If you're planning to visit a number of places, it may be worth buying a *CADW Explorer Pass*, valid for three days, £9.50 adult, £16.50 for two adults, £23 family; 7 days £15.50 adult, £26 for two adults, £32 family.

⁞ The Countryside Code

1 Drive carefully and behave courteously to other motorists and cyclists on narrow, winding roads. Park vehicles where they will not be a hazard or disruption to other motorists, residents or businesses.
2 Keep to public paths through farmland to minimize crop damage and avoid 'short-cuts' on steep terrain to prevent soil erosion and damage to vegetation.
3 Litter is an eye-sore, harmful to farm animals, wildlife and the water supply. Leave no waste and take all your rubbish home.
4 Protect wildlife, plants and trees.
5 Respect ancient monuments, buildings and sites of religious importance. Do not vandalize or cause graffiti.
6 Avoid damaging crops, walls, fences and farm equipment; leave all gates as you find them.
7 Do not collect wild flowers, seabird eggs or historical artefacts.
8 Avoid pollution of the water supplies – there are few toilets outside of villages so when walking in the countryside bury human waste and toilet paper in the ground and at least 30 metres from water courses.
9 Guard against risk of fire from matches, cigarettes, stoves and campfires.
10 Keep dogs under control, especially when near to sheep at lambing-time, seabird nesting sites at cliff edges. Avoid dog-fouling in public places.
11 Respect the peace, solitude and tranquillity of the countryside for others to enjoy – keep noise to a minimum.
12 The landscape can be spectacular but dangerous – take particular care along precipitous cliff edges, hilltops and slippery coastal paths.
13 Stay away from working areas on the moors and hills during game shooting, lambing season, deer culling and heather burning, and respect other locally or nationally imposed access restrictions.
14 Report any damage or environmental concerns to the landowner or the Environment Agency for England and Wales, T08708 506506, www.environment-agency.gov.uk/regions/wales.
15 Be adequately prepared when you walk in the hills – check the weather forecast, carry warm, waterproof clothing and adequate food and water supplies, and know how to use a map and compass.

Local customs and laws

In general, customs and laws are the same as you would encounter in any other western country. Informal clothing is acceptable throughout Wales, except at special events that specify a dress code. If you are planning to work in Wales, business clothes may be appropriate. Visitors may find the British to be reserved, and, as in most countries, politeness is appreciated.

Tipping

Tipping in Wales is at the customer's discretion. In a restaurant you should leave a tip of 10-15% if you are satisfied with the service. If the bill already includes a service charge, you needn't add a further tip. Tipping is not normal in pubs or bars. As in most other countries, porters, bellboys and waiters in more upmarket hotels rely on tips to supplement their meagre wages.

Prohibitions

If you use mace or pepper spray for self defence at home, you should note that both are illegal in the UK, and if you are caught carrying or using them, you may be arrested. Marijuana is illegal, as are all the usual drugs. However, under a recently introduced law, police in most cities turn a blind eye to possession of small amounts of cannabis.

Responsible tourism

Sustainable or ecotourism has been described as, "...ethical, considerate or informed tourism where visitors can enjoy the natural, historical and social heritage of an area without causing adverse environmental, socio-economic or cultural impacts that compromise the long-term ability of that area and its people to provide a recreational resource for future generations and an income for themselves..."

Many parts of Wales are areas of outstanding natural beauty, and home to both wildlife and people who make their living from the land. Please behave responsibly in the countryside, and around ancient monuments. For further information on what action is being taken throughout UK or across the world to control the negative aspects of tourism on the natural environment and traditional cultures, contact **Tourism Concern** ① *277-281 Holloway Road, London, T020 77533330, www.tourismconcern.org.uk.*

Safety

Generally speaking, Wales is a safe place to visit. However, Welsh cities have their fair share of crime, and you should take heed of the usual advice and avoid wandering alone around unlit city centre streets, parks and lonely railway stations. Trust your instincts and, if in doubt pay for a taxi. (See Women travellers, page 18.) Remember to look right, not left, when crossing the road. Footprint is a partner in the Foreign and Commonwealth Office's Know Before You Go campaign, www.fco.gov.uk/travel.

Getting around

Compared to the rest of Western Europe, public transport in Britain is generally poor and can be expensive. Rail, in particular, can cost an arm and a leg, and is notoriously unreliable. Coach travel is cheaper but much slower. Some areas are poorly served by public transport of any kind, and if you plan to spend much time in rural areas, it may be worth hiring a car, especially if you are travelling as a couple or group. A useful website for all national public transport information is www.pti.org.uk.

Rail

The rail network in Wales is less extensive than the bus network and generally a more expensive way to travel, and trains can be unreliable. However, there are some wonderfully scenic journeys across the middle of the country and many heritage railways still exist (see box, The rail thing). Most trains operating within Wales are run by **Arriva Trains Wales** ① *T08456 061660, www.arrivatrainswales.co.uk.*

Reservations

The system of fare pricing is complex. To help you navigate the railways, enlist the help of **National Rail Enquiries** ① *T0845 7484950, www.nationalrail.co.uk,* who will

The rail thing

Wales is a great place for lovers of scenic railway journeys – the country is full of them. The railways were vital to the development of the country's industries in the 19th century and trains, hauled first by horses and then by steam, were used to transport goods such as coal and slate from mines and quarries (often set in inaccessible mountain regions) to ports where they could then be loaded onto ships and exported all over the world. It was in 1804 that the first steam locomotive travelled on iron rails, going along the Merthyr tramroad in south Wales. And the world's first passenger railway service was launched in Wales in 1807, taking people around Swansea Bay. When the industries declined so did the railways – and the final death knell for many were the beeching cuts of the 1960s, which axed lines throughout Britain, badly affecting rural areas of Wales. However, many old railway lines that were abandoned have been carefully restored by volunteers who now run vintage trains (usually steam) along the tracks. The best known scenic routes are in the north, but there are a few in the south of Wales too. Wales also boasts Britain's only mountain railway, which travels up Snowdon (see box, page 187).

South Wales
Brecon Mountain Railway, Merthyr Tydfil, T01685 722988.

Mid Wales
Talyllyn Railway, Tywyn, T01654 710472.
Vale of Rheidol Railway, Aberystwyth, T01970 625819
Welshpool & Llanfair Light Railway, Llanfair Caereinion, T01938 810441.

North Wales
Bala Lake Railway, T01678 540666
Ffestiniog Railway, Porthmadog, T01766 516073.
Llanberis Lake Railway, T01286 870549.
Welsh Highland Railway, Caernarfon, T01766 516073.
Welsh Highland Railway, Porthmadog, T0870 321 2402.
Information on these services can be found at www.greatlittletrainsof wales.co.uk, T01654 710472.

Other scenic railways include:
Fairbourne & Barmouth Steam Railway, Fairbourne, T01341 250362; Gwili Railway, near Carmarthen, T01267 230666; Llangollen Railway, T01978 860979; Snowdon Mountain Railway, Llanberis, T01286 870223; and the Teifi Valley Railway, Cardigan T01559 371077.

provide advice on routes, timetables, fares and connections. You can book tickets and consult timetables online at **www.qjump.com** or **www.thetrainline.co.uk**. See Fares, page 25, for further detail on the types of ticket available; and box, Discount travel cards, page 35. Alternatively, you can contact each company direct: **Central** ① T0870 6091616, www.central.trains.co.uk, serving the Cardiff and border areas; **First Great Western** ① T0845 6001159, www.firstgreatwestern.co.uk, serving South Wales; **First North Western** ① T0845 6001159, www.firstnorthwestern.co.uk, serving South Wales; **Valley Lines** ① T0845 6061660, www.arrivatrainswales.co.uk, serving Cardiff and the Valleys; **Virgin Trains** ① T0845 7222333, www.virgintrains.co.uk, serving Cardiff and the north coast; **Wales & Borders** ① T0845 6061660, www.walesandwest.co.uk, serving the South and West.

See Ins and outs and Transport sections of each chapter for further local details.

Bicycle

Wales, like the rest of Britain, is less cycle-friendly than some countries, but with plenty of rivers, valleys, mountains, coast and moorland to explore, cycling is a great way to get out and about into the heart of the Welsh countryside. You don't need to go mountain biking off-road to enjoy the peace and quiet of the area; there are plenty of rural backroads, especially unclassified roads and country lanes, which are not numbered but are signposted and marked on OS maps. The only problem with more remote areas is the scarcity of spare parts should something go wrong with your bike.

There are also forest trails and dedicated routes along canal towpaths and disused railway tracks. These are part of the expanding National Cycle Network, which is covered by the *Official Guide to the National Network* (£9.99), published by the charity **SUSTRANS** ① *T0117 9290888, www.sustrans.co.uk*. There is also a series of demanding long-distance routes. The Wales Tourist Board provides good information at **www.cycling.visitwales.com**. The **Cyclists' Touring Club** (CTC) ① *T01483 417217, www.ctc.org.uk*, the largest cycling organization in the UK, provides a wide range of services and information on transport, cycle hire and routes, from day rides to longer tours. For off-road or mountain biking, see Sports and activities, page 45.

Transporting your bicycle You can cut down on the amount of pedalling you have to do by transporting your bike by train. Bikes can be taken free on most local rail services on a first come-first served basis, but only outside morning and evening rush hours (0730-0930 and 1600-1900). On long-distance routes you'll have to make a reservation at least 24 hours in advance and pay a small charge. Space is limited on trains so it's a good idea to book as far in advance as possible. Bus and coach companies will not usually carry bikes, with the exception of national park bus services, such as the **Beacons Bus** (see page 113) and the **Snowdon Sherpa** (see page 194). Details are given throughout the text, or are available on the CTC website.

Rental Bike rental is available at cycle shops in most large towns and cities and tourist centres. Expect to pay from around £10-20 per day, with discounts for longer periods, plus a refundable deposit. There are cycle shops and cycle hire companies in most large towns, and smaller towns and villages in popular tourist areas. Addresses and phone numbers are given under the transport sections of individual towns in this book.

Bus and coach

Travelling around Wales by bus is generally the cheapest form of public transport. Roads are well maintained and there are good bus links between towns and cities, but far less frequent in more remote rural areas. While it's possible to travel almost anywhere by bus, it can be slow-going and patience is required. There is a vast network of local and regional services throughout the country, including National Parks. When travelling on local buses, try to have the right money as change is not always available.

Postbus services Many rural areas not served by regular buses, can be reached by Royal Mail postbuses. These are minibuses that follow postal delivery routes and carry up to 14 fare-paying passengers. This is a slow way to travel as the bus stops to deliver mail, but it allows you to reach remote locations. A free booklet of routes and timetables is usually available from Tourist Information Centres (TICs), or visit www.postbus.royalmail.com/ RouteFinder.asp for a comprehensive route-planning service.

‡ Various companies offer backpacker bus tours operating on a jump-on/ jump-off basis. They are an affordable option for those on a modest budget, see Tours, page 14.

✦ Pedal power

Wales offers some superb opportunities for cyclists, with everything from gentle circuits for families to challenging mountain bike trails for the adventurous (and fit) biker. You can cycle alongside canal towpaths, down quiet country lanes, beside lakes and reservoirs and along forest and mountain tracks.

The country has two long-distance trails that can be ridden over about a week: The **Lôn Las Cymru National Cycle Route** (250 miles) runs north to south and takes you across the Snowdonia National Park and the Cambrian Mountains. It starts in Holyhead, Anglesey and cuts across the country to Cardiff or Chepstow.

The **Lôn Geltaidd Celtic Trail** (220 miles) goes from west to east, starting at Fishguard on the lovely Pembrokeshire coast and going across the country to Chepstow. It follows canal towpaths, disused railway tracks and quiet lanes.

Wales also boasts some of the finest mountain biking in the world. The best known tracks and bike bases are: **Afan Forest Park**, T01639 850564, Southeast, near Neath, with four trails; **Brecon Beacons National Park**, www.breconbeacons.org, the active heart of Wales with 16 mountain bike routes, suitable for novices and the more experienced; **Coed y Brenin**, T01341 422289, in North Wales, near Dolgellau, Wales' best known mountain biking centre, with good facilities and five trails; **Cwmcarn Forest**, T01495 272001, in the southeast corner, half an hour from Cardiff and close to Newport, has the **Whyte Twrch Trail**; **Gwydyr Forest**, T01341 422289, in the north near Betws y Coed, has a long mountain trail; **Llanwrtyd Wells**, Mid Wales, is a good base for exploring on a bike as it offers access to fine, unspoilt countryside and a variety of trails; **Machynlleth**, Mid Wales, has three trails that start from the town centre and a purpose built trail in the nearby Dyfi forest; **Nant yr Arian**, T01341 422289, in the northwest, near Aberystwyth, is set in the remote mountains, it has three trails including the challenging **Syfydrin Trail**.

These aren't the only places to cycle in the country though – there are cycle paths and trails everywhere. Just ask at local TICs and check out the following websites for loads more information on everything from maps, trail guides, bike repair shops and places to stay: **www.mbwales.com** for mountain biking; **www.cycling. visitwales.com** for all sorts of cycling info; **www.sustrans.org.uk** for maps and general info. There are also packs available on taking a cycle break in Wales, they cost £5.99 and can be ordered on T08701 211254.

Reservations A number of travel passes are available (see box, page 35 for details). Information on services throughout Wales is available from **Traveline Cymru**, T0870 608208, www.traveline-cymru.org.uk. Bus companies include: **Arriva Cymru**, T08701 201088, www.arriva.co.uk, serving north and west Wales; First Cymru, T01792 582233, www.firstcymru.co.uk, serving southwest Wales; **National Express**, T08705 808080, www.nationalexpress.com, serving major towns and cities throughout the country; and **Stagecoach**, T01633 838856, www.stagecoachbus.com/south_wales, serving southeast Wales.

Car

Travelling with your own transport is the ideal way to explore the country. This allows you the freedom to explore remote places in your own time. The main disadvantages

Discount travel cards

Full-time students or those aged under 25 or over 50, can buy a **Coach Card** for £9 which is valid for one year and gets you a 20-30% discount on all fares. Children normally travel for half price, but with a **Family Card** costing £15, two children travel free with two adults. The **Tourist Trail Pass** offers unlimited travel on all National Express services throughout Britain. Passes cost from £49 for two days' travel out of three, up to £190 for 15 days' travel out of 30. They can be bought from major travel agents, at Gatwick and Heathrow airports, as well as from bus stations. In North America these passes are available from **British Travel International**, T1-800-3276097, www.britishtravel.com, or from **US National Express**, T502-2981395.

There are a variety of **railcards** which give discounts on fares for certain groups. Cards are valid for one year and most are available from main stations. You need two passport photos and proof of age or status. **Young Person's Railcard**: for those aged 16-25 or full-time students in the UK. Costs £18 and gives 33% discount on most train tickets and some ferry services. **Senior Citizen's Railcard**: for those aged over 60. Same prices and discounts as above. **Disabled Person's Railcard**: costs £14 and gives 33% discount to a disabled person and one other. **Family Railcard**: costs £20 and gives 33% discount on most tickets (20% on others) for up to four adults travelling together, and 81% discount for up to four children.

Within Wales, the **Freedom of Wales Flexi Pass** allows you to travel on all mainline trains and almost all its buses for a specified period. There are further reductions for children. The **4 in 8 Pass** allows four days rail travel and eight days bus travel. Peak (mid June to mid Sept £55; Off Peak (Jan-mid Jun and mid Sep-end Dec) £45. The **8 in 15 Pass** allows 8 days rail and 15 days bus travel. Peak (dates as above) £92, Off Peak £75. The **Freedom of South Wales Flexi Rover** allows three days rail and seven days bus travel in South Wales. Peak £35, Off Peak £30; as does the **Freedom of North and Mid Wales Rover**, Peak £30. For further information contact T0845 6061660.

are traffic congestion and parking, but this is only a problem in the main cities and on major roads, particularly at weekends and on bank holidays. Roads in Wales are generally a lot less busy than those in England, and driving is relatively stress-free, especially on the B-roads and minor roads.

Rules and regulations To drive in the UK you must have a current **driving licence**, although foreign nationals may use their own licence for one year. International driving permits, available from your country of origin, may be required for some rentals, especially if your own licence is not in English. Visitors importing their own vehicle should also have their vehicle registration or ownership document. Make sure you have adequate **insurance**. In all of the UK you drive on the left. **Speed limits** are (unless otherwise indicated) 30 miles per hour (mph) in built-up areas, 70 mph on motorways and dual carriageways and 60 mph on most other roads. Further details on all aspects of driving in the UK an be found at www.dvla.gov.uk.

Organizations Britain has two main motoring organizations, which can help with route planning, traffic advice, insurance and breakdown cover. These are the **Automobile Association** (AA) ① T0800 444999, www.theaa.co.uk, and the **Royal Automobile Club** (RAC) ① T0800 550550, www.rac.co.uk. One year's membership starts at £43 for the AA and £39 for the RAC, which will cover you for emergency assistance. They also provide many other services, including a reciprocal agreement for free assistance with many overseas motoring organizations – check to see if your organization is included. Their emergency numbers are: **AA** To800 887766; **RAC** To8000 828282. You can still call these numbers if you're not a member, but you'll have to a pay a large fee.

Car hire

Car hire is expensive and you may be better off making arrangements in your home country for a fly/drive deal through one of the main multi-national companies: The minimum you can expect to pay is around £150 per week for a small car. Always check and compare conditions, such as mileage limitations, excess payable in the case of an accident. Small, local hire companies often offer better deals than the larger multi-nationals. Most companies prefer payment with a credit card otherwise you'll have to leave a large deposit (£100 or more). You need to have had a full driver's licence for at least one year and to be aged between 21 (25 for some companies) and 70. Motorcycle hire is very expensive, ranging from around £200 up to £350 per week. See individual town Transport sections for more information on local car hire companies.

Car hire companies

Avis, T08705 900500, www.avis.co.uk, in the US T1-800 3311084.
British Car Rental, T0113 2376879, www.bcvr.co.uk.
Budget, T0800 181181, www.budget.rentacar.co.uk, in the US T1-800 5270700.
Car Hire Express, T0870 4000024, www.carhireexpress.co.uk.
Easycar, www.easycar.com.

Europcar, T08457 222525, www.europcar.com.
Hertz, T08705 996699, www.hertz.co.uk, in the US T1-800 6543001.
Holiday Autos, T08705 300400, www.holidayautos.co.uk, in the US T1-800 4227737, www.holiday/colauto.com.
National Car Rental, T08705 365365, in the US T1-800-CAR-RENT, www.nationalcar.com.
Thrifty, T02072622223 (Cardiff), www.thrifty.com, in the US T1-800 3672777.

Hitching

As in the rest of the UK, hitching is never entirely safe, and is certainly not advised for anyone travelling alone, particularly women travellers. Those prepared to take the risk should not find it too difficult to get a lift, especially in rural areas where people are far more willing to stop for you. Bear in mind, though, that you will probably have to wait a while to even see a car in remote parts.

Maps

You'll find a good selection of maps of Wales in most bookshops and at the main tourist offices. Road atlases can be bought at service stations. The best of these are the large-format ones produced by the **AA, Collins** and **Ordnance Survey,** which cover all of Britain at a scale of around three miles to one inch and include plans of the major towns and cities. The **Michelin** and **Bartholomew** fold-out maps are also excellent, as are the official regional tourist maps published by **Estate Publications,** which are ideal for driving and which are available from most tourist offices.

The best detailed maps for walking are the **Ordnance Survey** maps, which are unsurpassed for accuracy and clarity. These are available at different scales. The **Landranger** series at 1:50,000 (1¼ inches to a mile) covers the whole of Britain and is good for most walkers. The new **Explorer** and **Outdoor Leisure** series are 1:25,000 and offer better value for walkers and cyclists. An excellent source of maps is **Stanfords** at 12-14 Longacre, London WC2E 9LP, www.stanfords.co.uk.

Sleeping

Accommodation in Wales is plentiful, and the quality of what's available has improved greatly in recent years. Hotels range from world-class luxury, for which you can expect to pay at least £100 to over £250 a night, to dilapidated concerns with dodgy plumbing and threadbare carpets, though thankfully the latter are decreasing in number. For the privilege of staying at one of these less charming places you can still expect to pay £50 a night for a double room. Most of the more salubrious hotels, the ones that can afford to pay the cleaner but may not offer full room service, are likely to cost between £80-£140 for a double room for a night. Generally it's still true to say that guests paying over £80 a night can expect a superior level of comfort and service: from well-sprung mattresses to fluffy bath towels and flowers in the room.

Hotels

Hotels range from top-notch country houses, with extensive grounds and sometimes spa facilities to smaller establishments like cosy inns. Wales also has an increasing number of boutique hotels which are small, classy and contemporary. You'll also find some restaurants with rooms – where accommodation tends to be good quality but simpler, as the emphasis is on the food – and inns, which are offering increasingly decent rooms.

At the lower end of the scale, there is often little to choose between cheaper hotels and guesthouses or B&Bs – in fact a good B&B can often be far better than a low-grade hotel, offering higher standards of comfort (and often cleanliness) and a more personal service. However, many small hotels are really just guesthouses, and are often family-run and every bit as friendly. Note that some hotels, especially in town centres or in fishing ports, may also be rather noisy, as the bar can often be the social hub. Rooms in most mid-range to expensive hotels almost always have bathrooms en suite. Many upmarket hotels offer excellent room-only deals in the low season. An efficient last-minute booking service is **www.laterooms.com**, which specializes in weekend breaks. Also note that many hotels offer cheaper rates for online booking through agencies such as **www.lastminute.com**.

Some of the best accommodation is collected in the brochure by **Welsh Rarebits** ① *T01686 668030, (Toll free from USA, T800-8737140), www.welsh.rarebits.co.uk.*

See inside the front cover for a quick guide to the hotel price codes used in this book.

Guesthouses

Guesthouses occupy the middle ground between hotels and B&Bs. The quality of accommodation in guesthouses varies wildly: some provide exceptional value for the money in houses of great character; while others have seen much better days. They can usually charge anything from £50-£100 for the night, occasionally quoting initially for half-board (dinner, bed and breakfast). Some have a restaurant, which may or may not be open to non-residents.

Guesthouses are often large, converted family homes with five or six rooms. They tend to be slightly more expensive than B&Bs, charging between around £35 and £55 per person per night. Although they are often less personal, they can provide better facilities, such as en suite bathrooms, TV in each room and private parking. In many instances they are more like small budget hotels. Many guesthouses offer evening meals, but this may have to be requested in advance. Information is available from the Wales Tourist Board, where you can book online at www.visitwales.co.uk. Some of the best small hotels, inns and guesthouses can be found in the brochure published by **Great Little Places** ① *T01686 668030, www.wales.little-places.co.uk.*

Hotel price codes explained

Accommodation prices in this book are graded with the letters below and are based on the cost per person, for two people sharing a double room with en suite bathroom, during the high season. Cheaper rooms with shared bathroom are available in many hotels, guesthouses and Bed and Breakfasts (B&Bs). Many places, particularly larger hotels, offer substantial discounts during the low season and at weekends. All places listed are recommended as providing good quality and value within their respective price category.

L over £160
A £100-160
B £80-100
C £50-80
D £30-50
E £15-30
F under £15

Bed and Breakfasts (B&Bs)

Bed & Breakfasts (B&Bs) provide the cheapest private accommodation. As their name suggests, they usually offer fairly straightforward accommodation in a private home, with a heart-stopping breakfast fry-up thrown in. Many are run by empty-nesters with beautiful period houses and gardens; elsewhere, the best of them tend to be on working farms. These days most have en suite or private bathrooms and TVs in the rooms – though do check beforehand to be sure. Again, their standards are extremely variable, but they're unlikely to cost much more than £70 per room per night, some as little as £45 – depending on their location as much as the quality they offer – and some hosts can really bring their area to life. Many hotels, guesthouses and B&Bs offer discounts for stays of more than one night, weekend deals, and high and low season prices. They can be booked through Tourist Information Centres (TICs). Some TICs charge a booking fee. Note that many B&Bs charge more than 50% of the room rate for single occupancy, so check beforehand.

Hostels

For those travelling on a tight budget, there is a large network of hostels offering cheap accommodation. These are also popular centres for backpackers and provide a great opportunity for meeting fellow travellers. Hostels have kitchen facilities for self-catering and some include a continental breakfast in the price or provide cheap breakfasts and evening meals. Advance booking is recommended at all times, and particularly from May to September and on public holidays.

In most major cities, national parks and other areas of outstanding natural beauty, budget accommodation can be found at **backpackers hostels** and **YMCAs**. Many campsites and youth hostels are run by the **Youth Hostel Association** ① *Trevelyan House, Dimple Rd, Matlock, DE4 3YH, T01629 592600 or T0870 8708808, www.yha.org.uk.* A bed in a dormitory usually costs less than £15 a night.

Self-catering

One of the most cost-effective ways to enjoy Wales is to hire a cottage with a group of friends or family. There are lots of different types of accommodation to choose from, to suit all budgets, ranging from high quality serviced apartments and luxury homes to windmills and lighthouse keeper's houses and basic cottages with few facilities.

The minimum stay is usually one week in the summer peak season, though many offer shorter stays of two, three or four nights, especially outside the peak season. Expect to pay at least £150-200 per week for a two-bedroom cottage in the winter, rising to £300-500 in the high season, or more if it's a particularly nice place.

Some TICs and a large number of private organizations keep lists of **self-catering** options on their books. Two of the more interesting are **The Landmark Trust** ① *Shottisbrooke, Maidenhead, Berks, SL6 3SW, T01628 825925, www.landmark trust.co.uk,* who rent out renovated historic landmark buildings, at a price; and **The National Trust** ① *36 Queen Anne's Gate, London, SW1H 9AS, T0870 6095380, brochure T0870 4584411, www.nationaltrustcottages.co.uk,* who provide a wide range of accommodation on their estates, from an old rectory to a gas-lit cottage.

Contacts

There's lots of information and contacts at www.cottages.co.uk. Also see:
Brecon Beacons Holiday Cottages, T01874 676446, www.breconcottages.com;
Coast and Country Cottages, T01239 881297, www.welsh-cottages.co.uk;

Menai Holiday Cottages, T01248 717135, www.menaiholidays.co.uk;
Nefyn Holidays, T01758 720674, www.nefynholidays.co.uk;
Snowdonia Tourist Services, T01766 513829, www.sts-holidays.com;
Wales Cottage Holidays, T01686 628200, www.wales-holidays.co.uk.

Campsites

There are plenty of campsites around Wales. Many are geared towards caravans and vary greatly in quality and level of facilities – some have large, luxury static caravans and electricity, others are just fields on a farm. The most expensive sites, which charge up to £10 to pitch a tent, are usually well-equipped. Sites are usually only open from April to October. If you plan to do a lot of camping, you should take a look at www.freedom-hols.co.uk, T01202 252179, which lists parks graded by the Wales Tourist Board.

Campus accommodation

Several Welsh universities open their halls of residence to visitors during the summer vacation (late June to September). Many rooms are basic and small with shared bathrooms, but there are also more comfortable rooms with private bathrooms, twin and family units and self-contained apartments and shared houses. Bed and Breakfast, and self-catering options are all available. Prices for B&Bs tend to be roughly the same as most B&Bs, but self-catering can cost as little as £50 per person per week. Local tourist offices have information, or contact the **British Universities Accommodation Consortium**, T0115 9504571, for a brochure. Details for Cardiff are given under the Cardiff sleeping section. For Swansea contact T01792 295665, www.swan.ac.uk; and for Aberystwyth contact T01970 621960, www.aber.ac.uk.

Eating

Food

The quality of food in Wales has improved enormously in recent years. Since the 1980s the British in general have been shrugging off their reputation for over-boiled cabbage and watery beef and although the food revolution took a bit longer to reach Wales, the Welsh have now made determined efforts to improve the quality of food on offer. Annual awards are made to restaurants and pubs serving high-quality food, as well as to outstanding Welsh food producers. Although Wales has never had a cuisine that's particularly distinct to that of the rest of Britain, it does have some excellent local produce, such as lamb and fish, as well as a number of traditional native dishes. Organic produce is also widely available. Many chefs are now making the most of

⚏ Restaurant price codes explained

The price ranges in this book are based on a two-course meal (main course plus starter or dessert) without drinks for one person. We have tried to include an equal number of choices in each category, though this is not always possible. All places listed are recommended as offering relatively good value, quality and standards of service within their respective price category.

♨♨♨	over £20
♨♨	£10-20
♨	under £10

this, combining ingredients in imaginative ways, and creating lighter, fresher versions of traditional dishes to create what's generally known as 'modern Welsh' cuisine. An increasing number of contemporary restaurants, bistros and so-called 'gastropubs' (where the emphasis is on good food rather than boozing) are opening throughout the country. The cities also generally have Italian and Indian restaurants and most places, including pubs, will offer at least one choice for vegetarians. Not surprisingly, the capital Cardiff has the most cosmopolitan food culture and you can eat anything there, from Mexican to Japanese. You shouldn't go hungry in Wales as even the smallest places usually have a takeaway outlet, generally offering Chinese food, baked potatoes with fillings or, of course, fish and chips – which can be excellent if well cooked. The situation's not perfect and plenty of places still do fatty pies, greasy chips and overcooked veg but things are improving all the time.

So what should you look out for in Wales? Well, meat eaters can try Welsh **lamb** and Black **beef**, which have been farmed on the local pastures and hills for centuries. There is also salt marsh lamb, which is raised on coastal areas feeding on saline rich vegetation which gives it a distinctive, delicate flavour. Lamb is used to make *cawl*, a traditional broth made with leeks, potatoes and other veg.

Then there's a wide range of **seafood**, perhaps the best known of which are the Penclawdd cockles which are collected on the Gower peninsula and sold at Swansea market. You'll also find oysters from Pembroke and Anglesey, crabs and lobsters from places like Milford Haven, and other delicacies like scallops and clams. The coastline, as well as Wales' lakes and rivers, mean that lots of fresh **fish** is available, from salmon to less familiar Arctic char and *sewin* (sea trout). The shore also gives Wales one of its most distinctive native dishes – **laver bread** (bara lawr). This is a sort of lettuce-like seaweed that is mixed with oatmeal and generally fried and eaten for breakfast with bacon – it's a Swansea favourite.

Lots of **vegetables** in Wales are produced organically – look out for the famous Welsh leek, often combined with potatoes in soups and stews. Then there are some wonderful Welsh **cheeses** varying from the famous Caerphilly, which is mild, white and crumbly to Llanboidy, a smooth, hard cheese. Most of the cheese-making production is in West Wales, especially the Teifi and Towy valleys. There are some delicious soft goat's cheeses available too. Hard cheeses are often flavoured with other ingredients such as laverbread, chives or garlic to create more intense flavours. Cheese, of course, features in some of Wales' native dishes such as **Welsh rarebit** – essentially cheese mixed with beer (or sometimes Worcester sauce) and grilled on toast, and **Glamorgan sausages**, made from cheese, herbs and vegetables.

Traditional Welsh baking recipes are simple but flavoursome. In tea rooms you might see **bara brith**, (speckled bread) which is a sort of dried fruit loaf made with tea, and Welsh cakes, which are made with fruit and cooked on a griddle. Welsh producers are also making **ice cream**, sometimes flavoured with local honey, yoghurts, preserves and handmade chocolates. Keep an eye out for them in delis and markets.

⚏ See inside front cover for a quick guide to eating price categories.

Eating out

For a cheap meal, your best bet is a pub, hotel bar or café, where ⌐
one-course meal for £6-7 or less, though don't expect gourmet food. The
often at lunch time, when many restaurants offer three-course set lunches ⌐
lunches for less than £10. You'll need a pretty huge appetite to feel like
three-course lunch after your gigantic cooked breakfast, however. Also good value ⌐
pre-theatre dinners offered by many restaurants in the larger towns and cities (you d⌐
need to have a theatre ticket to take advantage). These are usually available from aroun⌐
1730-1800 till 1900-1930. The biggest problem with eating out in the UK is the limited
serving hours in many pubs and hotels outside the main cities. These places often only
serve food between 1230 and 1400 and 1700 and 1900, seemingly ignorant of the eating
habits of foreign visitors, or those who would prefer a bit more flexibility during their
holiday. In small places especially it can be difficult finding food outside these times.

Drink

Drinking is taken as seriously in Wales as the rest of Britain and **beer** (flat, brown and
made with hops) is still the national drink – although it faces serious competition
from continental lagers and alcopops. **Real ale**, made from small independent
breweries, is available in many pubs in Wales. Pubs are still the traditional places to
enjoy a drink: the best are usually 'freehouses' (not tied to a brewery) and feature log
fires in winter, pretty gardens for the summer, and thriving local custom. Those that
also have accommodation are known as 'inns', while more and more are offering
good food. The local brews are Brains beer, which is made in Cardiff and ale made at
the Felinfoel brewery near Llanelli. As well as widely available 'bitter' you'll also find
'dark' in Wales, a sweeter, darker coloured beer.

Welsh **wines** are also now produced in the south (see box, Grape Expectations,
page 98), while the most recent additions to the local drinks industry are distilled
drinks made in Penderyn near the Brecon Beacons. There's Penderyn Welsh **whisky**,
Brecon gin, vodka and a creamy liqueur, www.welsh-whisky.co.uk. Pubs are usually
open from around 1100-2230 or 2300 Monday to Saturday, and on Sunday from around
1200-1500 and 1800-2230, though those in bigger cities might open for longer.

Entertainment

Not surprisingly, Cardiff has the most vibrant entertainment scene in Wales. Its bars
and clubs attract everyone from celebrities (local girl Charlotte Church is frequently
spotted living it up with friends) to visiting stags and hens. Friday and Saturday nights
can get extremely raucous – especially if there's been a big match on – but the crowds
are generally pretty good humoured. Outside Cardiff, you'll find the liveliest bars and
clubs in university towns and cities like Swansea, Aberystwyth and Bangor. Rural life
still tends to focus on the pub.

Cardiff, like other major British cities, plays host on a regular basis to world-class
theatre, music and dance – the new Wales Millennium Centre, the St David's Hall and
the Millennium Stadium all providing fine venues. Smaller towns and villages have
also made a name for themselves with their festivals and events – notably with
typical Welsh eisteddfodau (see box, page 43). Also keep an eye out for performances
and rehearsals of local **Male Voice Choirs** (details in individual town listings and on
www.malevoicechoir.net), a distinctive Welsh musical institution.

Gruffudd
herine Zeta
es – then
thony
Rhys
big
surprising that
as an increasingly fertile film
scene. There's an excellent film school
situated at Caerleon, near Newport,
and work started in 2004 on Dragon
Studios, a state-of-the-art film studio
complex near Bridgend. Some films
are set in Wales, such as the cult film
Human Traffic (1999) which was set in
Cardiff. Welsh locations are also often
used as a dramatic backdrop: the
sand dunes of Merthyr Mawr in

Lawrence of Arabia (1962); Raglan
Castle in *Time Bandits* (1981);
Caerphilly Castle in *Restoration* (1995),
Snowdonia in the second *Tombraider*
(2003). A number of big-budget
Bollywood films have also been shot
at locations in Cardiff, Caerphilly and
the Brecon Beacons. The Brecons
also featured in *King Arthur* (2004)
which starred Keira Knightley, and
Ioan Gruffudd as heroic Sir Lancelot.
Due for release in 2005 are *The
Libertine*, a period romp starring
Johnny Depp shot at Tretower Court
and Castle, and *Half Light*, a
contemporary drama starring Demi
Moore which was filmed on the
northwest coast.

Festivals and events

The most famous cultural festivals in Wales are the eisteddfodau (singular
eisteddfod) which are held annually all over the country. The biggest event is the
National Eisteddfod which is held in different venues each year, alternating between
North and South Wales. Other eisteddfodau include the Urdd National Eisteddfod,
aimed at young people, www.urdd.org. There are also folk festivals, music festivals,
agricultural shows and beer festivals held in towns and villages, mainly in the Spring
and Summer. The wackiest festivals and events are held in the Mid Wales town of
Llanwrtyd Wells, which hosts everything from bog snorkelling championships to a
man versus horse race.

Festivals and events calendar

Details are provided in the listings for each
area. Also check www.cerdddystwyth.co.uk.
Jan Hen Galen (13 Jan). Celebration of 'Old
New Year' according to the Julian calendar in
the Gwaun Valley, Pembrokeshire.
Feb Six Nations Rugby Championship,
Cardiff Millennium Stadium.
Mar St David's Day. Celebrations
throughout Wales, on 1 May.
Apr Cardiff International Festival of
Musical Theatre, www.cardiffmusicals.com.
Biennial celebration of the musical. Various
venues, next in 2005.
May Hay Festival, Hay-on-Wye, www.hay
festival.com. Festival of Literature, end May-

early Jun.
St David's Cathedral Festival, www.stdavids
cathedral.org.uk. Classical concerts at St
David's Cathedral.
Tredegar House Folk Festival, www.tredegar
housefolk.ik.com. Music and dance festival
near Newport.
Urdd National Eisteddfod, www.urdd.org.
The Welsh youth eisteddfod, held end
May-early Jun. Venue changes annually,
2005 venue is Millennium Centre, Cardiff.
Jun Abersoch Jazz Festival, Abersoch,
www.abersoch.co.uk. Jazz festival on the Llŷn.
Cardiff Singer of the World,
www.bbc.co.uk/cardiffsinger. BBC Wales'
biennial singing competition, usually held in
the St David's Hall. Next held in 2005.

⦂ The eisteddfod

Meaning a 'meeting of bards' or 'a gathering' the eisteddfod (plural eisteddfodau) is a uniquely Welsh event. Its origins stretch far back in history to the days when poets, singers and musicians would gather to compete for positions in the households of the gentry. The first major eisteddfod was held in 1176 in Cardigan Castle and after that they were held regularly, until the practice began to die out in the 17th and 18th centuries. They were revived in the 19th century, the first modern one taking place at Carmarthen. Now they take place all over Wales, with two major annual festivals – the **International**

Musical Eisteddfod (see box p218) and the **Royal National Eisteddfod**. The latter alternates between locations in north and south Wales and involves ceremonies in which prizes are awarded for poetry, prose, and music. Proceedings are conducted in Welsh and it's a fascinating insight into the country and its traditions. Visitors come from all over the world. The 2005 **Royal National Eisteddfod** will be held from 30 July-6 August at the Faenol Estate, Felinheli, near Bangor, T0845 1222003 or T01286 682430. The 2006 event will run from 5-12 August in Swansea, T02920 763777. Further details at www.eisteddfod.org.uk.

Gregynog Music Festival, Gregynog Hall near Newtown, Powys, www.wales.ac.uk. Classical music fest.

Gwyl Ifan, www.gwylifan.org. Major dance festival with events in locations in and around Cardiff, including the Museum of Welsh Life, St Fagans.

Man versus Horse Marathon, Llanwrtyd Wells, T01591 610666. A big cash prize if a runner can beat a horse.

Ruthin Festival, www.ruthinfestival.co.uk. Music festival in Ruthin.

Snowdon Fiddle Festival, Nantperis, T01286 871042. Music festival held in little village of Nantperis, late Jun-early Jul.

Jul Cardiff Festival, T02920 872087, www.cardiff-festival.com. Annual free arts festival held in late Jul-early Aug, aiming to be the new Edinburgh Festival, with theatre, music, street entertainment and fairground.

Gower Folk Festival, www.halfpenny folkclub.com. Music fest held in Swansea.

International Music Eisteddfod, Llangollen, www.international-eisteddfod.co.uk. See box, p218, for further information.

International Storytelling Festival St Donat's Castle, Vale of Glamorgan, T01446 799100, www.beyondtheborder.com. Held on the 1st weekend in Jul.

Llandudno Arts and Music Festival, www.llandudnofestival.org.uk. Held in

Llandudno in North Wales in mid-Jul.

MusicFest, www.aberfest.com. Chamber music in Aberystwyth.

National Eisteddfod of Wales, www.eisteddfod.org.uk. Over 6,000 competitors at this annual Welsh event held end Jul-early Aug. 2005 is in Bangor.

North Wales Bluegrass Festival, www.northwalesbluegrass.co.uk. Music fest held in Conwy in 2005.

Sesiwn Fawr, www.sesiwnfawr.com. Major music fest with sounds from around the world, in Dolgellau, Gwynedd.

Welsh Proms, T02920 878444. Classical music concerts in St David's Hall, Cardiff.

Aug Brecon Jazz Festival, www.breconjazz.co.uk. Lively weekend of jazz in Brecon.

Faenol Festival, www.brynfest.com. Bryn Terfel's festival of opera and other music genres, Faenol, Gwynedd.

Llandrindod Wells Victorian Festival, www.victorianfestival.co.uk. Exhibitions, street theatre, talks and more in the former spa town of Llandrindod Wells.

Machynlleth Festival, www.mornawales.org.uk. Classical music, jazz and art exhibitions in Machynlleth.

Pontardawe Festival, www.pontardawefestival.org.uk. Music, dance and craft festival aimed at families.

Kiss and tell

If you hear anyone mention SWS, (pronounced soos), it stands for Social, Welsh and Sexy, www.sws uk.com – a sort of social club for ex-pat Welsh people and anyone else with an interest in Wales (you don't have to be sexy either). There are branches in London, New York and Moscow, and members include Catherine Zeta-Jones and Ioan Gruffudd. Sws is also Welsh for kiss. They've set up their own dating agency, www.cwtsh.com, but don't think you'll get a date with Ioan...

Presteigne Festival, www.presteigne festival.com. Major festival of classical and orchestral music in the border town of Presteigne.
World Bog Snorkelling Championships, www.llanwrtyd-wells.powys.org.uk. Eccentric sporting event held in Llanwrtyd Wells on the Aug Bank Holiday.
Sep Abergavenny Food Festival, www.abergavennyfoodfestival.com. Weekend of masterclasses, talks and streets filled with stalls in Abergavenny.
Cardiff Mardi Gras, T02920 871260, www.cardiffmardigras.co.uk or www.gaywales.co.uk. Lively lesbian and gay festival which includes dance, music, stalls and information tents. Held end-Aug or Sep.
North Wales International Music Festival, www.northwalesmusicfestival.co.uk. Classical concerts in the cathedral at St Asaph.
Swansea Festival of Music and the Arts, www.swanseafestival.co.uk. Opera, ballet, drama and music, late Sep and early Oct.
Tenby Arts Festival, www.tenbyartsfest.co.uk. Lively performances, talks and art in seaside town of Tenby.
Nov Cardiff Screen Festival, T02920 333300, www.cardiffscreenfestival.co.uk. Annual film festival with European and UK premieres. Welsh-language films and films shot in Wales are also shown.
Dylan Thomas Festival, Swansea, www.dylan thomas.org. Events and readings celebrating the life and works of the national poet.
Winter Wonderland, www.cardiff.gov.uk/ winterwonderland. Cardiff celebrates Christmas and the New Year with an open-air ice rink in front of the City Hall, music and fireworks from end Nov-early Jan.

Public holidays

New Year's Day (1 Jan); **Good Friday** and **Easter Monday**; **May Day Bank Holiday** (the first Mon in May); **Spring Bank Holiday** (the last Mon in May); **Summer Bank Holiday** (the last Mon in Aug); **Christmas Day** (25 Dec) and **Boxing Day** (26 Dec). There are also local public holidays in spring and autumn. Dates vary from place to place. Banks are closed during these holidays, and sights and shops may be affected to varying degrees. Contact the relevant Area Tourist Board for more details.

Shopping

Shopping in Wales, as in the rest of Britain, is expensive when compared to the rest of Europe and the US. Even so, the variety of different opportunities makes browsing a real treat, even in some of the smallest villages. Although the brand names of the big retail chains may come to seem depressingly familiar in town centres and high streets up and down the country, independent retailers are still just about holding out. The Victorian arcades in Cardiff are crammed with independent stores selling everything from trendy clothes to unusual books and, together with the big chains, make the city one of the best shopping cities in Britain. Shop hours are generally Monday to Saturday from 0900 to 1730 or 1800. In larger towns and cities, many shops also open on Sundays and late at night, usually on a Thursday and Friday. Big supermarkets and retail complexes found outside large towns are open until 2000 or later Monday to Saturday and until 1600 on Sunday. In more remote parts few shops are open on Sunday. In many rural areas there is an early-closing day when shops close at 1300. This varies from region to region, but the most common day is Wednesday.

Look out for locally made crafts and silverware, as well as items such as blankets and jumpers made from Welsh wool. Rural towns and villages may well have antique or charity shops in which you might find curios or larger items like traditional Welsh dressers, or quirky agricultural implements. Markets and food shops are also worth checking out for good quality Welsh produce. Items like Welsh whisky or Welsh chocolates can easily be carried home.

Sport and activities

The Welsh terrain, complete with mountain ranges and a rugged coastline, is ideal for outdoor activities. Consequently, the country is littered with outdoor activity centres. You name it and you can do it, walking, riding, surfing, mountain biking, climbing, sailing, canoeing, birdwatching... A publication called *Adventure Wales* available from the tourist board (T02920 499909) is a helpful guide to sporting activities throughout Wales. A good website covering all sorts of outdoor activities – from white water rafting to caving is www.adventure.visitwales.com.

Cycling and mountain biking

According to some, mountain biking in Wales is better than the Alps. With plenty of upland terrain, a network of bridleways and a series of trails developed by the Forestry Commission, two-wheeled outdoor enthusiasts are well catered for. Information on trails is available at **www.mbwales.com**. Note that cyclists are not permitted on some coastal paths, such as the Pembrokeshire Coast Path. Off-road cyclists must give way to walkers and horse riders, and should be courteous and considerate to farmers and landowners whose land they are crossing. For further information about cycling in Wales, see Getting around, page 33. For details of routes, see box Pedal Power, page 34.

Golf

The Welsh Tourist Board produce a useful brochure to golfing, *Golf Wales*, T08701 211252. Useful websites include: www.golfasitshouldbe.com; www.back2wales.com; www.breakoutworld.com; www.golfwales-ghs.com; www.walesgolfvacations.com; www.welshgolfingholidays.co.uk; and www.welshrarebits.co.uk.

Hang-gliding and paragliding

Having launched a paraglider from a 500-foot hill it's possible to soar on the thermals to an altitude of 5,000 feet. A number of centres throughout the country offer instruction. Tandem jumps are also a possibility. The **British Hangliding and Paragliding Association** has seven clubs in Wales; for details, contact www.bhpa.co.uk.

Walking in Wales

Beacons Way, Wales' newest long distance walk, due to open 2005.
Stretching 98 miles across the Brecon Beacons National Park, from Holy
Mountain (north of Abergavenny) to Bethlehem in the west. It can be split
into sections over 8-10 days and is a great way of exploring the wilder
reaches of the area. Further details on www.breconbeaconsparksociety.org.

Cambrian Way, 274 miles, the longest and toughest path from Cardiff to
Conwy via Snowdon. Guidebook by Tony Drake, available from the
Ramblers' Association, www.cambrianway.com.

Coed Morgannwg Way, 36 miles, in the Valleys follows forest tracks from
Gethin Woodland Park near Merthyr Tydfil, to Margam, near Neath.
Guide published by Neath and Port Talbot County Borough Council.

Dyfi Valley Way, 108 miles, goes from Aberdovey to Bala lake (Lake Tegid)
then round to Aberystwyth.

East Clwydian Way, 122 mile circuit, start/finish Prestatyn. Guidebook by
David Hollett, available from North Wales area of the Ramblers' Association.

Edge of Wales Walk, 95 miles from Clynnog Fawr along the pilgrim's route to
the tip of the Llŷn Peninsula and Bardsey Island, www.edgeofwales.co.uk.

Glyndŵr's Way, 132 miles, National Trail, opened in 2002, starts in Knighton, on
the border and runs through Llandiloes, on to Machynlleth, then back through
Llanwddyn and on to Welshpool, T01654 703376, www.glyndwrsway.org.uk.

Landsker Borderlands Trail, 60 miles, circular walk in Pembrokeshire, start/
finish Canaston Bridge.

Millennium Heritage Trail, 72 miles, is a circular walking route from
St Fagans and around the villages and towns of the Vale of Glamorgan.
Information from Valeways, Unit 7 Barry Enterprise Centre, Skomer Rd,
Barry, Vale of Glamorgan CF62 9DA, T01446 749000.

Hiking and climbing

Wales is a brilliant destination for walking. It's a small country with a large amount of
outstanding, unspoiled countryside and all of it is readily accessible – you can be
shopping in the heart of Cardiff in the morning and walking in the green heart of the
Wye Valley in the afternoon. The best known areas for walking are the three national
parks: **Snowdonia,** the **Brecon Beacons** and the **Pembrokeshire Coast**. These offer
everything from gritty mountain climbs, bracing hill walks and scenic coastal treks.
But you don't have to restrict yourself to these hiking honeypots – there's hardly a
corner of Wales that doesn't offer some decent walks. While Snowdon is the big
attraction for mountain lovers and pulls large numbers of visitors, you can escape the
crowds on the wild **Rhinnogs** in South Snowdonia. There are also lovely walks in the
lush **Ceiriog Valley** in the northeast, round the coast of the remote **Llŷn Peninsula** in
the northwest, through the former coal mining valleys in the south, and on the lonely
mountains of mid Wales. For those who prefer their walks flat, there are also easy
strolls along canal towpaths, like the **Brecon and Monmouthshire canal,** beside
rivers, or round the reservoirs of the **Elan Valley** – Wales' lakeland. Even seemingly
industrial areas like Newport in the southeast have easily accessible and pleasant
strolls – there's one just in the shadow of the Llanwern steelworks.

Since May 2005 more of the Welsh countryside has been opened up to walkers
with the new Countryside and Rights of Way Act (CROW Act). What it means is that
certain areas (delineated by an orange line and coloured pale yellow on new OS

Monnow Valley Walk, 40 miles, Hay-on-Wye to Monmouth. Guidebook from
Eira and Harry Steggles, Treffynon, Lower Prospect Rd, Monmouth NP25 3HS.
The North Wales Path connects Prestatyn and Bangor, with information
from Conwy Countryside Service T01492 575200.
Offa's Dyke Path, 182 miles, follows, as far as possible, the line of Offa's Dyke
from Prestatyn to Chepstow, meandering along the border of England and
Wales. It runs through Knighton and passes very close to Montgomery and
Welshpool, T01547 528753, oda@offasdyke.demon.co.uk.
The Pembrokeshire Coast Path, 186 miles, is a waymarked National Trail
that runs around the coast from St Dogmaels near Cardigan to Amroth near
Tenby. The National park Authority produce a booklet on accommodation along
the path T01437 764636, £2.50 and luggage-carrying services are available. An
official guide to the route is published by Aurum Press. More information from
the National Park, T01437 764 636, www.nationaltrail.co.uk.
The Severn Way, 210 miles, traces the course of the River Severn from its
source on Plynlimon to the Bristol Channel; 55 miles of the route are in Powys.
Environment Agency guide.
Three Castles Walk, 19 mile circuit, links castles at Grosmont, Skenfrith and
White Castle. Guidebook from Monmouthshire County Council.
Wye Valley Walk, 136 miles, from Chepstow to Plynlimon in Powys. The walk
takes you through some lovely pastoral landscapes – including that round
Tintern Abbey – and passes several market towns, such as Monmouth, Ross-on-
Wye and Hay-on-Wye. An official route guide is available from Wye Valley AONB
Office, Hadnock Road, Monmouth, T01600 710846, approx £9 including p&p,
www.wyevalleywalk.org.
Other walks are detailed throughout the text.

Essentials Sports & activities

maps) you will be allowed to wander over open country, rather than sticking to the
footpaths. This introduces new areas to walkers such as the Berwyn mountain range,
the Hiraethog Moors and the Preseli hills. Large areas of forest are also opening up.
For more details check the website www.ccw.gov.uk, or www.ordancesurvey.co.uk.
Some of the most popular walks are detailed throughout the text or in the box above.

Safety The weather can change rapidly so don't set off unless properly equipped with
a map, compass, layers of warm clothes and waterproofs. Check weather conditions in
advance on T09068 500449, www.metoffice.com or www.metcheck.com/mountain.

Books and maps There are loads of specialist books detailing walks in Wales, many
of them giving route instructions, background and maps of the route. Try and get hold
of those that have been most recently revised – walks change over time. Always take
an Ordnance Survey (OS) map too, don't rely on the maps in the books – Explorer
1:25000 are the best. OS maps can be found at tourist offices and also at outdoor
shops. Don't just stick to the well-known trails either. Go into local TICs and
bookshops where you'll generally find loads of leaflets.

Contacts There are a number of organizations that can help with suggested routes,
maps or people to get in touch with. The biggest is the **Ramblers' Association**
① *Cathedral Rd, Cardiff CF11 9HA, T02920 343535, www.ramblers.org.uk*, which has
resources in different languages. Other good sources of information are www.walking
britain.co.uk, and the **British Tourist Authority**, www.visitbritain.com/walking.

⁝ Blue Flag beaches

The Blue Flag is an eco-label awarded to resort beaches and marinas throughout the world. Run by the independent non-profit organization **Foundation for Environmental Education** (FEE), the Blue Flag works towards sustainable development at beaches through strict criteria including water quality, environmental management, safety and facilities. Around 40 of Wales' beaches have been awarded Blue Flag status, for details see www.blueflag.org.uk.

For **guided walks** with an Arthurian and Earth Mysteries theme contact Laurence Main, 9 Mawddwy Cottages, Minllyn, Dinas Mawddwy, Machynlleth, T01650 531354. Two useful websites are **www.walking.visitwales.com** and the British Mountaineering Council at **www.thebmc.co.uk**. Also useful for climbers is **Plas y Brenin**, The National Mountaineering Centre, www.pyb.co.uk.

Horse riding

Wales has plenty of opportunities for horse riding, and details of those offering pony trekking and hacking are in area listings. Check out the website www.horse backwales.com. The **Wales Riding and Trekking Association** also have lots of information. You can contact them at North Barn Glanirfon, Llanwrtyd Wells, T01591 610818, www.ridingwales.com.

Watersports

Information on water-based activities throughout Wales are provided in the listings of each chapter or can be obtained from **Wales Watersports**, T0845 0873287, www.waleswatersports.com, or **Waterscape**, www.waterscape.com/wales.

Canoeing and rafting
Canoeing and whitewater rafting are popular on Wales' many rivers such as the Wye Valley or Elan Valley. **Sea kayaking** is also a popular pastime around the coastline of Anglesey, the Llŷn and Pembrokeshire. Contact www.welsh-canoeing.org.uk or www.ukrafting.co.uk for further details.

Coasteering
The novel activity of coasteering is said to have originated at Twr-y-Felin in St Davids, Pembrokeshire. Simply don your wetsuit and get the adrenalin going with a low-level scramble along the cliffs. If you fall off, it's just a small drop to the water, and you're prepared for a ducking anyway. The great thing about coasteering is that you need no previous experience whatsoever to get a kick out of it. However, it should only be undertaken with a qualified instructor, and participants should be capable swimmers. A good company to get in touch with in St David's is **TYF No Limits**, www.tyf.com.

Diving
Wales has some of the best diving in the UK, particularly around the Pembrokeshire coast, including the marine reserve of Skomer Island. Contact for information: www.ukdiving.co.uk, www.celticdiving.co.uk and www.divewales.co.uk

A rugby nation

Until their victory in the 2005 Six Nations Championship the Welsh rugby team had taken a bit of a battering. The glory days of the 1970s, when the Welsh game basked in the triumphs of players like Gareth Edwards and JPR Williams, had seemed well over.

The bell began to toll for Welsh rugby with the arrival of professionalism in 1995. Once the game became a business, something of its gutsy spirit was lost, and Wales found it hard to find a foothold in this acquisitive commercial world.

Although hugely popular throughout the country, the notion of Wales as a rugby nation was never entirely accurate. In terms of clubs and top players, the game was mainly the preserve of the industrialized south. In the rural north, soccer, an import from nearby Liverpool and Manchester, took precedence.

The Millennium Stadium, a state-of-the-art venue, constructed bang in the centre of Cardiff, was built to replace the legendary Cardiff Arms Park, scene of many Welsh rugby wins (for 28 years the English side did not win once in Cardiff).

In 1999, the Rugby World Cup was hosted by Wales (the team reached the quarter finals). So far so traditional. But this rugby venue is now also the home of the FA Cup, at least until a replacement for Wembley Stadium is up and running.

So football versus rugby? Chances are the two passions will run side by side, just as they always have. However with glamorous young players like Gavin Henson, one of Welsh rugby's hottest international stars, and new confidence and pride in the game, Welsh rugby is in a better state than it has been for years. Welsh Women's Rugby is also doing well. And if you wanted proof that the game still rouses intense passions look no further than the Welsh rugby fan who was so convinced England would beat his team that he told his mates he would 'cut his balls off' if they won. Wales won – and he did. For further information look up Welsh Rugby Union www.wru.co.uk.

Sailing

Where there's wind there'll be sailing. It's particularly popular on lakes such as Llangorse near Brecon, or on the coast around Conwy, Cardigan Bay or the Gower. Contact www.rya.org.uk for information on yacht charter, adventure cruises, recreational sailing or dinghy courses.

Surfing, kitesurfing and windsurfing

It might not be Hawaii, but all the same Wales has some stunning surf beaches. One of the favourites among aficionados is **Rhossili Bay** on the Gower Peninsula. In Pembrokeshire, **Freshwater West** has an awesome reputation. Wales also has some of the cleanest beaches in the UK. Generally, the best surf is to be found in late summer/early autumn. To find a break and get information on facilities including board rental, accommodation, tide charts and surf reports, try www.surf-uk.org.uk,or the **Welsh Surfing Federation** at www.welshsurfingfederation.co.uk. For **windsurfing**, try www.ukwindsurfing.com.

Kitesurfing is currently the hottest thing in watersports. Propelled along at dizzying speeds by a wind buffeted kite, it's not hard to see where the thrill comes in. Wales has miles upon miles of coastline, so finding some wind, somewhere, shouldn't be a problem. For further information, try www.kitesurfing.org.

Spectator sports

Cricket

Cricket is widely played in Britain. The most important club in Wales is **Glamorgan County Cricket Club** ① To871 2823400, www.glamorgancricket.com. Two teams will battle it out for four or five days and then at the end, having had to spend most of the time watching from the pavilion as the rain pours down, settle for a draw. Tickets for internationals are very hard to come by. If you can't get a ticket, and don't fancy watching on TV, then you can witness the zen-like atmosphere of a county cricket match, which takes place over four days, from the comfort of a deckchair. There are also one-day competitions. Ticket prices for international Test matches range from £15 to £40 for one day. One-day international cost £20-50, while county games cost less than £10. Information on cricket in Wales can be found on; www.welshcricket.org. For details of forthcoming Tests and county fixture, contact Glamorgan CC or the **England and Wales Cricket Board** (ECB) ① *Lord's Cricket Ground, St John's Wood, London NW8 8QN, To20 74321200, www.ecb.co.uk.*

Football

Football is the king of British sport. The passion generated by the game is unmatched – not only in any other national sport but also in almost any other walk of life. Anyone with more than just a passing interest should certainly endeavour to catch a game while they're here. The football season runs from mid-August to early May. Most matches are played on Saturday, at 1500, and there are also midweek games (mostly on Wednesdays) and some games on Sunday afternoons and Monday evenings. Ticket prices range from £20 and upwards for top-class games, to £15 and less for the lower divisions. Further information is available from the **Football Association of Wales**, www.faw.org.uk.

Rugby

The 'hard game' is actually two distinct games: **Rugby Union** and **Rugby League**. While the latter (13-a-side) variety is of working-class origins, the former (15-a-side) variety originates from Britain's fee-paying public schools, hence the name – Rugby. 'Rugger' as the latter is called, no longer lags behind football and cricket in terms of mass appeal and has, in recent years, been earning plenty of column inches in the sports pages. The annual **Six Nations Championship** (comprising England, Scotland, Wales, Ireland, France and Italy) is held around February and March and matches draw huge crowds. The Welsh side were given a huge confidence boost when, after a long spell when success just wouldn't go their way, they won the Grand Slam in the 2005 Six Nations Championship. See also box, A rugby nation.

Health

No vaccinations are required for entry into Britain. Citizens of EU countries are entitled to free medical treatment at National Health Service (NHS) hospitals on production of an E111 form. As a result of recent changes to European law a new E111 form has been introduced for travel during 2005. The new E111 form and the booklet " Health Advice for Travellers" can be obtained from the Post Office. Forms are also available to download from the Department of Health's website: www.dh.gov.uk/travellers. From 31 December 2005, the UK will adopt the European Health Insurance Card (EHIC), which will replace the E111. Also, Australia, New Zealand and several other non-EU European countries have reciprocal health-care arrangements with Britain. Citizens of other countries will have to pay for all medical services, except accident and emergency care given at Accident and Emergency (A&E) units at most (but not all) National Health hospitals. Health insurance is therefore strongly advised for citizens of non-EU countries.

❗ *Medical emergency: dial 999 or 112 (both free) for an ambulance. See individual town directory sections for hospital and medical services listings.*

Pharmacists can dispense only a limited range of drugs without a doctor's prescription. Most are open for normal shop hours, though some are open late. Local newspapers carry lists of which are open late. **Doctors' surgeries** are usually open from around 0830 or 0900 until 1730 or 1800. Outside surgery hours you can go to the casualty department of the local hospital for any complaint requiring urgent attention. For the address of the nearest hospital or doctors' surgery, T0800 665544.

Keeping in touch

Communications

Internet
Many hotels and hostels offer internet access to their guests, and cybercafés are springing up all over the place (these are listed in the directory sections of individual towns in the main travelling section of this book). Email works out far cheaper than phoning home, and is also useful for booking hotels and tours and for checking out information on the web. However, some internet cafés are expensive, and it may be worth enquiring whether they operate a discount card scheme. In the absence of any internet cafés listed under a particular town listing, try the public library for internet access or ask at the tourist office.

Post
Most **post offices** are open Monday to Friday from 0900 to 1730 and Saturday 0900 to 1230 or 1300. Many smaller sub-post offices operate out of a shop. Some rural offices may close on Wednesday afternoon.

Telephone
Telephone operator, T100; International operator, T155; national directory enquiries, 118 500 (calls to this number cost £0.20); overseas directory enquiries, T153. Any number prefixed by 0800 or 0500 is free to the caller. Note that many cell phones from the USA/Canada/Latin America will not work in the UK.

❗ *The IDD code for the UK is +44. See box, page 29, for further details.*

Most payphones are operated by **British Telecom (BT)** and can be found everywhere, BT payphones take either coins (20p, 50p, £1 and occasionally £2) or phonecards, which are available at newsagents, post offices and supermarkets displaying the BT logo. These cards come in denominations of £3, £5, £10 and £20. Some payphones also accept credit cards (Delta, Visa and Diners Club). For most countries (including Europe, USA and Canada) calls are cheapest between 1800 and 0800 Monday-Friday and all day Saturday and Sunday. For Australia and New Zealand it's cheapest to call from 1430 to 1930 and from midnight to 0700 every day. To call Britain from overseas, dial 011 from USA and Canada, 0011 from Australia and 00 from New Zealand, followed by 44, then the area code minus the first zero, then the number. To call overseas from Britain dial 00 followed by the country code and the number (minus the first zero). Country codes include: Australia 61; France 33; Ireland 353; New Zealand 64; South Africa 27; USA and Canada 1. Most phone boxes display a list of international dialling codes.

Media

Newspapers

There is a huge variety of national newspapers and competition between them is fierce. The national dailies are divided into tabloids, which are more downmarket, and broadsheets, which are generally of a higher standard. Foreign visitors may find the broadsheets easier to understand as they tend to use less slang than the tabloids. The broadsheets include the *Times* and the *Daily Telegraph*, which are politically conservative, and the *Guardian* and the *Independent*, which have more of a liberal/left-wing leaning. There's also the distinctively coloured and very serious *Financial Times*, which focuses on business and finance. The Saturday editions of these papers carry their own listings guides with useful reviews of movies, clubs, restaurants and theatre. The tabloids comprises the *Sun* and the *Mirror* which are the most popular and provide celebrity gossip and extensive sports coverage, the *Daily Mail* and *Daily Express* which are right-wing.

The Welsh daily broadsheet is the *Western Mail*, while Cardiff's regional daily is the *South Wales Echo*. In Swansea you can get the *Swansea Evening Post*. The main North Wales daily is the *Daily Post*. The national Sunday paper is the tabloid *Wales on Sunday*. In Cardiff and Swansea you can pick up a free listings magazine called *Buzz*.

Television

There are five main television channels in the UK; the publicly funded BBC 1 and 2, and the independent commercial stations ITV, Channel 4 and Channel 5. The BBC and ITV both offer regional programming, some of which is aimed at local special interest.

There is a Welsh language television station **S4C** (Sianel Pedwar Cymru): established in 1982 it broadcasts for several hours in Welsh each day. Shows include the long-running BBC Welsh soap *Pobol y Cwm* or 'People of the Valley', set in the fictional village of Cwmderi. The digital **S4C2** channel shows the proceedings of the Welsh Assembly, and viewers can choose to watch in English or Welsh.

Radio

The BBC network also broadcasts several radio channels, most of which are based in London. These include: **Radio 1** aimed at a young audience; **Radio 2** targeting a more mature audience; **Radio 3** which plays mostly classical music; **Radio 4** which is talk-based and features arts, drama and current affairs; and **Radio 5 Live** which is a mix of sport and news. In addition, the BBC broadcasts on local and regional affairs, through a network of local radio stations. There are a large number commercial radio stations including **Jazz FM** (102.2), **Virgin FM** (1215AM, rock), **Classic FM** (99.9-101.9FM), and hundreds of local radio stations, which can all be found at the touch of a dial.

Welsh language radio includes the BBC's **Radio Cymru** and a number of commercial stations such as **Radio Ceredigion**, which is bilingual. More information on the BBC services at www.bbc.co.uk/cymru.

⦙ Footprint features

Introduction

Cardiff is the energetic and good-humoured capital of Wales. Only becoming the capital city in 1955, it promotes itself as 'Europe's youngest capital' and is certainly the liveliest city in the country. The most striking thing about the city is its energy; it practically bubbles with optimism. Elegant arcades teem with shoppers, tables from busy bars and cafés spill on to the streets and glistening structures of glass and steel rise phoenix-like from the regenerated Cardiff Bay waterfront.

Although Cardiff has ancient origins, its past is just that – past. With no weighty history to hold it back, it's keen to embrace the new. The historic castle asserts no brooding presence but sits meekly on low ground, upstaged by the Millennium Stadium. The most distinctive buildings are 19th-century – a legacy of the lucrative trade in coal or 'black diamonds'. There is the Washington-white Civic Centre in Cathays Park; the glass-domed labyrinth of Victorian shopping arcades; and the exuberant red Pierhead building in the Bay. These have now been joined by the 21st-century Wales Millennium Centre.

The city's compact size makes it a lively weekend destination (don't expect a quiet Saturday night – stags and hens love it), and good transport links make it a great base from which to explore the heritage coastline and little towns of the nearby Vale of Glamorgan. Cardiff's main sights are its castle and excellent museum and art gallery, which boasts a fine Impressionist collection. There's a thriving cultural scene and it has a well-deserved reputation as Celtic heaven for shopaholics. The city that once meant industry, rugby and beer, now has a five-star hotel, award-winning restaurants, lively bars and a growing café culture. Yet for all that's going on, Cardiff's greatest asset is surely its people, who are refreshingly cheery, friendly and helpful.

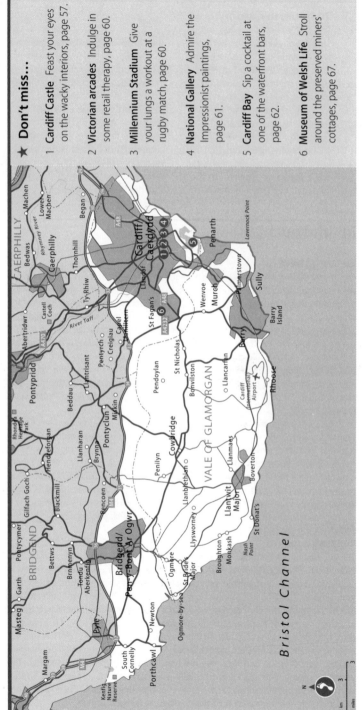

Cardiff & around

★ Don't miss…

1 **Cardiff Castle** Feast your eyes on the wacky interiors, page 57.

2 **Victorian arcades** Indulge in some retail therapy, page 60.

3 **Millennium Stadium** Give your lungs a workout at a rugby match, page 60.

4 **National Gallery** Admire the Impressionist paintings, page 61.

5 **Cardiff Bay** Sip a cocktail at one of the waterfront bars, page 62.

6 **Museum of Welsh Life** Stroll around the preserved miners' cottages, page 67.

⁞ 24 hours in Cardiff

Start the day like the sportier locals, with a gentle jog or stroll through **Bute Park** on the River Taff. Head back to your hotel for a leisurely breakfast, then put on a pair of comfy shoes and head off to the **National Museum and Art Gallery** to admire the collection of Impressionist paintings. Now it's just a short walk back to the heart of the city for some lunch – try the contemporary Welsh food at **Haze**.

Then head to the cashpoint or flex your credit card and treat yourself to an afternoon of retail therapy in the **arcades**. If you start to flag there are plenty of cafés to revive you. There'll be time for an early evening drink at the trendy **Ha Ha Bar**, before you head off to a restaurant in Cardiff Bay for something to eat overlooking the water. If you've got the energy after that, go clubbing – **Club Ifor Bach**'s a good choice.

Ins and outs → *Colour map 2, grid C5*

Getting there

Cardiff International Airport ① *Rhoose, near Barry, T01446 711111, www.cial.co.uk or www.cardiffairportonline.com*, is 12 miles southwest of Cardiff's city centre and a 30-40 minute car journey. The terminal's facilities include a few small bars selling drinks, snacks and teas and coffees, newsagents, duty free shops, and a children's play area. The airport is easily reached by car via the A4055, or taking the A4225 from the A48 or junction 33 off the M4. The **taxi office** ① *T01446 710693*, is in the arrivals hall and taxis can be booked in advance; it costs around £20 to central Cardiff. The **Air Bus** ① *X91, Mon-Fri 0650-1800 every 30 mins, 1936-2236 every hr; hourly at weekends, single fare £4*, operates between the city's central train, the main bus station and the airport. A rail link is due to open in the future. ▸▸ *For flight information, see Essentials, page 22.*

The city's main **bus station** ① *T02920 666444*, is situated between Cardiff Central Railway Station and Wood Street. The bus station is served by long distance **National Express** buses as well as local Cardiff services, regional and trans-Wales routes. The few buses that don't stop at the bus station itself pull up on Wood Street, directly outside the station. **Cardiff Central Railway Station** ① *T02920 430554*, is in the heart of the city, next to the bus station. Regular trains run between Cardiff Central Railway Station and London Paddington, with onward connections to Swansea. If driving, follow signs from the M4. ▸▸ *For further details, see Transport, page 84.*

Getting around

The city has an efficient **bus** network that makes getting around easy. **Cardiff Bus** offers a one day **City Rider** ticket ① *£3.50, £2.30 children, £7 families*. The centre is small with many pedestrianized streets. All the main sites can easily be explored on foot, although Cardiff Bay is about a 20-minute walk away, so you might prefer to take one of the regular buses. If **driving**, note that city-centre parking is heavily restricted and the presence of eagle-eyed traffic wardens encourages the use of the pay and display NCP car parks spread around the city centre, as well as the use of the voucher parking system. Vouchers are available from local shops approx (£1.20 per hour). If **cycling**, Cardiff is flat and it is also the start of the Taff Trail (see page 84). The **waterbus** leaves Mermaid Quay in Cardiff Bay to Penarth (see page 83). Further information on public transport is available from **Traveline Cymru** ① *T0870 6082608, www.traveline-cymru.org.uk.* ▸▸ *For further details, see Transport, page 84.*

Tourist information

Cardiff Visitor Centre ① *The Old Library, The Hayes, T02920 227281, www.visit cardiff.info, open all year Mon-Sat 1000-1800, Sun 1000-1600*. Helpful centre with information on both Cardiff and the rest of Wales, with plenty of leaflets/books on activities and places to go. They can also book accommodation.

Passes If you're exploring outside the city centre, it's worth buying a **CADW Explorer Pass**, three days £9.50 adult, £16.50 for two adults, £23 family; seven days £15.50 adult, £26 for two adults, £32 family, giving admission to castles like Caerphilly, www.cadw.wales.gov.uk. The **Cardiff Welcome Card**, £5, offers 10-15% discounts on entry to various attractions and in some shops. It's available from the Cardiff Visitor Centre.

Sights

The centre of the city is bounded by the River Taff on the west, on which lies the new Millennium Stadium. The stadium is close to Cardiff Castle, which is separated from the Taff by the green parklands of Bute Park. East of the park, north of the centre, is the university and the studenty/arty Cathays and Roath districts. West of the Taff, close to the city centre, is the increasingly exclusive Pontcanna – popular with Welsh media mafia. South of centre is the revitalized docklands area of Cardiff Bay, reached by Lloyd George Avenue; the walk to the Bay is pleasant during the day, but locals advise you not to do it at night. ▸▸ *For Sleeping, Eating and other listings, see pages 70-86.*

City centre

With its bustling streets, busy shops, and numerous bars and cafés, the centre of Cardiff feels very new – yet this is the oldest part of the city. Roman soldiers once trod this ground, possibly even building their temples on the same sites that are now occupied by the city's shopping malls – today's temples to consumerism. The castle was the site of the Romans' fort, though all that is left of their presence is a section of Roman wall. Later invaders built on the same site, and the castle today – the focus of tourist activity – bears the fingerprints of many generations. Close to the River Taff is a more recent addition to the city skyline, the mighty Millennium Stadium. When an important sports match is being played, Cardiff grinds to a standstill, and pubs and bars fill with fans sporting Welsh red dragons and enthusiastically sampling pints of Brains – the local brew. Shopping in the centre is a treat, for as well as the modern malls there are numerous atmospheric arcades filled with quirky shops. You can always escape the hordes by strolling along the Taff Walkway that runs behind the Millennium Stadium, or opting for quiet contemplation in a church.

Cardiff Castle

① *Castle St, T02920 878100, www.cardiffcastle.com, daily Mar-Oct 0930-1800, Nov-Feb 0930-1700, last entry 1 hr before closing. Grounds only £3.20 adults, £2 children, £9.20 family; grounds and tour £6.30 adults, £3.90 children, £18.40 family.* The castle is the historic and geographical heart of city, though it seems slightly incongruous so close to the road and the busy shops and bars. Once inside the high stone walls you can see the motte, or artificial hill, on which is perched the ancient Norman keep – the oldest part of the castle buildings – dating back to the 11th century

● *"A deserted pigeon house on top of a truncated sugar loaf." Unimpressed 18th-century*
● *visitor on Capability Brown's 'improvements' to the Castle keep.*

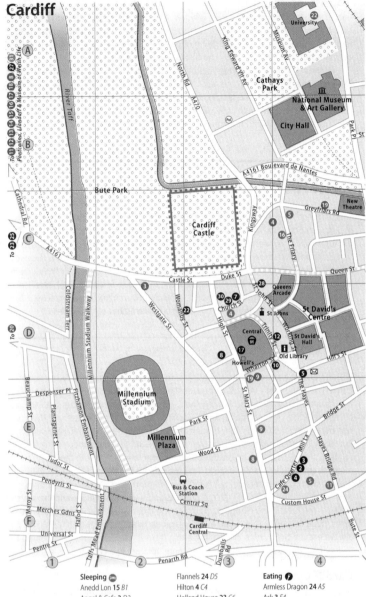

Sleeping 🛏️
Anedd Lon **15** *B1*
Angel & Cafe **3** *D2*
Beaufort Guest
 House **12** *B1*
Big Sleep **7** *E5*
Cardiff Backpackers **20** *D1*
Cardiff University **22** *A4*
Cardiff Youth Hostel **21** *A6*
Cathedral **8** *B1*
Church **16** *B1*
Courtfield **14** *B1*
Express by Holiday
 Inn **2** *F5*

Flannels **24** *D5*
Hilton **4** *C4*
Holland House **23** *C6*
Ibis **10** *E5*
Marriott **5** *F4*
Maxine's **17** *B1*
Park Plaza **19** *C4*
Penrhys **13** *B1*
SACO Apartments
 11 *B1*
Sandringham **9** *D3*
Thistle **6** *C5*
Town House **18** *B1*

Eating 🍴
Armless Dragon **24** *A5*
Ask **3** *E4*
Atlantic Coffee
 Company **30** *D3*
Bar Essential **11** *C5*
BSB 'The Place' **20** *C5*
Capsule **9** *D5*
Cibo **27** *B1*
Cornish Bakehouse
 29 *D3*
Da Venditto **1** *C5*
Graze at Aveda **17** *D3*
Greenhouse **26** *A5*

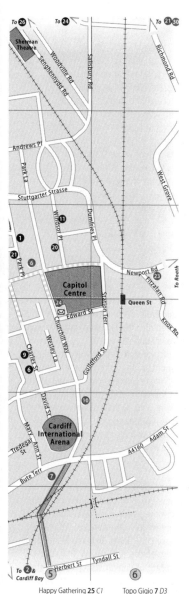

(although the site here was in use even earlier by the Romans). Throughout the Middle Ages, successive owners reinforced and added to this ancient fortification, but many of their additions were demolished in the late 18th century by the landscape gardener and designer Capability Brown, who had a penchant for 'improving' old buildings. If you climb the well-worn steps of the keep you'll get a great panoramic view of the city and surrounding countryside.

In the 1420s separate lodgings were built, which became the main living quarters. As the need for defences decreased, the house was extended and gradually became more luxurious and comfortable – although it fell into disrepair after the Civil War. Eventually the castle came into the possession of the Bute family, the wealthy Scots who owned vast areas of land in south Wales. By the time the elaborately monikered John Patrick Crichton-Stuart, third Marquis of Bute (1847-1900) inherited it, the family had more money than they knew what to do with, so the Marquis (possibly the richest man in the world at that time) was able to indulge his architectural whims by completely redesigning the house. He commissioned architect William Burges, who shared his passion for the gothic, and the two worked together to create a medieval fantasy. A taster of this style is provided in the façade of the Clock Tower, which is decorated with allegorical statues of the planets and heraldic shields. To see the lavish interior you have to take one of the guided tours, but it's worth it. Decorations are exotic, eccentric and ethereal with monkeys, parrots, knights and nymphs all jostling for your attention. Every riotously colourful room has its own theme. They include the Winter Smoking Room in the Clock Tower, which has stained-glass windows, a flamboyant carved chimney piece and richly gilded ceiling. Then there is the Bachelor Bedroom with a luxurious marble bath; the Eastern-influenced Arab Room with intricate patterned ceiling; the Fairytale Nursery, which is decorated with hand-painted tiles depicting stories from the Arabian Nights and the Brothers Grimm; Lord Bute's gilded bedroom with a mirrored ceiling; and the Banqueting Hall where Royals, from Edward VII to Charles and Diana, were entertained. Quiet taste it isn't but it's certainly worth seeing.

Cardiff & around City centre

Happy Gathering **25** *C1*
Haze **8** *D3*
Henry's **21** *C5*
Is it? **10** *D4*
Juboraj **2** *E4*
La Fosse **5** *D5*
Las Iguanas **4** *F4*
Le Gallois **23** *C1*
Metropolis **6** *D5*
St John the
  Baptist Church **28** *C3*
Sugar **22** *D3*
Toad at the
  Exhibition **12** *D4*

Topo Gigio **7** *D3*
Union Undeb **22** *D2*

Bars & clubs 🍸
Cayo Arms **31** *B1*
Claude **30** *A6*
Cottage **19** *E3*
Cuba **16** *C4*
Golden Cross **11** *F4*
Ha!Ha! **5** *C4*
Life **8** *E3*
Moloka **24** *F4*
Old Arcade **4** *D3*
Sodabar **9** *E3*

⁝ Victorian fantasist

William Burges (1827-1881) was the so called 'eccentric genius' who realized the Marquis of Bute's extravagant dreams for Cardiff Castle. Burges studied medieval architecture in Europe and travelled widely, soaking up influences from Byzantine, Renaissance and Islamic art. He adored and idealized the medieval world, which seemed more beautiful, stylish and natural than the vigorously industrial Victorian society he inhabited. He designed grand buildings like Brisbane Cathedral and Cork Cathedral, as well as everyday items such as teapots and chamber pots. He loved using the finest and most luxurious materials, such as marble, amber and cedarwood. When he met the Marquis of Bute he found someone who not only shared his passion for the medieval, but was able to spend lavish amounts of money on bringing a fairytale to life. After the castle, Bute commissioned him to work on Castell Coch (see page 91), his country retreat. Burgess died before it was finished.

St John's Church

ⓘ *St John St, Mon-Sat 1000-1600 and during services on Sun, free.*

In amongst the pubs and bars of central Cardiff is this ecclesiastical island – the oldest building in the city centre and the only significant medieval building. The first record of the church was in 1180, though it was rebuilt after Owain Glyndŵr's men sacked Cardiff in the mid 15th century. The 130-ft tower dates to about 1475 and is one of the finest examples in Wales of the late perpendicular style. Inside you can see the Herbert Chapel which contains a Jacobean monument to the Herbert brothers, one of whom was Keeper of Cardiff Castle, and the other Private Secretary to Elizabeth I and James I. There's also a Chapel of the Order of St John containing memorials to the great and the good, including Edward VIII (the king who abdicated before he was crowned) and Lord Kitchener, the World War One Commander in Chief famously depicted in contemporary 'Your Country needs YOU' posters. The Victorian stained glass is also considered to be some of the finest in Wales.

The Arcades

Cardiff is one of the best cities in Britain for anyone needing a bit of retail therapy and, just south of the castle, these elegant Victorian and Edwardian glass-canopied arcades are one of the highlights of the city. Crammed with individual shops that stock everything from designer clothes and contemporary homewares to Welsh gold rings and Harlech cheese, they are Cardiff's answer to places like the Burlington Arcade in London. They were erected between the 1850s and 1890s and covered existing alleyways. They escaped demolition (the fate of similar structures in other cities) only because Cardiff had little money after the collapse of the coal trade and could not afford redevelopment. The oldest is the Royal Arcade, around 1856.

Millennium Stadium

ⓘ *Westgate St, To2920 822228, www.millenniumstadium.com. Shop open Mon-Sat 0930-1700, tours 1000-1700 (Sun 1000-1600) run every hour on the hour, booking advised and subject to events, go to Gate 3 near the bus station. £5.50 adults, £3 children, £3.50 concession, £17 family.*

● On pedestrianized Queen Street in the city centre is a statue of Aneurin Bevan, the
● firebrand Labour MP from the Welsh Valleys, who founded the National Health Service.

The top sporting venue in Wales, with seating for 72,500 spectators and a retractable roof that contains a whopping 8,000 tons of steel. It was built on the site of the old National Stadium that stood on the famous Cardiff Arms Park. It's now the home of Welsh rugby and hosts matches in the annual **Six Nations Championship,** as well as international football matches, and major English footballing events, such as the FA Cup, during Wembley's closure. In Spring 2005, the Welsh rugby team were crowned Grand Slam winners of the Six Nations Championship here, reviving national pride. It was also the setting for the Tsunami Relief gig, the biggest in Britain since Live Aid, which raised over £1,300,000 for victims of the Asian tsunami disaster. Sixty one thousand people turned up to watch performers including Katherine Jenkins, the Manic Street Preachers and Eric Clapton. Take a tour to see the dressing rooms, the tunnel, the Royal box and, of course, the pitch.

Cathays Park and around

The area occupied by Cathays Park was sold to Cardiff by the wealthy Bute family in 1898. It was turned into the centre of administrative power, with serious and impressive buildings arranged around the National War Memorial and broad, tree-lined boulevards cutting through the smooth grass. The grandest building is the **City Hall,** which was officially opened in 1905 by Edward VII, who at the same time gave Cardiff official city status. It's an area that has a rather sedate feel, a serene and green corner of the city centre. The area's main feature is the **National Museum and Gallery,** one of Cardiff's greatest assets. The university is also here and the surrounding studenty districts of **Cathays** and **Roath** have lots of reasonably priced places to eat.

National Museum and Gallery

① *Cathays Park, T02920 397951, www.nmgw.ac.uk, Tue-Sun 1000-1700, free. Cathays is the nearest train station.*
This excellent museum and art gallery could hold its head up anywhere in the world. It covers everything from a hi-tech, interactive look at the evolution of Wales – a good spot for children on a rainy day – to conventional displays of art.

The story of Wales is told through its archaeology and natural history. There are galleries on animals and the environment, Viking-Age crosses, finds from Crannogs, displays on the early church and some beautiful Celtic jewellery. There are also some Roman relics found in Wales, which include delicate statuettes of dogs. The section on Wales in the Middle Ages includes the **Levelinus Stone** which was raised between 1198 and 1230 by the monks of Aberconwy Abbey in Gwynedd to commemorate a gift of land from Llywelyn the Great. It's inscribed with a mixture of Welsh and Latin.

If you're a connoisseur of china then head upstairs to the extensive collection of Welsh ceramics – it contains around 3,000 pieces of Welsh pottery and porcelain. But if you're short of time give it a miss and focus on the art collection instead. It is intended to illustrate the art history of Wales and put it in context and, as you would expect, contains many works by Welsh artists from Thomas Jones and Richard Wilson 1713-1782 (the first painter to capture the Welsh landscape on canvas) to Augustus John and Ceri Richards. Gallery 5 focuses on Art in Wales from 1780-1860. There are also works by Poussin, Cuyp, Claude and Canaletto. British artists in general are well represented and there's a good selection of works by Pre-Raphaelites such as Dante Gabriel Rossetti, Ford Madox Brown and Burne-Jones.

In Gallery 3 look out for the large **tapestry cartoons**. These have aroused some controversy in the art world as they were once thought to be the sole work of Rubens,

It's often said that 100 years ago, Cardiff was the energy equivalent of the Persian Gulf. The international price of coal was set in the Cardiff Coal Exchange, in what is now Cardiff Bay.

but now no-one is sure to what extent the master worked on them. They were produced by his workshop, but this was a major commercial operation, something like a modern design studio. Rubens certainly died before they were finished.

The highlight in the gallery is the **Davies collection** of 19th- and early 20th-century French art, the bequest of Gwendoline and Margaret Davies. It's a remarkable collection by two sisters, and one of the best collections of Impressionist art in the UK. Room 12 contains several sculptures by Rodin, including a large copy of *The Kiss*; a Degas bronze of a dancer; and paintings by Boudin, Manet, Monet and Pissarro. There's also Renoir's *La Parisienne* (1874) better known as '*The Blue Lady*'. Room 13 has Van Gogh's *Rain – Auvers* (1890), as well as paintings by Cézanne. Look out for the small picture of *A Shepherdess* by Anton Mauve – he gave painting lessons to Van Gogh. Galleries 14 and 15 focus on **20th-century art**, with Magritte, Lucien Freud, Stanley Spencer and others all represented. There's also a gallery that has a changing collection of contemporary art, which features Welsh artists as well as people like Rachel Whiteread. In Gallery 15 there's a view of Six Bells Colliery, Abertillery in Ebbw Fach Valley, painted by LS Lowry. He was taken to Wales by his Welsh friend and patron Monty Bloom.

City Hall

ⓘ *Cathays Park, T02920 872000/871727, www.cardiff.gov.uk, open Mon-Fri office hours, sometimes on Sat, no access if a function is taking place, free. Cathays is the nearest train station, but it is easy to walk from the centre.*

This is Cardiff's answer to the White House, the heart of the **Civic Centre** built at the start of the 20th century when Cardiff was a wealthy coal port. It's a confident neoclassical building, the focus of civic pride, with a façade of white Portland stone and an ornate clock tower. On the large dome is a snarling Welsh dragon that looks as if it's guarding a precious egg – presumably Wales. The bells in the clock tower are engraved, some in Welsh and some in English. The interior is impressive and well worth a look. Various paintings hang from the walls including a triple portrait of Princess Diana, painted when she still had her Royal HRH title. The **Marble Hall** is lined with columns of Siena marble and statues depicting 'Heroes of Wales'. Each statue is by a different sculptor, and the figures represented include Owain Glyndŵr, Harri Tewdwr (Henry VII), St David and Boudicca (Boadicea) – the woman who led the Celtic Iceni tribe in revolt against the Romans. Nearby buildings that help to make up the Civic Centre include the **Welsh National War Memorial** and the **Temple of Peace**.

In the main entrance to City Hall is a statue of a woman carrying a young child and wearing a chain round her waist. It commemorates the 36 women, four children and six men who in 1981 marched from Cardiff to Berkshire to protest against the siting of American cruise missiles at RAF Greenham Common. The site became known worldwide as a focus of anti-nuclear protest.

Cardiff Bay

About a mile from the city centre, Cardiff Bay is the city's former docklands area, built in the 19th century by the Bute family, and the key to the city's growth and wealth. It's separated from the city by parallel streets: Bute Street – to the west of which are the less affluent areas of Butetown and Grangetown; and Lloyd George Avenue – a characterless stretch lined with bland and pricey, new housing. Once better known as Tiger Bay, this was a cosmopolitan, working-class area, home to people from all over Britain as well as around 50 other nations including Somalis, Scandinavians, Russians and Indians. After the decline of the docks, the area became increasingly run down, but has been given a serious – and expensive – facelift. It's now full of hope and energy with shiny new buildings going up all the time, as well as retail outlets and a liberal splash of bars and restaurants. It has certainly helped regenerate the area, although the downside is the consequent loss of its working-class character and sense of community. Property in the Bay is expensive, but doesn't guarantee privacy – Charlotte Church bought one of the showpiece flats here, only to discover that she was on the tourist bus route and easily glimpsed by those peering in from the top deck. It feels very different to the rest of Cardiff, a shiny new appendage that hasn't yet grown onto the main body. But it's the site of the new Welsh Assembly building, as well as the Wales Millennium Centre – home to the Welsh National Opera – and there are loads of bars and restaurants, many of which offer outdoor seating with views of the water; a very pleasant option on a sunny day.

Further developments in the Bay will include a £700 million **International Sports Village**. The first phase of this will involve the construction of an Olympic-standard swimming pool, with plans for a snowdome and an ice arena. There's enough to see and do to occupy half a day and it's changing all the time. The centre of the waterfront is taken up with the shops, bars and restaurants of the new **Mermaid Quay** development. From here you can get boat trips into Bay and out to the **Barrage**, see page 83.

National Assembly Exhibition

① *Cardiff Bay, T02920 898200/898222, www.wales.gov.uk, Mon-Fri 0930-1630, Sat-Sun 1030-1700, free. Bus 6 Bay Xpress.*

This exhibition is housed in the lovely red-brick Victorian Pierhead Building on the waterfront, which is topped with a distinctive clock tower and contains fine stonework and tiling. It was built in 1897 as home for the Bute Dock Company. The exhibition focuses on the background of the setting up of the Assembly, an explanation of devolution and how the Assembly operates. There's also a scale model of the new

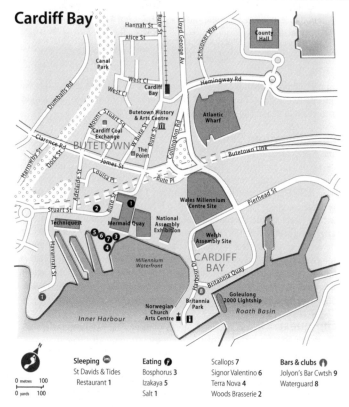

Cardiff Bay

Sleeping 🛏
St Davids & Tides
Restaurant 1

Eating 🍴
Bosphorus 3
Izakaya 5
Salt 1

Scallops 7
Signor Valentino 6
Terra Nova 4
Woods Brasserie 2

Bars & clubs 🍸
Jolyon's Bar Cwtsh 9
Waterguard 8

0 metres 100
0 yards 100

⁝ The desire for autonomy

It was in the mid-19th century that the modern campaign for greater autonomy for Wales really began. There was a revival of interest in Welsh culture – as evidenced by the reintroduction of the eisteddfod into Welsh life – the first being the National Eisteddfod of 1858. In 1885 the Welsh Language Society was started, which succeeded in ensuring that Welsh (which had been banned) was taught in schools. A political movement for a separate Wales was formed in 1886 as part of the Liberal party. The political scene in Wales became increasingly radical and in1900 Merthyr Tydfil elected a Scot, **Keir Hardie** as their MP – Britain's first Labour MP. World War One saw a Welshman, **David Lloyd George** become Prime Minister. The Labour Party continued to grow in importance in Wales, but there was dissatisfaction at their failure to introduce Home Rule – and the lack of safeguards for the Welsh language. In 1925 **Plaid Cymru**, the National Party of Wales was established. One of the founders was Saunder Lewis. He and two other Plaid members, DJ Williams and Lewis Valentine, gained notoriety (and Welsh support) when they set fire to buildings at an RAF station in North Wales. Over the years demands for home rule increased again and in 1979 a **referendum** was held – the result was huge disappointment for the nationalists with 80% of people voting against a Welsh assembly. After the Thatcher government was finally defeated and Labour took power again, another referendum was held in 1997. This time there was a tiny majority in favour and elections to the **National Assembly for Wales** took place in May 1999. Unlike the Scottish Parliament it has no tax raising powers. The new Assembley is based in Cardiff.

Assembly building, which is currently being erected on adjacent land and is due for completion late in 2005. For now the Assembly functions from a nearby building and tours to see it in action can be arranged (T02920 898477).

Wales Millennium Centre

ⓘ *Bute Place, T08700 402000, for tickets T02920 636400, www.wmc.org.uk.*
This £100 million performing arts centre opened in November 2004, and provides a home for seven arts organizations including Welsh National Opera. It's a controversial structure, said to have been inspired by the Welsh landscape (ironically many locals consider it looks 'too Welsh') and has layers of slate flanking a distinctive, steel-skinned mound. It looks a bit brooding from the outside and has already been nicknamed the 'bump' and the 'slug', but it's sleek and welcoming inside with a sparkling steel reception, champagne bar and a main auditorium with contemporary polished wooden floors and balconies made of layers of Welsh wood. Inscribed above the entrance is a poem which mixes lines of Welsh and English: the English reads 'In these stones horizons sing'. There are shops and cafés inside, and events range from classical ballet to Bugs Bunny.

Techniquest

ⓘ *Stuart St, T02920 475475, www.techniquest.org, Mon-Fri 0930-1630, Sat-Sun 1030-1700, school holidays Mon-Fri 0930-1700. £6.75 adults, £4.65 children, £18.50 family. Bus 6, Bay Xpress.*
This is a family-friendly, interactive science centre with a whole load of 'hands-on' exhibits covering everything from firing a rocket to forecasting the weather. In the

'wet' area exhibits range from building a dam to the importance of recycling water. There's a **planetarium**, where a changing programme of audio-visual presentations covers matters such as light pollution, and whether or not the moon landings were faked by the Americans. At weekends and during holidays, demonstrations are held in the **Science Theatre**, covering themes like dinosaurs and inventions.

Scott Memorial
① *Millennium Waterfront. Bus 6, Bay Xpress.*
In 1910 Captain Scott's ill-fated expedition to the South Pole set sail from Cardiff on the *Terra Nova*. The trip was largely funded by Cardiff's mercantile community and a grand farewell banquet was held in the city before the ship and its crew departed. Scott didn't sail with them on the first leg of the no doubt extremely uncomfortable journey – he travelled by luxury steamer and joined them later. There's a memorial to the explorers near the Norwegian church in the Bay and also in Roath Park.

Norwegian Church
① *Millennium Waterfront, T02920 454899, daily 0900-1700, free. Bus 6, Bay Xpress.*
An incongruous sight among the Victorian red brick and contemporary glittering glass, this church is a reminder that Cardiff was once an internationally important seaport. With its white wooden walls and black roof, it looks rather quaint and rustic. Originally a Norwegian Church and Seamen's Mission, it was moved here from a former site in the Bay. The author Roald Dahl was baptized here; he was born in Cardiff, but his father was Norwegian. It's now a cultural centre and café (see Entertainment, page 80).

Butetown History and Arts Centre
① *4/5 Dock Chambers, Bute St, T02920 256757, www.bhac.org, Tue-Fri 1000-1700, Sat-Sun 1100-1630, free. Cardiff Bay station or bus 6, Bay Xpress.*
A small but fascinating gallery which focuses on the multi-racial history of the Bay. There are changing exhibitions of photographs and documents, with a lot of emphasis on local memories and stories.

Goleulong 2000 Lightship
① *Harbour Drive, T02920 487609, www.lightship2000.org.uk, Mon-Sat 1000-1700, Sun 1400-1700, free. Bus 6, Bay Xpress.*
This lightship (*goleulong* in Welsh) was in use until the early 1990s, to warn ships away from the dangerous areas on Wales' treacherous coast. It used to be manned with a crew of seven who would be airlifted in and out by helicopter. You can see their cabins and the signal light. The ship now contains a chapel and a Christian café.

Cardiff Bay Barrage
① *Cardiff Bay, T02920 700234, www.cardiffharbour.com, Apr-Sep daily 0800-2000 , reduced hours in winter, free. From land train or waterbus from Cardiff Bay.*
This striking and controversial structure was built across the Taff and Ely estuaries to keep the tide out and create the enormous lake which forms the heart of the Bay development. The barrage, which cost over £200 million to build, is an advanced piece of engineering with locks, sluice gates and a fish pass. It allowed the marina to be developed but meant that a huge expanse of mudflats – a precious habitat for thousands of wading birds – disappeared. The birds you're most likely to spot today are the resident swans and cormorants. On a clear day the views from the barrage are superb – you can see right across the Bristol Channel to England – and if you visit in late September to December, you might see salmon leaping up the fish pass as they return to spawn in the waters of the Taff. You can walk here from Penarth, or take a boat trip from Mermaid Quay (see page 83).

⁝ King Coal

Cardiff might have remained a small coastal town had it not been for the industrial revolution, which dramatically transformed it from backwater to big city. The metamorphosis was largely due to the local landowners, the Scottish Bute family, who owned much of the land in both Cardiff and the surrounding coal rich valleys. The first Marquis built the Glamorganshire Canal in 1794 linking Cardiff with Merthyr Tydfil in the valleys. This was a far quicker and cheaper way of transporting coal than the previous method - mules. The second Marquis built the first dock on the Taff, soon followed by several more, and a lucrative export trade in 'black diamonds' was established.

King Coal made Cardiff one of the busiest ports in the world, and the Butes – who were in a position to insist that only their docks be used for trading the valleys' coal – one of the richest families. As the Welsh travel writer Jan Morris put it: "… from… his castle at the top of the town, the Marquis looked over the rooftops of his indefatigable fief – to the sea one way, where the coal of Wales went streaming off to the markets of the world, to the hills the other, where in valleys hidden from his view the miners toiled to dig it out."

Cardiff suburbs

Only part of Cardiff since 1922, Llandaff – the 'place on the Taff' – retains a distinctive, villagey feel. Its attraction for visitors is that it's the site of Llandaff Cathedral, the city's most famous church, which is tucked away in a sheltered hollow surrounded by grass and trees. The village of St Fagans, four miles west of the city centre, is quite picturesque, but what visitors come to see is the Museum of Welsh Life. It's situated in the grounds of St Fagans Castle, a Grade One listed building that dates back to Elizabethan times. In 1946, the Earl of Plymouth donated the castle and its surrounding land to the National Museum of Wales – on condition that they build an open-air museum there.

Llandaff Cathedral

ⓘ *Llandaff, T02920 564554, www.llandaffcathedral.org.uk, daily, free. Approximately 2 miles northwest of the city centre along Cathedral Rd. Buses from city centre.*
The cathedral at Llandaff is Cardiff's most important religious site. It stands on the site of a sixth-century church, founded by St Teilo, although the present building dates from the 12th century when the Norman stone church was built by Bishop Urban. The cathedral suffered during the Reformation and by the 18th century was almost a ruin. However, it was saved by restoration work, particularly in the mid-19th century, when Pre-Raphaelite artists made a great contribution to its renewal. There's a triptych, *The Seed of David*, by Dante Gabriel Rossetti (with figures modelled by his friends William Morris – King David; Jane Burden, his wife – the Virgin Mary; and Burne-Jones – a shepherd), and stained glass by William Morris and Burne-Jones. The cathedral was badly damaged in 1941 and further restoration and rebuilding was undertaken. An enormous Jacob Epstein statue, *Christ in Majesty*, was added during this period.

 In 1713 Francis Lewis, one of the signatories to the American Declaration of Independence, was born in Llandaff.

Museum of Welsh Life

① *St Fagans, 6 miles west of Cardiff, T02920 573500, www.nmgw.ac.uk, daily 1000-1700, free. Bus 32 or 320 from centre, hourly, less frequent Sun, £2.50. Taxis £10.*
This excellent open-air museum is four miles west of the city centre in the grounds of St Fagans Castle, and could easily take up a full day – especially if you've got kids. The museum brings to life 500 years of Welsh social history. The **indoor galleries** (handy if it's raining) include a wide collection of agricultural implements; a costume gallery with traditional Welsh clothing; a fascinating section on folklore, including elder tree crosses, believed to give protection against witches; and displays of gruesome old-looking surgical instruments. Outdoors, around 44 acres (18 ha) of ground have been given over to a collection of 40 period Welsh buildings, moved from their original locations and carefully rebuilt here. They provide an evocative glimpse of old Wales. The buildings range from tiny **Nant Wallter Cottage**, a two-room, 18th-century thatched cottage with walls made of clay/mud mixed with straw and stone dust, to **Kennixton Farmhouse**, a comfortable 17th-century farmhouse with red painted walls – for protection against evil spirits. There's also a chapel, a stylish stone pigsty, a mill, a Victorian school and a recreated Celtic village. Perhaps most fascinating are the **Rhyd-Y-Car** ironworker's houses, a 19th-century terrace from Merthyr Tydfil complete with gardens. Each of the six houses is furnished in a different period, ranging from 1805 to 1985. Close by there's a post-war **pre-fab bungalow**, an example of the kit homes that were constructed to replace houses bombed in the Second World War.

St Fagans castle itself is furnished as it would have been at the end of the 19th century. It is in the process of being refurbished, following problems with the roof, so not all the rooms are currently open. It's got some fine tapestries, dark wood panelling and a red silk bed. When you've exhausted all the buildings you can also explore the lovely **Castle Gardens**, with terraces, 18th-century fishponds and a recently restored **Italian Garden**. The **Victorian Gwalia Stores**, situated on top of an old fashioned ironmongery (once the corn store), are a great place to browse. You'll find things like bile beans, Sloan's liniment, loose biscuits and tins labelled 'Ringer's Shag – The Old Favourite'. Next door is a shop selling traditional items like laverbread, Welsh cheeses and Welsh cakes, while upstairs is a tea room.

Cardiff & around
Vale of Glamorgan

Vale of Glamorgan

Tucked away in the corner southwest of Cardiff, south of the M4, is the gentle, pastoral scenery of the Vale of Glamorgan. It's easily accessible from the city, with trains to Bridgend, buses to towns like Cowbridge and a water bus to Penarth. In 2005, the Vale of Glamorgan rail line should open going from Cardiff to Bridgend and stopping at places like Llantwit Major. The heritage coastline is varied, with the fish, chips and fairground rides resort of Barry mingling with the pleasant, but decidedly snoozy, Victorian town of Penarth. There are craggy cliffs, some award-winning beaches and good walks – notably the coastal walk around Dunraven Bay. Inland is Cowbridge, a pretty and very prosperous town (think Surrey with a Welsh accent) filled with independent shops, including lots of antique shops, and some good places to eat. A great little place to stroll around and window shop, but don't expect to find any bargains.

Penarth

① *TIC on the pier, T02920 708849, Easter-Sep, town trail leaflets available.*
Penarth is a Victorian seaside town just south of Cardiff, with a small promenade, a rather genteel little pier and a good vegetarian restaurant (see page 76). It's linked to

● *French impressionist painter, Alfred Sisley, came to Penarth in 1897 and stayed for four*
● *weeks at 4 Clive Place. The town and its seafront feature in a number of his works.*

Cardiff by waterbus (see boat trips, page 83) and in summer you can also take trips on the *Waverley*, the world's last sea going paddle steamer (ask the helpful TIC for details, also see Essentials page 56). The town also contains the **Turner House Gallery** ① *1 Plymouth Rd, T02920 708870, www.ffotogallery.org, Wed-Sun 1100-1700, free,* which displays the works of **Ffotogallery** – a national agency for contemporary and historic Welsh photographs, as well as international works.

Lavernock Point

At the little church at Lavernock Point, two miles south of Penarth, is a plaque informing you that in 1897 'near this spot the first radio waves were exchanged across water by Guglielmo Marconi and George Kemp/Between Lavernock and Flat Holm'. The historic message was disappointingly prosaic in content: 'Are you ready?' – not much better than 'Testing, Testing' really.

A few miles offshore, **Flat Holm** is a tiny island, once a retreat for monks, refuge for smugglers – and reputedly the burial place of the murderers of Thomas à Beckett. It has Viking associations and was mentioned in the Anglo Saxon Chronicles as Bradan Relice. It's now a Site of Special Scientific Interest and a Nature Reserve, home to the largest colony of gulls in Wales. Boats to the island are run by the **Flat Holm Project** ① *Pier Head, Barry Docks, T01446 747661, flatholmproject@ btinernet.com, £10,* at weekends in summer from Barry Harbour. Day trips allow around three hours on the island or limited overnight accommodation is available, book well in advance.

Cosmeston Medieval Village

① *Lavernock Rd, T02920 701678, Nov-Mar 1100-1600 (last tour 1500), Apr-Oct 1100-1700 (last tour 1600), £3.50, £2 children, £8 family.*
Go back to the days of the plague at this reconstructed 14th-century village. The original village grew up around a fortified manor house, but began to decline during the Black Death and was eventually deserted. It was rediscovered during archaeological work, and gradually recreated on the excavated ruins. Villagers wear medieval costume and give tours; it's a good place to bring kids.

Dyffryn Gardens

① *St Nicholas, off the A48, T02920 593328, www.dyffryngardens.org.uk, Easter-Sep 1000-1800, Oct 1000-1700, £3.50 adults, £7 family, free in winter.*
These are Grade 1 listed Edwardian gardens around a grand country house. There are lawns, fountains, an herbaceous border, Italian garden, arboretum and physic garden. In the 1900s Reginald Cory, a former owner of the estate, helped to sponsor several plant hunting expeditions which brought rare and exotic species back to Dyffryn. The arboretum contains a huge Paper Bark Maple (*Acer griseum*), which was grown from a seed collected in China by Ernest Wilson, a famous plant hunter.

Llantwit Major and around

① *TIC, Town Hall T01446 796086.*
A little village 15 miles southwest of Cardiff where you'll find **St Illtud's Church**, off Burial Lane. St Illtud founded a church and religious school on this site around AD 500. It was the first Christian college in Britain and alumni are said to include St David and St Patrick. Local kings were buried here and the church contains an important collection of Celtic stones. The building you see today dates back to Norman times.

A couple of miles west of Llantwit Major is **St Donat's Castle**, a medieval pile which was bought by American newspaper tycoon William Randolph Hearst in 1925. Various well-known names have stayed here including Charlie Chaplin, Bing Crosby, Marilyn Monroe and JFK. It's now home to **Atlantic College** ① *T01446 799010, tours available in Aug, ring to book,* the international private school, and also the **St Donat's Art Centre** ① *T01446 799100, www.stdonats.com,* which hosts various

Dragons, daffodils and leeks

The red dragon that adorns the Welsh flag first makes its appearance in a legend in which Vortigern, a fifth century Celtic king, tried to build a fortress on Dinas Emrys in Snowdonia. It kept collapsing, and Merlin advised him that it was because two dragons were sleeping beneath it. The land was dug up and sure enough, a red dragon and white dragon popped up and started fighting. Merlin explained that it symbolized the struggle between the Celts and the Saxons. The red dragon won – a prophecy that was realized when Henry Tudor took the throne as Henry VII.

The leek may have been introduced to Wales by the Romans and then became closely associated with St David; some say he ate leeks, others that he advised the Welsh to wear leeks in their helmets to distinguish them from the Saxons. Later, Welsh bowmen are said to have worn them at the Battle of Crecy and at Agincourt. They're still worn by Welsh regiments on St David's Day. The Welsh for leek is *cenhinen*, and the daffodil is known as *cenhinen Pedr* – Peter's leek. Hence the adoption of the daffodil as the national flower.

festivals (see page 80) as well as acting as a venue for theatre, film and dance events.

Just round the headland from St Donat's is **Nash Point**, a lovely lonely spot with two lighthouses, craggy cliffs and a warning bell floating in the bay, clanging eerily in the wind. Further west is **Southerdown** and lovely **Dunraven Bay**, a wide sandy beach. Just 100 yards behind the beach car park is the **Glamorgan Heritage Coast Centre** ① *T01656 880157, Mon, Thu-Fri 0900-1500, check to find out other times*, which has information and displays on the 14 mile stretch of protected Heritage Coast.

Ogmore and around

Travel further west along the coast and you come to Ogmore by Sea, where there's a lovely sandy beach that's a real favourite with kite surfers. About a mile inland are the remains of **Ogmore Castle**. It was built in the 12th century and was once an important stronghold. The grounds are said to contain buried treasure and are meant to be patrolled by the ghost of The White Lady. You can cross the river by stepping stones here (but check the tides first) to walk across to the pretty village of **Merthyr Mawr** – a picturesque place with thatched cottages and tranquil rural charm. It's on the edge of an extensive area of sand dunes, Merthyr Mawr Warren, a Site of Special Scientific Interest (SSSI). In the dune system are the remains of **Candleston**, a 15th-century fortified mansion house. It stood by the lost village of Treganllaw which has now disappeared beneath the sands.

A couple of miles east of Ogmore is Ewenny, where you can see the remains of **Ewenny Priory**, which was founded by a Norman lord in 1141 as a Benedictine priory. It was heavily fortified to withstand attacks from resentful Welsh and dissolved in the Dissolution. Close to the village is **Ewenny Pottery** ① *T01656 653020*, which dates back to 1610 and is the oldest working pottery in Wales.

Kenfig Nature Reserve

① *Near Porthcawl, T01656 743386, daily 0900-1700, visitor centre 1400-1630, free.*
Bug-lovers and botanists will love this National Nature Reserve which covers 1,300 acres of ground. Kenfig Pool is an enormous freshwater lake and forms the heart of the reserve. It provides a habitat for migratory birds as well as many rare plants and insects. Among the 13 species of orchid that grow here is the rare Fen Orchid. The site even has its own unique species of weevil.

Cardiff & around Vale of Glamorgan

There's an increasing variety of places to stay in Cardiff and the trend looks to continue as the city grows. Most places are located in the city centre where there are several well-established, traditional hotels and a clutch of newer chains, which offer reliable and comfortable accommodation. There are also some funkier places to kip, aimed very much at 20- and 30-something travellers. Cardiff Bay has less choice but there are a number of places opening up. It's also the place to find the city's swishest hotel, St David's Hotel and Spa (see p71), offering a chance to indulge in some luxurious living. Most of the city centre hotels offer good deals during the low season (though never on big match weekends) and prices can vary enormously, so it's always worth ringing around and asking what they can do. Many of the smaller hotels, guesthouses and B&Bs are concentrated on Cathedral Road to the west of the city centre, while there are some others along the busy Newport Road to the east. At the lower end of the scale there are a couple of hostels, and the university also offers campus accommodation.

City centre p57, map p58
L Angel Hotel, Castle St, T02920 649200, www.paramount-hotels.co.uk. This reliable Victorian hotel is sandwiched between Cardiff Castle and the Millennium Stadium. A mere Gareth Edwards sidestep from the shops, it is a perennial favourite with locals and regular visitors. The restaurant serves traditional British food and afternoon teas. If you're in the ground floor bar on a Sat afternoon, you may find yourself as an extra at the wedding of one of Cardiff's finest.
A Hilton Hotel, Kingsway, T02920 646300, www.hilton.com. Elegant and tasteful, this hotel attracts the great and the good (and its fair share of star guests) thanks to its fab location looking over to the creamy-stoned Civic Centre and Cardiff Castle. They've got a Health Club with a 20-m stainless-steel pool and a well-equipped gym, sauna and spa. The upmarket bar and restaurant attract a mixed crowd of visiting business people, well-heeled tourists and smart locals thanks to its reputation for discreet service.

A Holland House Hotel, 24-26 Newport Rd, T0870 1220020, www.macdonaldholland house.co.uk. This large 4-star chain has 165 rooms and opened in 2004. It caters mainly for the business and conference market and also has a spa with treatment rooms, 18-m swimming pool, sauna and steam room.
A Marriott Hotel, Mill Lane, T02920 399944 or T0870 400 7290www.marriott.com. With 182 rooms and standing cheek by jowl with Cardiff's Café Quarter, this 4-star hotel claims to be Cardiff's premier hotel and offers the standard facilities you'd expect of a major chain, though the exterior is less than enticing. Not funky but reliable. There's a gym, sauna and solarium, and a restaurant serving Mediterranean food.
B Park Plaza, Greyfriars Rd, T02920 111111. Cardiff's newest hotel is this 129-room, 4-star in the centre of the city. Rooms are crisp and comfortable with a contemporary look. There are plans to open a swimming pool and health club. Very slick, very cool, one of the best options in the city.
B Thistle Hotel, Park Place, T02920 383471, 0870 3339257, www.thistlehotels.com/cardiff. Confident Victorian building, with 136 rooms decorated in traditional style with comfy furnishings and swagged curtains. The hotel's location in the heart of the pedestrianized zone makes it handy for shopping and schlepping around town.
C Big Sleep Hotel, Bute Terrace, T02920 636363, www.thebigsleephotel.com. Listed as one of the best budget boutique hotels in the world and co-owned by John Malkovich, this high rise is chic and comfortable, with 81 chilled rooms offering views right across the city. Breakfast is a continental buffet with cereals and pastries. Style on a budget and very popular with a younger crowd. Parking.
C Sandringham Hotel, 21 St Mary St, T02920 232161, www.sandringham-hotel.com. This may not be in the most peaceful location in town, but if you want somewhere central and handily- placed for the Millennium Stadium, then this bustling family-run hotel with 28 rooms will float your boat. The jazz café adds to the ambience.
D Ibis Hotel, Churchill Way, T02920 649250, www.ibishotel.com. 102 rooms. Close to

Cardiff International Arena, these small but modern and functional en suite rooms are rather sterile, but the central location and friendly welcome more than compensate.

D-F Cardiff Backpackers, 98 Neville St, Riverside, T02920 345577, www.cardiff backpackers.com. 5 mins walks from Cardiff Central. Funky and friendly hostel about ½ mile from Cardiff Central station. Cheerful single, double, triple and bunk bedroom options are available. The bright and welcoming communal areas include café-style chairs and tables, a fully licensed bar and great squashy sofas.

Cardiff Bay *p62, map p63*

L St David's Hotel and Spa, Havannah St, T02920 454045, www.roccofortehotels.com. Rocco Forte's luxurious waterfront hotel dominates the Bay's skyline. Decor is light and contemporary and all 132 rooms have balconies and fabulous views across the Bay. The swish spa offers all kinds of indulgent new-agey treatments like hot stone therapy and Balinese massage, and has a swimming pool, fitness centre and solarium – it's a favourite with visiting celebs like Nancy dell'Olio. Parking is available but costs £4.20 for 24 hrs. Special deals often available.

A-B Jolyon's, 5 Bute Crescent, T02920 488775 or T07815 125130, www.jolyons.com. This non-smoking boutique hotel opened in autumn 2004 in a former seamen's lodge, one of the few Georgian buildings left in Cardiff Bay. 6 rooms, all individually designed – one has a veranda, another a 4-poster bed. Furniture has been imported from Holland and France and there's Welsh slate in the bathrooms. It's just across from the new Wales Millennium Centre. There is free use of the internet and you can arrange to be picked up from the airport. Veggies, vegans and those with special diets are well catered for – while anyone wanting a kick start to the day should ask for porridge punch, Jolyon adds a generous dash of Welsh whisky to it.

C Express by Holiday Inn Hotel, Longueil Close, Schooner Way, T02920 449000, www.exhicardiff.co.uk. Less pricey (and less luxurious) than St David's, the 87 modern, functional rooms are ideal for easy access to the Bay. Good access from the M4 makes it a popular stopover for business travellers.

Cardiff suburbs *p66*

C Beaufort Guest House, 65 Cathedral Rd, T02920 237003, www.beauforthouse cardiff.co.uk. About 10 mins' walk from the castle, this guesthouse is in a large Victorian semi that's recently been refurbished. All nine rooms are en suite and each is slightly different. Private car parking.

C Cathedral Hotel, 53 Cathedral Rd, T02920 236511, www.cathedral-hotel.com. This is a family-run hotel on a tree-lined road out to the leafy suburb of Pontcanna, but 10 mins' walk from the city centre. 40 rooms, facilities include a gym, bar, restaurant and parking.

C The Old Post Office, Greenwood Lane, St Fagans, T02920 565400, www.old-post-office.com. Situated a few miles outside Cardiff, opposite the Museum of Welsh Life in the village of St Fagans, this former post office and police station has been converted into a restaurant and guesthouse with 6 rooms. Decor is clean, crisp and modern; all the rooms are en suite and there's a little garden. Very popular with couples who want to treat themselves.

C Penrhys Hotel, 127 Cathedral Rd, Pontcanna, T02920 230548, www.penrhys hotel.com. Family-run hotel with 20 rooms offering en suite with TV. The Victorian building boasts a splendid period dining room complete with beautiful stained glass and dark wood.

C-D Church Hotel, 126 Cathedral Rd, Pontcanna, T02920 340881, www.church hotelcardiff.com. Nine rooms in large Victorian house, recently taken over by Charlotte Church's parents. Most rooms en suite with colour TV, but no off-road parking available. There are 3 family rooms sleeping up to 4 people. Veggie breakfasts by advance request. Don't expect to see Charlotte serving the toast though.

C-D Courtfield Hotel, 101 Cathedral Rd, Pontcanna, T02920 227701, www.court fieldhotel.com. Well-run B&B with 8 rooms set up in 1950 and still going strong. Some en suite rooms, off-street parking and a licensed bar – handy before a day's rugby-watching or after a hard day hitting the shops. Gay friendly.

D Annedd Lon, 157 Cathedral Rd, Pontcanna, T02920 223349. Pretty hanging baskets welcome you to this comfortable, family-run B&B with 6 en suite rooms, non-smoking, in sedate Pontcanna. Reasonably convenient for city centre and off-street parking to the rear of the building.

D Maxine's, 150 Cathedral Rd, T02920 220288. Straightforward, no frills B&B in light, bright surroundings offering value for money in the leafy Pontcanna district. Handy for the smart parade of local stores further up Cathedral Rd. Not all 10 rooms are en suite.

D Town House, 70 Cathedral Rd, Pontcanna, T02920 239399, www.thetownhouse cardiff.co.uk. 8 pleasant rooms, non-smoking, in an imposing and recently restored 3-storey Victorian townhouse. Antiques and old fireplaces in the public rooms, while breakfast is taken round one big table in the conservatory. All rooms en suite, off-road parking.

E Cardiff Youth Hostel, 2 Wedal Rd, Roath Park, T02920 462303 or T0870 7705750, www.yha.org.uk, bus 28, 29, 29B from Cardiff Central. Handily placed near an Indian and Italian restaurant in the student district of Cathays, several bus stops and 2 miles north of the city centre. Popular hostel, continental breakfasts available.

Serviced apartments

B SACO apartments, Cathedral Rd, T0845 1220405. Serviced apartments are a great alternative to hotels or B&Bs. These are in refurbished Victorian buildings, with well-equipped kitchen, satellite TVs and maid service. They're close to Glamorgan cricket ground. 1- or 2-bed apartments available.

Campus accommodation

E Cardiff University, Cathays, T02920 874864 or 874702, www.cardiff.ac.uk/resi. Locations north of the city centre. Thousands of rooms, many en suite, available during vacation season (Jun-Sep) – room only, B&B, self-catering and sports facilities.

Vale of Glamorgan *p67*

A The Great House, Laleston, Bridgend, off A38. T01656 657644, www.great-house-laleston.co.uk. Reminders of old Wales in this restored 16th-century building with 16 rooms, complete with oak beams and mullioned windows.

B Egerton Grey Country House, Porthkerry, Barry, Jct 33 off M4, follow signs to airport then Porthkerry, T01446 711666, www.egertongrey.co.uk. 10 en suite rooms in a plush 17th-century country house, filled with antiques, paintings, oak panelling and period detail. It's set in secluded gardens – anyone for croquet? – but is convenient for the nearby airport. They've got a restaurant serving traditional, high-quality, British fare.

C Court Colman Manor, Pe-y-Fai, Bridgend, 2 miles off Jct 36 of M4, T01656 720212, www.court-colman-manor.com. 30 en suite rooms in a grand old manor house set in its own grounds, with a pleasant mixture of styles. There are open fires and comfy sofas in the wood-panelled public rooms, while the themed bedrooms have anything from traditional Indian to Moroccan styles. More basic, rooms are also available. Their restaurant serves widely acclaimed and great-value Indian and Mediterranean food.

C Llanerch Vineyard, Hensol, Pendoylan, 1 mile from Jct 34 of M4, T01443 225877, www.llanerch-vineyard.co.uk. High-quality B&B in a traditional farmhouse at Wales' best-known vineyard, 15 mins from Cardiff. There are 9 rooms plus self-contained studio rooms in converted farm buildings.

🍴 Eating

If you thought Welsh food meant stodgy meat and potatoes washed down with beer, then eating out in Cardiff is going to be a pleasant surprise. The capital has erupted with restaurants and brasseries and you can dine on French, Turkish or Thai food, if you wish. High-quality Welsh produce is well represented and you should look for Welsh mountain beef, Salt Marsh lamb, and all sorts of seafood. There are loads of great cheeses too. Chefs often take classic dishes and give them a Welsh twist, and the contemporary trend for mixing foods and flavours has found a place on many menus. Cardiff's many café/bars allow you to pick up a light meal or snack during the day – and many places do cheap lunchtime specials. Al-fresco dining is popular, and on fine days you can hardly move for shiny metal tables and chairs spilling on to the streets. Even Caroline Street, once known as 'Chip Alley' where you got delicacies known to locals as 'chicken-off-the-floor-and-chips', has now been pedestrianized and is much smarter. At night the atmosphere changes, with drinking taking precedence, especially at weekends, though there are still many cheap takeaway outlets catering for the post-pub crowd.

City centre p57, map p58

¶¶¶-¶¶ Da Venditto, 7-8 Park Place, T02920 230781, Tue-Sat 1200-1430, 1800-2245. Award-winning Italian restaurant offering sophisticated cuisine close to the theatre. Mains might include Gressingham duck with pea and broad bean risotto, or ravioli with spinach, baby courgettes and parmesan. Special lunchtime set menus make for a more affordable option.

¶¶ Ask, 24/32 Wyndham Arcade, Mill Lane, T02920 344665, Mon-Sat 1200-2300, Sun 1200-2230. Blue tablecloths and candles at this small, but sleek, contemporary Italian restaurant that attracts lots of couples. The menu includes all the usual Italian favourites and there's a long list of pizzas to choose from topped with everything from goat's cheese to white anchovies. There are plenty of veggie dishes on offer.

¶¶ Juboraj, 10 Mill Lane, T02920 377668. Mon-Sat 1200-1400 (not Fri) and 1800-2400, closed all day Sun. This highly-rated South East Asian restaurant in the Café Quarter is one of a chain – there are others in Newport and other parts of Cardiff. This one has a bustling city vibe. If you want to eat cheaply then come at lunchtime when they do a good-value special deal.

¶¶ La Fosse, 9-11 The Hayes, T02920 237755, Mon-Sat 1200-1430, 1900-2300, closed Sun. This contemporary seafood restaurant/oyster bar is awash with palms, blue glass and chrome. It's housed downstairs in the former fish market. As well as starters like fish soup and seafood, mains like seabass and monkfish, there are plenty of meaty mains and a few veggie choices. Plus, of course, those oysters.

¶¶ Las Iguanas, 8a Mill Lane, T02920 226373, www.iguanas.co.uk. Food Sun-Thu 1200-2300, Fri-Sat 1200-2330. This is a popular Latin American bar/restaurant in the Café Quarter, with a large outdoor seating

area that teems with people in summer. They do a wide selection of Mexican favourites like enchiladas and fajitas, as well as more unusual dishes like *moqueca*, a Brazilian stew with coconut and vegetables. Many are just here for the knock-out cocktails laced with tequila or Brazilian sugar cane rum. Shaken or stirred?

¶ Metropolis, 60 Charles St, T02920 344300, daily 1200-1500, 1800-2300. Sleek wooden floors, beige seats and cool customers, and a surprisingly reasonably priced menu. Mains might include pork and leek sausages with colcannon or stuffed aubergine and feta. They also have a good range of puds.

¶ Topo Gigio, 12 Church St, T02920 344794. Mon-Thu 1200-1500, 1730-2300, Fri- Sun 1200-2300. Enduringly popular Italian that squeezes them in night after night. It offers a wide range of tasty pasta and pizzas, some with a Welsh twist, such as pizza with traditional Welsh laver bread, leek and goat's cheese, or penne pasta with Welsh lamb.

¶ Capsule, 48 Charles St, T02920 382882, winter Mon-Thu 1100-1500, Thu-Fri also 1830-late, Sat 1100-late; summer Mon-Tue 1100-1800, Wed-Sat 1100-late, opens Sun for special events. Funky café/bistro which also functions as a gallery showcasing the work of young Welsh and international artists. There's a little garden for warm days. Good-value pasta, pizza and lunchtime ciabatta.

¶ Haze, Old Library, The Hayes. T02920 878451, Tue-Sat 1000-1600. Lovely contemporary café, all blond wood and chrome, showcasing the best Welsh produce. It's hidden away downstairs in the Old Library. Come in for cappuccino, organic soup, Welsh rarebit or one of the daily specials.

Cafés

Angel Hotel, Castle St, T02920 649200. Food 1100-2300. Come for a cream tea, coffee or a herbal brew for around £4.75. They also do Welsh cakes, sandwiches (no crusts cut off) and paninis.

BSB 'The Place', 11 Windsor Place, T02920 238228. Food daily 1100-1700, Thu-Fri until 1900. Café/bar attracting a young post-work and shopping crowd. Take your pick from a variety of sandwiches, salads, paninis and main courses like salmon and herb fishcakes. Service can unfortunately be a little variable.

Graze at Aveda, 7 St Mary St, T02920 233005, Mon-Sat 0900-1800. Small but very sleek organic/health café in the new Aveda emporium – toy with juices, imaginative salads, organic soup or a delicious piece of lavender cake. Dress is slim black trousers rather than hand-knitted jumpers.

Flannels, Churchill Way, T02920 374079, Mon-Sat 1000-1700, Sun 1100-1600. Chilled café upstairs in designer clothes store, with a large terrace for fine days. Style changing as go to press, so no information on menu.

Henry's, Park Chambers, T02920 224672. Food Mon-Sat 0900-2100, Sun 1200-1800. Busy chain café/bar popular with lunching shoppers and the post-work crowd who come for the cocktails. Sharing plates for £7.95, or more filling mains like chicken. Extra busy during happy hour.

Is it?, 12 Wharton St, T02920 413600. Food daily 1000-2100, Sun-Wed open until 0030, Th-Fri until 0100, Sat until 0200. Large, self-consciously trendy café/bar with an enormous mirror behind the bar and a seating area upstairs as well as down. Popular with shoppers during the day, much noisier at night. Sandwiches, salads, pasta dishes and mains like burgers or mussels.

St John the Baptist Church, near Church St, Mon, Wed, Fri and alternate Thu lunchtimes. If you need to fill up on a budget, pop in here: the WI serve soup, rolls and homemade cakes in the church.

Thirty Three Windsor Place, 33 Windsor Place, T02920 383762. Food from1200-2100 daily. Recently refurbished café/bar with cool cream seats and polished wood. Serves all sorts of food from sandwiches, to pasta dishes and things like steak and chips. At night it's the choice of the city's young professionals and visiting business people.

Toad at the Exhibition, 18-19 Trinity St, T02920 666566. Food daily 1100-2000, bar until late. The Old Library is now partly given over to this chain bar, which has a few seats outside and is convenient if you're shopping. Choose from sandwiches, paninis or wraps.

Delis and takeways

Atlantic Coffee Company, High St Arcade/St Mary St, T02920 232202. Mon-Sat early-1800, Sun 1000-1700. Coffee shop serving lattes, frothy capps, and large sandwiches and cakes to go.

Central Market, High St, Mon-Sat 0800-1730. Stalls selling fruit, veg, fabulous cheeses, bread and enormous slices of cake.

Cornish Bakehouse, 11 Church St, T02920 665041. Mon-Sat 0900-1800, Sun 1100-1700. Enormous Cornish pasties to take away, with everything from the traditional filling to ones with lamb and mint, beef curry, and cheese and mushroom. Also thick-cut sandwiches.

Wally's Deli, 42 Royal Arcade, T02920 229265, Mon-Sat 0800-1730. Good deli stocking Welsh cheeses, lots of Greek delicacies, Turkish Delight and other goodies.

Cathays Park and around p61

The Armless Dragon, 97-99 Wyeverne Rd, Cathays, T02920 382357. Tue-Fri 1200-1400, Mon-Wed 1900-2100, Fri-Sat 1900-2130, booking advised. Dull exterior hides an award-winning restaurant offering a new twist on Welsh dishes. Lots of lamb, chicken and fish as well as choices for veggies like, ahem, laverballs. There's a good choice of Welsh wines and cheeses – and cinnamon bread and butter pudding.

The Greenhouse, 38 Woodville Rd, Cathays, T02920 235731, Tue-Sat from 1830. A good vegetarian and seafood restaurant out in Cathays, offering imaginative dishes. Influences are international, while the produce is fresh and local – often organic. Look out for things like roquefort tart with red onion jam, or leek, black olive and goats' cheese in filo pastry. Puddings might include an almond and quince tart.

Delis and takeways

Forum Deliciae, corner of Richards St and Crwys Rd, Cathays, T02920 373077, Mon-Sat 0900-1800. Fab European deli run by friendly George Exintaris, who also imports food and wine from Europe.

Cardiff Bay p62, map p63

Tides, St David's Hotel and Spa, Havana St, T02920 313018, Mon-Thu 1200-1430, 1800-2215; Fri-Sat 1230-1430, 1830-2230, Sun 1230-1500, 1800-2200. A former Savoy hotel chef presides over this sophisticated restaurant in the 5-star hotel. You also get some lovely views over Cardiff Bay, crisp white cloths and fresh flowers on the table. Dishes might include roasted cod with parsley mash and cockles, or barley couscous with grilled vegetables. Definitely the place to bring those you want to impress.

Woods Brasserie, Pilotage Building, Stuart St, T02920 492400, Mon-Sat 1200-1400, 1900-2200, Sun 1200-1430, booking recommended. Upmarket modern brasserie in a listed building in the Bay, now light and modern inside with lots of glass and an open-plan kitchen. They serve excellent food with a distinct Asian influence – perhaps oriental crispy beef salad or sweet and sour salmon. Traditional fish and chips with beer batter is also very popular.

Scallops, Mermaid Quay, T02920 497495. Mon-Thu 1200-1430, 1900-2200; Fri 1200-1430, 1900-2230; Sat 1200-1500, 1900-2230, Sun 1200-1600. This light, airy restaurant with views of the waterfront serves sophisticated seafood, as well as a few meaty dishes.

Bosphorus, Mermaid Quay, T02920 487477, Mon-Fri 1200-1500, 1800-2400; Sat-Sun 1400-1700, 1800-2400. Perched on a jetty, this glass-sided Turkish restaurant has great views around the Bay. The food's a reminder that Turkish cuisine doesn't have to be a dodgy doner kebab after the pub.

Izakaya, Mermaid Quay, T02920 492939. Lunch Mon-Sat 1200-1430, dinner Mon 1700-2200, Tue, Wed 1800-2300, Thu-Sat 1700-2300, Sun 1200-2200. If you fancy something light like tempura, then make for this Japanese restaurant. You can dine Japanese-style on low tables if you choose, and staff are kitted out in traditional happis. As you'd expect, there's lots of fish (including a dish featuring raw tuna) and you can wash it all down with sake or Japanese beer. Hai!

Signor Valentino, Mermaid Quay, T02920 482007, daily 1200-1430, 1800-2230. This airy eaterie pleases the punters by offering all the usual Italian eats coupled with some great views over Cardiff Bay.

Bar Cwtsh, 5 Bute Crescent, T02920 488775. Mon-Sat 1200-2300, Sun 1230-closing hours vary. Cwtsh means a 'hug' in Welsh and this cosy cellar wine bar at Jolyon's Hotel (see p71) is suitably relaxing with squashy leather sofas and a real fire. It's all non-smoking so it's clean too. They serve quality food like hearty homemade soups, sandwiches, and bangers and mash. Traditional organic Sunday lunches with lots of choice for veggies too.

Salt, Mermaid Quay, Stuart St, Cardiff Bay, T02920 494375. Sun-Thu 1000-2400, Fri-Sat 1000-0200. This slick bar/restaurant offers a range of pasta dishes and sharing plates in the heart of the revitalized Bay.

Terra Nova, Mermaid Quay, Stuart St, T02920 450947. Mon-Thu 1000-2400, Fri-Sat 1000-0200, Sun 1000-2400. The food in this bar/restaurant ranges from simple bar snacks to full meals, and the choice is excellent. They've also got a tapas bar.

Cardiff suburbs p66

Le Gallois, Y Cymro, 6-10 Romilly Crescent, Canton, T02920 341264, www.legallois-ycymro.com, Tue-Sat 1200-1430, 1830-2230, booking advised. This family-run bistro offers award-winning French-influenced food for discerning, well-heeled diners. One of Cardiff's top places to eat, it serves dishes like langoustine risotto and roast partridge. Very posh, very French.

The Old Post Office, Greenwood Lane, St Fagans, T02920 565400. Sun-Thu 1200-1400, Wed-Sat 1900-2130. A few miles outside the city centre, this restaurant serves high-quality, come-for-a-treat, modern European food. You might find goat's cheese soufflé, fillet of Welsh beef or duck ravioli on the menu. Leave room for a pudding though – the French pastry chef produces calorie-filled treats such as pistachio crème brûlée, and brioches filled with prunes and armagnac.

Cinnamon Tree, 173 Kings Rd, Pontcanna, T02920 374433, Mon-Thu and Sat 1200-1400, Mon-Sat 1800-2300. Shiny polished wood and not a hint of flock wallpaper at this very popular Indian restaurant. All the usual curries are on the menu but you'll also find more unusual dishes like 'flaming ostrich' (it's grilled, not burn-your-mouth spicy), spicy duck and Bangladeshi fish. Veggies aren't neglected and can look forward to the unpronounceable kathri kai kara kozumba (baby aubergine in a yoghurty sauce). Booking's essential at weekends.

Happy Gathering, 233 Cowbridge Rd East, T02920 397531, Mon-Thu 1200-2300, Fri-Sat 1200-2330, Sun 1200-2100. This large, busy restaurant is an enduring favourite serving an extensive range of Chinese food. It attracts a loyal following.

♛ **Stefanos**, 14 Romilly Crescent, T02920 372768, Mon-Sat 1700-2230. This is a popular, family-run Italian restaurant out in the Canton region of the city.

♟ **Cibo**, 83 Pontcanna St, T02920 232226. Mon-Fri 1200-2100, Sat-Sun 1000-2100, booking advisable. Great Italian place, good for daytime or evenings. Good value ciabatta, pizzas and pasta in friendly atmosphere.

Vale of Glamorgan *p67*

♛♛-♛ **Huddarts**, 69 High St, Cowbridge, T01446 774645, Tue-Sun 1200-1400, Tue-Sat also 1900-2130. Come here to taste good Welsh meats or fish – cockles and laver bread are also on the menu.

♛ **Valentino's**, 44 High St, Cowbridge, T01446 771155. Lunch Tue-Sun 1200-1445, dinner Mon-Sat 1730-2200. Italian restaurant serving the usual pizzas, pasta and meaty mains. Lunch and early-bird menus for £6.95.

♛♛-♟ **Bar 44**, 44c High St, Cowbridge, T01446 776630. Mon 1200-2300, Tue-Sat 1000-2300, Sun 1200-2230. Lively tapas and cocktail bar on the main street.

♛♛-♟ **Bokhara Brasserie**, Court Colman Manor, Pen-y-Fai, Bridgend, T01656 721122. Mon-Fri 1230-1430, 1900-2300, Sat 1900-2300, Sun 1200-1430. Great Indian cuisine in the very unlikely setting of a rambling former manor house that has now become a hotel. It offers very good value meals, especially for vegetarians. The kitchen at one end of the restaurant is open so you can see your food being prepared, if you want to keep tabs on the chef.

♛♛-♟ **Farthings**, 54 High St, Cowbridge, T01446 772990. Mon-Fri 0930-1530, Sat 0930-1330, Sun 1000-1500, and Tue-Fri 1830-2200, Sat 1900-2200. Good-value food at this bistro where you can fill up with baked potatoes, pasta or delicious salads during the day, and more substantial dishes at night.

Cafés
Gallery Espresso, 68 Eastgate, Cowbridge T01446 775093. Mon-Sat 1000-1700. Great little café serving range of fresh filled bagels, baguettes and other snacks, as well as yummy homemade cakes, tea and coffee.

Delis and takeways
Glanmor's, Unit 30, Castle Court, Brynau Rd, Bridgend T02920 888355. Mon-Sat 0830-1730. A great sandwich shop, near the castle, serving homemade pastries and meals.

◐ Pubs, bars and clubs

Most of the constantly changing bars, pubs and clubs are in the city centre and Cardiff Bay. Mill Lane, otherwise known as the 'Café Quarter', offers a fair choice of eating options and bars. The former Brains brewery site has also been transformed into a lively night time spot. Gay venues focus on Charles Street and elsewhere on the city's southern fringe. Wed night sees the university crowds descend on the town for student nights at various venues. Fri and Sat can be incredibly rowdy, when assorted South Walians and stag and hen crowds (hens generally wearing antlers or sprouting sparkly fairy wings) go largin' it in the big city. But many bars, pubs and clubs are now competing for punters during the rest of the week, with cheap drinks, late licences and live band nights. These days the city seems to be crammed with themed chain pubs. However, traditional pubs still exist. The locally brewed beer is Brains – shipped, so some said, to the US for Catherine Zeta-Jones and Michael Douglas' wedding bash in order to keep her Welsh relatives happy.

City centre *p57, map p58*
Pubs and bars
Bar Ice, 4 Churchill Way, T02920 237177. Sun-Tue, Thu-Fri 1100-2300, Wed and Sat 1100-0200. Popular with students and office workers, this rather clinical chrome bar is perfect if you're vain as there are plenty of mirrors in which to admire yourself. If you can see through the smoky atmosphere and hear yourself above the laughter and general buzz, as well as the sport on TV.
City Arms, Quay St, T02920 225258. Mon-Sat 1100-2300, Sun 1200-22.30. Busy bar that almost overflows on match days. Best not to say anything rude about the Welsh rugby or football teams here...

Copa, 4 Wharton St, T02920 222114. 1200-2300. Large, stylish mirrored bar in former glass factory offering a wide range (around 12 so far) of European beers from places like Belgium, Italy and Germany. They also serve food.

The Cottage, 25 St Mary's St, T02920 337194, Mon-Sat 1100-2300, Sun 1200-2230. Popular traditional Edwardian pub in the centre of the city, serving real ales and attracting people of all ages – Dads love it. Food at lunchtimes.

Creation, Park Place, T02920 377014, Mon, Fri-Sat 2130-0200. Three rooms at this club: one for r'n'b, one for dance, and a chill-out room with funky house music. There's also a bar that serves food and plays chart music that's open daily from 1000-late.

Ha!Ha! Bar and Canteen, The Friary, T02920 397997, Mon-Thu 0930-2300, Fri-Sat 0900-0100, Sun 0900-2230. This bar is perfect for chilling out after a hard day's shopping, or for posing after dark – it aims to be all things to all (thirty-something) people. A wide selection of snacks, main meals and desserts is also on offer – one of Cardiff's best new bars.

Life, St Mary St, T02920 667800. Mon-Sat 1900-0100. Popular with young professional types who are thirsty but wouldn't be seen dead in one of Life's pub-chain neighbours. This still does not explain the long queues on Fri and Sat.

Moloka, 7 Mill Lane, T02920 225592, Mon 1700-2400, Tue-Wed 1200-0100, Thu-Sat 2400-0200, Sun 1700-2400. Lively vodka bar with a small dance floor, doing a popular line in cocktails too. Regular DJ nights.

The Old Arcade, 14 Church St, T02920 231740, Mon-Sat 1100-2300, Sun 1200-22.30. An old-fashioned pub serving Brains beer as well as bar food. Packed on rugby international days, it is loved by locals and visitors alike.

Sugar, 23 Womanby St, T02920 343433. Mon-Sat 1700-0200, some daytimes too. This is Cardiff's newest style bar, located in a converted warehouse on a cobbled street. It covers several floors and each one is slightly different in shades of chocolate, pink and magenta. Lots of cocktails and eclectic, soulful music.

The Yard, Old Brewery Quarter, T02920 227577, Mon-Sat 1000-0100, Sun 1200-1230. Busy, contemporary bar on the old Brains brewery site. It gets packed at weekends. Food's served until 2200.

Clubs

Clwb Ifor Bach, 11 Womanby St, T02920 232199, www.clwb.net, Tue-Wed 2100-0200, Thu-Sat 2000-0200, sometimes earlier if live bands are playing. Situated over 3 floors, it is regarded as one of the coolest clubs in Cardiff thanks to a popular mix of regular live music and DJs. Saturday is for members only (be they Welsh speaking or Welsh learners).

Cuba, Unit 9, The Friary, T02920 397967. Mon-Sat 1100-0200, closed Sun. Small bar that gets cramped towards the weekend with drinkers, gawpers, pullers and people shaking their thing to salsa and merengue – take classes if your footwork isn't up to scratch, they run them on Tue.

The Emporium, 8-10 High St, T02920 664577, Tue, Fri and Sat. Dance club that hosts a variety of club nights with visiting big-name DJs, spread over 2 floors. Something for everyone, especially the diehard clubmonster.

Flares, 96 St Mary St, T02920 235825, open till 0100. This is a real blast from the past. An eclectic clientele from *Rocky Horror* wannabees to alcopopped teens – if you're up for dressing up in glittery Afros and grooving to 1970s hits, this one's for you.

Liquid, St Mary St, T02920 645464, www.liquid-online.com, Thu-Sat 0930-late. Large city centre club attracting a lively crowd. Thu is r'n'b, Fri and Sat have dance floor fillers.

Metros, Bakers Row, T02920 399939, Tue-Sat, entry £5. Rockers heaven, this club bangs out sweaty rock and metal music. At its loudest on Tue, student night.

No 10, 10 Mill Lane, T02920 645000. Mon, Thu, Sat 2100-0100. This classy club is in fact 3 clubs in one, full of designer-clad crowds of chic folk who happen to pass the No 10 doorstep test.

The Sodabar, 41 St Mary St, T02920 238181, www.thesodabar.com, Thu-Sat 2200-late. Pitching for the more discerning end of the clubbing market, its chic interior is packed to the gunnels with Italian furniture on flagstone floors. Great DJs and an excellent sound system add to the buzzy atmosphere. **Stylus**, Elgin House, Golate, T02920 376110. There are 3 bars at this small venue which majors on house music. There's quite a strict dress code so don't turn up in scruffy trainers. **Toucan Club**, 5-97 St Mary's St, T02920 372212, www.toucanclub.co.uk, Tue-Sun. A unique and independent venue in Cardiff, this chilled yet friendly club hosts live music with an eclectic global flavour upstairs, and often features salsa and Latin American music.

Cardiff Bay *p62, map p63*
Pubs and bars
City Canteen, 1-2 Mount Stuart Sq, T02920 331020, Mon-Fri 1000-2300, Sat 1200-2300, Sun 1200-2230. Cool bar in the Bay – unlikely to attract squealing crowds of celebrating hens or stags.
Salt, Mermaid Quay, Stuart St, T02920 494375, Sun-Thu 1000-midnight, Fri-Sat 1000-0200. New England-style bar, complete with arty driftwood over 2 floors and stylish comfortable sofas.
Terra Nova, Mermaid Quay, Stuart St, T02920 450947, Mon-Thu 1000-2400, Fri-Sat 1100-0200, Sun 1000-2400. Set on 4 levels, the building is shaped like a ship's bow. A seating area on the top floor resembling a crow's nest is ideal for people-watching on a summer's evening.
The Waterguard, Harbour Drive, T02920 499034, Mon-Sat 1200-2300, Sun 1200-2230. The main bar area is modern and open, with comfy sofas in light and airy surroundings.

Clubs
Evolution, UCI building, Atlantic Wharf, T02920 464444, Wed, Fri 2200-0200, Sat 2130-0400. The biggest club in Cardiff, it offers cheap booze, party anthems and mainstream house and dance. There's a free bus service to collect would-be groovers from outside the New Theatre in the city, every 15 mins from 2115.

Cardiff suburbs *p66*
Pubs and bars
Cayo Arms, 36 Cathedral Rd, Pontcanna, T02920 391910, Mon-Sat 1200-2300, Sun 1200-2230, food 1200-1500, 1700-2100, all day at weekends. Named after a commander of the Free Wales Army, this pub is popular with those who, in ale terms, like to keep it real. Several Camra awards, excellent beer and fresh food.
The Claude, Albany Rd, Roath, T02920 493896. Mon-Sat 1200-2300, Sun 1200-2230. It is unlikely that you will get bored in this popular pub, set in a large traditional building with pool tables, TVs showing live sporting events, a juke box and games machines. As if that's not enough, there's also frequent live music on offer.

Clubs
The Cameo Club, 3 Pontcanna St, Pontcanna, T02920 220466. Mon-Thu 0900-0100, Fri-Sat 0900-0200, Sun 1100-2230. This private members' club is a favoured haunt of Cardiff's media mafia, but non-members can usually get in before 2100 – although there's an extra charge. It's got big screen facilities so is popular on match days, and has good selection of food and wine.

Vale of Glamorgan *p67*
The Bush Inn, St Hilary, Cowbridge, off A48, T01446 772745, daily 1200-2300. This ancient inn is popular with locals as it serves good bar meals and real ales. Cosy in the winter, with a real fire.
Plough and Harrow, Monkash, off B4265 near Nash Point, T01656 890209, daily 1200-2300. Pub that's full of character (it's an old Welsh longhouse with an inglenook fireplace) with a good range of real ales. Serves good food too.
The Vale of Glamorgan, High St, Cowbridge, off A48, T01446 772252, Mon-Sat 1100-2300, Sun 1200-2230. Good traditional pub with real fires, real ales and a good atmosphere.
The Victoria Inn, Sigingstone, on B4270 near Cowbridge, T01446 773943, Mon-Sat 1145-1500, 1800-2300, Sun 1145-1530, 1900-2230. Popular pub serving good bar and restaurant meals. Especially noted for its Sun lunch. It may be worth booking in advance.

Cardiff has a lively entertainment scene and is particularly good if you like music; you might find anyone from Bryn Terfel to Robbie Williams. Homegrown bands like the Stereophonics have played here, of course, and it's a good place to keep your eye out for up-and-coming stars. The hot new opera venue is the Wales Millennium Centre, which opened in November 2004. There's a smattering of cinemas, a comedy club, and a clutch of theatres showing everything from old-fashioned panto to experimental works. The local press have details of what's happening in the city. Also look out for *Buzz*, a free, informative monthly guide to listings on gigs, galleries, film etc. Information on the arts in Cardiff is available from T0800 3899496, www.arts4cardiff.co.uk.

Cinema

The **Wales Screen Commission** website is worth checking out, www.walesscreen commission.co.uk. You can see all the usual big-budget films in Cardiff, but it's also got an art-house cinema for those who like something more thoughtful. The annual **Celtic Film Festival**, www.celticfilm.co.uk, takes place throughout the British Isles, with Cardiff playing host in 2005.

Chapter Arts Centre, Market Rd, Canton, T02920 304400, www.chapter.org. This popular venue has 2 screens showing art-house movies and mainstream pictures, as well as many foreign films. It's also got a theatre. Tickets cost around £5.

Ster Century Multiplex, Millennium Plaza, T0870 7672676, www.stercentury.co.uk. Cardiff's biggest cinema, with 14 screens and state-of-the-art facilities. They also show art-house films on Wed evenings.

UGC, Mary Ann St, T0870 9070739 or T0871 2002000. Mainstream city-centre multiplex

UCI, Atlantic Wharf, Cardiff Bay, T0870 0102030, www.atlanticwharf-cardiff.com. 12-screen multiplex showing almost exclusively mainstream movies.

Comedy

You can catch some of the biggest names on the stand-up circuit in Cardiff, which has a healthy comedy scene.

The Glee Club, Mermaid Quay, Cardiff Bay, T0870 2415093, www.glee.co.uk. Cardiff's main comedy club regularly stages live acts from comedy circuit regulars. Lee Evans, Mark Steel and Johnny Vegas have strutted their stuff here. Once the acts are over, the laughs continue as the club morphs into a boozy dance venue.

Jongleurs, Millennium Plaza, Wood St, T0870 7870707. The comedy's less edgy than at the Glee, but it's still worth catching. There's also a bar that stays open till late.

Dance

Traditional ballets have generally been staged at the **St David's Hall** (though the **Wales Millennium Centre** will probably become the main venue from now on) while more experimental dance might appear at the **Chapter Arts Centre** or **The Point**. However, you might also wish to catch some performances of traditional Welsh dance at an eisteddfod or street festival. Several dance festivals are held in Wales, see the **Welsh Folk Dance** website, www.welshfolk dance.org.uk.

Music

Wales is known as the land of song and Cardiff's venues manage to attract a wide variety of big names – from classical to cutting-edge contemporary. Classical music, including the Welsh Proms, is generally staged at the huge St David's Hall, while rock and pop acts play at the big stadiums. Everyone from The Strokes and The Flaming Lips to Shirley Bassey, Katherine Jenkins and Tom Jones has played in Cardiff. You can also find jazz, folk (often in pubs) and, of course, traditional Welsh Male Voice Choirs who hold open rehearsals. The Wales Millennium Centre is the main venue in Wales for opera, as well as many other arts events. For more information about the Welsh folk scene get hold of *Taplas*, a bi-monthly guide, also found online at www.taplas.co.uk.

Barfly Club, Kingsway, T0870 9070999, www.barflyclub.com. This bar hosts a wide range of live bands, both local and visiting. Chance to see bands that are on their way up. Check gig guides in local press or ance it and see.

Cardiff Coal Exchange, Mount Stuart Sq, Cardiff Bay, T02920 494917, www.coal exchange.co.uk. The former commercial centre is now a hub for live performances, and hosts the Welsh Music Awards. If it's been good enough for Jools Holland and Van Morrison...

Cardiff International Arena, Mary Ann St, T02920 224488, www.getlive.co.uk/cia. The prime venue for big-name rock and pop acts: past performers at these venues have included Atomic Kitten, Tom Jones, Blue, Iron Maiden, The Strokes, Robbie Williams and The Stereophonics, so pretty varied. Prices upwards of £20, depending on the act.

Clwb Ifor Bach and **Toucan Club** (see Bars and clubs, page 77) both have live music worth checking out.

Millennium Stadium, Westgate St, T08705 582582. Occasionally plays host to the same kind of acts as the International Arena. It was the venue for the Tsunami Relief concert.

St David's Hall, The Hayes, T02920 878444, www.stdavidshallcardiff.co.uk. This huge concert hall dominates much of the city centre. It's the prime venue for classical concerts as well as the Welsh Proms and other large-scale events.

University Student's Union, Park Place, Cathays Park, T02920 781458 or 781400, www.cardiff.ac.uk. Many events are restricted to NUS card-holders but others are open. Attracts a wide range of big-name bands and dance acts such as Catatonia, The Stereophonics, Travis, Coldplay and many more.

Wales Millennium Centre, Cardiff Bay, T08700 402000, www.wmc.org.uk. Cardiff's newest arts venue staging everything from classical ballets to crowd pleasing musicals.

Jazz

Café Jazz, Sandringham Hotel, St Mary St, T02920 387026, www.cafejazzcardiff.com. Home to the Welsh Jazz Society and hosts top local performers as well as international acts. Admission costs depend on acts. Call ahead to check.

Male voice choirs

Cardiff Male Voice Choir rehearses at Conway Rd Methodist Church, Canton on Wed 1930-2130, T02920 709098, www.malevoicechoir.net. Check beforehand.

Theatre

Cardiff has a thriving theatre scene and you can see anything from amateur productions and contemporary alternative pieces to classical dramas. This is the place to come to catch new works by Welsh writers.

Chapter Arts Centre, Market Rd, Canton, box office T02920 304400, www.chapter.org (see cinema). Home to several experimental theatre companies, and offers actors' workshops as well as an eclectic range of full performance pieces. Very lively programme.

New Theatre, Park Place, T02920 878889, www.newtheatrecardiff.co.uk. Traditional Edwardian theatre offers everything from opera, ballet, musicals and drama to the occasional pantomime at Christmas.

Norwegian Church Cultural Centre, Harbour Dr, Cardiff Bay, T02920 454899, norwegian.church@talk21.com, daily 0900-1700, plus evenings for performances. This attractive little church, where author Roald Dahl was christened, is the venue for all manner of exhibitions, workshops and concerts. Also has a good café.

The Point, Mount Stuart Sq, Cardiff Bay, T02920 460873, www.thepointcardiffbay.com. This converted church is used to host experimental theatre as well as dance and live music.

Sherman Theatre, Senghennydd Rd, T02920 646900, www.shermantheatre.co.uk. Concentrates on avant-garde and more serious drama and children's events. Welsh and English language productions here.

❀ Festivals and events

Apr Cardiff International Festival of Musical Theatre, various venues, celebration of the musical, www.cardiffmusicals.com, biennial event – next in 2005.

May Urdd National Eisteddfod, Wales Millennium Centre, Cardiff, www.urdd.org. The Welsh youth eisteddfod held late May/early Jun. Venue changes each year, 2005 venue is Cardiff.

Jun Cardiff Singer of the World, www.bbc.co.uk/cardiffsinger. BBC Wales' biennial singing competition, usually held in the St David's Hall. Next held in 2005.

Gwyl Ifan, Major dance festival with events in various locations in Cardiff and at the Museum of Welsh Life, St Fagans, www.gwylifan.org.

Jul International Storytelling Festival (1st weekend), St Donat's Castle, Vale of Glamorgan, T01446 799100, www.beyondtheborder.com

Cardiff Festival (late Jul/early Aug), T02920 872087, www.cardiff-festival.com. Annual free arts festival aiming to be the new Edinburgh Festival, with theatre, music, street entertainment, a food fest and fairground. The city's festival culminates in the **Big Weekend**.

Sep Cardiff Mardi Gras (end Aug/early Sep), T02920 871260, www.cardiffmardigras.co.uk /www.gaywales.co.uk. Lively lesbian and gay festival which includes dance, music, stalls and information tents.

Nov Cardiff Screen Festival, T02920 333300, www.cardiffscreenfestival.co.uk. Annual film festival in which over 100 films are screened, many of them European and UK premieres. Welsh-language films and films shot in Wales are also shown. Venues are the Chapter Arts Centre and sometimes the UGC.

Winter Wonderland (end Nov-early Jan), www.cardiff.gov.uk/winterwonderland. Cardiff celebrates Christmas and the New Year with an open-air ice rink in front of the City Hall, music and fireworks.

○ Shopping

Cardiff *p57, maps p58 and 63*

Cardiff is an excellent city for shopping. The centre is compact, so you can get around easily on foot, and while there are all the usual high-street chains (Next, Waterstones, HMV, Gap, you name them, they're here), you'll also find a brilliant choice of smaller, specialist outlets selling everything from cigars to guitars. The best places for individual shops are the splendid Victorian and Edwardian arcades, with their glass domes. There are also the usual modern, characterless malls like the huge St David's Centre and Capitol Centre. Pedestrianized Queen Street is the main drag, followed by St Mary Street. Late opening night is Thu, when most large outlets are open until 2000. In the next few years the city centre will be developed into one of the biggest shopping areas in Europe. Major chains like John Lewis are soon to open.

Arts and crafts

Capsule Gallery, 48 Charles St, T02920 382882. Contemporary art gallery that's a good place to pick up works by up-and-coming Welsh artists. Also a bistro.

Craft in the Bay, The Flourish, Lloyd George Av, Cardiff Bay, T02920 484611, daily. Co-operative retail gallery selling eclectic mix of contemporary Welsh furniture, ironwork, ceramics, jewellery and knitwear.

La Mostra Gallery, Mermaid Quay, Cardiff Bay, T02920 492225, www.lamostra gallery.com, Tue-Sat 1000- 1800, Sun 1100-1700. Wide range of contemporary international artworks. Come here and you might pick up an erotic work by Julian Murphy – or one of convicted art fraudster John Myatt's now celebrated fakes.

The Martin Tinney Gallery, Windsor Place, T02920 641411. Posh gallery for the minted, exhibiting artists like Kyffin Williams and Henry Holland.

Oriel Makers, 37 Pen-y-Lan Rd, Roath Park, T02920 472595, Wed-Sat 1000-1700. This is a platform for Welsh arts and crafts. Varying exhibitions of work including ceramics, glass, textiles, jewellery and watercolours, most of which is for sale. Work can be commissioned.

Books

Ian Allan, Royal Arcade, T02920 390615, Mon-Fri 0900-1730, Sat 0900-1700. Trainspotter heaven – a specialist train bookshop. It's also got titles on aviation.

Oxfam, 36 St Mary St, T02920 222275, Mon-Sat 0930-1730, Sun 1100-1600. Well-stocked 2nd-hand bookshop, a good

place to pick up Welsh titles – and cheap 'speak Welsh in 30 days'-type guides.
Waterstone's, The Hayes, T02920 665606, Mon, Wed, Fri 0900-1800, Tue 1000-1730, Thu 0900-1900, Sun 1100-1700. Well-known chain with a good choice of Welsh titles.

Clothing

Fab, High St Arcade. Mon-Sat 1000-1730. The place to come for women needing a special number – long dresses, pretty bags.
Drooghi, High St Arcade, T02920 230332, Mon-Sat 1000-1730. Cool clothes store for the about-town trendies.
Flannels, Churchill Way, T 02920 374079, Mon-Sat 1000-1700, Sun 1100-1600. One of a chain stocking designer clothes for men and women – enough stock to keep even minted footballers happy: Wayne Rooney reportedly spent £15,000 in 1 hr in the Manchester branch.
Hobos, High St Arcade, T02920 341188, Mon-Sat 1100-1730. Great retro shop with large and psychedelic range of 1960s and 1970s clothes.
Pussy Galore, High St Arcade, T02920 312400, Mon-Sat 1000-1730. Unfortunately named shop packed with women's 'dressing up for the evening' glam clothes.
The Pavilion, Wharton St. Men's clothing store with designer labels like Burberry, Timberland and Lacoste.
Woodenwood, Duke St Arcade, T02920 389592, Mon-Sat 1000-1730. Range of women's clothing including Chilli Pepper and FCUK with plans to introduce Gucci and Fendi in the future.
Woodies Emporium, 22-26 Morgan Arcade, T02920 232171, Mon-Thu 0900-1730, Fri, Sat 0900-1800. All sorts of designer labels to covet and drool over, from the likes of Paul Smith and Armani.

Department stores

Howells, St Mary St. Mon-Wed, Fri-Sat 0900-1800, Thu 0900-2000, Sun 1100-1700. House of Fraser store with everything from perfume to designer clothing. Handy toilets on the 2nd floor and a café/restaurant.

Food and drink

Central Market, off St Mary St. This good old-fashioned covered market has stalls selling everything from fruit and veg to books. Good place to stock up on fresh bread and Welsh cheese. Huge slabs of cake are also popular.

Furniture/homewares

Back to my Place, Bridge St, T02920 400800, www.b2mp.com, Tue, Wed, Fri-Sat 1000-1800, Thu 1000-1900, Sun 1100-1700. Come here for funky furniture and designer homewares such as Alessi, or the Dutch Pisa Vase goods.
Melin Tregwynt, Royal Arcade, T02920 224997, Mon-Sat 1000-1730. One of the places to shop in Cardiff, with all sorts of Welsh covetables, like fine woollen blankets, contemporary rugs, china and accessories.
Momentum, 31 Charles St, T02920 236266, Tue-Fri 0930-1730, Sat 1000-1800. 4 floors of designer homewares and furniture, stocking brands from the likes of B&B Italia to Vitra and Kartell.

Jewellery

Silver Studio, Royal Arcade, T02920 397111, Mon-Sat 1000-1700. Not a hint of bling. Come here for contemporary silver jewellery.
Time House Jewellery, Oxford Arcade, T02920 382050, Mon-Sat 0900-1730. This is the place to pick up that Welsh gold wedding ring, or Celtic-style jewellery.

Music

Spillers Records, 36 The Hayes, T02920 224905. Established record shop that's got a great selection of sounds by Welsh artists.

Shoes

Buzz and Co, High St Arcade, T02920 668788, Mon-Wed 1000-1730, Fri-Sat 1000-1800. Great shop for the shoe fetishist fed up with standard high-street offerings.

Souvenirs

Millennium Stadium, Westgate St, T02920 822228, Mon-Sat 0930-1700. Full range of merchandise, including the official Welsh Rugby and Welsh football strips.
Shop Wales, 9 St John St, T02920 373770, Mon-Sat 0930-1730, and Sun match days 1100-1600. Full to bursting with Welsh souvenirs with which to delight the folks back home. Among the T-shirts, baby-gros, mouse mats and blow-up dragons are kilts emblazoned with the Welsh dragon and an

enticing range of fly-the-flag underwear. If you know someone who would benefit from a pair of 'Unleash the Dragon' Y-fronts then this is the place to come.

Vale of Glamorgan *p67*
Arts and crafts

The Market Place, Penny Lane, Cowbridge, Vale of Glamorgan, Tue-Sat 0930-1630. Showcases work of local artists and craftspeople – a good place to find anything from a cute little bag to a painting.

Clothing

Goose Island, 50a High St, Cowbridge, T01446 771072, www.goose-island.co.uk, Mon-Sat 1000-1700. Lovely clothes from the Far East, as well as bags, jewellery and gifts.
McArthur Glen Designer Outlet Retail Park aka The Pines, www.mcarthurglen.com, off J36 off M4 near Bridgend, Mon-Fri 1000-2000, Sat 1000-1800, Sun 1100-1700. Has about 80 designer outlet stores, with up to 50% off RRP, you need at least ½ a day to get round it all.

Activities and tours

Boat trips

Bay Island Voyages, from Mermaid Quay, Cardiff Bay, T01446 420692, www.bay island.co.uk. Offer high-speed boat trips out to the barrage and around the bay. A ½ hr trip costs £7, £4 child. There is also a 1-hr Coastal Cruise that takes you through the barrage and along the coast round Penarth and Lavernock Point, £12, £6 child. They also offer a 2-hr trip that includes both Flatholm and Steepholm Islands, price £22.50, £12 child. There are only 12 seats on the boats so booking is required.
Cardiff Bay Cruises, from the Pierhead Building, T02920 472004, www.cardiffbay cruises.com. Operate ½ hr cruises of the Bay on an 'African Queen' lookalike (£3), and ½ hr (£3) and 1 hr (£6) trips on a luxury restaurant boat (weekends in holiday season).
Water Bus, Cardiff Cats, T07940 142409, www.cardiffwaterbus.com. Run water buses between Cardiff Bay or Taffmead Embankment (approximately 300 yds from Central station in the city centre) and Penarth and the barrage. Daily from 1040-1800, every 40 mins, £4 return, round trip £6.

Bus tours

City Sightseeing tour buses, Easter-Nov daily from 1000, T02920 384291, www.city-sightseeing.com, £7 adult, £2.50 children, £5 student. Open-top bus tours do a 50-min loop from the Castle, taking in 11 stops. You may hop off at any point before joining a later tour within a 24-hr period.

City tours

Creepy Cardiff, Ghost Tours, T07980 975135, www.creepycardiff.com, £5 adult. 1-hr ghost tours of the city. These are group tours only, but if there's availability they will let you join in. Check first.

Cycling

Taff Trail Cycle Hire Centre, off Cathedral Rd, in the Cardiff Caravan Park in Pontcanna Fields, T02920 398362. Bikes available for day rental from £10 for adults, £7.50 for children; shorter rents also possible. Bikes for disabled people available from £2.25 per hr, advance booking essential.

Football

Cardiff City FC, play at Ninian Park, Ninian Park Rd, T02920 221001, www.cardiffcity fc.co.uk. However, a huge new stadium is going up almost opposite, on the site of the Lecwith Stadium. Work starts in 2005.

Golf

Bridgend Golf Complex, Bridgend, T01656 647926, off A48. 9-hole 'pay and play' course, floodlit driving range.

Health and beauty

St David's Hotel and Spa, Havannah St, T02920 454045, www.roccofortehotels.com, Cardiff Bay. Voted 3rd best UK spa by *Condé Nast Traveller* readers, the spa at Cardiff's 5-star hotel is open to non-residents seeking some serious pampering. It's a hydrotherapy spa with an exercise pool, sauna and yoga studio and also has treatment rooms where

Cardiff & around Activities & tours

The Taff Trail

The Taff Trail extends from Cardiff Bay to Brecon, 87km (54 miles) to the north. It follows the river Taff and passes close to Castell Coch, through Merthyr Tydfil and past the Pontsticill Reservoir. The trail is used by walkers and cyclists and is mostly traffic free. Based on the former routes tramways, railways and canal towpaths, it passes through an area rich in industrial archaeology. See www.tafftrail.org.uk for further details. Detailed maps are available from TICs.

you can have aromatherapy or hydrotherapy massages, get your chakras sorted out and generally chill. Day packages cost from £95.

Ice hockey
The Ice House, Hayes Bridge, T02920 397198 or T02920 645 988, www.thecardiff devils.com. This ice rink is home to the Cardiff Devils, Wales' main ice hockey team, though it is due to close late in 2005. A new home has not been found at time of writing.

Rugby
The Millennium Stadium, Westgate St, T08705 582582, www.millenniumstadium. co.uk. The sporting venue in Wales, and the home of Welsh rugby, www.wru.co.uk. Hosts matches in the annual **Six Nations Championship** rugby, as well as international football matches.
Cardiff Rugby Club, T02920 302000 or T0870 0135213, www.cardiffrfc.com. Game are played at the Arms Park, Westgate St, by the Millennium Stadium.

Train trips
Cardiff Barrage Crossing, from Mermaid Quay, opposite Techniquest, Cardiff Bay, T02920 512729, www.cardiffroadtrain.com, 1100-1700 Easter-end Oct, £3 return adult, £2 return children. Family-friendly trip, with informative commentary, on a little train taking you from Mermaid Quay to the Port of Cardiff and on to the Barrage. The trip lasts just under 1 hr, but you can get off to see the Barrage if you wish and return later.

Walking
The Vale of Glamorgan has loads of possibilities for walks. Most of the 14 miles of Heritage Coast can be walked. A popular route is between Llantwit Major and St Donats, and there is also the **Valeways Millennium Heritage Trail**, www.valeways. org.uk, a 70-mile circular route that starts and finishes near the Museum of Welsh life at St Fagans (see p67). It takes you through pretty towns and villages and onto the coast. There are plenty of other walks on the Bridgend website, www.bridgend.gov.uk.

Transport

Further information on public transport and getting around Wales can be obtained if you contact **Traveline Cymru**, T0870 6082608, www.traveline-cymru.org.uk.

Air
There are direct flights to Cardiff from **London City airport** every day except Sat, as well as regular flights from provincial UK airports, Ireland and several European centres, including daily flights to **Amsterdam**. See p22 for further details.

Bus
Local Cardiff Bus (Traveline Cymru, T0870 6082608, www.cardiffbus.com) runs services all over the city from its base in Wood St, and its green, white and orange buses generally operate 0530-2320, with a reduced service at the weekend and on public holidays. Prices vary according to the system of colour-coded fare zones, Zone A (red) is the city centre, where tickets cost from 70p. Exact change is usually needed; tickets can be bought on the buses.

The main routes between the city centre and the Bay area include the following: Bus 6 **Bay Xpress**, www.cardiff.gov.uk/bayxpress (departing from Central Station), No 35 (from Wyndham Arcade on St Mary St to Mermaid Quay) and No 8 (from Wood St to Atlantic Wharf), and these services run every 10-15 mins 0730-2300. A 24-hr **City Rider pass**, costing £3.50, £2.30 children, £7 families allows unlimited travel on all Cardiff Bus services within Cardiff and its near neighbour Penarth. This can be purchased on the buses or from the bus sales office in Wood St.

Buses to **Caerphilly** leave from Cardiff bus station. **Stagecoach** bus A and B also to go Caerphilly. **Stagecoach** bus No 26 goes hourly to Caerphilly and continues to Castell Coch; both castles can be seen in a day (see p90-91). **Castell Coch** can also be reached by Stagecoach 132 which goes to **Tongwynlais** (£2.50 return, 30 mins, Mon-Sat every ½ hr, Sun every hr) from where it's a 10-min walk to the castle. Bus Nos 89 and 89A run from Cardiff to **Penarth** (£2.45 return, 20 mins, Mon-Sat every ½ hr, Sun every hr).

Long distance Buses leave from the city's main bus station to most of the major towns in Britain. **National Express** (T0870 5808080, www.nationalexpress.com) run direct bus services to **London** (Victoria coach station), 9 daily, 3½ hrs, £28 return; **Bristol** 4 daily, 1 hr 10 mins, £9.40; **Glasgow**, 1 daily, 10 hrs, £63; **Birmingham**, 4 daily, 2 ½ hrs, £19; **Newport**, approx every ½ hr, 25 mins, £4.10; **Swansea**, 11 daily, 1 hr 5 mins, £7.10; change at Swansea for **St David's** and **Tenby**.

Car

Car hire is available from **Hertz**, Cardiff Airport, T01446 711722, www.hertz.co.uk; and **Europcar**, Cardiff Airport, T01446 711924, www.europcar.com.

Train

For information call **National Rail Enquiries**, T08457 484950.

Local Arriva Trains Wales run most local train services (T08456 061660, www.arriva trainswales.co.uk) which run 0500-2430 on weekdays, with a reduced service at weekends/public holidays. A shuttle train service takes 3 mins from Queen St station in the city centre to Cardiff Bay station, from

where Cardiff Bay is a 5-min walk. There are 4 services per hr Mon-Fri, 2 per hr on Sat (from £1 off-peak), but no service on Sun. Travelling to **Cardiff Bay** from Central Station costs the same but takes longer, including a change at Queen St. Arriva also offer a **Day Explorer pass** for £6.50 adults, £3.25 children, allowing for 1 day of unlimited travel on their train services and **Stagecoach** buses, as well as discounts to some tourist attractions around the city. To **Caerphilly** and the Vale of Glamorgan **Valley Lines'** Rhymney or Bargoed train service from Cardiff, £3, 20 mins, Mon-Sat every 20 mins, Sun 3 times daily. **Penarth** is at the end of the line from Cardiff Central (£2, 10 mins, every 20 mins).

Long distance Arriva also runs services to **Swansea**, every ½ hr, £15, 1hr; **Newport**, every ½ hr, £3.40, 15 mins; **Abergavenny**, hourly, £15.50, 40 mins; **Trehafod** in the Rhonda Valley, twice hourly, £3.10, ½ hr and **Merthyr Tydfil** (from where there's a bus link to Brecon), hourly, £3.10, 1 hr. To visit Hay-on-Wye you'll have to get a train to Hereford, then a bus to Hay.

There are regular daily services to and from most major British cities. For further details, see Essentials p33 . **First Great Western** runs direct services to **London Paddington**, hourly, 2 hrs, supersaver return ticket £35. Regional railway lines provide a direct link to **Bristol**, every ½ hr, £12; **Plymouth** 3 direct daily or every ½ hr via Bristol, £40; **Birmingham** and the Midlands, direct every 2 hrs, or every ½ hr via Bristol, £36.80; **Manchester** and the Northwest, hourly, approx 4 hrs, £43.

Taxi

Taxis can be found in the ranks at Central Station, Queen St station and on Duke St by the castle. A taxi from Central Station/ Wood St Bus Station to Cardiff Bay costs around £4 one way. Taxis may be hailed on the street or, alternatively, can be ordered by telephone from dozens of firms, including: **Black Cab**, Riverside, T02920 222999; **Capitol**, T02920 777777; **Castle**, 27 Westgate St, T02920 344344; **Dragon**, City Rd, T02920 333333; and **Premiere**, T02920 555555/ 02920 565565.

Cardiff & around Transport

◑ Directory

Airline offices
Air Wales, T0870 7773131, www.air
wales.com; BMI Baby, T0870 264 2229,
www.bmibaby.com; KLM, T08705 074074,
www.klmuk.co.uk; Ryanair, T0871 2460000
or T0871 2460016, www.ryanair.com.

Banks and ATMs
Bank opening hours are Mon-Fri from
around 0930-1600-1700. You can withdraw
cash from selected banks and ATMs with
your credit/debit card. There is a branch of
Lloyds TSB on Queen St and other banks can
be found there or on High St. Several major
banks around the city have exchange,
Mon-Fri 0900-1700.

Cultural institutions
Royal Norwegian Consulate, High St,
Cowbridge, T01446 774018,
www.norway.org.uk, Mon-Fri 0900-1730.
American Welsh Affairs Office, T02920
786633 (no visa or consular services at this
branch), London office T0207 4999000,
www.usembassy.org.uk.

Embassies and consulates
All major embassies are based in London.
Australia, T020 73794334; Canada, T020
72586600; Denmark; T020 72351255;
France, T020 70731400; Germany, T020
78241300; Italy, T020 7312 2200; Japan,
T020 74656500; Netherlands, T020
75903200; New Zealand, T020 79308422;
South Africa, T020 74517299; Spain, T020
7589 8989; Sweden, T020 79176400;
Switzerland, T020 76166000; USA, T020
74999000. See also Cultural Institutions.

Emergency numbers
Police/Fire/Ambulance T999.
Penarth coastguard T01792 366534.

Language schools
Languages Direct, 61 Charles St, T02920
665677. Cardiff Language Academy, 16/17
High St, T02920 226047.

Laundry
Launderama, 60 Lower Cathedral Rd.
Canton Launderette, 244 Cowbridge Rd
East, T02920 341039.

Left luggage
Only available at Cardiff Visitor Centre (see
p57), though limited facilities.

Libraries
Cardiff Central Library, Frederick St, T02920
382116, Mon-Sat 0900-1730. Free internet
Tue, Wed, Fri 0900-1800, Thu 0900-1900, Sat
0900-1730.

Media
The Welsh daily broadsheet is the *Western
Mail*, while Cardiff's regional daily is the
South Wales Echo.

Medical
Dentists Riverside Health Centre,
Wellington St, Canton, T02920 371221. For
emergency-only dental treatment.
Doctors NHS Wales, T0845 4647,
www.wales.nhs.uk, can offer confidential
medical advice over the phone or let you
know the location of your nearest doctor.
The website also has some useful links for
local doctors surgeries and so on. Among
surgeries in the city are: Roath House
Surgery, 100 Penylan Rd, Roath Park, T02920
461100 and St Isan Road Surgery, 46 St Isan
Rd, T02920 612333. A useful website is
www.click-for-health.com. For serious
medical emergencies requiring an
ambulance, dial T999. Hospitals
University of Wales Hospital, Heath Park,
T02920 747747. Pharmacies There are
chemists all over the city. The main one is
Boots, 36 Queen St, T02920 231291.

Police
Cardiff Police Station, King Edward VIII
Avenue, Cathays Park, T02920 222111.

Post offices
Main Post Office, The Hayes. Mon-Fri 0900
-1730, Sat 0900-1230.

Southeast Wales

❗ Footprint features

Introduction

The southeast corner of Wales has something for everyone. The rugged Brecon Beacons National Park offers lovers of the outdoors everything from hill walking and horse riding, to canoeing and mountain biking. The famous Valleys have fascinating examples of 19th-century industrial architecture, Blaenavon, with its colourful workers' houses and ironworks, provides a sobering reminder of life during the Industrial Revolution. For those seeking more ancient relics, the Roman remains at Caerleon, near Newport, boast an impressive fortress, and the medieval castle at Caerphilly is the largest in Wales. Lovers of literature can make for the ruins of Tintern Abbey, which inspired romantic painters and poets, or browse in the second-hand bookshops that dominate the border town of Hay-on-Wye – home to the famous Hay Festival, which attracts literati from all over the world.

Swansea, the second largest city in Wales and birthplace of Dylan Thomas, has all the charm of a maritime hub – not to mention some excellent museums and a market well worth visiting for its seafood and Welsh specialities, such as laver bread. Next door, the Victorian seaside resort of Mumbles is popular with locals and visitors alike and has a fine array of pubs and restaurants. West of Swansea is the Gower Peninsula, Britain's first designated Area of Outstanding Natural Beauty, and a Mecca for surfers and lovers of soft, sandy beaches.

★ **Don't miss...**

1 **Big Pit** Don a hard hat and head down 'the pit', page 92.

2 **Tintern Abbey** Indulge your inner poet, page 99.

3 **Brecon Beacons** Get out and active, page 103.

4 **Hay-on-Wye** Browse for bargains in Britain's best book town, page 106.

5 **Rhossili** Watch the sun set over one of Wales' best beaches, page 118.

6 **Mumbles Mile** Dine out in one of the many restaurants, page 121.

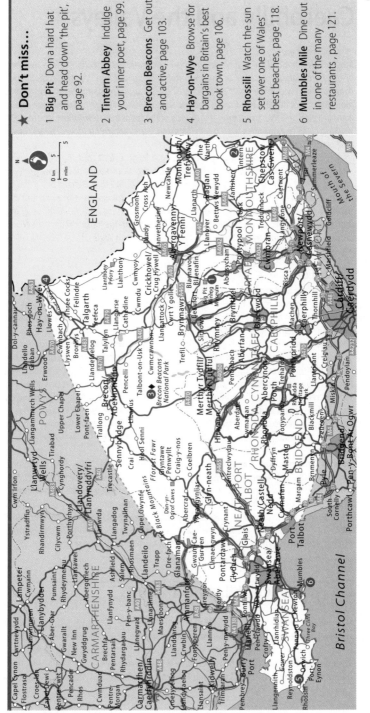

Southeast Wales

Caerphilly and the Valleys

→ *Colour map 2, grid C5*

Most tourists bypass the Valleys for the more conventional attractions of the beaches of the Pembrokeshire coast or the mountains of Snowdonia. Yet these distinctive communities, with their rows of terraced houses squeezed into the valleys of the mountains that lie between Cardiff and the Brecon Beacons, are full of history. These were the coal and iron producing heartlands of the Industrial Revolution, where close working class communities lived harsh lives under the gloomy shadow of hills scarred and blackened with slag heaps.

When the coal mining industry died so, to a large extent, did the Valleys, with unemployment devastating the population. But the slag heaps have now gone or been greened over, some coal mines are now museums and Blaenavon, a World Heritage Site, is reinventing itself as a booktown. The towns are still poor, but the people are very friendly; the surrounding hills are stunning and the glimpse of the industrial past is fascinating. Caerphilly itself is justly famous for its castle, the second largest in Europe and one of the most impressive sights in Wales. ➤ *For Sleeping, Eating and other listings, see pages 94-96.*

Ins and outs

Getting there and around Eight miles north of Cardiff, Caerphilly is easily reached by **road** from junction 32 of the M4, by taking the A470 and then following signs for Caerphilly. There are good **train** and **bus** links from Cardiff to Caerphilly and the main towns in the valleys like Merthyr Tydfil. **Arriva Valley Lines**, www.valleylines.co.uk, Rhymney service trains run every half an hour from Cardiff to Bargoed, stopping at Caerphilly railway station about a quarter of a mile from the visitor centre opposite the castle; the trip takes about 20 minutes. **Arriva Valley Line** trains also run along the Rhonda Valley and to Merthyr Tydfil. Bus No 26 runs hourly from Cardiff Bus station in Wood Street, takes about 45 minutes and will stop at Caerphilly Railway Station and on Castle Street near Caerphilly Visitor Centre. Towns like Merthyr Tydfil and Caerphilly are small enough to explore on foot. If you want to travel from valley to valley without returning to Cardiff it is easier to go by car. ➤ *For further details see Transport, page 95.*

Tourist information Caerphilly Visitor Centre ① *Lower Twin Sq, Caerphilly, T02920 880011, www.visitcaerphilly.com, daily Apr-Sep 1000-1800, Oct-Mar 1000-1700;* **Blaenavon TIC** ① *North St, The Ironworks, T01495 792615, blaenavon. ironworks@btopenworld.com, Apr-Oct Mon-Fri 0930-1630, Sat 1000-1700, Sun 1000-1630, can also help people to trace their local family history;* **Merthyr Tydfil TIC** ① *14a Glebeland St T01685 379884, tic@merthyr.gov.uk, Mon-Sat 0900-1600;* **Pontypridd TIC** ① *Bridge St, T01443 490748, www.pontypriddmuseum.org.uk, Mon-Sat 1000-1700.*

Caerphilly (Caeffili) and around

Nine miles north of Cardiff, at the foot of the Rhymney Valley, Caerphilly is famous not only for its vast castle, but also for its cheese. Crumbly, white and salty it is still made by traditional methods at dairies in the area and is sold in many places about town. The cheese is celebrated at the **Big Cheese festival** (see page 95) in July. Not far from Caerphilly are the beautiful Llancaiach Fawr Manor and the fairytale Castell Coch.

The vast medieval fortress of **Caerphilly Castle** ① *Caerphilly, T02920 883143, www.cadw.wales.gov.uk, daily Jun-Sep 0930-1800, Apr-May, Oct 0930-1700, Nov-Mar Mon-Fri 1100-1600, Sun 0930-1600, £3, £2.50 children, £8.50 family, CADW,* is the second largest castle in Europe and, despite the fact it was never a royal castle, bears comparison with even the mightiest of the castles of Edward I. It was built between 1268 and 1271 by 'Red' – as he was known after the fiery colour of his hair – Gilbert de Clare, Earl of Gloucester, one of Henry III's most powerful and ambitious barons, to prevent the area falling into the hands of the Welsh leader Llywelyn the Last. The castle is vast, spread over some 30 acres of land, inspiring the poet Tennyson to write: 'It isn't a castle – it's a town in ruins'.

Six miles north of Caerphilly, **Llancaiach Fawr Manor** ① *near Nelson on B4254, T01443 412248, Mar-end Oct Mon-Fri 1000-1700, Sat-Sun 1000-1800, closed Mon Nov-Feb, £4.95, £3.50 children, £14 family,* is a lovely old manor house. Built in 1530, it is now a living history museum focussing on the year of the Civil War (1645) when then owner Col Edward Prichard changed his allegiance from the Royalist to the Parliamentarian cause. The informative guides are dressed in period costume and speak and act as they would have in the 17th century. The rooms have been restored and furnished to the period and there are also 17th-century style gardens.

Four miles southwest of Caerphilly is **Castell Coch** ① *near Tongwynlais, T02920 810101, £3, £2.50 children, £8.50 family, daily Jun-Sep 0930-1800, Easter-May, Oct 0930-1700, Nov-Mar Mon-Sat 0930-1600, Sun 1100-1600 (due to close for conservation work Sun 4 Jan-11 Feb 2006), CADW,* whose lavishly eccentric interiors, like Cardiff Castle, are a result of the partnership of the Marquis of Bute and architect William Burges. Their joint love of gothic fantasy and Bute's vast fortune allowed them to create extravagant rooms, with gilded ceilings, walls painted with golden apples, monkeys and peacocks and elaborate furniture and fittings. You half expect to see Rapunzel letting down her hair from one of the turret windows.

The Valleys

The Valleys were hardly populated until the Industrial Revolution, when the discovery of rich seams of coal and iron turned them into blackened boom towns. Vast numbers of people flooded in seeking work, and distinctive close-knit communities grew up. Conditions in the mines were terrible and until 1842 women and children (some as young as six) worked underground alongside the men, crawling on their hands and knees through narrow seams, dragging carts laden with coal. The work was dangerous and there were frequent mining disasters. With life so hard people often took solace in the pubs and working men's clubs and, as a counter to this, the chapel and temperance movement also gained a firm foothold. Social divisions between those who owned the industries and those who worked in them were sharply polarized and the Valleys began to gain a reputation for radical politics.

Mining began to decline in the 20th century. The miners strike of 1984-1985, in which the Thatcher government 'took on' the National Union of Mineworkers (NUM), effectively rung the knell for mining in the Valleys (and in Britain). Now some industrial sites have become museums and there is an increasing emphasis on walking and cycling in the strikingly beautiful hills.

Blaenavon (Blaenafon)

In 2000 the industrial town of Blaenavon was designated a UNESCO World Heritage Site – a recognition of the important role it played in the Industrial Revolution. **Blaenavon Ironworks** ① *T01495 792615, mid Mar-Oct Mon-Fri 0930-1630, Sat 1000-1700, Sun 1000-1630, £2, £1.50 children, £5.50 family, pre-book for guided tours,* are

Aberfan

Coal mining disasters were once a terrible feature of life in the Valleys, yet the most horrific of all occurred above ground in the little village of Aberfan. In 1966, after heavy rain, a slag heap slid down the hill completely smothering the school beneath. It killed 144 people, 116 of whom were children. It tore the heart from the community. It was a disaster waiting to happen, as subsequent enquiries revealed that safety had long been given a low priority by the authorities. Today the graves of all those who died are ranged in rows in the local graveyard. They are a desperately poignant sight: one little boy's gravestone simply says that he 'Loved Light, Freedom and Animals.' The slag heaps are no longer there.

one of the best preserved 18th-century ironworks in Europe. Established in 1788 – the site being chosen for its abundance of coal, iron-ore, limestone and water – they were at the cutting edge of technology, using steam rather than water to power the furnaces. By 1796 Blaenavon was the second largest producer of iron in Wales. In later years the metallurgist Sidney Gilchrist Thomas worked from here, spawning the mighty steel industry. As well as the remains of the works, there's a colourful little terrace of iron workers cottages, inhabited until 1973.

Blaenavon is now in the process of re-inventing itself as a book town (www.booktownblaenafon.com), along the same lines as Hay-on-Wye. Bookshops are opening all the time, selling everything from cookery books to travel titles; cafés, bars and places to stay are all in the pipeline. They now have a book festival every year, usually in March (see festivals, page 95). Within the town is a small **Community Heritage and Cordell Museum** ① *Lion St, next to the library, To1495 790991, Apr-Sep Mon-Fri 1000-1600, Sat 1000-1300, Oct-Mar Mon, Tue, Thu 1000-1600, Sat 1000-1300, £1.* Inside is the recreated study of local author Alexander Cordell.

Blaenavon wasn't just an iron-working centre, it was also a coal-mining town as you can see at **Big Pit National Mining Museum** ① *approx 1 mile west of Blaenavon, To1495 790311, www.nmgw.ac.uk mid Feb-Nov daily 0930-1700, 1st tour 1000, last 1530, free.* This historic mine, high on the moors, gives an excellent insight into the life of the Valleys' coal miners. This mine opened in the mid-19th century and was one of the few in the Valleys that did not experience a major disaster. Coal was mined from 1880 until 1980, the site opening as a museum in 1983. In its heyday it employed 1,300 men and produced more than 250,000 tons of coal a year. The highlight of a visit is the tour, which takes you 300 ft (90 m) underground. You don a helmet, cap-lamp and battery pack and, guided by ex-miners, go down to the coal face where you see the miserable conditions under which people worked. Not just people either – the underground stables still bear the names of the pit ponies who spent their lives in darkness. The last ponies around here were only brought to the surface in 1972. Among the surface attractions are the listed 1930s **Pithead Baths**, and an exhibition in which you learn about the social history of the area. There's also a gallery focusing on modern mining and a café.

Just to the west of Blaenavon is the **Pontypool and Blaenavon Railway** ① *Furnace Sidings Station, off A4348, To1495 792263, www.pontypool-and-blaenavon.co.uk, Easter-Sep and around Christmas, £2.40, £1.20 children, £6 family,* the steepest and highest train line in the country, passing through dramatic moorland landscape. A round trip takes 20 minutes, but you can stop off as many times as you like; Garn Lakes are a good spot for a picnic.

The name of Merthyr Tydfil is synonymous with the country's industrial past, although the town has roots dating back to Roman times if not before. The town's name refers to Tydfil, a Welsh princess who was martyred for her Christian beliefs in the fifth century. In the 18th century the town was transformed when its rich supplies of iron ore and limestone were discovered and exploited. It became the most important iron producing town in the world. The population swelled rapidly as workers swarmed in, being housed as cheaply as possible by their wealthy masters. The appalling working conditions and poor cramped housing led to a wave of radicalism: in 1831 there was a violent workers uprising (when the Red Flag, which had been dipped in calf's blood, was raised for the first time) and in 1900 it became the first town in Britain to elect a Socialist MP – Keir Hardie. When the industry declined in the 20th century Merthyr suffered terribly from the consequent depression.

Today the history of the town, and the gulf that existed between the iron masters and their workers, can best be understood by visiting two contrasting sites. **Joseph Parry's Cottage** ① *4 Chapel Row, T01685 721858, Apr-Sep Thu-Sun 1400-1700, free,* is a preserved ironworkers' cottage, part of a terrace built in 1825 for skilled workers employed in the Cyfartha Ironworks. The ground floor rooms are furnished simply, as they would have been in the 1840s. Upstairs there's an exhibition about composer Joseph Parry who was born here and wrote a well known Welsh tune – *Myfanwy.*

Not far away, on the high ground, is the lavish **Cyfartha Castle** ① *Brecon Rd, T01685 723112, daily Apr-Sep 1000-1730, Oct-Mar Tue-Fri 1000-1600, Sat-Sun 1200-1600, free,* built at a cost of £30,000 in 1825 by the Crawshay family, who owned the Cyfartha Ironworks. It stands in 160 acres of parkland. Part of this opulent pile is now a school, the rest an excellent museum and art gallery. There's a good collection of pottery and ceramics, including local Nantgarw ware; Egyptian and Roman artefacts collected by a local man; and displays on male voice choirs, the Iron Industry, Welsh Nationalism and the miners strike of 1984-1985. You can also see paintings by artists such as Jack Butler Yeats (brother of the poet), Kyffin Williams, Cedric Morris and George Frederick Harris (Rolf Harris' grandfather who was born in Merthyr). There's a nice café too.

Around Merthyr Tydfil

The **Brecon Mountain Railway** ① *Pant Station, 3 miles north of Merthyr (signposted off the A470, or bus No 35 from Merthyr bus station) T01685 722988, www.brecon mountainrailway.co.uk, Easter-Oct, generally closed Mon and Fri Mar-May and Sep-Oct, £7.50, £3.75 child, family ticket available,* once carried coal and passengers and has now been restored. The narrow gauge steam railway now takes you into the Brecon Beacons National Park (see page 103), the journey takes about an hour, but you can hop off and on at Pontsticill.

Southeast of Merthyr, **Rhonda Heritage Park** ① *Coed Cae Rd, Trehafod, near Pontypridd, T01443 682036, www.rhonddaheritagepark.com, daily 1000-1800, last tour 1630, closed Mon Oct-Easter, £5.60, £4.30 children, £16.50 family,* is based at the former Lewis Merthyr Colliery; there's an interesting exhibition looking at life in the valleys, with recreated shops and house interiors. Panels tell the story of the colliery and the appalling Tynewydd Colliery disaster in 1877 when the pit was flooded and many men trapped underground. Tours of the site are available and there's also a good selection of books on life in the Valleys, as well as a café and gallery upstairs.

Towards Port Talbot

Margam Stones Museum ① *Near Port Talbot, T02920 500200, Wed-Sun 1030-1600, £2, £1.50 children, £5.50 family,* is small but fascinating. Situated next to it is **Margam Abbey Church** ① *T01639 871184, CADW,* which contains a fine collection of early Christian sculptured stones. There's the **Bodvoc Stone**, which once sat on Margam mountain, set into a line of prehistoric barrows; 10th- and 11th-century crosses found at a nearby farm; and a sixth-century memorial stone to Pumpeius Carantorius, with Ogham inscriptions which look rather like Morse code. The church itself is well worth a visit and contains 16th- and 17th-century tombs.

Margam Park ① *Near Port Talbot, junction 38 off the M4, T01639 881635, www.npt.gov.uk/margampark, daily Easter-Sep 1000-1730, winter 1000-1630, free, £2 car park*, is a delightful parkland surrounding an elaborate 19th-century house and the romantic ruins of **Margam Abbey**. In the gardens is an elegant 18th-century Orangery, designed by Antony Keck to house a citrus collection of around 100 orange and lemon trees. There's a walled garden, fuchsia collections and a play area for children. Contemporary artworks by artists such as Paul Williams and Elizabeth Frink are dotted around the grounds.

● Sleeping

Caerphilly *p90*

C Cottage Guest House, Pwll-y-pant, T02920 869160, www.s-h-systems.co.uk/hotels/cottagegh. This 300-year-old cottage is only a mile from Caerphilly Castle. Friendly welcome and hearty breakfasts.

C Lugano Guest House, Hillside, Mountain Rd, T02920 852672. Comfortable B&B with stone floors, a big bay window and garden. Some rooms have views of the castle and it's just 5 mins' walk to the centre of town.

The Valleys *p91*

B Heritage Park Hotel, Coed Cae Rd, Trehafod, near Pontypridd, T01443 687057, www.heritageparkhotel.co.uk. Comfortable and clean business-geared hotel that makes a good base for exploring the Valleys and is right next to the Rhondda Heritage Park. Character is added with old photographs of mining families and landscapes hanging from the walls. Staff are friendly and there are good leisure facilities, including a swimming pool, sauna, gym and beauty treatments.

C Mill Farm, Cwmafon, Pontypool, T01495 774588. This 15th-century farmhouse B&B in the Valleys has 3 en suite rooms, log fires and a small indoor heated swimming pool. It's adults only as the idea is to give you complete peace and quiet.

C Tyn-y-Wern Country House, Ynysybwl, Rhonnda Cynon Taff, 3 miles from Pontypridd on B4273, T01443 790551. A Victorian mine manager's house with 3 rooms, 1 en suite. They are happy to cater for walkers and cyclists. They also have self catering lodges sleeping 2-4 people.

● Eating

Caerphilly *p90*

Ⅱ Glanmor's, Unit 30, Castle Court, Brynau Rd, T02920 888355. Great sandwich shop, close to the castle, serving homemade pastries.

Ⅱ Take a Break, The Pavilion, next to the Post Office, T02920 889966. Serves all-day breakfasts, pies and things with chips.

Ⅱ Traveller's Rest, Thornhill Rd, Thornhill, T02920 859021. Sits astride the hill summit between Caerphilly and Cardiff. Essentially a chain pub, it does so-so food in pretty and quaint surroundings – still better than much of what Caerphilly itself can offer.

The Valleys *p91*

ⅡⅡ Heritage Park Hotel, Coed Cae Rd, Trehafod, near Pontypridd, T01443 687057, daily 1200-1400, 1900-2200. This hotel restaurant is worth checking out if you want a change from pub grub. Lots of steaks and roast meats, as well as some good veggie choices.

ⅡⅡ-Ⅱ The Cinnamon Tree, Tonteg Rd (Power Station Hill), Treforest, near Pontypridd, T01443 843222, Wed-Sat 1200-1400, Mon-Sat 1800-2230, Sun from 1200. If you're out and about and suddenly yearn for a curry this is the answer. It's a drive-through Indian restaurant. It's very popular so you'll need to phone in your order in advance – then turn up and tuck in.

Ⅱ Cyfartha Castle Tearoom, Cyfartha Castle, Merthyr Tydfil, T01685 723112, Apr-Sep, daily 1000-around 1700; Oct-Mar Tue-Fri 1000-around 1530, Sat, Sun 1200-1530. As it's free entry to the castle it's worth going just for this little tearoom.

🍺 Pubs, bars and clubs

The Valleys *p91*
Aberaman Hotel, Brynheulog Terrace, Aberaman, T01685 874695. Typical valleys pub serving real ales and bar meals.
Capel, Park Place, Gilfach Fargoed, near Bargoed, T01443 830272. Traditional pub serving real ales.
Falcon Inn, 1 Incline Row, Cwmaman, near Aberaman, T01685 873758. Popular pub on the riverside. Serves real ales and bar meals.
Glan Taff, Cardiff Rd, Quakers Yard, off A470 outside Caerphilly, near Abercynon, T01443 410822. Popular inn on the River Taff, serving real ales and good bar meals.

🎭 Entertainment

The Pop Factory, Jenkins St, Porth, The Valleys, T01443 688500, www.thepop factory.com. Off A4058 near Pontypridd. Good place to catch Welsh rock acts and new Valleys talent.

🎪 Festivals and events

Mar Blaenavon Booktown Festival, T08707 601093, www.booktownfestivals.com, literary talks, poetry and music.
Jul The Big Cheese is a 2-day event held on the last weekend of the month to celebrate Caerphilly, the pale, salty and mild cheese, once so popular with miners who needed to top up their salt levels. Cheese races, a medieval-themed fair, music, crafts events.

🧗 Activities and tours

Climbing
Welsh International Climbing Centre, Taff Bargoed Centre, Trelewis, Treharris, south of Merthyr Tydfil, T01443 710749, www.indoor climbingwalls.co.uk. Climbing (largest indoor climbing wall in Europe), caving, abseiling, high ropes courses and outdoor activities like gorge walking and kayaking. 2 hr and ½ day introductory tasters, adult lessons and longer breaks. 2 hr taster session for 4 people £48. Also have bunkhouse accommodation.

Cycling/mountain biking
Torfaen Cycle Route runs from Blaenavon through Pontypool into Cwmbran and on to Newport, using old railway lines and canal towpaths. Further details from: Countryside Section, Development Dept., Floor 4, County Hall, Cwmbran, NP44 2WN, T01633 648034.
The Taff Trail (55 miles/93 km route from Brecon to Cardiff) passes through Merthyr Tydfil and Pontypridd, see p84.
Cwmcarn Forest Drive, Visitor Centre and Campsite, Cwmcarn, Crosskeys, T01495 272001, www.caerphilly.gov.uk/visiting. Mountain biking track, the **Twrch Trail**, visitor centre, forest drive (£3 per car), guided walks and a campsite.

Horse riding
Caerphilly Riding School and Trekking Centre, Ty Canol Farm, Caerphilly, T02920 880500, www.caerphillyridingschooland trekkingcentre.com. Escorted trekking and riding lessons. Full day trek £25.

Quad biking
Taff Buggy Trails, Cwrt Y Celyn Farm, Eglwsilan, T02920 831658, www.adventure wales.co.uk, summer 0900-2000, winter daylight hours. Quad biking and activity centre. Quad biking from £15 for 45 mins.

Train trips
See Pontypool and Blaenavon Railway, p92 and Brecon Mountain Railway, p93.

Walking
Walking leaflets describing walks around Pontypool available from: Torfaen County Borough Council, County Hall, Cwmbran, Torfaen, NP44 2WN.

🚌 Transport

Caerphilly *p90*
Bus
Bus No 26 or **Stagecoach** bus A or B stop at the train station and on Castle St near the TIC, to **Cardiff** (£2.80, 45 mins, Mon-Sat every 20 mins, Sun 3 daily). The No 132 also runs to **Tongwynlais**, from where it's a 10-min walk to **Castell Coch**; the No 26 (Mon-Fri) stops at the castle gates.

Train
Valley Lines' Rhymney or Bargoed train service to **Cardiff** (£3, 20 mins, Mon-Sat every 20 mins, Sun 3 times daily).

Bus

From High St in Blaenavon, **Stagecoach** bus No 30 heads to **Newport** (40 mins, Mon-Sat every hr); in summer it also continues to **Big Pit Mining Museum**; Bus No X24 also goes to **Newport**. From Merthyr Tydfil **Stagecoach** bus No X4 goes to **Cardiff** (£3, 45 mins, every 15 mins), X78 to **Cardiff** (£3, 4 daily), X75 to **Swansea** (£4.50, 1 hr, every hr). Bus No 43 to **Brecon** (£2.80, 35 mins, Mon-Sat every 2 hrs, Sun twice daily).

Train

From Merthyr Tydfil **Valley Lines** run trains to **Cardiff**, (£5 return, 1 hr, every hr, Sun every 2 hrs). From just north of Merthyr, the **Brecon Mountain Railway** travels into the **Brecon Beacons National Park** (see p93).

ⓘ Directory

Caerphilly *p90*

Internet Free access in **Caerphilly** Library, Morgan Jones Park, near the town centre, T02920 852543, Mon, Wed, Thu 0930-1800 Tue 0930-1330, Fri 0900-1930, Sat 0930-1700.

The Valleys *p91*

Library Blaenavon Library, Lion St, T01495 790367, free internet access Mon, Thu, 0930-1730, Tue, 1400-1900, Sat 0900-1300.

Monmouthshire → *Colour map 2, grid B-C6*

When George Borrow wrote his famous travelogue 'Wild Wales', Monmouthshire was considered to be English rather than Welsh. Although now officially part of Wales, the county still feels less immediately Welsh than the borderlands further north. It was once the scene of fierce fighting as locals resisted first Roman and then Norman incursions on their land. There are vivid reminders of those times in the extensive Roman remains at Caerleon and the 'don't mess with me' Norman castle at Chepstow. The west of the county, particularly around the city of Newport, is industrialized, but as you move east it becomes increasingly green. There are good golf courses here; in 2010 the Ryder Cup will come to Newport. The most beautiful area is the lush, green Wye Valley – an area of Outstanding Natural Beauty formed as the River Wye ripples along the border from Monmouth to Chepstow. The valley, an excellent area for walking and canoeing, is home to one of the most celebrated sites in Wales – Tintern Abbey, a picturesque ruin, right on the border with England. ›› *For Sleeping, Eating and other listings, see pages 101-103.*

Ins and outs

Getting there and around By **road**, Monmouth is easily reached from Cardiff and southwest England by exiting at junction 24 of the M4 and taking the A449 and A40. From the Midlands and the northern England, leave M5 at junction 8 and follow the M50 and A40. Chepstow is just off the M48 and Newport off the M4. Newport is linked to Cardiff and Chepstow by **train**, as well as the Midlands. **Bus** service No 69 runs approx every two hours between Monmouth and Chepstow and the journey takes about 50 minutes. A useful booklet, *Discover the Wye Valley on Foot and by Bus*, is available from TICs. ›› *For further transport information, see page 102.*

Tourist information Chepstow TIC ⓘ *Castle Car Park, Bridge St, T01291 623772, www.chepstow.co.uk, daily 1000-1730, may be closed 1hr at lunch.* **Monmouth Visitor Centre** ⓘ *Shire Hall, Agincourt Sq, NP5 3DY, T01600 713899, www.monmouth.gov.uk, Easter-Oct 1000-1730, Oct- Easter 1000-1300, 1400-1700.* **Newport TIC** ⓘ *Museum and Art Gallery, John Frost Sq, T01633 842962, newport.tic@newport.gov.uk, Mon-Sat 0930-1700.* **Wye Valley Tourism** ⓘ *T01600 715781, www.wyevalleytourism.co.uk.* Other useful websites include www.wyevalleyaonb.co.uk, www.visitwyevalley.com and www.monmouthshire.gov.uk.

Background

Monmouthshire, like so many borderlands, has a turbulent past. This is the main southern route into Wales and was the obvious point of entry for invading forces. The Romans built the first bridge over the Wye, thus facilitating their incursions into Wales and they were followed by the Normans, who made their intentions obvious soon after the Battle of Hastings by building one of the first stone castles in Britain on the Wye at Chepstow. The Norman invaders moved west, building more castles in Monmouthshire all the time, and castles continued to be built here until the Middle Ages. After the Civil War the county became more peaceful – although the land was still disputed: it did not officially become part of Wales until 1974. In the 18th century the romantic beauty of Tintern Abbey in the Wye Valley began to attract large numbers of visitors, who gradually began to discover the rest of Wales as a holiday destination. Industrialisation, in the form of the coal and steel industries, transformed the area around Newport, but to the north and east Monmouthshire still retains much of its pastoral appeal.

Chepstow (Cas-Gwent)

Chepstow deserves the title 'Gateway to Wales': it's the first town you come to if driving to Wales from the south of England and is strategically situated on the Wye, which here marks the border. The main reason for stopping is to visit the magnificent Norman **castle** ① *T01291 624065, Mar-Oct daily 0930-1700; Jun-Sep daily 0930-*

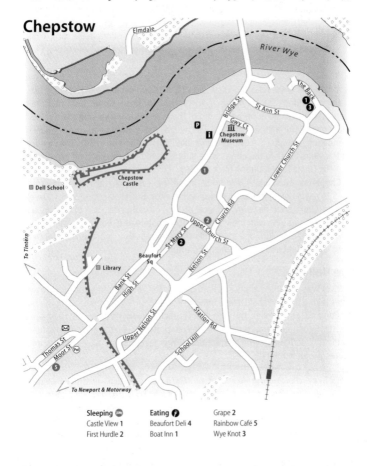

Chepstow

Sleeping 🛏
Castle View 1
First Hurdle 2

Eating 🍴
Beaufort Deli 4
Boat Inn 1

Grape 2
Rainbow Café 5
Wye Knot 3

⋮ Grape expectations

It might sound unlikely but there are now several vineyards clustered together in the southeast corner of Wales. Several Welsh wines have won medals at international competitions. It was the Romans who introduced wine making to Wales and one of their largest British vineyards was at Caerleon, where fossilized grape pips have been found. Later the monks at Tintern Abbey produced their own wine, but when Henry VIII dissolved the monasteries, the tradition died out. It was revived by the fabulously wealthy Marquis of Bute who sent his gardener to France to do some research, and then planted his first vineyard in 1875 at his country home of Castell Coch. More vineyards were established and became reasonably successful – in 1887 3,600 bottles were produced for Queen Victoria's golden jubilee. Production later faltered, particularly during WW1 and it wasn't until the mid-20th century that wine growing began again. Most Welsh wines are white, but some rosés are produced. Try visiting one of the following:

Cariad Wines ⓘ *Llanerch Vineyard, Hensol, Pendoylan, T01443 225877, www.llanerch-vineyard.co.uk, Easter-end Oct, daily 1000-1700, £3,* is the largest vineyard in Wales and has a six-acre vineyard and 10 acres of landscaped grounds. A tour includes a wine tasting.

Tintern Parva Wines ⓘ *Parva Farm, Tintern, T01291 689636, daily 1030- 1830, dusk in winter,* has two acres of vines on a 60-acre working farm. Free tastings in the shop, while the self-guided vineyard tour is £1.

1800; Nov-Mar Mon-Sat 0930-1600, Sun 1100-1600, last entry ½ hr before closing, £3, £2.50 children, £8.50 family, CADW, the first stone castle built in Britain. It occupies a superb position on a bend of the Wye with views along the river as you wander round. During the Civil War it was held by the Royalists and came under siege, surrendering in 1645 – the events are recalled in an exhibition inside. The castle grew over the years as its fortifications were strengthened but you can still see the oldest part – the Great Tower, dating back to 1067.

Chepstow Museum ⓘ *Bridge St, near the castle, T01291 625981, summer Mon-Sat 1030-1730, Sun 1400-1730; winter Mon-Sat 1100-1700, Sun 1400-1700, free,* has displays on the town and local history, including the story of local man Able Seaman Williams who won the VC at Gallipoli. Upstairs is a room containing a variety of old machines, including a 'permanent waving machine' (circa 1940) that bears a strong resemblance to an instrument of torture.

Wye Valley

The River Wye is worked almost as hard by canoeists and fishermen as it once was by barges taking the Forest of Dean's iron ore down to Bristol. Running along the border with England for 154 miles, the area wasn't officially recognized as part of Wales until 1974. It is treasured today, but still officially unprotected, for the ecological value of its broadleaf woodlands, which step down the steep sides of its gorge and its picturesque viewpoints.

● *In St Mary's churchyard in Monmouth you'll find a gravestone that would fox a Da Vinci Code cryptographer. It's a sort of puzzle on the grave of John Renie, a painter and decorator, who designed it himself. The puzzle is in the form of a grid and contains the words 'Here Lies John Renie' in thousands of different permutations - the message can be read from left to right and up and down. It was erected in 1823, a time when puzzles like this were very popular.*

The most beautiful stretch of the valley is between Chepstow and Monmouth, and the most spectacular site is **Tintern Abbey** ① *6 miles north of Chepstow, bus 69 from Chepstow, T01291 689251, Mar-May, Oct daily 0930-1700; Jun-Sep daily 0930-1800; Nov-Mar Mon-Sat 0930-1600, Sun 1100- 1600, £3.25, £2.75 children, £9.25 family, CADW*, founded in 1131 for Cistercian monks. The abbey became increasingly wealthy and its power was reflected in a grand rebuilding programme in the late 13th century. It flourished until dissolution in 1536, then gained a new lease of life as a romantic ruin in the 18th century, its picturesque beauty and glorious setting inspiring both Wordsworth and JMW Turner. The abbey, a beautiful shell with soaring archways and delicate stonework, still attracts bus loads of tourists today, so try to visit early in the morning or late in the day. To really see the ruins at their best you should cross the Wye at a nearby bridge and follow the path to view the abbey from the opposite bank. A mile from the abbey is **Tintern Old Station** ① *T01291 689566, Apr-Oct daily 1030-1730*, a Victorian station now converted into a visitor and information centre, with a camping area nearby.

There are good opportunities for walking in the area, including the 136-mile **Wye Valley Walk** from Chepstow to the Plynlimon mountains, and **Offa's Dyke Path** running from Chepstow to the northern coast near Prestatyn, following the Wye River for some distance. For further details of walks, see box page 46.

Monmouth (Trefynwy) and around

North of Tintern, where the Wye joins the Monnow, is the handsome town of Monmouth. The heart of the town is Agincourt Square, a reminder that Henry V was born here and won the Battle of Agincourt (1415) with the help of Welsh archers. There's a statue here of Charles Rolls, of Rolls Royce fame, holding a model of an aircraft. He was also a pioneer aviator and in 1910 became the first person to make a double crossing of the Channel. A month later he was killed when his plane crashed at an airshow. His mother, Lady Llangattock, was a distant relative of Lord Nelson and her collection of Nelson memorabilia can be seen at the **Nelson Museum and Local History Centre** ① *Priory St, T01600 710630, Mon-Sat 1000- 1300, 1400-1700, Sun 1400-1700, free*. Among the exhibits are various fake personal effects, manufactured to profit from the cult of Nelson that flourished after his death. They include a glass eye, presumably once proudly displayed in a cabinet along with the best china. However, the makers got it wrong: although Nelson was famously blind in one eye ('I see no ships'), he lost only the sight, never the eye itself.

Monnow Bridge was built in the 13th century to replace an earlier wooden crossing. The fortified medieval bridge spans the River at the west end of Monnow Street and the stone gatehouse is the only complete example of its kind in Britain.

Raglan Castle ① *8 miles southwest of Monmouth, T01291 690228, Mar-May, Oct, daily 0930-1700; Jun-Sep daily 0930-1800; Nov-Mar Mon-Sat 0930-1600, Sun 1100-1600, £2.75, £2.25 children, £7.75 family*, is an attractive mixture of castle and palace. Work began in 1435 and the owner, Sir William ap Thomas took the opportunity to show off his wealth and status.

Usk

Approximately midway between Monmouth and Newport, the little town of Usk has several good places to eat and drink, and a number of pretty buildings. The **Usk Rural Life Museum** ① *New Market St, T01291 673777, Easter-Oct Mon-Fri 1000-1700, Sat-Sun 1400-1700, £2, £1 children*, is a fascinating museum housed in three converted barns. It focuses on rural life from 1850 to the end of the Second World War and has a vast collection of old farming implements, with ploughs, tractors, scythes and grim items like castrating irons. There are also recreated domestic interiors like a farmhouse kitchen and an exhibition about the Great Western Railway.

Newport's most famous site is its **Transporter Bridge**, an extraordinary contraption built between 1902-1906 by a French engineer. The brief was to construct a bridge across the Usk that would not hinder shipping and which enabled road traffic to pass from one quay to another – better than a hazardous ferry trip on a stretch of water that has one of the highest tides on the world. Vehicles sit on a platform which then glides across the water; it's a bit like a huge, flat ski lift.

The **Newport Museum and Art Gallery** ① *John Frost Sq, T01633 840064, Mon-Thu 0930-1700, Fri 0930-1630, Sat 0930-1600, free*, takes you right through the history of Newport and its surroundings. It houses a cast of a 7,000-year-old footprint found in peat in the Severn estuary; part of a Roman mosaic floor from Caerwent; and displays on mining. Of note is the section on the 19th-century Chartist uprising when working people demonstrated in support of the People's Charter which demanded, among other things, the vote for all men. Demonstrations took place all over the country; one in Newport in 1839 resulted in the deaths of 22 protesters who were shot by soldiers. The leader of the rising, John Frost, was transported. Upstairs in the art gallery are works by a variety of British artists including Spencer, Lowry and Russell Flint. There's also a wartime work, *Home Front*, by Stanley Lewis portraying local civilian and volunteer services in the war – it was never finished. You can also see a collection of pottery and porcelain, with many items of Wemyss Ware, and the Wait Collection of over 300 novelty teapots.

Around Newport

Two miles west of Newport, **Tredegar House** ① *off the A48, T01633 815880, Easter-Sep Wed-Sun 1100-1600, £5.50, children free, entrance to grounds only free*, is a fine 17th-century mansion that was home to generations of Morgans, the local gentry. They essentially founded Newport and owned vast amounts of land in and around the city. They were a colourful family: Henry Morgan was a pirate, and Evan Morgan, who lived there in the 1930s held glamorous parties entertaining the likes of Charlie Chaplin, Evelyn Waugh, H G Wells and the spy Anthony Blunt. To see the house today you must join a guided tour, which takes you through the elaborate state rooms, as well as below stairs to the scullery and kitchen. There are 90 acres of parkland and formal gardens, too. In May it is the site of a popular folk festival, see page 102.

On the eastern outskirts of Newport **Caerleon** was a Roman town, Isca, founded in AD 75. It became a major base for the Roman legions – one of only three in Britain. Around 6,000 troops of the second Augustan Legion were housed here, in a sophisticated garrison complete with amphitheatre, baths and shops. The **amphitheatre** (free), which seated 6,000 people and had boxes for VIPs, is impressive and it is not too difficult to imagine bloodthirsty contests between gladiators and wild animals. It was only excavated in the 1920s; before this it was concealed by a grassy mound, once thought to be King Arthur's Round Table. By the Bull Hotel car park are the **Fortress Baths** ① *T01633 422518, Mar-Oct daily 0930-1700; Nov-Mar Mon-Sat 0930-1700, Sun 1100-1600, £2.50, £2 children, £7 family, CADW*, once a 'leisure centre' for the soldiers with a swimming pool, heated changing rooms, hot and cold baths and a gymnasium. Discoveries from local excavations are displayed in the **Roman Legionary Museum** ① *T01633 423134, daily, free*. The new-agey Ffwrrwm Centre (approx 0930-1730) focuses on Caerleon's Arthurian links and has a courtyard filled with wooden sculptures, as well as little shops and a bistro.

Dewstow Hidden Garden ① *Caerwent, 10 miles east of Newport off A48, T01291 430444, www.dewstow.com, Apr-Sep, Sun only, 1000-1500, £7, £3.50 children, £15 family*, is an extraordinary forgotten garden, still being restored. It's an underground garden created in Edwardian times by Henry Oakley, a director of the Great Western Railway. He had grottoes, caverns and tunnels built beneath a more conventional garden of pergolas and pools. It's now been designated a Grade One historic garden.

● Sleeping

Chepstow *p97*

C Castle View Hotel, 16 Bridge St, T01291 620349, www.hotelchepstow.co.uk. This comfortable hotel dates back 300 years. In the centre of town, it is very convenient for the castle – as the name suggests.
D First Hurdle, 9 Upper Church St, T01291 622189. Central, down-to-earth B&B that's handy for all the sights.

Monmouth and around *p99*

B The Bell at Skenfrith, Skenfrith, 6 miles north of Monmouth, T01600 750235, www.skenfrith.co.uk. On the banks of the River Monnow, this romantic former coaching inn has been restored to its 17th-century glory. 8 smart bedrooms complete with widescreen TVs and DVDs.
C Riverside Hotel, Cinderhill St, T01600 715577, www.riversidehotelmonmouth.co.uk. Originally a 19th-century coaching inn, this hotel is set in a quiet corner of Monmouth. 2 bedrooms are on the ground floor, ideal for guests who are less mobile.

Usk *p99*

A Cwrt Bleddyn Hotel and Country Club, Llangybi, near Usk, T01633 450521, www.cwrt-bleddyn-hotel.co.uk. This swish pink-painted hotel has extensive spa and leisure facilities.
A-B The Newbridge, Tredunnock, near Usk, T0871 9958248, www.thenewbridge.co.uk. The Newbridge is one of a growing band of high quality gastropubs/hotels in Wales. It's in a lovely spot by the river Usk and handy for visiting the Roman site of Caerleon.
B Glen-Yr-Afon-House, Pontypool Rd, Usk, T01291 672302, www.glen-yr-afon.co.uk. Secluded country house in its own grounds, just a few mins walk from the centre of Usk. Each room is slightly different. Home-cooked food and bar.

Newport and around *p99*

L Celtic Manor Resort, Coldra Woods, off M4, T01633 413000, www.celtic-manor.com. This huge 5-star hotel (over 300 rooms) is a sport lover's dream – it will host the Ryder Cup in 2010 and has 3 golf courses, as well as 2 health clubs with swimming pools. Masses of spa treatments are on offer so you can feel thoroughly pampered.

A-B The Inn at the Elm Tree, St Brides, Wentlooge, near Newport, T01633 680225, www.the-elm-tree.co.uk. Tucked away among flatlands and reed beds, in an area that looks more like Holland than Wales is this refreshingly comfortable 5-star inn. The rooms are individually designed and there is a relaxing feel.
C Pendragon, 18 Cross St, Caerleon, T01633 430871, www.pendragonhouse.co.uk. Friendly and accommodating B&B. Rooms are clean and comfy, and you eat breakfast at a large wooden table – homemade bread, lots of fresh fruit if you want and veggies catered for. Packed lunches on request.

● Eating

Chepstow *p97*

₩ The Boat Inn, The Back, T01291 628192, Mon-Sat 1200-1500, 1830-2130, Sun 1200-1500, 1800-2130. With a lovely waterside setting, outdoor seats and old beams, this inn is the best place in town for a drink, a snack or a good bar meal. From Sun-Thu early bird rates apply (from 1800) with £10.95 for 2 courses and £12.95 for 3.
₩ Castle View Hotel, 16 Bridge St, T01291 620349, daily 1200-1430, 1830-2100. Relaxed hotel serving tasty light meals during the day, such as ploughman's lunches and jacket potatoes, and more substantial evening meals that range from pork steaks to roast duck.
₩ The Grape, 24 St Mary's St, T01291 620959, food Mon-Thu 1200-2130, Fri-Sat 1200-1700. This wine bar/bistro serves baguettes, sandwiches and snacks – as well as wine of course.
₩ Wye Knot, 18a The Back, T01291 622929, Tue-Fri 1230-1430, 1900-2200, Sat 1900-2200, Sun 1230-1430. Winner of 2 AA rosettes, this restaurant down by the river is the best place to eat in Chepstow. Sun lunch here is a local favourite, with choices such as leg of lamb or sirloin of beef.
₮ Beaufort Deli, Beaufort Sq, T01291 626190, Mon-Sat 0900-1900, Sun 1000-1700. Good deli offering all sorts of tartlets, quiches, cheeses, pâtés, salads and imaginative sandwiches to eat in or take away. Good place to fill your pack before setting off to walk Offa's Dyke.

 ¶ **Rainbow Café**, Moor St, Mon-Sat 0930-1700. Friendly coffee shop and Christian bookshop serving good selection of coffees, hot chocolate, cakes, sandwiches and paninis.

Monmouth and around *p99*
¶¶¶ **The Bell at Skenfrith**, Skenfrith, 6 miles north of Monmouth, T01600 750235, Tue-Sun 1200-1430, 1900-2130. The 2 AA rosette dining room at this popular inn offers a range of modern dishes using largely seasonal and locally sourced ingredients and a fab award-winning wine list.

Usk *p99*
¶¶ **The Bush House Bistro**, 15 Bridge St, T01291 672929, daily 1900-2130, lunch Wed-Sat 1200-1400. Brightly coloured tablecloths and terracotta walls make this good quality restaurant a cheery choice on a damp evening. Modern British food with lots of fish and game and vegetarian options.
¶¶ **Three Salmons Hotel**, Bridge St, T01291 672133, daily lunchtimes and 1800-2130 (Sat 1830-2200). Lunchtime snacks like BLTs and ploughmans with a varied menu in the evening ranging from veggie dishes like cannelloni with wild mushrooms and goat's cheese or meaty choices such as breast of goose.

Newport and around *p99*
¶¶¶-¶¶ **The Inn at the Elm Tree**, St Brides, Wentlooge, near Newport, T01633 680225, Mon-Sat 1200-1430, 1730-2100, Sun 1200-1500. High quality food at this 21st-century inn. Light lunches include wild boar and apple sausages, or broadbean and tomato risotto, or splash out in the restaurant in the evening. Mains are strong on fish and local produce. Good vegetarian dishes too.

☻ Entertainment

Chepstow Male Voice Choir rehearse at Dell School, Welsh St, Chepstow, on Mon and Thu 1930-2115.

☻ Festivals

May Tredegar House Folk Festival, Tredegar House (see p100), Newport, www.tredegarhousefolk.ik.com. Popular folk music and dance festival.

▲▲ Activities and tours

Canoeing
Monmouth Canoe and Activity Centre, Castle Yard, Old Dixton Rd, Monmouth, T01600 713461, www.monmouthcanoehire.20m.com. Canoe hire and kayaking on the Wye, 2-seater Canadian canoes, ½ day £20; full day kayak hire £17.
Wye Valley Canoes, Glasbury-on-Wye, Herefordshire, T01497 847213, www.wyevalleycanoes.co.uk. Over the border in England, offer canoeing and kayaking on the Wye. From £10 per person for ½ day canoe hire.

Cycling/Mountain biking
Pedalabikeaway Cycle Centre, Cannop Valley, near Coleford (just over the border), T01594 860065, www.pedalabikeaway.com. Bike hire, maps and information. Trail bikes from £4 for 1 hr to £12 for a full day.
Pedalaway, Trereece Barn, Llangarron, Ross-on-Wye, T01989 770357, www.pedalaway.co.uk. Mountain bike trails and routes for casual cyclists, range of bikes to hire. Mountain bikes from £13 for ½ day.

☻ Transport

Chepstow *p97*
Bus
Bus No 73 runs to **Newport** (hourly, £3.60, 45 mins), no service Sun. Bus Nos X10, X11 and X14 run to **Bristol** (every hr, £3.30 single, 50 mins). **Stagecoach** buses Nos 65 and 69 run approx every 2 hrs to **Monmouth** (£3, 50 mins); No 69 also stops at **Tintern**.

Train
Direct daily services to **Newport** (hourly, £4.60, 15 mins) and **Cardiff** (£8.10, ½ hr).

Wye Valley *p98*
From Tintern Abbey, bus No 69 runs to **Chepstow** (Mon-Sat, every 2 hrs, £2.20, 20 mins) and **Monmouth** (£2.70, ½ hr).
Beacons Bus No B9 is the **Offa's Dyke** circular route to **Hay-on-Wye**, see p113.

Monmouth *p99*
Stagecoach bus No 69 runs approx every 2 hrs to **Chepstow** (£3, 50 mins); No 69 also stops at **Tintern**. Bus No 83 runs every 2 hrs to **Abergavenny** (£2.80, 40 mins) via **Raglan**.

Usk *p99*
H&H coaches bus No 60 runs to **Monmouth** (½ hr) and **Newport** (35 mins) 7 daily.

Newport *p99*
Bus
Bus No 73 runs to **Chepstow**, (hourly, £3.60, 45 mins), except Sun. Bus No 30 runs to **Cardiff** (every 20 mins, less on Sun, £2.60, 45 mins) and **National Express** to **Bristol** (3 direct daily, or via Cardiff, £9.40, 55 mins). Frequent bus connections to **London**, **Birmingham** and other major cities throughout the country.

Train
Frequent trains to **Cardiff** (every 10-15 mins, £3.40 return, 15 mins) and **Bristol** (every 15 mins, £7.50 return, 40 mins).

❶ Directory

Chepstow *p97*
Internet Chepstow Library, Manor Way, T01291 635730. Free access.

Monmouth and around *p99*
Internet Free access available at Monmouth library (T01600 775215).

Brecon Beacons National Park

→ *Colour map 2, grid B4-5*

Covering 520 square miles of wild countryside in southeast Wales, the Brecon Beacons National Park is a magnet for lovers of the outdoors. While none of the mountains are over that magical 3,000 ft, this still isn't 'walking for softies' country and the terrain can be rugged and windswept: it's not for nothing that the SAS train here, sending hopefuls up and down the highest peak Pen-y-fan (2,907 ft, 886m) in order to wear them down both physically and mentally. The wildest part of the National Park is in the west where Fforest Fawr, a former hunting forest, now an area of lonely uplands and waterfalls, leads to the bleak and barren expanse of Black Mountain – the least visited area with the most challenging walks. The central area is occupied by the eponymous Brecon Beacons range, to the north of which is the busy town of Brecon, a popular base for a wide range of outdoor activities. The Monmouthshire and Brecon Canal offers some less demanding walks, before the National Park stretches out to Abergavenny, and the famous book town of Hay-on-Wye, both of which are great bases for exploring the brooding Black Mountains. ›› *For Sleeping, Eating and other listings, see pages 107-113.*

Ins and outs

Getting there and around There is a **train** station at Abergavenny with trains running from Newport. The nearest train station to Hay-on-Wye is Hereford in England, from where a bus runs to Hay and on to Brecon. The only other station is at Merthyr Tydfil, south of the National Park, which is linked to Cardiff and the **Brecon Mountain Railway**, www.breconmountainrailway.co.uk. The **Heart of Wales** train line, www.heart-of-wales.com, runs to Llandeilo and Llandovery from where there are buses into the park. **Bus** services are better, most are run by **Stagecoach**, but they only link major towns like Abergavenny, Brecon and Hay-on-Wye. Sunday services and those between villages are poor or non-existent, especially out of season. In summer, **Beacons Bus**, a general term for local services, runs from mid-May to mid-Aug with some services on Sunday, and links Brecon with Carmarthen, Swansea, Bridgend, Cardiff, Newport and Hereford. Many services have cycle trailers. You can stop off at various points en route, T01873 853254, www.visitbrecon beacons.com. ›› *For further transport information, see page 113.*

● The highest mountain in the world is named after a Welshman. Sir George Everest
● (1790-1866) was born in Crickhowell and spent 25 years of his life completing the trigonometrical survey of India. The highest mountain, known first to westerners as Peak XV, was given Everest's name by his successor.

Southeast Wales Brecon Beacons National Park

Tourist information **Brecon TIC** ① *Cattle Market Car Park, Brecon, T01874 622485, Easter-Sep daily 0930-1730, winter Mon-Fri 0930-1700, Sat 0930-1630, Sun 0930-1530, www.breconbeacons.org.* Further information available at www.explore midwales.com. **Abergavenny TIC** ① *Monmouth Rd, Abergavenny, T01873 857588, www.abergavenny.co.uk. Daily Easter-Oct 1000-1730, winter 1000-1600, closed for 1 hr at lunch.* **Crickhowell TIC** ① *Beaufort Chambers, Beaufort St, T01873 812105, www.crickhowell.org.uk.* **Hay on Wye TIC** ① *Craft Centre, Oxford Rd, Hay-on-Wye, T01497 820144, www.hay-on-wye.co.uk, daily Easter-Nov 1000-1300, 1400-1700, rest of year 1100-1300, 1400-1600.* Further information is available at www.tourism. powys.gov.uk.

Brecon (Aberhonddu)

The undoubted hub of the National Park, the solid market town of Brecon can trace its roots back to pre-Roman times, but development only really began when the Normans arrived and built the castle and a Benedictine Priory – which later became the cathedral. The town continued to grow in importance, becoming the capital of the old county of Brecknockshire, and a centre of the cloth trade. Plenty of Georgian buildings still stand in the centre, which tends to be peopled by a mix of local farmers and visiting walkers. The highest peak in the National Park, **Pen-y-Fan**, can be reached easily from here, as can the Brecon Mountain Centre (see page 105) and the indoor climbing centre at **Llangorse**. The town is at the northern end of the **Monmouthshire and Brecon canal**, which runs 33 miles from Brecon to Pontypool and you can take trips along the calm waters. ▸▸ *For further information, see Activities, page 111.*

Brecon Cathedral ① *Priory Hill, T01874 625222, 0830-1800, free,* stands on a site that is thought to have been used for Christian worship for around 1,000 years. In 1093 a Benedictine Priory was established here and you can still see the Norman font in the cathedral today. In the 15th century it became a focus of pilgrimage; the central

Brecon Beacons

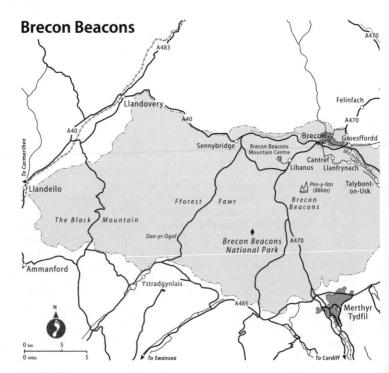

crucifix in the rood screen (destroyed during the reformation) was believed to have healing properties. After the dissolution of the monasteries the building became a Parish church, and was made a cathedral in 1923. After you've wandered round the cathedral, you can visit the small **Heritage Centre** ① *Mar-Dec Mon-Sat 1030-1630, Sun 1200-1500, free*, which has exhibits on the cathedral.

The **Brecknock Museum and Art Gallery** ① *Captain's Walk, T01874 624121, Mon-Fri 1000-1700, Sat 1000-1300, 1400-1700; Apr-Sep also Sun 1200-1700, £1*, has a number of interesting exhibits, including a dugout canoe discovered in Llangorse lake, a carved four-poster bed in which Charles I is said to have slept when he came to Brecon in 1645, and various recreated aspects of old Wales such as a smithy, village schoolroom and courtroom. Just down the road, the **South Wales Borderers Museum** ① *The Watton, T01874 623111, Apr-Sep daily 0900-1700, Oct-Mar Mon-Fri 0900-1700, £3, under 16 free*, is the place for anyone who's a fan of the film *Zulu* (1964); this is the regiment that fought the famous battle at Rorkes' Drift in 1879.

The **Brecon Mountain Centre** ① *Libanus, 5 miles southwest of Brecon, T01874 623366, www.breconbeacons.org, free*, is the main visitor centre for the National Park and a good starting point for a variety of walks. It offers great views of Pen y Fan, the highest mountain in South Wales, and has a popular café and shop.

Western Brecon Beacons

The Black Mountain and Fforest Fawr are noted for their wild, unspoilt landscapes. The main visitor attraction, and a good place to take kids on a rainy day, are the **Dan-yr-Ogof Showcaves** ① *off the A4067, T01639 730801, www.showcaves.co.uk, Apr-Oct daily 1000 around 1600, £9, children £6*. Discovered in 1912 by two local farmers, the three caves are an Indiana Jones-style labyrinth of subterranean lakes and caverns with stalactites and underground waterfalls. There are also exhibits on Bronze Age and Iron Age life aimed at children, a dinosaur park and dry ski slope.

Crickhowell (Crug Hywel)

With plenty of places to eat, drink and sleep, the pretty little town of Crickhowell is an excellent base for exploring the eastern Beacons. Its most prominent feature is the 16th-century Usk Bridge, which distinctively has 12 arches on one side and 13 on the other. Once an important stop for stagecoaches, the town is squeezed between the Usk and Table Mountain, on the summit of which is the 'crug' or hillfort, of Hywel – hence the town's name. It's a great place for walkers, with a choice of routes going up Table Mountain, along the river, or into the Black Mountains to the east. It's also easy to arrange activities such as paragliding, canoeing and caving.

Three miles north of the town is **Tretower Court** ① *(Tre-tŵr), T01874 730279, Mar-Sep daily 1000-1700, Oct daily 1000-1600, £2.50, £2 children, £7 family, CADW*. The first settlement here was a Norman earthwork castle, built around 1100 to guard an important route through the Black Mountains. In the 13th century, a stone structure replaced it and, although this was eventually abandoned in favour of the house, the round keep is still standing today. The house itself is a fine late medieval home with a galleried courtyard and well preserved Great Hall, with a huge hearth and high ceiling. The old kitchen contains displays of various herbs commonly used in medieval times, including dandelion, nettle, sage and sorrel. The main bedchamber is thought to have had a secret opening in the wood panelling so that the occupant could keep an eye on events in the Great Hall below. There's a re-created medieval garden too. *The Libertine*, starring Johnny Depp as a rakish Restoration poet, was filmed here in 2004.

Abergavenny (Y Fenni)

Just on the edge of the National Park, Abergavenny is surrounded by delightful countryside and is a good base for walking. There has been a settlement here since Neolithic times and the Romans later established a fort known as Gobannium. Development really took off when the Normans built the inevitable castle here around 1090 and in later years the town became an industrial centre, with flourishing tanning and weaving industries, as well as a busy market.

The castle is now ruined but was the scene of an infamous massacre at Christmas in 1175 when the Norman lord, William de Braose, invited local Welsh chieftains to a banquet and then murdered them. A hunting lodge, built in the 19th century from the castle's keep is now a small **museum** ① *T01873 854282, Mon-Sat 1100-1300, 1400-1700, Sun 1400-1700; Nov-Feb closes at 1600, £1*, with exhibits on the town's history including a recreated Victorian farmhouse kitchen and grocer's shop. **St Mary's Church** on Monk Street, was founded around 1090 as a Benedictine priory. It contains an important selection of medieval monuments and a 15th-century carving of Jesse, the father of King David, which was once part of an altarpiece showing Christ's family tree.

Around Abergavenny are the hills of **Blorenge** (1834 ft) to the southwest – a favourite with paragliders and hang gliders; **Skirrid-Fawr** (1596 ft/486 m) in the north east; and **Sugar Loaf** (1955 ft, 596 m) to the northwest.

From Abergavenny there is a wonderful scenic drive to the famous Welsh booktown of Hay-on-Wye, an effortless way of enjoying the striking beauty of the Black Mountains. You can pick up the road at Llanfihangel Crucorney, north of the town and then follow the unclassified road as it leads you to Llanthony Priory, then on to the hamlet of Capel-y-Ffin, past the viewpoint at Hay Bluff and down into Hay-on-Wye. It's single track much of the way.

Llanthony Priory (CADW, free), now a picturesque and sleepy ruin, was founded in 1108, probably on the site of a sixth-century hermitage. The medieval traveller Giraldus Cambrensis described it as 'truly calculated for religion' and the description still holds true today; there is a sense of peace and spirituality here that is missing from better known and more commercialized sites, such as Tintern Abbey. There's a hotel/inn built into the ruins but it doesn't seem to spoil the beauty of the site. Capel-y-Ffin was once the home of sculptor and typeface designer Eric Gill, who lived here from 1924-1928 with various family members and artistic friends.

Hay-on-Wye (Y Gelli)

From a lone second-hand bookshop in 1961, Hay-on-Wye now has over 30, specializing in everything from apiculture to erotica; the town is bliss for bibliophiles. The former cinema alone has a stock of around 200,000 books and every other building in town, including the old castle, seems to be filled with wonderful piles of dusty tomes, old school annuals and rare first editions. The widest selection of all is at **Richard Booth's Bookshop**, Lion Street, with over 400,000 titles for sale. Booth was the force behind Hay's rejuvenation as a booktown, opening the first second-hand bookshop here and

● Abergavenny's most famous resident was Hitler's deputy, Rudolf Hess, who was imprisoned
● at Maindiss Court near the town after the plane in which he was flying crashed in Scotland in 1941. He was allowed out once a week for walks and became a regular at a local pub.

promoting Hay to the extent that it is now known throughout the world as a centre for second-hand books. On 1 April 1977 (April Fool's Day), Booth declared Hay, right on the border of England and Wales, an independent state – proclaiming himself king in the process. The town is busiest during the annual **Hay Festival** (see Festivals, page 111), an excellent literary festival that attracts the biggest names in literature.

◉ Sleeping

Brecon and around *p104, map p107*
L Llangoed Hall, Llyswen, off A470 between Brecon and Builth Wells, T08719 958238, www.llangoedhall.com. Luxury all the way at this sumptuous hotel in a Jacobean mansion created by Sir Bernard Ashley, the late Laura Ashley's husband. Bedrooms decorated with Ashley textiles; lots of antiques and open fires.

A-B Peterstone Court, Llanhamlach, off A40 southeast of Brecon, T08719 958262, www.peterstone-court.com. Elegant country house hotel in the heart of the National Park. Great mountain views from the bedrooms and a spa and small, heated swimming pool.
B Felin Fach Griffin, 3 miles north of Brecon on the A470. T01874 620111, www.eatdrink sleep.ltd.uk. It's hard to miss this lovely rosy-

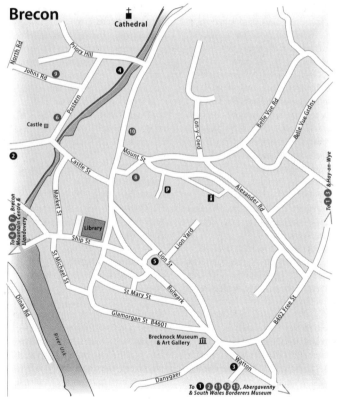

Brecon

Southeast Wales Brecon Beacons National Park Listings

red, refurbished pub. It's a very modern inn, which has 7 individually designed, simple and stylish bedrooms. It's all contemporary and unfussy but very comfortable, with emphasis on relaxation and good food. As it says outside, it's a place to 'Eat, Drink, Sleep'.

C Beacons Guest House, 16 Bridge St, T01874 623339, www.beacons.brecon. co.uk. Non-smoking, traditional guesthouse in a restored Georgian townhouse. It's situated just over the Usk bridge, a few mins from the centre of town.

C Blaencar Farm, Sennybridge, east of Brecon, T01874 636610, www.blaencar.co.uk. This is a working farm offering good quality B&B in a refurbished farmhouse. One of the 3 rooms has a 4-poster bed. It's a lovely relaxing place from which to explore the National Park.

C Castle House, Postern, T01874 623343, www.castle-house.co.uk. Crisp, light decor at this refurbished B&B. Wood burning stove in the breakfast room where they serve tasty 'dragon sausages'. Non-smoking.

C Felin Glais, Aberyscir, 3 miles east of Brecon, T01874 623107, www.felinglais. zookitec.com. A carefully restored 17th-century barn on the outskirts of Brecon and worth seeking out. 3 rooms, 2 of which have jacuzzi baths. They serve evening meals using fresh, seasonal produce and will cater for veggies and vegans.

C George Hotel, George St, T01874 623421, www.george-hotel.com, 17th-century building which retains some original features such as the 300-year-old staircase. Some suites have jacuzzi baths.

C Pickwick House, St Johns Rd, T01874 624322, www.pickwick-house.brecon.co.uk, 3 en suite rooms. Non-smoking B&B in estate just a few mins from the centre of town. Has small conservatory residents can use and drying facilities for walkers and cyclists. Happy to cater for special diets.

F Bikes and Hikes Bunkhouse, The Elms, 10 The Struet, T01874 610071, www.bikes andhikes.co.uk. Central bunkhouse that has cycle lock up and also does bike rental.

F Bunkhouse, The Held, Cantref, near Brecon, T01874 624646, www.theheld bunkhouse.co.uk. Converted barn offering 24-30 beds in bunkhouse accommodation across 6 rooms. Open year round.

F Canal Barn Bunkhouse, Ty Camlas, Canal Bank, T01874 625361, www.canal-barn.co.uk.

24 beds at this at this bunkhouse not far from the town centre. Book in advance.

F Cantref Bunkhouse, Upper Cantref Farm, Cantref, near Brecon, T01874 665223, www.cantref.com. This farm bunkhouse about 3 miles from Brecon accommodates 2-8 per shared room and also has grounds where you can pitch a tent.

Crickhowell and around *p105*

A-B The Bear Hotel, High St, T01873 810408, www.bearhotel.co.uk. Lovely old coaching inn dating back to 1432, the Bear has individually decorated rooms – some with jacuzzi baths or 4-poster beds. The bar has lots of character with oak beams and a flag stone floor. Johnny Depp apparently made lots of instant friends when he ordered drinks all round while filming nearby.

C The Manor Hotel, Brecon Rd, on A40 northwest of Crickhowell, T01873 810212, www.manorhotel.co.uk. Swish hotel perched on a hill outside Crickhowell, which also has leisure facilities. Dark wooden floors and heraldry shields on the walls downstairs, while bedrooms are lighter and brighter.

C Ty Croeso Hotel, Dardy, off B4558, just outside Crickhowell, T01873 810573, www.wiz.to/tycroeso. Small hotel overlooking the Usk Valley and close to the Brecon and Monmouthshire Canal. Good quality restaurant and welcoming atmosphere.

D Gwyn Deri, Mill St, T01873 810297, smith@gwynderi.fsnet.co.uk. 3 rooms, 2 en suite. Clean, comfortable B&B just on the edge of town.

Abergavenny *p106*

A Allt-yr-Ynys Country House Hotel, Walterstone, near Abergavenny, T01873 890307, www.allthotel.co.uk. Technically this comfortable and reliable hotel is in England, by about a foot – the border, the river Monnow flows, beside it. It's a secluded location, with many rooms in converted outbuildings dotted around the grounds, giving you extra privacy. There's also a swimming pool.

B The Angel Hotel, 15 Cross St, T01873 857121, www.angelhotelabergavenny.co.uk. Famous old coaching inn in the centre of town, offering plush rooms, 1 with 4-poster bed.

D Gaer Farm, Cwmyoy, 4 miles from Llanthony Priory, T01873 890345, www.gaer

farm.com. Remote farmhouse B&B in the lovely Llanthony Valley. En suite rooms with private sitting room. Beds have traditional wool-filled quilts made on the farm.

D Pentre House, Brecon Rd, T01873 853435, treardonsm@aol.com. This attractive B&B is out of town at the turning for Sugar Loaf mountain. There are 3 rooms, one en suite and very attractive gardens.

F Black Sheep Backpackers, Station Rd, T01873 859125, www.blacksheep backpackers.com. This bunkhouse by the station offers dormitory accommodation. Price includes a light breakfast.

Hay-on-Wye and around *p106, map p109*

C Ffordd-Fawr, Glasbury, near Hay-on-Wye, T01497 847332, www.ffordd-fawr.co.uk. Restored farmhouse offering non-smoking accommodation in countryside.

C Tinto House, Broad St, T01497 820590, www.tintohouse.co.uk. This central B&B is in a listed Georgian townhouse, with a garden that overlooks the River Wye.

C-D The Old Post Office, Llanigon, near Hay-on-Wye, T01497 820008, www.oldpost-office.co.uk. High quality, vegetarian B&B a couple of miles from Hay. The house is a 17th-century listed building with plenty of character, and is close to Offa's Dyke Path.

F YHA Hostel, Capel y Ffin, T01873 890650. Former hill farm now offering hostel accommodation in remote area.

Camping

F Radnors End Camping, Hay-on-Wye, T01497 820780. Seasonal campsite overlooking the River Wye, convenient for visiting Hay and walking Offa's Dyke.

● Eating

Brecon *p104, map p107*

⫶⫶-⫶⫶ Felin Fach Griffin, near Brecon, 3 miles out of town on A470, T01874 620111. One of a new wave of excellent 'gastropubs' in Wales.

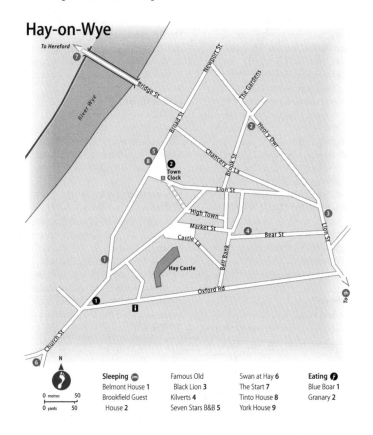

Hay-on-Wye

To Hereford

River Wye

Bridge St

Newport St

The Gardens

Broad St

Chancery La

Healy Dwr

Town Clock

Lion St

Broad St

High Town

Market St

Castle La

Bear St

Lion St

Bell Bank

Hay Castle

Oxford Rd

A470

Church St

N

0 metres 50
0 yards 50

Sleeping ●
Belmont House **1**
Brookfield Guest House **2**

Famous Old Black Lion **3**
Kilverts **4**
Seven Stars B&B **5**

Swan at Hay **6**
The Start **7**
Tinto House **8**
York House **9**

Eating ●
Blue Boar **1**
Granary **2**

The interior is an eclectic mix of oak beams, stone floors and laid-back leather sofas, and the food is based on fresh local produce such as saltmarsh lamb, cheeses and locally grown salad leaves. Even discerning food critic AA Gill liked it.

₸₸₸-₸₸ The White Swan, Llanfrynach, a few miles south of Brecon, T01874 665276, www.the-white-swan.com. Another revitalized pub, serving high quality food, tucked away in the countryside outside Brecon. Features fresh produce and has a daily 'specials' menu that features many fish dishes, also has several veggie choices.

₸₸ Beacons Guest House, 16 Bridge St, T01874 623339, Tue-Sat 1830-2100. Guesthouse serving non-residents. Mains include halloumi cheese with tomato and black olive sauce, or Welsh lamb with couscous.

₸₸ Castle of Brecon Hotel, Castle Sq, T01874 624611, www.breconcastle.co.uk. Food Thu-Sat 1200-2130, Mon-Wed 1200-2100, Sun 1800-2100. Sandwiches and salad available during the day, and heartier dishes such as beef and stilton pie, good old cod, chips and peas. Some veggie choices.

₸₸-₸ The Puzzle Tree, opposite museum, T01874 610005, Mon-Wed 1100-2300, Thu 1100-2400, Fri- Sat 1100-0100, Sun 1200-2230. Large modern-looking place attracting a younger crowd. Does a bit of everything, breakfasts in the morning, cream teas in the afternoon, and meals such as curries, steaks and veggie choices.

₸ Bull's Head, 86 The Struet, T01874 622044 food 1200-1430, 1830-2130. Good traditional pub serving bar meals, with some vegan choices. Real ales also on offer.

₸ The Café, 39 High St, Mon-Sat 1000-1700. Busy, popular licensed café with nice bright decor of white painted floors and shocking pink chairs. Fair trade coffees, soups, cakes and baguettes with fillings like brie and grape or goat's cheese, rocket and pine nuts.

Crickhowell p105

₸₸ The Bear Hotel, High St, T01873 810408, daily 1200-1400, Mon-Sat 1900-2130. Wide choice of very good food, with several vegetarian choices. Bar food might include homemade faggots in onion gravy; or fillet of salmon with asparagus in the restaurant.

₸₸ Nantyffin Cider Mill Inn, Brecon Rd, A40 out of Crickhowell, T01873 810212, food

1200-1400 and 1830-2100. Lovely old, pink-painted inn, serving excellent food and real ales. Mains might include baked vegetable tart or roast duck, and scrummy puds such as lemon tart. Very popular so worth booking.

₸ The Cheese Press, High St, T01873 810167, daily 0930-1500 (1330 on Wed). Coffee shop at the back of a gift shop serving good cakes, and light meals like toasties or curry and lentil pasties.

Abergavenny p106

₸₸₸ The Walnut Tree Inn, Llandewi Skirrid, T01873 852797, www.thewalnuttreeinn.com, closed Sun-Mon. Well established and highly rated restaurant that has been attracting food pilgrims for years.

₸₸-₸ The Angel Hotel, 15 Cross St, T01873 857121, bar meals 1200-1430 and 1830- 2200, restaurant 1900-2200. Formal meals in the restaurant of this revamped hotel include mains like seabass with chive sauce, cassoulet, or steak and chips. Lighter meals are available in the bar where you can snuggle by an open fire or sit out in the courtyard in summer.

₸ Mad Hatters, Cross St, T01873 859839, daily 0930-1730. Excellent sandwich/coffee bar. Delicious pattiserie, sponge cakes and sandwiches, such as brie, grape and apple, and mozzarella, tomato and avocado.

₸ The Trading Post, 14 Neville St T01873 855448, winter Mon-Wed 0900-1700, Thu-Sat 0900-2330; May-Oct daily 0900-2330. Very popular lunch spot serving baguettes, baked potatoes and snacks. In the evening has a full bistro menu.

Hay-on-Wye p106, map p109

₸₸₸-₸₸ Kilverts, The Bullring, T01497 821042, food 1200-1400, 1900-2130. Very popular pub that serves great bar food. Seats outside on fine days.

₸₸₸-₸₸ Old Black Lion, Lion St, T01497 820841, food 1200-1430, 1830-2130. Highly rated food (awarded a Michelin star) in this atmospheric old inn. Splash out in the restaurant or eat more cheaply in the bar.

₸₸-₸ Blue Boar, Castle St, T01497 820884. Coffee from 0930, light meals 1200-1800, more expensive choices in the evening. Friendly café offering snacks like hummous with pitta bread and and cakes or mains like Tuscan bean casserole with couscous.

₸ The Granary, Broad St, T01497 820884,

food daily 1000-2100. Another very popular, relaxed self-service café, with wooden floors and good food. Great spot for soup, salads, sandwiches or just a coffee, cake and a read of the newspaper. Plenty of veggie and vegan main meal choices.

Ÿ Oscars, High Town, T01497 821193, daily 1030-1630. Very busy, good value self service café, with scrubbed pine tables and wooden floors – hard to get a seat at peak times. Great for bowls of soup, delicious cakes, or substantial main meals. Plenty for veggies.

⊕ Pubs, bars and clubs

Abergavenny *p106*
Hen and Chickens, 7 Flannel St, T01873 853613, food daily 1100-1500, 1900 on. Nice traditional pub with lots of old pictures and fittings. During the day you can get 'doorstep sandwiches' such as beef with dripping or larger meals. Sun lunches and live jazz every Sun night, folk music every other Tue.
King's Head, Cross St, T01873 853575. Popular bar serving real ales and offering bar lunches during the week. Live music on Fri.
The Lounge, 21a High St, T01874 611189, Mon-Wed 1100-2300, Sun 1200-2230. Newly opened café/bar serving cocktails and coffees – popular new spot with locals.

⊕ Entertainment

Brecon *p104, map p107*
Male voice choirs
Male voice choirs rehearse on the following nights, visitors welcome (except Aug): **Brecon**, Fri 1930-2100, Llanfeis Primary School, T01874 624776; **Talgarth Male Voice Choir**, Mon 2000-2200, except late Jul-Aug, Gwernyfed Rugby Club, Talgarth, T01874 625865; **Ystradgynlais Male Voice Choir**, Mon 1900-2100, Tabernacle Chapel, Ystradgynlais or Fri, **Coronation Club**, Glanrhyd, T01639 843845.
Theatr Brycheiniog, Canal Wharf, T01874 611622, www.theatrbrycheiniog.co.uk, stages a wide range of concerts, dance, opera and plays.

○ Shopping

Hay-on-Wye *p106, map p109*
There are almost 40 2nd-hand bookshops in Hay, with a vast range of literature. Many of

the bookshops are to be found along Castle Street. Some of the best include:
Castle Street Books, Castle St, good for contemporary and historical guides, maps.
Hay Cinema Bookshop, Castle St, T01497 820071, the former cinema, plenty of choice.
Richard Booth's Bookshop, Lion St, T01497 830322, has huge range with over 400,000 titles from Anglo-Welsh literature to erotica.
Y Gelli Auctions, Broad St, T01497 821179, regular auctions for maps, prints and books.

⊛ Festivals and events

Mar Three Peaks Challenge, T02920 238576. Annual sporting challenge over 3 main peaks around Abergavenny.
May Hay festival, Hay-on-Wye, T01497 821217, www.hayfestival.co.uk. Internationally known literary festival. Past speakers have included Bill Bryson and Bill Clinton,
Aug Brecon Jazz Festival, Brecon, T01874 625557, www.breconjazz.co.uk. International festival attracting all the great names in jazz.
Sep Abergavenny Food Festival, T01873 851643, www.abergavennyfoodfestival.co.uk. A celebration of the area's local produce, with demonstrations and entertainment.

▲ Activities and tours

Canal cruising
Monmouthshire and Brecon Canal, near Rich Way, Brecon, T07831 685222, www.dragonfly-cruises.co.uk. 2½ hr cruise on the canal, £6, Mar-Oct, twice daily.
Brecon Boats, Travellers Rest Inn, Talybont on Usk, near Brecon, T01874 676401. Self-drive boat hire on Monmouthshire to Brecon Canal.

Canoe and kayak hire
Paddles and Pedals, 15 Castle St Hay-on-Wye, T01497 820604, www.canoehireuk.com. Canadian canoe hire, instruction and tours.

Caving
Good caves for beginners are **Porth yr Ogof**, near Ystradfellte and **Chartist Cave** on the Llangynidr Moors. Permission is needed and you should go as part of a group. More on caving from www.caving.uk.com.
Llangorse Rope Centre, Gilfach Farm, T01874 658272, www.activityuk.com.

Indoor climbing centre with natural rock faces, an abseiling wall, high wires and an introductory pot-holing system. Also a range of other activities including horse riding. Open Mon-Sat 0930-2200, Sun 0930-1800,1 hr climbing taster £12; horse treks £46 full day. Bunkhouse accommodation.

Cycling/mountain biking
Brecon Cycle Centre, 10 Ship St, Brecon, T01874 622651, www.breconcycles.com. Bicycle hire.
Pedalaway, Hopyard Farm, Govilon, near Abergavenny, T01873 830219, www.pedalaway.co.uk.

Horse riding
Cantref Riding Centre, Upper Cantref Farm, Cantref, T01874 665223, www.cantref.com. Everything from 1hr to full-day rides on the Brecon Beacons.
Grange Trekking Centre, Capel-y-Ffin, near Abergavenny, T01873 890215, www.grangetrekking.co.uk. Trekking holidays in the Black Mountains, Apr-Oct.
Llanthony Riding and Trekking, Court Farm, Llanthony, T01873 890359, www.llanthony.co.uk. Trekking for beginners and hacks for more experienced riders. Easter-Oct, ½-day ride £18.
Mills Bros, Newcourt Farm, Felindre, Three Cocks, T01497 847285, www.newcourt-horseriding.co.uk, ½ and full-day treks in the Black Mountains.
Tregoyd Mountain Rides, Three Cocks, near Hay-on-Wye, T01497 847351, www.tregoydriding.co.uk. Hourly or full-day rides and treks. Accommodation available.
Wern Riding Centre, Llangattock Hillside, Crickhowell, T01873 810899, www.wiz.to/wern, Apr-Oct. Trekking and trail riding.

Mountain activities
See also **Brecon Mountain Centre**, p105 and **Llangorse Rope Centre**, under Caving.
Black Mountain Activities, Three Cocks, near Hay-on-Wye, T01497 847897, www.blackmountain.co.uk. 1-5 day multi-activity breaks, with whitewater rafting, mountain biking and caving. Mountain bike and canoe hire.
Kevin Walker Mountain Activities, 74 Beacons Park, Brecon, T01874 625111, www.mountain-acts.freeserve.co.uk. Runs

mountain craft, climbing and caving courses in the Brecon Beacons.
Mountain and Water, 2 Uppe Cwm, Nant Gam, Llanelli Hill, T01873 831825, www.mountainandwater.co.uk. Activities include abseiling, coasteering, gorge walking and caving. Days adventures, holidays and courses.

Paragliding
Welsh Hang-gliding and Paragliding Centre, T01873 850910, www.hg-pg.com, for information about paragliding at Blorenge mountain near Abergavenny.

Sailing
Llangorse Lake, near Brecon, is a general outdoor activity area, good for sailing, rowing, canoeing or fishing. **PGL Llangorse Sailing School**, T01874 658657 and **Llangorse Sailing Club** T01874 658596. Camping available at **Lakeside**, T01874 658226, www.lakeside-holidays.net.

Sauna
The **Forestry Commission**, T01550 720394, have opened a woodland sauna in Pen Arthur wood near the village of Capel Gwynfe, in the shadow of the Black Mountain.

Walking
Brecon Beacons Mountain Centre, Libanus, 6 miles from Brecon off A470, T01874 623366, www.breconbeacons.org, daily Mar-Jun, Sep- Oct 0930-1700; Jul-Aug 0930-1800; Nov-Feb 0930-1630, free. This centre has plenty of maps, guides and information on outdoor activities in the area. It's a good starting point for walks, whether gentle or challenging. There's a good café and an exhibition on the National Park.
Beacons Way, Wales' newest long-distance walk stretching 98 miles across the Brecon Beacons National Park, from Holy Mountain (north of Abergavenny) to Bethlehem in the west. For further details see box p46 or www.breconbeacons parksociety.org.
Taff Trail, www.tafftrail.org.uk, the Taff Trail is a 55 miles (93km) cycling/walking route that starts in Brecon and runs through the Valleys to Cardiff. Free leaflets are available from TICs in the area. See also box, p84.

Beacons Bus services

Beacons Bus services operate from Carmarthen, Swansea, Brigend, Cardiff, Newport and Hereford, on Sundays and bank holidays from June to August. They are Ideal for cyclists or walkers, the B5/B8 services run beside the canal for much of their route. A **Beacons Bus All Day Ticket** can be purchased and used on all Beacons Bus Sunday services, £5.50, £3.75 children, £11 family, allowing unlimited journeys for one day. Free timetables and a useful leaflet '*One Way Walks*' are available from TICs. For further information contact: T01873 853254, www.visitbreconbeacons.com. Useful services include:

B1 Cardiff - Brecon
B2 Swansea - Brecon
B3 Brigend - Treorci - Brecon
B5 Newport - Abergavenny - Brecon
B6 Roundabout service (including Brecon Mountain Railway)
B8 Brecon - Crickhowell (canal walk service)
B9 Offa's Dyke Circular (including Hay-on-Wye)
40 Hereford - Hay-on-Wye-Brecon

⊖ Transport

Brecon *p104, map p107*
Bus Roy Brown and Stagecoach run several daily buses around the area, including No G14 to **Llandovery** (5 daily, £1.80, 40 mins) and **Llandrindod Wells** (3 daily, £2.70, 1 hr); No 43 to **Myrthr Tydfil** (6 daily, £2.80, 40 mins); No X4 to **Cardiff** via Merthyr Tydfil (6 daily, £4.50, 2 ½ hrs); and No 63 to **Swansea** (3 daily, £4.25, 1 ½ hr).
Train The Brecon Mountain Railway train runs to **Merthyr Tydfil**, see p93.

Crickhowell *p105*
Bus No 21 runs to **Abergavenny** (£2.35, 15 mins) and **Brecon** (£3.10, 35 mins).

Abergavenny *p106*
Bus Stagecoach Bus No 21 travels to **Brecon** (6 daily, £3.70, 1 hr) and Crickhowell (£2.35, 15 mins); **Stagecoach** bus No X3 to **Cardiff** (Mon-Sat hourly, £4.50, 1 ½ hrs); No 83 to **Monmouth** (5 daily, £2.80, 35 mins).
Train Trains to **Cardiff** (£7.80, 40 mins) via **Newport** (£5.50, 15 mins) run hourly Mon-Sat, less often on Sun.

Hay-on-Wye *p106, map p109*
Bus Stagecoach bus No 39 connects Hay-on-Wye with **Brecon** (8 daily, £3, 45 mins) and **Hereford** (£4.50, 1 hr).
Train The nearest train station to Hay-on-Wye is **Hereford** in England. Trains travel hourly from Hereford to **Abergavenny** (£7, 25 mins), **Newport** (50 mins, £13.20) and on to **Cardiff** (1 hr 15 mins, £13.20).

⊕ Directory

Hospital Neville Hall Hospital, Abergavenny, T01873 732732. **Internet** Free access at **Crickhowell Library**, T01873 810856, Tue 1000-1300, 1530-1900, Thu 1000-1230, 1330-1730, Fri 1000-1230, 1330-1630, Sat 0930-1300; **Brecon library**, T01874 623346, Mon, Wed-Fri 0930-1700, Tue 0930-1900, Sat 0930-1300; **Hay-on-Wye library**, Chancery Lane, T01497 820847. **Crickhowell Resource and Information Centre**, in Market Hall (location may change), has internet access all day for £8, and shorter chargeable slots, Mon-Fri 1000-1600, T01873 811970.

Swansea and the Gower → *Colour map 2, grid C1*

This is, above all, Dylan Thomas territory. The poet was born in the industrial city of Swansea and spent his final years further west in the evocative village of Laugharne, where his last home, the simple Boathouse, is set on a glorious silvery spot on the Taff Estuary. Most of his greatest works, including his 'play for voices' ,Under Milk Wood, were written and inspired by this little chunk of Wales and if you're a fan of his work – or want to learn more about it – then this is the place to come.

Swansea itself has some worthwhile museums and the nearby resort of Mumbles offers a great choice of places to eat and drink. Best of all, for anyone looking for accessible yet unspoiled countryside, is the Gower peninsula, a tourist hotspot that famed for its award-winning beaches (great for surfing) in the south, and its quieter marshlands in the north. This is a place best explored leisurely on foot or by bike.

▸▸ *For Sleeping, Eating and other listings, see pages 119-124.*

Ins and outs

Getting there Swansea is just off the M4, about 45 minutes' drive from Cardiff and 35 minutes' from Carmarthen. The central **bus** station, T01792 456116, is right next to

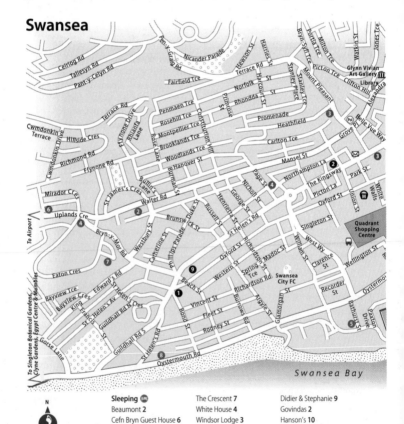

Swansea

Sleeping	The Crescent **7**	Didier & Stephanie **9**
Beaumont **2**	White House **4**	Govindas **2**
Cefn Bryn Guest House **6**	Windsor Lodge **3**	Hanson's **10**
Devon View **8**		Joe's Ice Cream **1**
Marriott **5**	**Eating**	La Braseria **11**
Morgan's & Restaurant **1**	Chelsea Café **8**	

N

0 metres 500
0 yards 500

the city's Quadrant shopping centre. **National Express** run coaches to Swansea from most major towns and cities, as well as direct from Heathrow and Gatwick airports. **First Cymru**, To870 6082608, operate the Swansea area bus routes, as well as an hourly shuttle bus No 100 between Swansea and Cardiff bus stations. Swansea railway station is 10 minutes' walk north of the centre at the top of the high street. There are frequent direct **train** services to Swansea from Cardiff Central station; the journey takes approximately 40 minutes. There are also direct services from London (three hours), Carmarthen and Fishguard. Swansea is also the southern terminus for the **Heart of Wales** line, www.heart-of-wales.co.uk, which runs across the top of the Gower to Llanelli, then up through Llandeilo and Llandovery to Shrewsbury. **Swansea Cork Ferries** run during peak seasons to and from Cork in the Republic of Ireland, www.swansea-cork.ie, from the ferry terminal by the mouth of the Tawe river about one mile east of town. ›› *For further information, see Transport page 123.*

Getting around Swansea can easily be explored on foot. There are regular buses to Mumbles as well as the toy-town train. The Gower is well served by buses from Swansea; North Gower is good for cycling as traffic is light.

Tourist information Mumbles TIC ① *2 Dunns Lane, Mumbles, To1792 361302, www.mumbles.info, Mar-Oct Mon-Sat 1000- 1600, longer hours in school holidays and Jul-Aug,* very helpful office with books on walking in the Gower. **Swansea TIC** ① *Plymouth St, off West Way by bus station, To1792 468321, www.swansea.gov.uk, Mon-Sat 0930-1730, Jul-Aug also Sun 1000-1600.* The following websites also provide useful visitor information: www.visitswanseabay.com, www.dylanthomas.org, www.neath-porttalbot. gov.uk/attractions/index.html and www.gog wa.com (Gower Watersports).

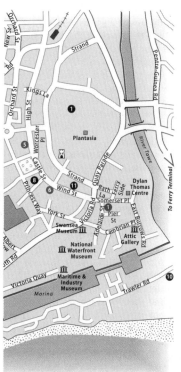

Bars & clubs ①
Cafe Mambo 3
Escape 4
Monkey Cafe Bar 5
No Sign Wine Bar 6
Palace 7

Swansea (Abertawe) and around

Swansea, the second city of Wales, is a far more Welsh place than its great rival, Cardiff, and Welsh is spoken by far more people. Its origins go back to Norman times at least, when a castle was built here as part of William the Conqueror's strategy to suppress the troublesome Welsh. Its maritime location and proximity to Wales' rich coalfields led to its inevitable development as an industrial town. By the 18th century it was a thriving coal port, as well as a copper smelting centre. The city was very badly damaged by bombing in the Second World War and most of its historic heart was flattened. It might not be pretty enough to have you reaching for the camera but it's a relaxed city with a welcoming atmosphere. Dylan Thomas himself once described it as 'ugly', then later described it as 'marble town, city of laughter, little Dublin'.

Keep it clean!

All Saints Church in Oystermouth was built on the site of an old Roman villa. Buried in the graveyard is Thomas Bowdler (1754-1825) the original man with a blue pencil. He became famous as the prudish editor of the Family Shakespeare in which he removed '…words and expressions… which cannot with propriety be read aloud in a family' - ie he took out all the rude bits. Hence emerged the term 'to bowdlerize'.

Today, Swansea is trying to re-invent itself as a tourist spot, making use of natural features like its seemingly endless arc of sand. The city centre and Maritime Quarter (the former docks) have some fine collections in the art galleries and museums, and the traditional Labour Club on Wind Street now rubs shoulders with sharp bars and restaurants. High above the amphitheatre of Castle Square, sit the remains of Swansea Castle, which had its heydey in the 13th century. If you've only one day to spend here, try not to make it Monday when most of the sights are closed.

Sights

The **Dylan Thomas Centre** ① *Somerset Place, T01792 463980, www.swansea.gov.uk/dylanthomas, www.dylanthomas.org, Tue-Sun 1000-1630*, is based in a beautiful colonnaded Victorian listed building. It celebrates Thomas through memorabilia like original manuscripts and letters and also hosts literature festivals, author readings, lectures and discussions. It also has a good second-hand bookshop and a nice café.

Swansea's hot house, **Plantasia** ① *Parc Tawe shopping complex, T01792 474555, www.plantasia.org, Tue-Sun 1000-1700, £3, £2.10 children*, is home to 850 species of tropical and sub-tropical plants as well as Tamarind monkeys, rainforest birds and butterflies and other exotic animals. There are three different climate zones where you can find bananas, coconuts, giant bamboo, a wonderful lush collection of ferns and plenty of prickly cacti.

Dylan Thomas pilgrims should walk up to 5 Cwmdonkin Drive, Uplands where a blue plaque is affixed to the wall. He was born here in the upstairs front bedroom on 26 October 1914.

Located in the Old Maritime Quarter, the **Attic Gallery** ① *14 Cambrian Place, T01792 653387,www.atticgallery.co.uk, Tue-Fri 1000-1730, Sat 1000-1630*, is Wales' longest established private gallery; it highlights the work of some of the principality's most important artists and promotes new artists. The **Glynn Vivian Art Gallery** ① *Alexandra Rd, T01792 516900, Tue-Sun 1000-1700, free*, has a good collection of work by 20th-century Welsh artists such as Ceri Richards and Gwen and Augustus John. There's also an internationally important collection of porcelain and china.

Swansea's newest museum is the **National Waterfront Museum** ① *Swansea Marina, T01792 459640, www.waterfrontmuseum.co.uk, daily 0930-1730, free*. Built at a cost of £31 million, it covers the industrial history of Wales – and also takes a peep into the future. Galleries cover themes such as coal, metal and the sea and exhibits include a replica of the *Penydarren locomotive*, the world's first steam train. There's also an original copy of the 1851 census which stated that Wales was the world's first industrialized country. It covers two floors and has several cafés and lots of audio visual exhibits, so it's great for kids.

Swansea Museum ① *Victoria Rd, T01792 653763, Tue-Sun 1030-1730, free*, is the oldest museum in Wales (Dylan Thomas called it 'a museum that should be in a museum'); it's best known for its ancient 2,200-year-old mummy of a priest called

● Mumbles' most famous daughter is Catherine Zeta Jones, who still returns occasionally to see her family and has a £3 million house here.

66 99 Ugly, lovely town, crawling, sprawling, slummed, unplanned, jerry-villa'd, and smug suburbaned by the side of a long and splendid curving shore. Dylan Thomas on Swansea.

Hor, but also has a good collection of Nantgarw pottery and porcelain. There's also a memorial to Edgar Evans, a Swansea man who was one of Captain Scott's companions on the ill-fated polar expedition. You will find more Egyptian antiquities at the **Egypt Centre** ① *Taliesin Arts Centre, Swansea University, T01792 295960, www.swansea.ac.uk/egypt, Tue-Sat 1000-1600, free*. There are over 1,000 artefacts dating as far back as 3,500 BC, with statues of gods and goddesses, jewellery, the painted coffin of a musician from Thebes – and even a mummified crocodile. Interesting even if you wouldn't know Tutunkhamen from Nefertiti.

Swansea Market ① *off Castle Sq and the A4067, by the Quadrant Shopping Centre, Mon-Sat 0930-1700*, is the biggest covered market in Wales. Swansea's salty maritime heritage means you can come here to try local grub such as fresh cockles with loads of vinegar and pepper. It's renowned for fresh seafood from the estuary, as well as Welsh cheese, laver bread and bacon (Swansea's traditional breakfast dish) and freshly baked Welsh cakes. **Joe's Ice Cream**, also available in nearby Mumbles (where they even queue in the winter), is proclaimed by locals, and many sweet toothed visitors, to be the best ice cream in the world.

Outside the town, **Singleton Botanical Gardens** ① *T01792 298637, daily, winter 0900-1700, summer 0900-1800, Aug 0900-2000, free*, have glass houses for desert, temperate and tropical regions, as well as a herb garden, huge magnolias and ornamental gardens. In the economic greenhouse you can see lots of exotic plants that are of economic importance, such as sugar cane, olives, coffee and coconut. **Clyne Gardens** ① *T01792 401737, www.swansea.gov.uk/leisure/allparks.html, daily, free*. This is largely a woodland garden and covers 46 acres of land surrounding Clyne Castle, purchased in 1860 by millionaire William Graham Vivian. As well as a great collection of rhododendrons and azaleas there's a bog garden, wildflower meadow and bluebell wood. It's a good place to bring kids and a picnic.

> ❗ Swansea's local delicacy – laver bread – is a type of seaweed, collected from the coast and cooked in oatmeal. It's eaten with bacon or ham and is said to be highly nutritious.

Mumbles (Mwmbwls)

West of Swansea Bay and the gateway to the Gower, is the cheery stretch of seafront known as Mumbles (Dylan Thomas called it 'a rather nice village, despite its name'). This name originally referred to a couple of little offshore islands and is a corruption of the name *mamelles* (breasts) that French sailors gave them. Today it's a general term for the village of **Oystermouth** (Ystumllwynarth), an historic oyster fishing port, and the long stretch of seafront to Mumbles Lighthouse and the blue-flag beach **Bracelet Bay**. It's noted for its generous number of pubs (some patronized by the ever-thirsty Mr Thomas) along the legendary Mumbles Mile and has some fine places to eat (see Eating, page 121). Nearby, **Caswell Bay** offers some great urban surfing. The winding streets behind the promenade contain the ruins of **Oystermouth Castle** ① *Apr-Sep, £1*, a former Norman stronghold. The surrounding parkland offers great views out over the Mumbles headland and across the sweeping sands of Swansea Bay.

The Gower (Gwyr)

West of Mumbles is the 19 mile long Gower, a small and scenic peninsular, which resembles a toe dipping tentatively into the Bristol Channel. The Gower was Britain's first designated Area of Outstanding Natural Beauty and much of the coastline is owned by the National Trust. Its lovely beaches have become a favourite with surfers and windsurfers. Its cliff tops and narrow lanes offer some good walking – there's a Gower Coastal Path – and cycling. The peninsula is sprinkled with ancient churches, small villages and lovely heathlands. If you want to escape the crowds make for the north coast, where there are lonely stretches of grazed saltmarshes, rich in rare plants.

The Gower is dotted with pretty and historic little churches; if you're interested in things ecclesiastical, pick up a copy of the leaflet '*In the Steps of the Saints*' which has details of all the Gower's churches. These include St Cadoc's, Cheriton – known as the Cathedral of the Gower, and St Mary's, Pennard, the burial place of Welsh poet Harri Webb.

South Gower

Three Cliffs Bay is the closest of the Gower beaches to Swansea and has a glorious three-mile stretch of sand with dramatic rock formations, popular with climbers. At nearby Parkmill, on the main A4118 is the **Gower Heritage Centre** ① *T01792 371206, www.gowerheritagecentre.co.uk, daily Apr-Oct 1000-1730, Nov-Mar 1000-1600, £3.70, £2.60 children, £12 family*, a child-orientated attraction based around an old water-powered corn mill, with craft workshops and displays and a tea shop. They also offer guided walks for groups and have plenty of leaflets on the area; it's the place to take the kids on a rainy day.

Further round the peninsula, is **Oxwich Bay**, a National Nature Reserve encompassing dunes, marshes and woodlands, as well as a popular sandy beach and plenty of accommodation. The relatively sheltered bay offers good opportunities for windsurfing; the surf picks up at high tide. Here you'll find **St Illtyd's Church** (open 1100-1500), which stands on the site of a sixth-century Celtic monastic cell, and **Oxwich castle** ① *May-Sep, daily 1000-1700, £2, CADW*, the ruins of a Tudor manor.

A couple of miles on from Oxwich, the road brings you to the quiet village of **Horton** – which has a good beach popular with windsurfers – and livelier, but more touristy, **Port Eynon**. At the western end of the beach, signposted from the YHA, is **Culver Hole**, a man-made cave built into the cliffs, thought to have been used by smugglers. From here the spectacular five-mile Gower Coastal Path winds its way around the cliff tops to Rhossili. Along the walk look out for **Paviland Cave**, where human remains were found dating back over 20,000 years.

The picturesque village of **Rhossili** is the end of the A4118 road, at the far western tip of the Gower peninsula. Steps lead down to the vast three-mile stretch of sand that is **Rhossili Bay**, one of the most stunning beaches in the country and very popular with surfers. It's a good spot for lunch or a cream tea, and at low tide it's possible to walk out across the causeway to **Worm's Head**, a rocky outcrop supposedly resembling a Welsh dragon. Information and tide times are available from the **National Trust information centre** ① *T01792 390707, Apr-Oct, 1030-1730.*

North and west Gower

Along the northern stretch of Rhossili Bay a narrow road winds up to the little village of **Llangennith**. To get here by car follow the B4291 from Swansea, or if coming from

"*We sank to the ground, the rubbery, gull-limed grass, the sheep-pilled stones, the pieces of bones and feathers, and crouched at the extreme end of the Peninsula*".
Dylan Thomas at Rhossili

⚡ Surf's up!

"I think the most important things you need to be a surfer in Wales is that you have to be very keen to deal with the cold, the wind and the pollution. And you need a good sense of humour! But on the plus side, you get to share the ocean with Welsh people." Carwyn Williams, former World Tour surfer and Welshman.

The Gower Peninsula is the surfing heartland of Wales, a series of sandy bays with reefs and points that provide no end of surfing possibilities. Some recommended places include

Three Cliffs Bay, one of the most scenic beaches on the Gower and usually an uncrowded spot; Oxwich Bay, which can get busy and tends to be best at high tide; and Llangennith beach, with three miles of sand a very good place for beginners, with a surf shop, campsite and parking nearby. More experienced surfers might like to head for Pete's Reef which can get very crowded and holds up to 5 ft, a favourite with locals.

From *Footprint Surfing Europe* by Chris Nelson and Demi Taylor.

South Gower, there's a cut through at **Reynoldston**. Llangennith can get very busy in summer with hoards of day trippers heading down to the beach. There's a good pub, surf shop and a little church, dedicated to St Cenydd who founded a priory here in the sixth century. Even older is the massive dolmen near Reynoldston known as **King Arthur's stone**, which sits alone on a windy ridge. A giant capstone, weighing around 25 tons, balanced on smaller rocks, it marks a Neolithic burial chamber. The views from this isolated spot seem to stretch forever.

🛏 Sleeping

Swansea *p115, map p114*

L-A Morgan's Hotel, Somerset Place, T01792 484848, www.morganshotel.co.uk. This is Catherine Zeta-Jones and Michael Douglas's hotel of choice and the place to come if you want to treat yourself. All 20 rooms are named after local ships and are individually designed. There are lovely wooden floors, crisp sheets and comfy beds and plasma TVs set into the walls. Bathrooms have scented candles and lovely big baths. There's also a posh restaurant and plans to open a spa.

A Marriott Hotel, Maritime Quarter, T01792 642020/T0870 4007282, www.marriott.com. Its location redeems the uninspiring exterior of this 4-star chain hotel with 122 rooms, small swimming pool, sauna and fitness equipment. It is well placed next to the marina and most rooms have lovely views, either of the marina or Swansea Bay. Ask for a view when you book.

B-C Beaumont Hotel, 72-73 Walter Rd, T01792 643956, www.beaumonthotel.co.uk, Family-run 2 star hotel with 16 well-

furnished and comfortable bedrooms. The executive rooms are larger and have sunken bath tubs.

C Cefn Bryn Guest House, 6 Uplands Crescent, Uplands, T01792 466687, www.cefnbryn.net. Conveniently located in sedate suburban Uplands, yet just 1 mile from Swansea train station and close to the city centre, a genuinely warm welcome awaits in this smart late-Victorian setting. Recently refurbished. Non-smokers only.

C The Crescent, 132 Eaton Crescent, Uplands, T01792 466814, www.crescent guesthouse.co.uk. 6 en suite bedrooms in a roomy Edwardian guesthouse that overlooks the Bay. There are superb panoramic views from the lounge. Free private parking.

C Devon View, 394-396 Oystermouth Rd, T01792 462008, www.devonview.co.uk. 16 rooms, mostly en suite. This 3-star guesthouse is on the seafront and some rooms have great views. It's in a Victorian terrace and vies with the White House (below) for best floral displays. They do a full breakfast and also have a restaurant carvery.

C **White House Hotel**, 4 Nyanza Terrace, T01792 473856, www.thewhitehouse hotel.co.uk. This is a beautifully refurbished and maintained Victorian hotel with 9 rooms, located 1 mile from the city centre. The en suite rooms are comfortable and warm and the owners are friendly. They'll do you a packed lunch if you ask and evening meals are also available. The exterior's wonderfully colourful in summer – they win 'Swansea in Bloom' nearly every year.

C **Windsor Lodge Hotel**, Mount Pleasant, T01792 642158, www.windsor-lodge.co.uk, Small and friendly hotel with 19 rooms in a welcoming grade II listed building has the air of a country hotel yet in the city. There are elegant en suite rooms, a restaurant and convenient parking.

Mumbles p117

A **Patrick's with Rooms**, 638 Mumbles Rd, T01792 360199, www.patrickswithrooms.com. 8 en suite rooms, each individually furnished and all facing the sea. Convenient for the sleek restaurant downstairs.

B **Hillcrest House Hotel**, 1 Higher Lane, Langland, T01792 363700, www.hillcrest househotel.com. Small, comfortable hotel with individually themed rooms (lots of daffodils for the Welsh room for instance, including a giant triffid-like standard lamp). All rooms are en suite, private parking.

C **Glenview Guest House**, 140 Langland Rd, T01792 367933, www.mumblesglen view.co.uk. B&B in a Victorian house overlooking Underhill Park. It has en suite rooms, pretty gardens and real fires in the lounge in winter.

C **Tides Reach**, 388 Mumbles Rd, T01792 404877, www.tidesreachguesthouse.co.uk. High quality 4-star B&B on the seafront. All rooms en suite and extremely clean and comfortable. The lounge has good views over the Bay and is furnished with antiques.

Gower p118

L-A **Fairyhill**, Reynoldstone, T01792 390139 or T0871 9958220, www.fairyhill.net. This is the Gower's only 5-star hotel but its reputation has spread much further. An ivy covered, 18th-century house tucked away in the quiet of the countryside; it's a great place to treat yourself and luxuriate – if you can afford it.

B-C **Oxwich Bay Hotel**, Oxwich Bay, T01792 390329, www.oxwichbayhotel.co.uk. Large, traditional hotel with great situation overlooking by Oxwich Bay. Try and get a room with a sea view.

C **King Arthur Hotel**, Higher Green, Reynoldston, T01792 390775, www.king arthurhotel.co.uk. Lovely newly refurbished rooms at this warm and popular inn, situated on the village green. Ask for a room in the new annexe and you won't have to worry about noise from the bar.

C **Surf Sound Guest House**, Long Acre, Oxwich, T01792 390822, www.surf sound.co.uk. Good value, non- smoking, B&B with en suite rooms, convenient for Oxwich beach. Closed in winter.

C **Woodside Guest House**, Oxwich, T01792 390791, www.oxwich.fsnet.co.uk. With 5 rooms, this is a 200-year-old cottage that's been converted into a 4-star guesthouse, conveniently situated near Oxwich beach. It's a good bet for surfers who can't wait to get into the water.

C-D **Parc-le-Breos**, Parkmill, T01792 371636, www.parc-le-breos.co.uk. 19th-century hunting lodge set in its own grounds. The rooms are clean, with en suite facilities and many have pleasant views of the gardens. Popular with those on horse riding, surfing or walking holidays. Evening meals available.

D **Tallizmand**, Llandmadoc, T01792 386373, www.tallizmand.co.uk. Small, comfortable B&B, with 2 en suite rooms and 1 with shared bathroom. In the quiet village of Llandmadoc and convenient for nearby beaches and walks. Evening meals and packed lunches available.

F **Port Eynon Youth Hostel**, Old Lifeboat House, Port Eynon, T01792 390706, porteynon@yha.org.uk, 28-bed seasonal hostel close to the beach.

Camping

Campsites in the Gower are very popular and often full at weekends during the summer, phone ahead for availability or arrive early on a Friday. See www.the-gower.com/campsites or www.gower-camping.co.uk for further information. Some good sites include:

Hill End Campsite, Llangennith, T01792 386204. Popular site, often full, just behind the dunes of Rhossili Bay, car park and shop.

Kennexstone Farm, Llangennith, T01792 391296, before you reach the village on the B4291, basic facilities, friendly.

North Hills Farm, between Parkmill and Penmaen, T01792 371218, good views of Three Cliff's Bay.

The Oxwich Camping Park, 1 mile back from the beach, on the Penrice Rd, T01792 390777, swimming pool and laundry.

Pitton Cross Caravan & Camping, on the B4247 near Rhossili, 01792 390593, www.pittoncross.co.uk, spacious pitches, laundry facilities.

◑ Eating

Swansea *p115, map p114*
♈♈♈ Morgans, Somerset Place, T01792 484848, Mon-Fri, Sun 1200-1500, Tue-Sat 1900-2100. This is Swansea's special-occasion venue. There are 2 restaurants in this upmarket hotel that's situated in the former Victorian Port Authority building. It's all non-smoking, the food's highly rated and there's a champagne bar too.

♈♈ Chelsea Café, 17 St Mary St, T01792 464068, Tue-Sat 1200-1430, 1900-2130. Lots of fresh Welsh produce at this popular restaurant which serves lots of produce from the local fish market, like cockles, black bream and sea bass. There's a separate veggie menu and lots of diet-defying desserts such as bread and butter pudding.

♈♈ Didier and Stephanie, 56 St Helens Rd, T01792 655603, Tue-Sat 1200-1400, 1900-2100. Swansea's only French restaurant serves everything from snails in garlic to guinea fowl in port. There are also several vegetarian dishes. Desserts are worth saving room for and include pistachio crème brûlée and meringue with coffee cream. Good choice of French wines.

♈♈ Hanson's, Pilot House Wharf, Trawler Rd, T01792 466200, Tue-Sat 1200-1400, Mon-Sat 1830-2130. Catherine and Michael have been spotted in this pleasant, out-of-the-way restaurant. It's big on fish, which is bought locally, and you might find turbot, cod, lobster or mussels. There are also a couple of options for veggies and they're happy to cater for special diets. The 3-course set lunch is good value.

♈♈ La Braseria, 28 Wind St, T01792 469683, Mon-Sat 1200-1430, 1900-2330. Situated on Wind St, the heart of Swansea's drinking and dining area, this large restaurant/wine bar serves fresh meat and fish dishes and a dash of Spanish music. It's popular so gets busy.

Mumbles *p117*
♈♈♈-♈♈ Knights Restaurant, 614-616 Mumbles Rd, T01792 363184, Tue-Sat 1200-1400, 1830-2130, Sun 1200-1400. Lively, contemporary restaurant with extensive fish menu – look out for sewin (sea trout) and monkfish as well as lots of unusual meat choices like wild boar, ostrich or guinea fowl. Separate veggie menu.

♈♈♈-♈♈ PA's Wine Bar, 95 Newton Rd, T01792 367723, daily 1200-1430, Mon-Sat 1800-2130. This little wine bar serves Welsh food in a relaxed setting and is very popular. In summer the doors open and you can look out on to the garden. They do lots of fish, bought from the market – you might find Penclawdd mussels with white wine and garlic on the menu.

♈♈♈-♈♈ Patrick's with Rooms, 638 Mumbles Rd, T01792 360199, Mon-Sun 1200-1400, Mon-Sat 1830-2150. Imaginative British cuisine in this very popular restaurant with accommodation (see Sleeping). There's a daily specials board and they use lots of Welsh produce like cockles, laverbread and Welsh beef. Dishes might include pan-fried duck with honey plum sauce, or game pie, and they also have a good choice for veggies with things like ravioli with wild mushrooms.

♈ Café Valance, 50 Newton Rd, T01792 367711, Mon-Sat 0800-1800. Great café with lots of comfy sofas and a good choice of filled baguettes, paninis, cakes and coffees.

♈ Claudes, 93 Newton Rd, T01792 366006, www.claudes.org.uk, Tue-Fri 1200-1430, 1800-2200, Sat 1200-1430, 1800-2145, Sun 1200-1500 (also open Mon Jun-Dec). Inventive Welsh cuisine with dishes such as homemade meatballs, roast cod with red pepper sauce, or saffron risotto. 2-course set lunch is a worthwhile choice on a budget.

♈ The Coffee Denn, 34 Newton Rd, T01792 360044, Mon-Sat 1000-1730, Sun 1100-1730. Good place for snacks, light meals like jacket potatoes, and heartier options such as chicken casserole or cottage pie.

♈ G&Ts Bistro, 602 Mumbles Rd, T01792 367309, Mon 1830-2130, Tue-Sat 1200-1400, 1830-2130, Sun 1200-1500, 1900-2130.

Warm red interior and flickering candles at this bistro which serves mains like Welsh beef and lamb, as well as tapas. **Govindas**, 8 Cradock St, T01792 468469, Sun-Thu 1200-1500, Fri-Sat 1200-1800. Established Hare Krishna veggie diner offering good-value grub. Good karma if not sophisticated. **Verdi's Knab Rock**, Mumbles Rd, T01792 369135, www.verdis-café.co.uk. Daily 1000-2100 (Jul-Aug until 2200), earlier closing Mon-Thu in winter. Relaxed Italian ice cream parlour and restaurant, with great views across Swansea Bay. Great for relaxing outside with an ice cream sundae, pizzas, foccacia or just coffee.

Delis and takeaways

Deli 28, Newton Rd, T01792 366828, Tue-Sat 0930-1730. This is a great place to pick up cheeses, olives and other picnic items.

Gower p118

Fairyhill, Reynoldstone off B4295, T01792 390139, daily 1230-1330, 1730-2045. If you can't afford to spend the night at this luxurious country hotel you can still enjoy some of its comforts in the restaurant, which uses local produce and serves classical food with a contemporary twist. Good choice of wines and delicious desserts too. Lunch is good value.

Welcome to Town Inn, Llanrhidian, Gower, T01792 390015, www.thewelcome totown.co.uk. Tue-Sun 1200-1400, Tue-Sat 1900-2130. Highly acclaimed food at this award-winning bistro. Lots of Welsh produce on the menu with some good-value set lunches. There's a good choice of Welsh cheeses, homemade bread and fresh vegetables.

King Arthur Hotel, Higher Green, Reynoldston, T01792 390775, 1200-1430, 1800-2100 (2130 at weekends). Lively inn on the village green, with a nautical theme in the cosy bar. Wide choice of bar meals with several veggie options.

Oxwich Bay Hotel, Oxwich Bay, T01792 390329, food available all day. Plenty of choice of no-nonsense food here with dishes like

baked potatoes, sausages or burgers as well as pricier food like steaks and seabass. The terrace offers a great outlook over the beach. **King's Head**, Llangennith, T01792 386212, food Mon-Sat 1100-2130, Sun 1200-2130. Popular pub serving bar meals like lamb balti, goulash or sweet and sour chicken. Good selection of real ales. **Three Cliffs Coffee Shop**, 68 Southgate Rd, Penard, off A4118 near Southgate, T01792 233885, daily 0900-1800. Marple top tables, outside seating and good homebaking at this lovely little café tucked away on the south Gower coast. Serves a good selection of filled baguettes, snacks and coffees.

♦ Pubs, bars and clubs

Swansea p115, map p114

Café Mambo, 46 The Kingsway, T01792 456620. Primarily a restaurant, the bar section is very small yet the atmosphere is very good in this Latino themed bar offering cocktails by the glass or pitcher. **Escape**, Northampton Lane, T01792 652854, www.escapegroup.com. Balearics come to Swansea Bay in this venue hosting varied club nights. Open 2200-0400 at weekends. **Monkey Café Bar**, 13 Castle St, T01792 480822, www.monkeycafe.co.uk. Cool bar offering DJ nights and live music as well as good pub grub in relaxed surroundings. **No Sign Wine Bar**, 56 Wind St, T01792 465300. One of the oldest bars on Wind Street and yet another of Dylan Thomas' old haunts. The warm atmosphere of this café bar tends to attract an eclectic mix of local drinkers, DT fans and clubbers. **Palace**, 156 High St, www.thepalace swansea.co.uk. Loud house in club conveniently close to railway station.

Mumbles p117

Antelope, Mumbles Rd. One of those 'Dylan Thomas drank here' pubs along the popular Mumbles Mile. Has a beer garden.

Gower p118

Greyhound Inn, Oldwalls, T01792 391027. Traditional pub said to serve the best beers on the Gower. Real ales and pub grub.

⊙ Entertainment

Theatre
Swansea Grand Theatre, Singleton St, Swansea, T01792 475715. Drama, pantomime, opera, ballet, concerts.
Taliesin Arts Centre, University of Wales, Mumbles Rd, Swansea, T01792 602060, www.taliesinartscentre.co.uk. The centre is home to a wide variety of performances, exhibitions, activities and events, with a cinema, gallery and conference facilities.

⊛ Festivals and events

May-Sep Swansea Bay Summer Festival, events run through the summer months, www.swanseabayfestival.net.
Aug Escape into the Park, big name DJs playing funk and trance music.
Oct Swansea Festival of Music and the Arts, everything from opera to jazz, www.swanseafestival.co.uk.
Oct/Nov Dylan Thomas Festival, events to celebrate the poet and his work, T01792 463980, www.dylanthomasfestival.org, run by the Dylan Thomas Centre, Swansea (see p116).

⚠ Activities and tours

Boat trips
Gower Coast Adventures, T07866 250440, www.gowercoastadventures.co.uk. Jet boat trips from Port Eynon Bay to Worms Head (2 hrs, £25 adults) and Knab Rock, Mumbles to Three Cliffs Bay (1½ hrs, £18 adults). Reductions for children and families.

Cycling
The Millennium Coastal Park has a 20-km cycle trail along the Loughor Estuary and runs from Bynea in the east to Pembury in the west.
Pedalabikeaway, North Dock, Llanelli, T01554 780123, www.pedalabikeaway.com, mountain bikes to tandems for hire.
Swansea Cycles, 10 Wyndham St, Swansea, T01792 410710. Hire, ½ day £8, full day £14.

General activities
Clyne Farm, Westport Ave, Mayals, Swansea, T01792 403333, www.clynefarm.com. Weekend and school holiday activity days for all ages from 8 upwards. Can include archery, riding, indoor climbing – booking necessary. Also offer hacks and beach rides.

Horse riding
Pitton Moor Trekking, Pilton Cross, Rhossili, Gower, T01792 390554, WTRA approved trekking on the Gower.
Parc le Breos, Parkmill, Gower, T01792 371636, www.parc-le-breos.co.uk. Daily rides and pony trekking holidays.

Walking
Gower Guided Walks, T01792 652040, www.gowerguidedwalks.co.uk. Variety of guided walks on the Gower.

Watersports
Bay Watersports, Oystermouth Rd, Swansea, T01792 534858, www.bay watersports.co.uk. Offer windsurfing lessons and kit hire. 1 lesson £20, 2 day course (4 lessons) £65.
Euphoria Sailing, T0870 7702890 or T01792 234502, www.watersports4all.com. Offers a variety of watersports in Oxwich Bay from sailing and windsurfing to wakeboarding.
Hot Dog Surf Shop, Kittle, Gower T01792 234073, www.hotdogsurf.com. For surf gear.
PJs Surf Shop, Llangennith, Gower, T01792 386669. Good range of wetsuits and surfboards for hire, (from £9) also have a surf hotline T09016 031603 (60p per min).
Welsh Surf School, Llangennith, Gower, T01792 386426, www.wsfsurfschool.co.uk. Run surfing lessons from Apr-Oct in Rhossili Bay (Llangennith).

⊙ Transport

Swansea *p115*, map *p114*
Boat
Swansea-Cork Ferries (T01792 456116, www.swanseacorkferries.com) runs both car and foot passenger services to **Cork** from mid-Mar to mid-Jan. They sail 4 times a week – more frequently in high season. Prices cost from £22 single for foot passengers. The journey takes 10 hrs (see p27).

Bus
The **Beacons Bus** B2 connects Swansea with **Brecon** (see p113). **First Cymru** run a shuttle bus between Swansea and **Cardiff** bus

stations (Mon-Sat hourly, Sun 5 daily, £5.90, 1 hr). **National Express** buses travel from Swansea to major cities including: **Pembroke** (3 direct daily, 1 hr 50 mins, £9.90); **Tenby** (3 direct daily, 1 hr 35 mins, £9.90); **Haverfordwest** (3 direct daily, 2 ½ hrs, £10.50); and **Carmarthen** (3 direct daily, £6.90, 1 hr). For **Brecon**, change at Cardiff (1 daily, 3 ½ hrs, £14). Buses to North Wales travel via **Birmingham** (8 ½ hrs, £62.50). Direct buses to **Cardiff** (10 daily, £8.90, 1hr 15 mins) or change at Newport; to **Bristol** (4 daily, £33, 4 ½ hrs) or change at Cardiff; to **London** (4 daily, £36, 4 hrs 45 mins) or change at Cardiff. Bus No 201 goes directly to **Heathrow Airport** (11 daily, £34.50 return, 4 ½ hrs) and **Gatwick** (£40.50, 5 ½ hrs).

Train

First Great Western run direct trains from Swansea to **London Paddington** (hourly, £47, 3 hrs) stopping at **Cardiff** (£15, 40 mins), **Bristol** (£16.40, 1 ½ hrs) and Reading (£34, 2 ½ 30 mins). **Arriva Trains Wales** run to **Carmarthen** (hourly, £5.80, 50 mins) and **Fishguard** (2 daily, £9.50, 2 hrs). The **Heart of Wales**, www.heart-of-wales.co.uk, line cuts right across the middle of Wales via **Llandeilo** (3 daily, £2, 50 mins), **Llandovery** (£3.70, 1 hr 20 mins), **Llandrindod Wells**

(£4.20, 2 hrs 10 mins) to **Shrewsbury** (£8, 3 hrs 40 mins).

Mumbles *p117*

First Cymru bus Nos 1,2, 2A and 3A run to **Swansea** bus station (every ½ hr, £.1.60, 15 mins), or during term time Nos 82A or 83 run between the University and the bus station along Oystermouth Rd.

In the summer months the **Swansea Bay Rider** toy-town train runs from 1130-1500 along the Swansea promenade stopping at Oystermouth (£1.65 single tickets only).

Gower *p118*

Pullman run hourly bus services to and from **Swansea** to the Gower. Bus No 118 to **Oxwich** (30 mins), **Rhossili** and South Gower; Bus No 116 to **Llangennith** (1 hr) and North Gower.

❶ Directory

Swansea *p115, map p114*
Hospital Singleton Hospital, Sketty Park Lane, T01792 205666. **Internet** Swansea library, Alexandra Rd, T01792 516757 Mon-Sat. **Pharmacy** Kingsway Pharmacy, 39 The Kingsway. **Police** main station on Alexander Rd, T01792 456999.

Southwest Wales

❧ Footprint features

Introduction

Carmarthenshire is a land of green hills, farms and ancient castles, extending out to the edge of the brooding Black Mountain. It's a quiet county full of history and mystery – the Romans mined gold here and legend has it that it's the birthplace of Merlin the magician. On its sleepy coast is Laugharne, where the gifted poet Dylan Thomas spent his final years.

West of Carmarthenshire, Pembrokeshire is the most westerly county in Wales and one of the most beautiful. Its coastline of dramatic sea cliffs, glorious beaches and secluded coves has been attracting tourists for years – and its importance was recognized in 1952 when it was designated a National Park. Punctuating this rugged coastline are pretty villages and seaside towns: on the south coast is the traditional – but far from tacky – bucket and spade resort of Tenby; on the north coast is the quietly comfortable little town of Newport. Far to the west is delightful St David's – Britain's smallest city and a spiritual centre since the sixth century. Today the best way to appreciate this unspoilt landscape is on foot; the Pembrokeshire Coast Path clings to the coastline as much as possible and provides some of the best walking in Britain.

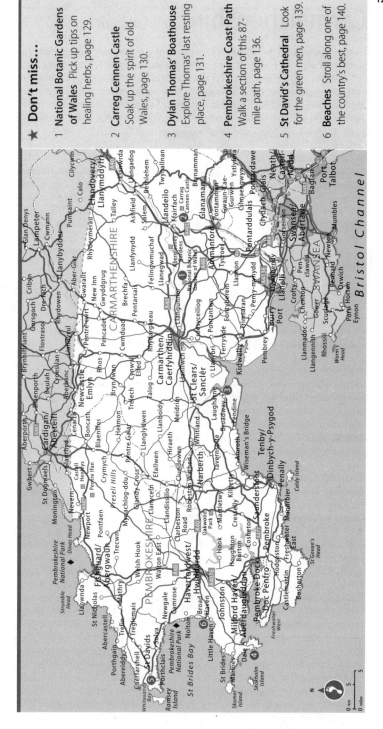

★ Don't miss...

1 **National Botanic Gardens of Wales** Pick up tips on healing herbs, page 129.

2 **Carreg Cennen Castle** Soak up the spirit of old Wales, page 130.

3 **Dylan Thomas' Boathouse** Explore Thomas' last resting place, page 131.

4 **Pembrokeshire Coast Path** Walk a section of this 87-mile path, page 136.

5 **St David's Cathedral** Look for the green men, page 139.

6 **Beaches** Stroll along one of the country's best, page 140.

Carmarthenshire → *Colour map 2, grid B1-2*

Carmarthenshire is often overlooked by visitors rushing westwards to Pembrokeshire or north to Snowdonia. However, it's one of the most Welsh parts of Wales – green, rural, with fine gardens, the poignant ruins of ancient castles and a landscape steeped in myth and legend. The Welsh language is still widely spoken here. It's perhaps appropriate that the national poet, Dylan Thomas, chose to live in Carmarthenshire and a visit to his former home in Laugharne on the soft, sleepy coastline is a highlight of any trip to Wales. ⇥ *For Sleeping, Eating and other listings, see pages 132-133.*

Ins and outs

Getting there and around Carmarthen has good public transport links. **National Express** run daily **buses** via Haverfordwest, to Swansea, Cardiff and London. **First Cymru** buses run to Cardigan, Swansea and Haverfordwest. The **Beacons Bus** (see box, page 113) links Carmarthen with Brecon. **Trains** run to Cardiff, Fishguard, Pembroke, Haverfordwest and Milford Haven. The **Heart of Wales** line, www.heart-of-wales.co.uk, travels from Swansea, through Llanelli and follows the Tywi Valley up through Llandeilo and Llandovery, to Shrewsbury. Trains to Pembrokeshire pass through Carmarthen.

Information **Carmarthen TIC** ① *113 Lammas St, near the Crimea Monument, T01267 231557, www.carmarthenshire.gov.uk, Mon-Sat 1000-1330, 1400-1715.*

Carmarthen (Caerfyrddin) and around

Often regarded as the gateway to West Wales, the town on the River Tywi (also known by its anglicized name, Towy) is the ancient capital of the region. Although it was founded as a Roman fort, legend claims that it is the birthplace of Merlin (Myrddin). Once a busy trading port and wool town, Carmarthen is now a flourishing market town and stronghold of the Welsh language. Sights of interest within the town include the **Oriel Myrddin** ① *Church Lane, T01267 222775, Mon-Sat 1000-1700, free*, a craft centre and imaginative gallery showcasing local artists.

Around Carmarthen

Two miles east of Carmarthen, the former seat of the Bishop of St David's between 1542 and 1974, now houses the regional history museum. The **Carmarthenshire County Museum** ① *Bishop's Palace, Abergwilli, T01267 228696, Mon-Sat 1000-1630, free*, has an interesting and eclectic exhibition of well-presented displays of local castles, pottery and archaeological finds, wooden dresses, and the origins of one of Wales's first eisteddfodau (Welsh cultural festivals), held nearby in 1450.

Three miles north of Carmarthen on the A484, is the **Gwili Railway** ① *T01267 230666, www.gwili-railway.co.uk, May-Sep, check times, £5, £3 children, £13 family.* This steam railway starts at Bronwydd Arms and follows a river much of the way, before stopping at Llwyfan Cerrig, where there's a picnic site and miniature railway. You can get off here or continue to Danycoed and return. The round trip is four miles.

● *Merlin the magician was thought to have been based on Myrddin a sixth-century holy*
● *man, famed for his prophecies born near Carmarthen. The 12th-century writer Geoffrey of Monmouth in his 'Vita Merlini' essentially re-invented him as King Arthur's advisor and wizard and created the romantic figure we know today. The son of a Breton princess and a wicked spirit, some say he's buried on Bryn Myrddin (Merlin's Hill) near Carmarthen.*

National Botanic Garden of Wales

ⓘ *T01558 668768, www.gardenofwales.org.uk, Llanarthne, summer daily 1000-1800, winter 1000-1630, £7, £2 children (free at weekends and holidays), £16 family.*

Opened in May 2000, this is one of Wales' most important millennium projects – its own botanic garden. It's a bit like a mix of Kew and the Eden Project – though on a smaller scale. The Middleton estate on which it's built dates from the 1600s and the old double-walled garden (cleverly designed so as to produce more heat) has been restored and has beds containing all sorts of vegetables and flowers, with interesting old varieties like yellow raspberries and funny shaped tomatoes. There's an excellent exhibition on the Physicians of Myddfai – the name referring to a line of Welsh physicians who used natural remedies to cure people. It has displays on herbal remedies/treatments from all over the world. There's also a 19th-century apothecaries' hall from Anglesey – complete with bottles with labels like 'Dr Rooke's Solar Elixir and Reanimating Balm of Life'. At the heart of the garden is the newly built Great Glasshouse designed by Norman Foster. This is divided into different climate zones, with plants from Australia, South Africa, the Mediterranean, Canary Islands, Chile and California. Other attractions include a summer 'maize maze', a Japanese garden and a bog garden.

Llandeilo and around

Llandeilo is a small market town in the Tywi Valley. It's just a mile from Dinefwr castle and about four miles from Carreg Cennan castle so makes a convenient spot for a bite to eat if you're exploring the area.

Aberglasney Gardens

ⓘ *Llangathen, 2 miles west of Llandeilo, T01558 668998, www.aberglasney.org.uk, daily summer 1000-1800, winter 1030-1600, £6, £3 children, £15 family.*

East of Middleton, off the A40, is Wales' answer to Heligan – a lost garden surrounding a fine manor house, both of which had suffered badly from neglect and looked doomed to disappear. Both the house – a listed building – and the weed choked grounds, were saved in the mid 1990s and a unique garden was discovered, which has now been carefully restored. The formal Cloister Gardens are a rare and authentic Jacobean survival as almost all such gardens were swept away in the 18th century. You can also see Victorian aviaries, a Pool Garden, Kitchen Garden and an atmospheric Yew Tunnel. There's a good café where you can sit outside on fine days.

Dinefwr Castle and Park and Newton House

ⓘ *T01558 823902, west of Llandeilo, Easter-Oct Thu-Mon 1100-1700; house and park £3.80, £1.90 children, £9 family; park only £2.60, £1.30 children, £6.30 family, unrestricted access to the castle.*

Legend has it that the first castle at Dinefwr was built in AD 877 by Rhodri Mawr, King of Wales. It became the principal court of Hywel Dda (the 'Good') who in AD 920 ruled much of Southwest Wales, known as Deheubarth. He was responsible for creating the first uniform legal system in Wales. The ruined stone castle visible today was built on the same site and was the 12th-century stronghold of Lord Rhys, who united Welsh rulers against the English.

In the 17th century the more comfortable Newton House was built (about a 25-minute walk across parkland from the castle), and the park was landscaped in the 1770s by Capability Brown. The house is gradually being restored by the National Trust and you can see the period rooms, hung with paintings. The park is notable for its indigenous rare White Park cattle, which are white with long horns and black noses. They have a lineage stretching back to the time of Hywel Dda – in the event of any injury to the King of Deheubarth tribute had to be paid in the form of these cattle.

⦂ The Welsh Robin Hood

Not far from Llandovery, on the RSPB's Dinas Nature Reserve, is a cave that was said to be the lair of Twm Sion Cati, often known as the Welsh Robin Hood. Born in 1530 near Tregaron, his real name was the less romantic Thomas Jones. Myths have grown up around him and he inspired many works of fiction. His early 'career' was that of highwayman – it's said he only robbed the rich, though whether he gave to the poor is much disputed.

He was a fast talker (it's said he could sell a farmer a cow he'd only stolen from him the day before) and in 1557 he fled to Geneva to escape the law. He returned in 1559 when he was given a Royal Pardon and became a pillar of the community. He used to draw up family trees for wealthy gentry, and was a published poet – some of his works are in the British Library. He also became a Justice of the Peace – a supreme irony for a former thief. It's said that he married a local heiress in his old age and died around 1620.

Aberdeunant

This tiny **traditional farmhouse** ⓘ *Taliaris, 3 miles north of Llandeilo, T01558 650177, National Trust, Apr-Sep, first Sat and Sun of each month, tours 1200-1700, £2, children £1,* gives a rare insight into a rural way of life that's now been lost. Guided tours are available, but it's so small only a few people can fit into it at once.

Carreg Cannen Castle

ⓘ *Southeast of Llandeilo, near Trapp, T01558 822291, Easter-Oct daily 0930-1830, Nov-end Mar daily 0930-dusk, £3, £2.50 child, £8.50 family, CADW.*
Carreg Cennen is probably the most dramatically situated castle in Wales – perched high on a precipitous crag above the River Cennen, the views down the valley are stunning. Legend has it that a castle was built here by King Arthur's knights; one of them is still said to sleep under the existing structure, a seemingly impenetrable stone stronghold which dates from around 1300. It was dismantled by the Yorkists in the Wars of the Roses and is now a romantic ruin. A visit here includes taking a torch and walking along the dark passageway that leads to a cave beneath the fort.

Llandovery and around

In the northern part of Carmarthenshire, Llandovery is a good base for exploring the **Twyi Valley**. The town was once an important stopping place for drovers taking cattle to market in London; it was so important that a drover's bank, the Bank of the Black Ox, was founded here. In 1909 it became part of Lloyds Bank. The town has Roman origins, though the site of the Roman fort is now occupied by **St Mary's Church** at Llanfair-ar-y-Bryn just north of the town. William Williams Pantycelyn, one of Wales most famous composers of hymns (he wrote '*Guide me O Thou Great Jehovah*') is buried there.

Dolaucothi Gold Mines

ⓘ *Pumsaint, llanwrda, T01558 650177, Easter-end Oct daily 1000-1700, £3.20, £1.60 children, family £8; underground tour £3.80, family £9.50, National Trust.*
To the northeast of Llandovery the Dolaucothi Gold Mines were first mined by the Romans. These ancient gold mines were opened again in the 19th century and worked until 1938. There are underground tours, exhibitions and a chance to pan for gold.

A 10-minute drive southwest of the mines, off the B4302, is remote Talley Abbey, founded in 1185. The building project ran out of money early on and the abbey was never as large as was first envisaged. It was an early victim of Edward I's assault on Wales and was later dissolved by Henry VIII. It had become a ruin by the 19th century and is a lonely sight today – little more than a shell.

Carmarthenshire Coast

The coastline of Carmarthenshire has a different character to the wild interior and is notable as the final home of Dylan Thomas, who spent his last years in the simple boathouse at Laugharne. As you travel west from the Gower along the A484 over the Loughor estuary, you come to the excellent **National Wetland Centre** ① *Penclacwydd, Llwynhendy, near Llanelli, T01554 741087, www.wwt.org.uk, summer daily 0930-1700, winter 0930-1630, £5.50, £3.50 children, £14.50 family*. This is twitcher heaven, but you don't have to be a bino-clutching beardie to enjoy a visit. The centre covers 500 acres around the Burry Inlet, with salt marshes, mudflats and a landscaped area that's home to flamingos, geese and ducks. Hides give you the opportunity to see a wide range of wildfowl and wading birds; in winter around 50,000 birds come here. Species you might spot include herons, ringed plovers and little egrets. There's also a good interactive **Discovery Centre** for kids and a café.

Further west, just off the A484, is one of Wales' lesser known castles, well-preserved **Kidwelly** ① *T01554 890104, daily Easter-May, Oct 0930-1700; Jun-Sep 0930-1800; Nov-Easter Mon-Sat 0930-1600, Sun 1100-1600, £2.50, £7 family, CADW*. Founded by the Normans, the castle was a link in a chain of coastal strongholds. Its most prominent feature is the great gatehouse, completed in 1422.

Laugharne (Talacharn)

The undoubted highlight of the Carmarthenshire coast, described by Dylan Thomas as 'a legendary lazy little black magical bedlam by the sea' – and the most likely inspiration for fictional Llareggub of *Under Milk Wood*, which he wrote here. On this glorious spot on the Taff estuary, you can feel the spirit of this most quotable of poets. He came here several times, once to chase after Caitlin – whom he later married – and lived in several houses around the town until in 1949 his benefactor, Margaret Taylor, bought him and his family the famous Boathouse where he lived until his death in 1953. **The Dylan Thomas Boathouse** ① *T01994 427420, www.dylanthomasboat house.com, daily May-Oct 1000-1730, Nov-Apr 1030-1530, £3, £1.50 children*, is a simple building with an idyllic location, perched on the clifftop with glorious views over the estuary and its 'heron-priested shores'. It's reached by a narrow track from the town (and is so poorly signposted you're sure to miss it at first) and his tiny writing shed, originally a garage, is laid out much as it was when Thomas worked here, with scrunched up pieces of paper and a bottle of beer on the table. The house itself is the simply furnished living room, with some copies of his manuscripts and other memorabilia. Nearby, in the township is St Martin's Churchyard, where Thomas and his wife are buried.

Close to the Boathouse, on the shore, is **Laugharne Castle** ① *T01994 427906, Apr-Sep daily 1000-17000, £2.50, £7 family*, an atmospheric ruin built in the mid- to late-13th century. In Elizabethan times it was turned into a mansion, but after the Civil War it fell into decline. JMW Turner painted it and Dylan Thomas sometimes worked in its summerhouse. A short drive inland from Laugharne is the village of **St Clears**, where there's a good craft centre and excellent café (see Eating, page 133).

● *Dylan Thomas was having a sly joke when he came up with the name Llareggub for the*
● *fictional town in* Under Milk Wood. *Spell it backwards and you'll see why.*

⊜ Sleeping

Carmarthen and around *p128*

B Ivy Bush Royal Hotel, Spilman St, T01267 235111, www.ivybush.co.uk. Recently refurbished hotel, once a retreat for Nelson and Lady Hamilton. Rooms well equipped and comfortable with standard hotel furnishings.

B Ty Mawr Country House, Brechfa, near Carmarthen, T08719 958284, www.wales-country-hotel.co.uk. Lovely rural feel to this ancient whitewashed farmhouse with original beams and log fires. It's noted for its good Welsh food, which is mostly organic.

C Allt y Golau Uchaf, Felingwm Uchaf, T01267 290455, www.visit-carmarthenshire.co.uk/alltygolau. Comfortable and clean rooms in a restored farmhouse in a peaceful location. Immaculate residents' lounge.

C Boar's Head, Lammas St, T01267 222789, Reasonably priced clean en suite rooms in a quaint old coaching inn in central location.

C Glasfryn, Brechfa, T01267 202306, www.glasfrynbrechfa.co.uk. 3 en suite rooms at this little village B&B. Good breakfasts.

D Drovers Arms, Lammas St, T01267 237646. A family-run hotel, proud of its history with the early cattle drovers who travelled long distances from rural Wales to the cattle markets. Comfortable en suites, cosy bar and open fire in pub serving real ale.

Laugharne and around *p131*

L-A Hurst House, East Marsh, T01994 427417, www.hurst-house.co.uk, off A4066 near Laugharne. One of actor Neil Morrissey's hotels, this goes in for contemporary luxury and is aimed at the wealthy weekender market.

tbc Browns Hotel, King St, T01994 427320. Another of actor Neil Morrissey's properties, this hotel was once a favourite haunt of Dylan Thomas. At the time of writing it is being refurbished, but due to re-open late 2005. The grade-3 listed bar will be left much as it was in Thomas' time.

B Llwyn Hall, Llwynhendy, Llanelli, T01554 777754, www.llynhall.com. Lovely old house with lots of antiques and fine furnishings. It's next door to the wildlife reserve.

C Coedllys Country House, Llangynin, near St Clears, T 01994 231455, www.coedllys countryhouse.co.uk. This cosy retreat in the heart of the countryside is a great place to get away from it all. 4 en suite rooms.

C The Cors, Newbridge Rd, Laugharne, T01994 427219. 2 clean and contemporary rooms available at this central restaurant.

D Glan Gwendraeth Farm, Priory St, Kidwelly, T01554 890309, www.glangwen draeth.co.uk. Clean and comfortable, good value farmhouse B&B, all rooms en suite, some with views of Kidwelly's stunning castle.

⊙ Eating

Carmarthen and around *p128*

₸₸₸-₸₸ Ty Mawr, Brechfa, T01267 202332, Mon-Sat 1900-2130, Sun 1200-1400. Restaurant with rooms with lots of Welsh lamb and beef on the menu. Desserts include fresh farmhouse cheeses.

₸₸₸-₸₸ Y Polyn, Nantgaredig, T01276 290000, lunches 1200-1500, evenings from 1800. Lots of Welsh produce on the menu in this pub which has both a restaurant and bar. Serves real ales too.

₸₸ Falcon, Lammas St, T01267 234959, daily 1200-1400, Mon-Sat 1830-2100. Traditional roast meats, such as salt marsh lamb, as well as local fish dishes.

₸₸ Glasfryn, Brechfa, T01267 202306, evening meals by arrangement. This B&B happily cooks for non residents if you book. Food served in the conservatory. Mains might be lamb in redcurrant sauce, or cheese and parsnip roulade with apricot stuffing.

₸₸ Halfway Inn, Nantgaredig, T01558 668337, Tue-Sat 1130-1430, 1800-2130, Sun 1200-1400. Standard bar lunches, and more filling meals like roast duck or steak and mushroom pie. Some veggie choices.

₸₸ Quayside Brasserie, The Quay, T01267 223000, Mon-Sat 1200-1430, 1800-2130. Well prepared and presented fresh food on the Tywi quay.

₸₸-₸ Y Capel Bach Bistro at The Angel, Rhosmaen St, Llandeilo, T01558 822765, Mon-Sat 1200-1430; Mon-Thu 1900-2115, Fri-Sat 1900-2130. Popular pub with a restaurant serving good food at modest prices.

₸ Barita, 139 Rhosmaen St, Llandeilo, T01558 823444, Mon-Sat 0930-1700. Excellent deli/café serving great coffee, cakes and imaginative tarts, filled rolls and baguettes. Try your chosen cheese from the counter with sticky onion marmalade.

The Plough, Felingwm Uchaf, T01267 290019, food Mon-Fri 1800-2100, Sat 1200-2100. Traditional pub with oak beams and wood burning stove. Serves 'farmers' portions' with veggie choices and real ales.
The Railway Inn, Nantgaredig, from 1800. Unpretentious, but great value food at this family-run pub. Good curries and steak.

Laugharne p131

The Cors, Newbridge Rd, T01994 427219, Wed-Sun from 1900, booking essential. Highly rated food at this cosy restaurant offering contemporary Welsh dishes such as sewin (sea trout) with samphire, or organic beef; let them know in advance if you're veggie.
Hurst House, East Marsh, T01994 427417, off A4066 outside Laugharne, daily 1200-1600, 1900-2200. With an emphasis on fresh Welsh produce, you might find Welsh beef, lamb, or local lobster on the menu.
Owl and the Pussycat Tearooms, 3 Grist Sq, T01994 427742, Tue-Wed, Sun 1000-1700, Thu-Sat 1000- 2200. Traditional tearoom with Welsh cakes and bara brith, or evening meals like crab salad or salmon.
Portreeve Restaurant and Tavern, Market Sq, T01994 427476, daily 1215-1430, and Tue-Sat 1830-2130, and Sun 1215-1430. Booking advised. Good bar meals, with Welsh produce, pizzas and other dishes. Real ales.
Talents Coffee House, Pentre Rd, St Clears, T01994 231826, Mon-Sat 1030- 1630. Great contemporary café serving fresh local produce like Salt Marsh lamb hot pot, or Welsh black beef casserole, as well as veggie dishes, cakes and local ice cream.

Pubs, bars and clubs

Carmarthen and around p128
The Plough, Felingwm Uchaf, T01267 290019. Real fires and real ales.
The Salutation, Llandeilo, T01558 823325, Traditional pub serving real ales with live music. Sometimes has jazz on Tue and folk on Wed; always has bluegrass on Thu and tunes on the piano on Sat.

Laugharne p131
New Three Mariners, Market St, T01994 427426, food 1200-1500, 1700-2100. Established pub now refurbished and part owned by actor Neil Morrissey. Also bar food.

Festivals and events

May/Jun Merlin Festival, Carmarthen. Celebration of the famous magician. Street entertainers, magic and storytelling. T01554 747500
Jul Kidwelly Carnival and Air Display, T01554 890203. Does what it says on the tin. Llandeilo Fawr Festival of Flower and Music, T01558 823294. Mid-Jul.

Activities and tours

Penlan Outdoor Activity Centre, Meidrim Rd, St Clears, T01994 230559, www.penlan activitycentre.co.uk. Offers everything from archery to canoeing and horse riding. Also has self-catering accommodation.

Transport

Carmarthen p128
Bus
Carmarthen bus station is on Blue St, just on the north side of the bridge. Services run to **Swansea**, **Cardigan** and **Haverfordwest**. Bus No 1, the **Towy Valley Bus** is the most useful for visitors as it runs twice daily and links **Carmarthen**, **Llandeilo**, **Llandovery** and **Brecon**; it also runs to the National Botanic Gardens. The **West Wales Rover** ticket (£5) applies to this route and can be purchased on board the bus. See www.pembrokeshiregreenways.co.uk, T01437 776313, for further information.

Train
Carmarthen train station lies over Carmarthen Bridge, on the south side of the river and about 500 m from the bus station. Trains run to **Swansea** and **Cardiff** (6 daily, £16, 2 hrs) and west to **Tenby**, **Pembroke**, **Milford Haven**, **Haverfordwest** and **Fishguard**.

Laugharne p131
No direct services to Swansea, change at Carmarthen or St Clears. **First Cymru** bus No 222 to **Carmarthen**, every 2 hrs (£3.60, ½ hr).

Directory

Internet Free access is available at Carmarthen library, St Peter's St, T01267 224830, open Mon-Sat.

Pembrokeshire → Colour map 1

Everyone loves Pembrokeshire: sun-tanned surfers, bearded birdwatchers, history lovers and families all flock here. No wonder it's been dubbed the 'new Cornwall'. Its craggy cliffs, honeyed beaches and offshore islands make its coastline one of the finest in Britain. There are plenty of cultural attractions when you want a break from the beach, from the cathedral at St David's to ancient archaeological sites, castles and sleepy churches. And inland there are tranquil nooks like the Gwaun Valley, a pastoral haven that many overlook. ▸▸ *For Sleeping, Eating and other listings, see pages 144-150.*

Ins and outs

Getting there

There are good road links via the A40 from Haverfordwest to Fishguard, and the M4 beyond to the south. The A487 leads northeast up the coast towards Cardigan Bay and Aberystwyth. There are **train** stations at Tenby, Haverfordwest, Milford Haven, Fishguard and Pembroke, with direct daily services from Swansea and Carmarthen. **National Express** run **buses** from Swansea to Tenby, Pembroke, Haverfordwest and Milford Haven. St David's can only be reached by **Richards Brothers** bus from Haverfordwest or Fishguard; it is also the last stop of the **Puffin Shuttle** (see below), which runs during the summer. **Ferries** from Rosslare in Ireland run to Pembroke Dock (10 minutes from Pembroke) and Fishguard. ▸▸ *For further details, see Transport, page 150.*

Getting around The area is served by **First Cymru**, www.firstcymru.co.uk; **Richards Brothers**, T01239 613756, www.richardbros.co.uk; and **Silcox Coaches** T01646 683143. During the summer public transport along the coastal path is pretty good with bus services linking the main areas. The **Coastal Cruiser** bus service runs all year round (daily May-September, three buses a week October-April) between Pembroke, Angle, Freshwater West, Bosherston, Stackpole and Freshwater East. There are other buses running daily in summer: the **Poppit Rocket** runs from Cardigan to Fishguard; the **Strumble Shuttle** runs from Fishguard to St David's; the **Puffin Shuttle** runs along the coast from Milford Haven to St David's; and the **Celtic Coaster** runs around St David's Peninsula – details are available from TICs or www.greenways.co.uk. As you go inland it's generally easier to get around if you've got your own transport; however remote areas can sometimes be reached by **postbus** (www.postbus.royalmail.com).

The best way to travel is to buy a **West Wales Rover** ticket, £5, for all day travel on any of these buses and can be purchased on the bus. For further information, see www.pembrokeshiregreenways.co.uk, T01437 776313.

Tourist information Tenby TIC ⓘ *The Croft, Tenby, T01834 842404, tenby.tic@ pembrokeshire.gov.uk, Apr-May 1000-1700, Jun-Sep 1000-1730, Jul-Aug 1000- 2100, Oct 1000-1700, Nov-Apr 1000-1600.* **Pembroke Visitor Centre** ⓘ *The Commons Rd, Pembroke, T01646 622388, pembroke.tic@pembrokeshire.gov.uk, Jun-Sep 1000-1730, otherwise 1000-1700.* **Newport TIC** ⓘ *Long St, T01239 820912, Apr-Sep Mon-Sat 1000-1730, shuts for lunch.* **St David's TIC/National Park Visitor Centre** ⓘ *The Grove, St David's, T01437 720392, www.stdavids.co.uk, daily Apr-Oct 0930-1730, Mon-Sat Nov-Mar 1000-1600.* **Fishguard TIC** ⓘ *The Library, High St, T01348 873484, www.fishguard.tic@pembrokeshire.gov.uk, Easter-May daily 1000-1700, Jun-Sep daily 0930-1700; Oct Mon-Sat 1000-1700, Nov-Easter Mon-Sat 1000-1600.* **Fishguard Harbour TIC** ⓘ *Ocean Lab, T01348 872037, www.fishguardharbourtic@pembroke shire.gov.uk, daily 1000-1700 Easter-Oct, Nov-Easter 1000-1600.* **Haverfordwest Visitor Centre** ⓘ *Old Bridge St, T01437 763110, Easter-Oct Mon-Sat 0930-1730; Jul-Aug also Sun 1000-1600; Mon-Sat 1000-1600 at all other times.* Useful websites include:

Background

Pembrokeshire has been inhabited since at least Neolithic times and the north of the county in particular is still dotted with mysterious reminders of its prehistoric past. The **Preseli Hills** (Mynydd Preseli) – a brooding range of hills south of Newport – was an important Celtic stronghold and it was from here that the bluestones of Stonehenge were quarried. **Pentre Ifan**, a vast Neolithic burial chamber, is the most impressive of a number of cromlechs (tombs) that have survived. In the fifth and sixth centuries, early Christian missionaries began to arrive in western Wales. The most notable was St David, the patron saint of Wales, who founded St David's Cathedral in AD 550. It became an important place of pilgrimage – and two visits here were considered to be equal to one pilgrimage to Rome.

Norse invaders periodically attacked Pembrokeshire, colonising the most fertile lands in the south – and giving distinctive Viking names to outlying islands such as **Skomer** and **Grassholm**, now renowned for their rich birdlife. The Vikings were followed by the Normans, who arrived late in the 11th century and consolidated their hold on the south by building a line of fortifications through the heart of the county. Known as the **Landsker** (frontier) it effectively divided Pembroke into a Celtic, Welsh speaking north and a more racially mixed – eventually Anglicized, south. Largely English speaking, and less rugged than the north, the area south of the Landsker became known as 'Little England beyond Wales'. The difference is still evident today – in place names, church architecture and language.

Although coal and iron were mined in Pembrokeshire, today the main industries are agriculture and tourism. The **Pembrokeshire National Park** was established in 1952 and is one of the smallest National Parks, covering 240 sq miles (620 sq km). Disaster struck in 1996, when the oil tanker Sea Empress, hit the rocks spilling oil onto this unique coastline. Vast numbers of seabirds died and many beaches were smothered in oil. But the clean-up operation was successful and the pristine beaches and clear seas are now something close to heaven for water sports enthusiasts: surfers, windsurfers, kite surfers, sailors, kayakers – you name them, you'll find them here. You can even try coasteering, a mix of rock climbing, scrambling and swimming. The marine wildlife is thriving too – with huge colonies of puffins, kittiwakes, gannets and other seabirds on the islands, and dolphins, seals and porpoises easily spotted in the waters.

Newport (Trefdraeth) and around

Lovely little Newport makes a great base for exploring the northern part of Pembrokeshire. The town's small streets, which stretch either side of the A487, provide easy pedestrian access to the Pembrokeshire Coast Path to the north. Head south and you can walk up the distinctive, brooding hill known as **Carn Ingli** – or 'Hill of Angels' – which was once topped with an Iron Age hillfort. You can still see the outlines of 25 ancient houses; archeologists think around 150 people may have once lived here. The views from the top are great. There are more reminders of Newport's prehistoric past at **Carreg Coeltan**, a Neolithic burial chamber reached via Feidr Pen-y-Bont road. Inevitably it was once claimed to be the burial spot of King Arthur. The TIC has plenty of information on walks and cycle routes in the area.

Nevern

Around two miles east of Newport is the little village of **Nevern**, site of the fascinating church of St Brynach, which was founded in the sixth century. Dark yew trees line the

Pembrokeshire Coast Path

The Pembrokeshire Coast Path is a long-distance waymarked walking trail, which clings to the stunning coastline of the Pembrokeshire National Park. It stretches 186 miles (299 km) between Amroth in the south to St Dogmaels in the north. It takes in a National Nature Reserve, a Marine Nature Reserve and 17 Sites of Special Scientific Interest (SSSIs). Walking it gives you the best chance of seeing the wildflowers, sea birds and seals that inhabit coastal Pembrokeshire. There are some steep ascents and descents so some sections are quite challenging. The whole route can be walked in a couple of weeks, and individual sections can be done as day walks. If you want to walk the path do make sure you plan it carefully, checking tide times locally, working out how far you can comfortably walk in one day, booking accommodation in advance, and making sure you have good maps, boots etc. Going from north to south the route can be split into easy chunks.

Day 1 St Dogmaels to Newport (approx 16 miles) – the most challenging section of the walk (less fit walkers should do this over two days, staying overnight at Moylegrove).
Day 2 Newport to Goodwick (approx 13 miles) – clifftops and some minor roads (this can be done over two days, staying overnight at Dinas, near Pwllgwaelod).
Day 3 Goodwick to Trefin (approx 19 miles) – a long section over high clifftops (can be done over two days with an overnight stay at Pwll Deri).
Day 4 Trefin to Whitesands (approx 11 miles) – a very popular stretch, takes you past pretty Porthgain, with the remains of old industry and a great pub. If you want to stay overnight at St David's it's easiest to stop at Caerfai.
Day 5 Whitesands to Solva (approx 13 miles) – one of the most popular stretches, with no road walking, above Whitesands Bay and round to St Bride's Bay.
Day 6 Solva to Little Haven (approx 12 miles) – some road walking on

path, one of which (the second on the right) is known as the 'bleeding yew' on account of the reddish sap that oozes from it. Legend has it that a man was hanged from the tree for stealing a church plate. The churchyard is older than the church and beside the porch is an ancient stone known as the **Vitalianus Stone**, a fifth-century stone inscribed both in Latin and in Ogham (an Irish branch of Celtic then used in parts of Wales) and commemorating a British chieftain, or a Briton who served in the Roman army. The churchyard also contains the **Great Cross**, a Celtic Cross 13-ft high, probably carved in the 10th century. Inside the church is another bilingual stone, the Maglocunus Stone and a Celtic carved Cross Stone. From the church you can bear right and uphill to visit **Pentre Ifan**, a vast Neolithic burial chamber that is probably one of the finest in Wales.

Unclassified roads that stretch between Nevern and Cardigan bring you to hidden sections of stunning coastline. Head for Moylegrove and you can get to Ceibwr Bay, where you can walk a section of the Coastal Path or simply gaze at the dramatic cliffs and swooping sea birds. Further north, a little road leads from St Dogmaels to the lovely beach at Poppit Sands, then to a tranquil estuary and the headland of Cemaes Head.

Castell Henllys

Four miles east of Newport, just off the A487, is **Castell Henllys** ① *T01239 891319, www.castellhenllys.com, Easter-Oct daily 1000-1700, guided tours at 1130 and 1430, £3, £2 children, £8 family*, a fascinating reconstructed Iron Age village, built on the site of an original hillfort. A footpath through the woods takes you to the circle of this section, which takes you past Newgale Sands.

Day 7 Little Haven to Dale (approx 20 miles) – this long stretch could be split over two days, with a stop at Marloes.

Day 8 Dale to Neyland, by Milford Haven (approx 15.5 miles) – lower cliffs and quite a bit of road walking, involves a causeway crossing that can only be crossed at low tide.

Day 9 Neyland to Angle (approx 15.5 miles) – more road walking involved, can split into two days, with an overnight stop at Pembroke.

Day 10 Angle to Bosherston (approx 18 miles) – no road walking on this section which takes you past popular spots like Barafundle Bay and Stackpole Quay.

Day 11 Bosherston to Manorbier (approx 11 miles) – a very popular section and a good day walk, can be combined with a visit to Manorbier Castle.

Day 12 Manorbier to Amroth (approx 15 miles) – the last stretch if you've done it north to south, but worth doing over two days and stopping at the charming resort of Tenby, which is about half way along.

A couple of firms offer a baggage transport service – well worth considering unless you enjoy lugging a pack around. They are: **Pembrokeshire Discovery**, T01437 710720, www.pembrokeshire discovery.co.uk and **Tony's Taxis**, T01437 720931, www.tonystaxis.co.uk.

You can also use public transport to help do the walk or sections of it: T01437 776313, www.pembrokeshire greenways.co.uk. Maps that cover this area are OS Explorer OL 35/36 and Landranger 145, 157 and 158.

For further information covering everything from maps to where to stay, contact the **National Park Authority**, T0845 3457275, info@pembrokeshirecoast.org.uk, www.pembrokeshirecoast.org.uk.

Southwest Wales Pembrokeshire

thatched roundhouses, where smoking fires burn and informed staff give demonstrations of weaving and other crafts. This is a working archeological site and it is still being excavated – it's a great place for both children and adults.

Gwaun Valley (Cwm Gwaun)

This must be one of the least explored areas of Pembrokeshire and there's a lovely 'land that time forgot' feel to it; things change so slowly here that they still celebrate New Year (or Hen Galan) on 13 January, which is according to the ancient Julian calendar instead of the new fangled Gregorian one.

The Gwaun Valley is easily reached if you take the A487 from Newport towards Cardigan, and turn first right after the Golden Lion pub. A couple of miles further on there's a T-junction, where you turn right again and into the heart of this deep, wooded valley. Part way along you can turn off to visit lovely **Penlan-Uchaf gardens** ① *T01348 881388, Easter-Nov 0900-dusk, £2.50*, where there are 3 acres of award-winning landscaped grounds with views to die for – it's a great spot for tea and homemade cake too. Further along is exquisite **Pontfaen church** – a real ecclesiastical treasure. The church was founded in AD 540 but, after the Dissolution, was neglected and was almost ruined by the 19th century. However, it was later lovingly restored. In the churchyard are two pre-Conquest Latin crosses, while inside is a glistening icon painted by an Italian in 1902 – it's a copy of '*The Tabernacle of the Madonna of the Stars*' by Fra Angelico. On the road near the church is the blue-painted, and wonderfully time-warped, *Dyffryn Arms* (see Pubs, page 148).

Shortly after this you can take the B4313 left, to reach the eccentric village of **Rosebush**. It was once a slate-mining village but when the railway arrived the Victorian owners tried to turn it into a spa resort. Buildings were erected quickly in corrugated iron, but the visitors stayed away. The residents of this frontier style settlement remained and it feels as if little has changed in the intervening years. The proposed hotel became a pub – the *Tafarn Sinc* or *Zinc Inn* (see Pubs, page 146), the name is a reference to the fact it's made of corrugated iron. It's full of atmosphere. Outside is what remains of the railway station; the last train ran in 1949.

Fishguard (Abergwaun) and around

Fishguard is rarely regarded as anything more than a stop-off to and from the nearby ferry port serving Ireland. Its Lower Town was used extensively as a film location when Richard Burton made *Under Milk Wood* in the early 1970s and it attracts its fair share of Dylan Thomas fans.

The town was the location of one of Wales's most remarkable and historic battle victories; in 1797 an army of local women forced the surrender of French troops, the last invading army to land on the British mainland. Having arrived nearby at Carreg Wastad, legend has it that the invading troops mistook the traditional Welsh dress (black stovepipe hats and red flannel dresses) of the local women marching towards them for the outfit of British soldiers and instantly capitulated. One woman, pitchfork- wielding Jemima Nicholas, a 47-year-old cobbler, is known to have single-handedly captured 14 of the French soldiers; she is buried in the local church. At the time of writing, the Fishguard Tapestry depicting this episode is out of public view, but may be displayed during the school summer holidays at the junior school on West Street (ask at the TIC).

Halfway along the seafront is **OceanLab** ① *Goodwick, T01348 874737, www.ocean-lab.co.uk, Easter-Oct 1000-1700, Nov-Easter 1000-1600*, which features an exhibition gallery about sea and shore life and displays of fossils. Other facilities include a cyber café, soft play area for young children and coffee shop.

Fishguard to St David's

The stretch of coast between Fishguard and St David's is less commercialized than in the south and is better known for its rugged beauty and ancient landscape dotted with interesting little villages and beaches. For walkers, this stretch of the Pembrokeshire Coast Path (see box, page 136) is one of the most beautiful and remote; the path winds its way precariously over the cliffs, with secret coves tucked away beneath.

To the west of Fishguard, **Strumble Head**, with its lighthouse, is a good place for walking or for spotting migrating birds, seals, dolphins and even whales. Further down the coast, **Abercastell** is a tiny but charming fishing village with a few houses and a pub. The village's claim to fame is that in 1876 the first man to sail solo across the Atlantic in a fishing dory, landed here. Half a mile west of the village, just off the coastal path is Carreg Samson – a fine example of a Bronze Age burial chamber. Further south, you come to **Trefin**, the largest village on this stretch of coast. The nearby beach is easily accessible, and near the shore stands the ruin of Trefin Mill, abandoned in 1918 but immortalized in the famous Welsh poem by William Williams, *Melin Trefin*. Perhaps the loveliest village is nearby **Porthgain**, with its ivy-covered remains of its former brickworks. It boasts a lively community, an attractive harbour and a great pub, *The Sloop Inn* (see Eating, page 147). You can take boats out into the harbour to spot dolphins (see Activities and tours, page 149). The village grew to prominence in the mid-19th century as the port of export for slate and granite mined at nearby **Abereiddy**; the stretch of coast between the two is one of the most beautiful.

St David's (Tyddewi) and around

No visit to Pembrokeshire is complete without a trip to St David's, Britain's smallest city famed for its magnificent cathedral, founded in AD 550 by St David, who was born and baptized near here. The city is the most important religious site in Wales and has been a place of pilgrimage since the sixth century attracting saints, sinners and sightseers; although it gets extremely busy, it somehow never loses its air of tranquillity. It's a lovely place to stay, with plenty of decent accommodation, and some good pubs and restaurants.

St David's Cathedral ⓘ *T01437 720199, www.stdavidscathedral.org.uk, Mon-Sat 0800-1830, Sun 1230-1730, donations welcome, guided tours T01437 720691*, is one of the oldest in Britain. It is built on the spot St David selected for his monastery, an area known as *Glyn Rhosyn* in Welsh, meaning 'valley of the little marsh'; it would have been a wild, deserted spot but well hidden from raiders. Early pilgrims included William the Conqueror, who came here in 1081, and Henry II who visited twice in 1171 and 1172. You can still see St David's shrine, although it was damaged during the Reformation. Set in its own grassy hollow on the edge of the city, the cathedral is a delightful place to explore, with lots of tombs, statues and ornate carvings to examine.

The building you see today dates back to the late 12th century, although there were many later additions and alterations – an earthquake damaged the building around 1247 and the floor of the nave has a discernible slope. As you enter you are struck by the fine carved ceiling, made of Irish oak. It was built in the late 15th century to conceal restoration work, when the building looked in danger of collapse again. If you look carefully you can see several Green Men carved here – the attendants can help you spot them – they are an ancient pagan symbol, thought to be associated with fertility and harvest, but considered by some to represent evil. The carved misericords in the choir are also worth a look, and include a particularly vivid depiction of a man being sick over the side of a boat. The choir contains a stall reserved for the monarch, unique in Britain – the Queen being an automatic Canon of the cathedral. Behind the choir, the presbytery has a brilliantly coloured 15th-century ceiling, which was restored and repainted in the 19th century by Sir George Gilbert Scott.

Close to the cathedral is the **Bishop's Palace** ⓘ *T01437 720517, Mar-May, Oct daily 0930-1700; Jun-Sep daily 0930-1800; Nov-Mar Mon-Sat 0930-1600, Sun*

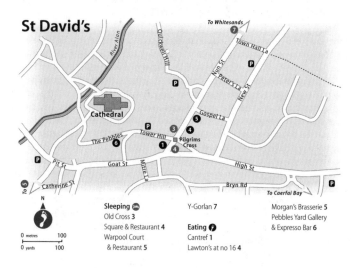

St David's

River Alan
Quitkwell Hill
To Whitesands 7
Town Hall La
Nun St
St Peter's La
New St
Cathedral
Gospel La
Tower Hill 3 4 5
The Pebbles 6
Pilgrims Cross 1 4
Pit St
Goat St
Mitre La
High St
Catherine St
To St
Bryn Rd
To Caerfai Bay

N

0 metres 100
0 yards 100

Sleeping	Eating	
Old Cross **3**	Y-Gorlan **7**	Morgan's Brasserie **5**
Square & Restaurant **4**		Pebbles Yard Gallery
Warpool Court	Cantref **1**	& Expresso Bar **6**
& Restaurant **5**	Lawton's at no 16 **4**	

Southwest Wales Pembrokeshire

5 of Pembrokeshire's best beaches

Whitesands, beautiful beach in a lovely setting with stunning walks, p140.
Newgale, exposed to the Atlantic gales, great waves for watersports, p140.
Broad Haven, magnificent stretch of sand with good facilities, p140
Marloes Sands, rugged and remote, with dramatic rock formations, p140
Barafundle, charming, sheltered cove, accessible from the Coast Path, p142

1100-1600, £2.50, £2 children, £7 family, CADW, a magnificent ruin, built between 1328-1347 by Bishop Henry de Gower, who pulled out all the architectural stops to create a building that reflected the power and wealth of the church – and the bishop. You can see the remains of many of the fine carvings, ornate windows and grand state rooms, and there is also an exhibition on the life of the palace.

St David's Peninsula

This is a good place for walking, with inlets and coves around every corner. The peninsula is also served by the **Celtic Coaster** bus. From the city you can walk south to the beach at **Caerfai** where the purple sandstone cliffs were quarried to provide masonry for St David's Cathedral. Just west of here is **St Non's Bay**, the spot at which St Non was said to have given birth to David – a spring suddenly appearing in the ground when he was born. There's a shrine here that still attracts pilgrims and the ruins of a 13th-century chapel, as well as a 20th-century chapel. Further round is the picturesque inlet of **Porthclais**, which was the port of the monastic community of St David's and supposedly the place where St David was baptized. Due west of St David's is the little harbour of **St Justinians** from where boats leave to **Ramsey Island** (see Activities, page 149), noted for its rich bird life, while the waters are great for spotting seals, whales and dolphins. Perhaps the most stunning beach on the peninsula, a couple of miles northwest of St David's, **Whitesands Bay** ① *£2 car parking, no dogs May-Sep*, is a clean, sandy stretch popular with surfers and windsurfers, with a couple of campsites nearby. If you follow the Coast Path north from here, you reach the small, secluded beach at **Porthmelgan**.

St Bride's Bay and the islands

To the south of St David's, the Coast Path takes you round the curve of St Bride's Bay, past some stunning scenery with plenty of camping and caravanning spots. The first place you come to is the picturesque little village of **Solva**, a beautiful rocky inlet providing a natural harbour for yachts and pleasure boats. In the 19th century it was a busy port where passenger services left for New York, today it has a number of little shops, art galleries and several good places to eat. Further round the bay are the endless sands of **Newgale** beach, fully exposed to the Atlantic winds, it is the longest beach on the bay and an excellent spot for all sorts of watersports. Further south, the lively holiday village of **Broad Haven** has a magnificent beach and some interesting rock formations while, tucked away nextdoor, **Little Haven** has a small attractive sandy cove and craggy harbour and is one of the centres for scuba diving in the area (see Activities, page 149). Out on the southern peninsula, there is a glorious clifftop walk, accessible from the National Trust car park (£2) at **Marloes**, from where you can reach the quieter sandy beach of Marloes Sands. The village of **Dale** is a popular watersports centre while Martins Haven, near Marloes, is the usual starting point for trips to the islands of Skomer, Skokholm and Grassholm (see below).

These offshore islands are nature reserves famed for their huge population of seabirds in the spring and summer months. The boats usually run from April to October, weather permitting. Contact the **Wildlife Trust West Wales** (WTWW) ① *To1239 621600* or **Dale Sailing Company** ① *To1646 601636, www.dale-sailing.co.uk*, for details.

Skomer is home to one of the most the most easily accessible of all seabird colonies in northwest Europe, and has been a National Nature Reserve (NNR) since 1959. Puffins and Manx shearwaters are the island's most famous residents, to be seen throughout the summer until August. There is a huge range of other wildlife including grey seals, which pup in September, the common porpoise and dolphins. The island also contains the remains of Iron Age huts and ancient field systems. To the south is **Skokholm**. Walkers may enjoy guided trips in the summer around this WTWW reserve to view the puffins, Manx shearwaters and storm petrels up close. Eleven miles off the coast, and the smallest of the three islands, is **Grassholm**, an RSPB reserve housing 35,000 breeding pairs of gannets. These give rise to the island's nickname the 'Wedding Cake' as, from a distance, it appears to be covered in a white icing. Landing is not allowed but boat trips can take you close to the island.

Haverfordwest (Hwlffordd) and around

The main transport hub and shopping centre of Pembrokeshire, Haverfordwest offers little in the way of tourist attractions, though there's a ruined castle and small museum and art gallery. The 12th-century castle was the focus around which the town developed, later becoming a prosperous port in the 17th and 18th centuries. If you head three miles east of the town, off the A40, you'll find **Picton Castle and Woodland Gardens** ① *The Rhos, To1437 751326, www.pictoncastle.co.uk, Apr-Sep Tue-Sun 1030-1700, £4.95, guided tours of castle between 1200-1600; gardens open Mar-Oct, honesty box*, a 13th-century castle set in 40 acres of beautiful grounds, including woodlands, ferns, a maze and a walled garden. The Walled Garden contains a large collection of culinary and medicinal herbs.

Scolton Manor Museum and Country Park ① *Spittal, off B4329 4 miles northeast of Haverfordwest, Museum To1437 731328, Easter-Oct daily 1030-1730; Park, To1437 731457 Apr-Oct 0900-1730, Nov-Mar 0900-1630, £2*, is an early Victorian manor house set in 60 acres of grounds, with a nature reserve. The museum concentrates on the history and natural history of Pembrokeshire and there are period furnished rooms in the house. There's a visitor centre, country trails, picnic sites and play areas.

Narbeth (Arbeth)

The town of Narbeth lies at the hub of the Landsker Borderlands. It was one of the homes of the Princes of Dyfed and is even mentioned in the *Mabinogion*, an early collection of Welsh folk tales. Among the art studios in town is the **Creative Café** ① *Spring Gardens, Narberth To1834 861651, Easter-Oct daily until 1730; otherwise Tue-Sun 1000-1700, www.thecreativecafe.co.uk*, a studio/café with a difference. Kids can enjoy painting designs on ready-made pottery, leave it to be glazed and collect in a couple of days (postal service available). There's also a coffeeshop.

Oakwood Park

Just to the west of Narbeth is **Oakwood Park** ① *Canaston Bridge, To1834 891373, www.oakwood-leisure.com, Easter-Sep 1000-1700, Jul-Aug until 2200, £13.75 adults, £10 children, £49 family*, Wales' answer to Alton Towers. Oakwood has a watercoaster, sky-coaster and large wooden rollercoaster. CC2000, Oakwood's indoor family entertainment centre is an all-weather complex including a Crystal Maze and a ten-pin bowling alley.

St Govan's Chapel

One of the most striking sights here is St Govan's Chapel, a tiny chapel squeezed into a cleft in the rocks. It's thought to be 13th century but could be earlier. St Govan, an Irish monk, was said to have been visiting Pembroke when he was attacked by pirates. The rock is said to have miraculously unfolded allowing him to hide. He spent many years living in this remote spot and is meant to be buried under the altar. A well here was said to offer miraculous cures for eye complaints and rheumatism. You can visit the chapel by a long stairway, but access is sometimes limited because it is within military grounds. Ask at the local TIC or ring T01646 662340 for details.

Pembroke (Penfro) and around

On Pembrokeshire's south coast is the pleasant, but rather uninspiring, market town of Pembroke, which developed after the building of a castle here in 1093 – the mightiest of the Norman castles in the south west of Wales. The heart of the town is the Main Street, an attractive jumble of Georgian and Victorian buildings that runs down from the fine castle – undoubtedly the main reason for visiting.

Pembroke Castle ① *T01646 681510, www.pembrokecastle.co.uk, daily Apr-Sep 1000-1800, Mar, Oct 0930-1700, Nov-Feb 1000-1600, £3, £2 children, £8 family,* was first built in 1093 by Roger de Montgomery, cousin of William the Conqueror. This first building was made of timber, but was strong enough to withstand a long siege from the Welsh. In 1204 work began to reconstruct the castle in stone, a task finished around 1247. In 1452 Jasper Tudor was granted the castle, and in 1457 his nephew, the future Henry VII and first Tudor king, was born here. During the Civil War the castle withstood another long siege, until the garrison surrendered – after which much of the building was destroyed on Cromwell's orders. Today the ruins you see have been restored. There's a Keep or Great Tower, a Norman Hall, dating from c1150-1170, and a spiral staircase leading to **Wogan's Cavern**, an unexpectedly large, dank cave that was used as a shelter as far back as the Palaeolithic Period, and continued intermittently into the Mesolithic age. There are re-enactments of historical events every weekend in the summer holidays and a café on site.

Pembroke to Tenby

South of Pembroke is a gloriously unspoiled coastline. The Stackpole Estate is owned by the National Trust and encompasses sheer cliffs and quiet beaches. **Stackpole Quay**, a tiny natural harbour, has a good tearoom (see Eating, page 147) and is a good starting point for walks on the cliffs. From here you can follow an easy path for half a mile over the clifftops to **Barafundle Bay**, a lovely stretch of sand and dunes. Footpaths continue to Stackpole Head, Broad Haven and Bosherston – where the rugged offshore rock formation known as Stack Rocks teems with birdlife, including a large colony of guillemots. Just inland, near Bosherston, are **Bosherston Lakes**, a series of man-made lakes created in the late 18th and early 19th centuries. They now support a range of wildlife, including otters, toads and kingfishers. Further west the land is owned by the MOD, within which lies the enigmatic **St Govan's Chapel**, tucked away in the cliffs (see box, page 142). The **Coastal Cruiser** bus service runs between Pembroke and Broadhaven, Stackpole and Lamphey, £3 return.

The A4139 south east of Pembroke takes you first to the ruined **Bishop's Palace** ① *Lamphey, T01646 672224, daily 1000-1700, £2.50, £2 children, £7 family, CADW.* This was the country retreat of the bishops of St David's and has everything from fishponds to orchards. Further along the road you come to a turning for Manorbier, where there's a lovely ruined castle overlooking a sandy beach. **Manorbier Castle** ① *Bus No 349, T01834 871317, Easter-Sep 0930-1730, £3.50, £1.50 children*, was the birthplace in 1146 of Giraldus Cambrensis, or Gerald of Wales, the medieval churchman who travelled widely through Wales and chronicled the country and its people.

East of Pembroke, off the A477, is **Carew Castle and Tidal Mill** ① *T01646 651782, www.carew castle.com, daily Easter-Oct 1000-1700, £3, £2 children, £8 family*. The castle was built by the Normans but altered and extended over the years, eventually becoming an Elizabethan country mansion. It's now ruined but is often used as the setting for events in summer. The Tidal Mill was built in Elizabethan times and was powered, as the name suggests, by the force of the tides. It is one of only three in Britain, and retains the original machinery.

Tenby (Dinbych y Pysgod) and around

Tenby must qualify as one of the most delightful seaside towns in Britain. Perched on a rocky promontory above endless sandy beaches, with a fringe of pastel-coloured buildings set around a cosy harbour, it has a genteel, but lively, charm. The town's mix of award-winning beaches, winding medieval streets, and busy bars and

Southwest Wales Pembrokeshire

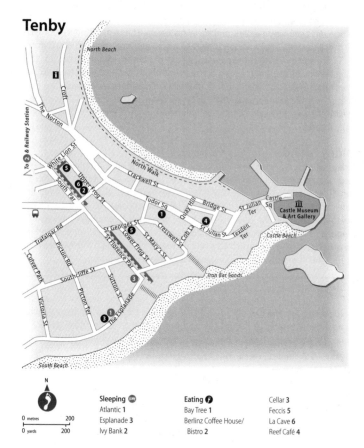

Tenby

Sleeping 🛏	**Eating** 🍴	Cellar **3**
Atlantic **1**	Bay Tree **1**	Feccis **5**
Esplanade **3**	Berlinz Coffee House/	La Cave **6**
Ivy Bank **2**	Bistro **2**	Reef Café **4**

0 metres   200
0 yards   200

restaurants allow it to appeal to a wide range of people, whether young surfers, city slickers on a weekend break or families on holiday. It's also an important stop on the Pembrokeshire Coast Path, and there's plenty of accommodation for weary walkers.

The town's Welsh name means 'Little Fort of Fishes'. It grew up around the Norman castle, first mentioned in records in 1153, the remains of which are perched on the headland. In the 13th century the town was partly enclosed by protective walls, which were later extended and strengthened. Tenby gradually developed into a thriving port and, although trade declined during the Civil Wars, enjoyed a revival in the 18th century as a salt water spa. The arrival of the railway in the 19th century attracted large numbers of visitors keen to enjoy the health-giving benefits of the seaside. It became a fashionable Victorian resort and attracted a wide range of people, from the naturalist PH Gosse to artists and authors like Lewis Carroll, George Elliot and JMW Turner.

In the heart of the town is **St Mary's Church**, with its 152-ft spire. Among those commemorated is Robert Recorde, a mathematician born in Tenby circa 1510, who was said to have invented the 'equals' sign. On Quay Hill is the **Tudor Merchant's House** ① *To1834 842279, Easter-Oct Mon-Fri, Sun 1100-1700, £2.20, £1.10 child, £5.50 family, National Trust,* one of the oldest buildings in town dating back to the 15th century. A former wealthy merchant's house, it is on three floors. You can see the remains of 18th-century seccos on the walls (they're like frescoes but painted onto dry rather than wet plaster) and see how the family would have lived. It was a family home until 1915 so there's plenty of atmosphere.

In the remains of the castle is the **Museum and Art Gallery** ① *To1834 842809, www.tenbymuseum.free-online.co.uk, daily 1000-1700, £2.50.* This includes exhibits on the town's geology, maritime and social history, and has a permanent art collection which includes works by locally bred artists Augustus and Gwen John and Nina Hamnett.

To the east of Tenby is the pleasant village of **Amroth**, with its sheltered, south-facing beach. It's the end (or start) of the **Pembrokeshire Coast Path** (see box, page 136). Further east is the sandy beach of **Wiseman's Bridge**, which was used for the D-Day rehearsals in 1944, supervised by Sir Winston Churchill himself. At low tide it is possible to walk to neighbouring **Saundersfoot**, one of the area's most popular family resorts.

Caldey Island

Caldey Island, just a few miles south of the mainland, has been a monastic settlement since around the sixth century and is now a popular destination for **boat trips** ① *To1834 844453, www.caldey-island.co.uk, Easter-Oct Mon-Sat, £8,* from Tenby. In the early Middle Ages a Benedictine order founded a priory here, but it was deserted after the Dissolution. The island is now home to a small community of monks of the Reformed Cistercian Order, who manufacture a range of products including perfumes and toiletries inspired by the island's wild flowers, gorse and herbs. The abbey church is open, and there's a little museum and tea garden on the island.

● Sleeping

Newport and around *p135*
C **Cnapan Hotel**, East St, T01239 820575, www.online-holidays.net/cnapan. Well established, popular 4-star hotel, noted for its good food. Closes during the winter.
C **Gellifawr Hotel and Cottages**, Pontfaen, Gwaun Valley, T01239 820343, www.gelli fawr.co.uk. Lovingly restored 19th-century stone farmhouse and cottages in tranquil setting. Comfortably furnished, spacious

rooms. Friendly bar and excellent restaurant.
C **Llysmeddyg**, East St, T01239 820008, www.llysmeddyg.com. Lovely large, airy rooms in this clean, friendly guesthouse. Breakfast from local and organic foods, with imaginative veggie options.

Self-catering
Tregynon Farmhouse and Country Cottages, Gwaun Valley, T01239 820531,

www.tregynon-cottages.co.uk. Award-winning self catering cottages, with great views of the Gwaun Valley. Wonderful base for walking.

Fishguard and around *p138*
B Fishguard Bay Hotel, Quay Rd, Goodwick, T01348 873571, www.smoothound.co.uk/hotels/fishguard.htm. Originally a mansion converted to accommodate passengers on the mail steamers to Ireland, this renovated grande dame of an hotel is comfortable and rather old-fashioned in its faded elegance and the views of Fishguard Bay are stunning.
B Three Main Street, 3 Main St, T01348 874275. This excellent restaurant just off Market Square has 3 stylish rooms and the breakfasts are great.
C Glanmoy Lodge Guesthouse, Tref-Wrgi Road, Goodwick, T01348 874333, www.glanmoylodge.co.uk. 10 mins' walk from the port, comfortable and clean en suite rooms in a secluded location. Chance to watch badgers at night.
C Ivy Bridge Guesthouse, Drim Mill, Dyffryn, Goodwick, T01348 875366, www.ivybridge.cwc.net. Popular B&B with an indoor swimming pool. Evening meals if required.
E Hamilton Backpackers Lodge, 21-23 Hamilton St, T01348 874797, www.hamiltonbackpackers.co.uk. Just a 1-min walk from the tourist office. 2 doubles as well as dorm accommodation available.

Camping
Fishguard Bay Caravan and Camping Park, Garn Gelli, Fishguard, T01348 811415, www.fishguardbay.com; Mar-Dec.

St David's and around *p139, map p139*
A-C Trevaccoon, Llanrhian, near St Davids, T01348 831438, www.trevaccoon.co.uk. Restored Georgian house with crisp, comfy rooms. Lots of fresh flowers and fluffy towels.
B Crug-Glas Country House, near Abereiddy, T01348 831302, www.crug-glas.co.uk. On large working farm, with carefully designed, 5-star comfortable rooms and en suite bathrooms. Luxurious base for exploring the coast.
B Old Cross Hotel, Cross Sq, T01437 720387, www.oldcrosshotel.co.uk. Rather old fashioned but comfortable hotel in the centre of St Davids. Closed Christmas-early

Feb. Good food and pleasant garden.
B Warpool Court Hotel, T01437 720300, www.warpoolcourthotel.com. Pay the extra for a sea view if you can, at this comfortable, friendly hotel on the edge of town. Relaxing gardens and 3,000 exquisite hand-painted tiles dotted all over the hotel.
C The Square, Cross Sq, T01437 720333, www.thesquarecafegallery.co.uk. Closed Jan and Feb. Small but cool B&B with stripped wooden floors, sleek chrome fittings and lush pot plants. Egyptian cotton sheets on the beds and imaginative breakfasts.
C Y-Gorlan, 77 Nun St, T01437 720837, www.stdavids.co.uk/gorlan. Clean and comfortable B&B. 2 rooms have a view over Whitesands Bay, as does the large residents' lounge. Healthy options for breakfast.

Camping
Campsites in the area include:
F Caerfai Farm Camp Site, close to Caerfai Bay, T01437 720548, www.caerfai.co.uk. Toilets and showers, May-Sep.
F Newgale Camp Site, Wood Farm, Newgale, T01437 710253, www.newgale campingsite.co.uk. Easter-Oct. Camp in the field just across the road from gorgeous Newgale beach.

Haverfordwest and around *p141*
A-B Wolfscastle Country Hotel, Wolfscastle, near Haverfordwest, T08719 958290, www.wolfscastle.com. Recently refurbished hotel, well placed for exploring St David's or the Preseli Hills. The restaurant's noted for its fresh fish dishes.
C The County Hotel, Salutation Sq, T01437 762144, www.countyhotel.com. Reasonably cosy en suite rooms in family-run hotel.
C Lower Haythog Farm, Spittal, near Haverfordwest, T01437 731279. Cosy dairy farm with clean, comfortable rooms and great farmhouse breakfasts.
D College Guesthouse, 93 Hill St, St Thomas Green, T01437 763710, www.college guesthouse.com. Decent B&B in former Baptist college about 5 mins' walk from town centre.

Pembroke and around *p142*
A Lamphey Court Hotel, Lamphey, T08719 958236, www.lampheycourt.co.uk. Imposing colonnaded mansion with good leisure

facilities including an indoor pool and 2 tennis courts.

C **Portclew House**, Freshwater East, T01646 672800, www.portclewhouse.co.uk. Listed Georgian building with large rooms, set in its own grounds.

C **Poyerston Farm**, Cosheston, near Pembroke T01646 651347, www.poyerston farm.co.uk. Lovely clean and comfortable rooms on this friendly working farm. Flowery fabrics and traditional touches throughout. Breakfast is taken in the conservatory.

C **Williams of Solva**, 10 Main St, Solva, T01437 729000, www.williamsofsolva.co.uk. High quality B&B at this Georgian house. Egyptian cotton sheets, en suite facilities and good organic food for breakfast.

Tenby and around p143, map p143
A **Penally Abbey**, Penally, near Tenby, T0871 9958254, www.penally-abbey.com. Secluded country house on the site of an ancient abbey, set in 5 ha of grounds. Lots of antiques and period furniture. Conveniently close to an 18-hole golf course.

A-B **Atlantic Hotel**, The Esplanade, T01834 842881, www.atlantic-hotel.uk.com. Traditional flowers and flounces at the swishest hotel along the seafront. Worth paying a bit extra to get a sea view. 2 restaurants, spa, sauna and pool.

B **The Esplanade Hotel**, The Esplanade, T01834 842760, www.esplanadetenby.co.uk. Traditional seafront hotel, cheaper but less luxurious than the Atlantic.

C **Ivy Bank**, Harding St, T01834 842311, www.ivybanktenby.co.uk. 4-star B&B in Victorian house. All rooms en suite and non-smoking.

C **Wychwood House**, Penally, near Tenby, T01834 844387. 3 large, en suite rooms and lovely views at this attractive B&B.

⊙ Eating

Newport and around p135
♙♙♙ **Gellifawr**, Pontfaen, Gwaun Valley, T01239 820343, www.gellifawr.co.uk. Excellent restaurant, with traditional stone and wood burning fire, serving à la carte and bistro meals using fresh local produce. Friendly and welcoming.

♙♙♙ **Llysmeddyg**, East St, T01239 820008, Sun lunch 1200-1430, daily for dinner 1900- 2200; opens daily for lunch Mar- Oct 1200- 1430, booking advised. Fresh seasonal produce. Dishes such as lamb cutlets on a bed of pernod, spinach and roasted garlic. Veggie options available. Desserts include grilled peaches with rosemary and vanilla ice cream.

♙♙♙ **Tregynon Farmhouse Restaurant**, Gwaun Valley, T01239 820531, Fri-Sat from 1930, booking required. Fresh local produce served at this farmhouse in the peaceful Gwaun valley. 4-course meal with meat, fish and vegetarian options.

♙♙♙-♙♙ **Cnapan**, East St, T01239 820575, Mon, Wed-Sat 1200-1400, and 1845-2045. Country house atmosphere at this well-established restaurant serving modern British dishes with a twist. Fresh local produce is used and they make their own bread. You might find Welsh beef, seafood chowder or spicy fish cakes on the menu. Plenty of choices for veggies too. Desserts include an apricot and almond tart.

♙♙-♙ **Café Fleur**, Market St, T01239 820131, Wed-Sat 1030-1700, Sun 1100-1500, Fri-Sat from 1930. Good café/restaurant serving a wide range of sweet and savoury pancakes, paninis and more substantial meals in the evening. Plenty of veggie dishes.

♙♙-♙ **The Golden Lion**, East St, T01239 820321, food daily 1200-1400, 1830-2100. Popular pub serving good bar meals. Also has rooms – some 2-star, some 4-star.

♙ **Old Post Office Tea Rooms**, Rosebush, T01437 532205, Tue-Sun lunchtime and Tue-Sat 1830-2300. Pretty little tea rooms tucked away behind the distinctive corrugated iron buildings of Rosebush.

♙ **Penlan-Uchaf Gardens**, Gwaun Valley, 5 miles from Newport, T01348 881388, Mar-Nov daily until dusk. Outstanding views across the valley from the tea rooms of this garden. Homemade cakes and hot drinks, and ploughman's lunches in winter.

♙ **Tafarn Sinc**, Rosebush, T01437 532214. Tue-Sat 1200-1400, 1800-2100 and Sun lunch. Atmospheric pub serving traditional dishes like faggots in gravy or Glamorgan sausages.

Fishguard p138
♙♙♙ **Three Main Street**, 3 Main St, T01348 874275. An excellent restaurant with rooms overlooking the Bay, serving modern European cuisine with its focus on top-class seafood, set in a Georgian townhouse. Beautiful interiors and fresh flowers.

¶ **Royal Oak**, Market Sq, T01348 872514, Oct-Easter daily 1200-1430 and Tue-Sat 1800-2100; Easter-Oct daily 1200-2100. Near the town hall, this old inn has a brass memorial plaque outside which gives information about the invasion and has memorabilia dating back to the actual event – including musket balls and muskets. Great pub food, folk music nights on Tue and live music on Fri and Sat.

St David's and around *p139, map p139*

¶¶¶ **Lawton's at No 16**, 16 Nun St, T01437 729220, Mon-Sat in summer 1800-2130, check for hours in winter. Stylish contemporary restaurant offering a modern twist to traditional favourites. Starters might include crab and gruyère tart, and you might find mains such as organic beef on horseradish suet pudding with red wine sauce. There are vegetarian choices and delicious desserts like sticky toffee pudding.

¶¶¶ **The Old Pharmacy**, Main St, Solva, T01437 720005, daily from 1730, booking recommended. Best place to eat in the area, with lots of local dishes. Several veggie choices and selection of desserts. You don't have to have a main meal – dessert and coffee in the garden is fine.

¶¶¶ **Warpool Court Hotel**, T01437 720300. For formal dining in St David's come to the restaurant of this comfortable hotel. Mains like guinea fowl casserole, or roast teal and several veggie options.

¶¶¶-¶¶ **Morgan's Brasserie**, 20 Nun St, T01437 720508, Easter-Sep daily from 1800, otherwise Thu-Sat from 1900. Booking essential at this popular brasserie. Blackboard menu for fresh fish dishes, while other mains might include salt marsh lamb and caramelized onion and red pepper tarte tatin.

¶¶¶-¶¶ **The Shed**, Porthgain, T01348 831518, daily in school holidays from 1000-1600 for teas and lunches and 1800 for dinner; otherwise Wed-Sun. This bistro/tea room serves snacks, light meals and cream teas, as well as set meals. Lots of fish, booking recommended.

¶¶ **The Nest Bistro**, Grove Place, Little Haven, T01437 781728, daily from 1900, closes in winter. Lots of fish on the menu here. Mains cost around £13-15, with veggie choices slightly cheaper.

¶¶ **Williams Restaurant and Deli**, courtyard off Main St, Solva T01437 720802, Oct-Easter, Thu-Sun 1230-1530, 1830-2030, Easter-Oct also Wed. You're advised to book if you want dinner at this cosy restaurant which serves dishes like mussels in white wine, or salmon and sea bass fishcakes. Veggie options available and lots of Thai influenced dishes.

¶¶-¶ **The Sloop Inn**, Porthgain, T01348 831449, food daily breakfasts 0930-1130, bar meals 1200-1430, 1800-2130. Dating back to 1743, this great inn serves a good range of bar meals, and pricier specials with lots of fresh fish and lamb shanks – around £13. Maritime theme inside with old ropes and floats. Serves real ales.

¶ **Cantref**, 22/23 Cross Sq, T01437 720422, 1100-1430, 1830-2100, closed Fri and in winter. Good choice for old favourites like jacket potatoes and burgers, as well as filled Yorkshire puds and veggie dishes.

¶ **Pebbles Yard Gallery and Espresso Bar**, The Pebbles, T01437 720122, daily 1000-1730. Relaxed contemporary café above a gift shop, with outside seating area. Good for filled pitta breads, sandwiches, cakes and coffee.

¶ **The Square**, Cross Sq, Tue-Sun 1030-1700, closed Jan-Feb. Lovely little café, hung with the owner's artworks and serving cakes, light lunches and many varieties of sandwich (even peanut butter and tomato).

Haverfordwest and around *p141*

¶¶¶ **Stone Hall**, Welsh Hook, T01348 840212, Tue-Sat 1900-2130, closes Jan-Feb. Small country inn serving French influenced food with fresh Welsh produce. There's a good wine list, too.

¶¶ **George's**, 24 Market St, T01437 766683, Mon-Sat 1200-1700, Fri-Sat also 1900-2100. Established eatery offering good value lunches, real ales and wines and evening meals such as lemon sole or veggie crêpes.

Pembroke and around *p142*

¶¶-¶ **Renaissance Bar One**, Main St, T01646 687895, Mon-Thu 1000-1700, Fri 1000-2300, Sat 1000-late. Lively bar/bistro serving drinks, and Mediterranean style light meals and salads during the day, as well as more substantial dishes in the evening.

¶ **Boathouse Tearoom**, Stackpole Quay, T01646 672058, daily 1030-1730, 1200-1530, closes Nov-Easter but sometimes open from Boxing Day for 2 weeks. Lovely licensed tea room close to beautiful Barafundle Bay. Homemade cakes, filled baguettes and jacket potatoes as well as imaginative dishes like tomato and chive tart with feta.

Henry's Coffee Shop, Main St, T01646 622293, Mon-Sat 0900-1700, also Sun Easter-Sep 1100-1600. Hidden away at the back of a gift shop this tea shop caters for those just wanting slices of cake, or light meals during the day.

Rowlies, 2 Main St, T01646 686172, Mon-Wed 0900-2000, Thu-Sat 0900-2100. Award-winning fish and chips that you can take away or sit in and eat (sit down meals stop 1hr before closing).

Tenby *p143, map p143*

The Cellar, The Esplanade, T01834 845566, daily 1200-1430, 1800-2200. Bistro of the swish Atlantic Hotel (see p146) offering modern Welsh dishes. If you fancy something more formal try dining in The Carrington, also in the Atlantic Hotel, which has 4-course meals for £18.

La Cave, Upper Frog St, T01834 843038, daily from 1830. Good wine bar/bistro offering a good range of veggie dishes as well as meaty mains that range in price from £8.95 to £15.95 (for tournados).

The Reef Restaurant, St Julian St, T01834 845258, daily in summer 1000-2200, winter Wed-Thu from 1830, Fri-Sat 1200-1430 and from 1830, Sun 1200-1600. Lively Mediterranean style restaurant with wooden tables and lots of warm terracotta paint. Dishes like lemon sole or lobster thermidor.

The Bay Tree, Tudor Sq, T01834 843516. daily 1200-1400 and from 1800; summer daily from 1200-2200. One of the most popular of the mid-range places to eat, wide range of meat dishes and plenty of veggie options.

Berlinz Coffee House/Bistro, Upper Frog St, T01834 842143, daily 1000-1700 and 1800-2230. Lots of pasta dishes, steaks and chicken at this café/bistro.

Feccis, Upper Frog St. Well-established Italian ice cream parlour, where you can settle down to a huge knickerbocker glory, or buy a cone to slurp on the beach. Also have a fish and chip shop on Lower Frog St.

Pubs, bars and clubs

Newport and around *p135*

Dyffryn Arms, Pontfaen, daily 1100-2300, winter 1200-2300. Fantastic old pub untouched by the 20th, let alone 21st century. Bessie, the landlady, whose family has owned it since 1845, serves beer poured into jugs from behind a serving hatch. Simple living room lined with seats and a real fire in winter.

Tafarn Sinc, Rosebush, T01437 532214. Red corrugated iron exterior hides a great little pub inside, with sawdust on the floor, old settles and lots of old photos. Real ales.

Fishguard *p138*

Ship Inn, Newport Rd, Lower Town, Cluttered yet cosy, this rather eccentric little inn is a great place to while away the hours.

St David's and around *p139, map p139*

Druidston Hotel, Druidston T01437 781221. Bohemian hotel and bar high up on the cliffs with great views.

Farmers Arms, Goat St, T01437 720328. The liveliest and most popular pub in St David's. Serves real ales and has a garden. Bar meals available lunchtimes and evenings.

Haverfordwest *p141*

The Fishguard Arms, Old Bridge Close, T01437 768123, Mon-Fri 1200-1400, and Thu-Sat 1900-2200; Sun 1200-1400. Excellent food at reasonable prices and real ales in a friendly atmosphere with live music (jazz, folk, soul) at weekends.

Pembroke and around *p142*

The Watermans Arms, 2 The Green, T01646 682718, food 1200-1430, 1800-2130 in winter; in summer 1200-2200. Situated just over the bridge, this pub has a veranda where you can sit and look over the water nursing a pint or eating one of their bar meals.

Festivals and events

May/early Jun St Davids Cathedral Festival, annual classical music festival, T01437 720271, www.stdavidscathedral.org.uk.
Jul Fishguard International Music Festival, T01348 873612, week long classical and popular music festival.

Aug Pembrokeshire County Show, County showground, Haverfordwest, T01437 764331, 3-day agricultural show in mid-Aug.
Sep Tenby Arts Festival, annual week-long music and arts festival, T01834 84229, www.tenbyartsfest.com.

▲▲ Activities and tours

Boat trips
Porthgain Boat Trips, Quayside, Porthgain, T01348 831518, www.porthgainboats. ndo.co.uk. Coastal cruises and fishing trips on small, traditional boat from Apr-Nov. 1hr dolphin search trip. Times vary, so check.
Thousand Islands Expeditions, Cross Sq, St Davids, T01437 721721, www.thousand islands.co.uk. RSPB cruises to Ramsey Island wildlife reserve, opportunity to land on the islands and chance to see various sea birds. £14 adults, trips at 1000 and 1300 daily. Also run sea trips to watch basking sharks, pilot whales and dolphins, £50.
Voyages of Discovery, 1 High St, St Davids, T0800 854367, www.ramseyisland.co.uk, whale and dolphin watching May-Sep; tours of the coast, £18 adults, Easter-Nov daily.

Cycling
The western section of the long-distance **Celtic Trail** (see box, p34) runs through Pembrokeshire; information from celtic-trail@tsww.com. For information on general cycling in Pembrokeshire, the *Freewheeling Pembrokeshire* pack is available from TICs.
Mikes Bikes, 17 Prendergast, Haverfordwest, cycle hire for all the family, Mon-Sat.
Newport Bike Hire, from Wholefoods of Newport, East St, Newport, T01239 820773, hire of a range of mountain bikes, children's bikes, helmets. Also have maps.

Diving
There are several diving centres/ schools in Pembrokeshire:
Celtic Diving, Main St, Goodwick T01348 874752, www.celticdiving.co.uk. Courses in snorkelling, scuba and specialist courses.
Dive Pembrokeshire, The Old School House, Little Haven, T01437 781117, www.dive pembrokeshire.com. SSI and PADI training centre, dive charters and specialist courses.
Pembrokeshire Dive Charters, Neyland Marina, T01646 602941, www.gopdc.co.uk.

Dive charters and courses.
St David's Scuba Diving Centre, Caerfai Bay Rd, St Davids, T01437 721788, www.dive wales.com. Boat charters, dive school, scuba courses and holiday packages.
West Wales Divers, Hasguard Cross, near Little Haven, T01437 781457, www.westwales divers.co.uk. Diving gear for sale and hire.

Horse riding
East Nolton Riding Stables, Nolton, Haverfordwest, T01437 710360, www.eastnolton.com. Riding and trekking for all abilities, also have accommodation.
Sycamore Ranch Western Riding Centre, Llawhaden, Narberth, T07079 308941, www.sycamoreranch.com. Western style treks from 2 hrs to a full day. Pre book.

Outdoor activities
Sealyham Activity Centre, Wolfcastle, Haverfordwest, T01348 840763, www.sealy ham.com. Run courses from 1-5 days in kayaking, surfing, rock climbing, coasteering or dinghy sailing. Pre booking needed.
Tyf Adventure, 1 High St, St Davids, and 16 Julian St, Tenby, T0800 132588, T01437 721611, www.tyf.com. Offer coasteering, surfing, kayaking and climbing – taster sessions, ½ day, full day and longer programmes available.

Sailing
Solva Sailboats, 1 Maes-y-Forwen, Solva, T01437 720972, www.solva.net/ solvasailboats. 2-hr taster sailing sessions, accompanied sails and longer courses in dinghy and keelboat sailing. Powerboat courses also available.

Surfing
Ma Simes Surf Hut, 28 High St, St Davids, T01437 720433, www.masimes.co.uk and www.whitesandssurfschool.co.uk. Surf hire and surfing lessons, on Whitesands beach, also sell surfing kit. From £20 for 2 ½ hrs.
Newsurf, Newgale, T01437 721398, www.newsurf.co.uk, daily surf reports T01437 720698, hire out and sell surf skis, surfboards, body boards and wet suits, and also offer instruction.
West Wales Wind, Surf and Sailing, Dale, T01646 636642, www.surfdale.co.uk. Variety of watersports for all levels – from ½ day

windsurfing and catamaran sailing, to full-week courses. Also offer powerboat courses and have a surf school. Equipment for hire.

Walking

See box Pembrokeshire Coast Path, p136. There are plenty of opportunities to walk short sections of the route, using buses (summer) to get back to your starting point – details of the **Poppit Rocket**, **Strumble Shuttle** and **Celtic Coaster** bus services are available from TICs or www.greenways.co.uk.
Pembrokeshire Discovery, www.pembroke shirediscovery.co.uk. Guided walking tours.
Pembrokeshire Greenways Holidays, T01834 862109/861975, www.greenways holidays.com. Offer walking packages with luggage transfer, as well as self-guided walks using public transport – a special *Walk and Ride* leaflet is available T01437 776313.

⊙ Transport

Fishguard *p138*
Boat

Fishguard's ferry terminal is in **Goodwick** (Wdig) about a mile from the town centre and is served by rail and bus connections. **Stena Line** ferries (T0870 5707070, www.stena line.com), operates 2 types of vessel between **Rosslare** in Ireland and **Fishguard**: a high speed catamaran which completes the crossing in just under 2 hrs (Apr-mid Sep) and a conventional superferry which completes the journey in about 3 ½ hrs. Buses usually meet ferries. A taxi (T01348 873774 or 875129) into town costs around £3-5.

Bus

Buses stop in Market Sq. **Richards Brothers** bus No 411 runs to **Haverfordwest** every 2 hrs (£3.40, 1½ hrs) and **St David's** every hr (£2.30, 50 mins); bus No 412 runs hourly to Haverfordwest and **Cardigan** (£2.50, 45 mins). The **Strumble Shuttle** runs during summer to **Strumble Head**, **Trefin**, **Porthgain** and **Abereiddy**.

Train

Fishguard train station is next to the ferry terminal on Quay Rd. Currently, there is a twice daily service to and from **London Paddington** (£45, 5 hrs).

St David's *p139, map p139*

Buses stop at the corner of New St and High St. **Richards Brothers** bus No 411 runs to **Haverfordwest** every hr (£3.40, 45 mins) and to **Fishguard** (£2.30, 50 mins). The **Puffin Shuttle** runs during summer along the coast to **Milford Haven**. The **Celctic Coaster** runs around **St David's Peninsula**.

Haverfordwest *p141*

Richards Brothers bus No 411 runs to **Fishguard** every 2 hrs (£3.40, 1½ hrs), **St David's** every hr (£3.40, 45 mins) and **Cardigan** every hr (£2.50, 45 mins). **First Cymru** bus No 349 runs hourly to **Pembroke** (£2.40, 45 mins).

The train station is a 10-min walk east of the town centre. There are up to 7 daily services link the town with **Swansea** (£11, 2 hrs), **Cardiff** (£15, 2 hrs 45 mins) and **London Paddington** (£45, 5 hrs).

Pembroke *p142*

Buses stop on Main St except for buses to **Pembroke Dock** which leave from near the castle entrance on Westgate Hill. **First Cymru** No 349 runs hourly to **Tenby** (£2.10, 45 mins) and **Haverfordwest** (£2.40, 45 mins). **National Express** coaches run to **Swansea** (2 daily, £9, 1 hr 45 mins), **Carmarthen** (£5, 1 hr) and **Tenby** (£3.50, 15 mins).

Trains run 4-6 times daily to **Tenby** (£3.10, 35 mins) and **Carmarthen** (£5.30, 1 hr 15 mins) and **Swansea** (£8.20, 1 hr 50 mins).

Tenby *p143, map p143*

First Cymru bus No 349 runs to **Haverfordwest** (£2.30, 40 mins) and **Pembroke** (£3.50, 15 mins). **National Express** coaches run 3 times daily to **Carmarthen** (£5.50, 40 mins), **Pembroke** (£3.50, 15 mins) and **Swansea** (£9, 1 hr 40 mins).

Several trains daily run to **Swansea** (£8.60, 1½ hrs) and **Pembroke** (£3.10, 35 mins).

⊙ Directory

Internet Public internet access is available at **Fishguard TIC** in the CyberCafe, £2 per ½ hr. **Tenby library**, Greenhill Rd, Mon-Fri 0930-1300, 1400-1700, Sat 0930-1230 has free access as does **Newport Library**, Bridge St, Mon 1400-1700, Wed 1000-1300, Fri 1000-1200, 1400-1700.

Mid Wales

⁞ Footprint features

Introduction

Mid Wales is the place to come if you really want to escape the crowds. It encompasses a variety of landscapes, including the southern part of the Snowdonia National Park, where Cadair Idris and its surrounding peaks provide wild and challenging walking. There are gentler walks in the east, where towns like Knighton give ready access to the Offa's Dyke Path, which runs along the border with England.

It is here that you'll find the Wells towns, a cluster of Victorian spa towns that might have lost their original lustre but still retain an air of faded grandeur. And then there's Rhayader, gateway to the Elan Valley – the lakeland of Wales, with enormous reservoirs that can be easily explored on foot or by bike.

Rhayader is also a great place for wildlife watching, its surrounding hills now home to a thriving population of red kites – distinctive birds of prey that have all but disappeared from the rest of Britain. Remote farms operate as feeding stations and you can watch from hides as hundreds of kites swoop down to feed.

There are more wildlife-watching opportunities along the coast, where plenty of operators run boat trips that give you the chance to see dolphins, porpoises and seabirds. It's along this stretch of coastline that you'll find places like Harlech, famed for its well preserved castle; Aberystwyth, famed for its university; and fishing villages like Aberaeron and New Quay which are less well known but are charming all the same.

Mid Wales

★ **Don't miss...**

1 **Harlech** Walk barefoot on the soft sands or visit the stunning castle, page 154.

2 **Centre for Alternative Technology** Go green, page 158.

3 **Dolphin watching** Take a boat trip, page 171.

4 **Powis Castle** See how the rich lived, page 173.

5 **Red kites** Drop in for feeding time at Gigrin Farm, page 176.

6 **Abergwseyn Pass** Explore Mid-Wales' wild beauty, page 178.

South Snowdonia National Park

→ *Colour map 4, grid C3-4*

Anyone who thinks the wildest parts of Wales are to be found in northern Snowdonia should think again. It is the southern part of the National Park, in Mid Wales, that boasts brooding Cadair Idris – the mountain that both horrified and inspired Romantic painters and poets – as well as the rough and empty Rhinogs, east of Harlech. Cadair Idris, or the Chair of Idris, was famously painted by Richard Wilson, and is a distinctive mountain on which survive rare alpine plants. The Rhinogs might not attract much attention, being below 2,500 ft, but they still present some challenging walking – and are where Welsh walkers come when they want to escape the crowds that flock north to Snowdon. South Snowdonia is also etched with an almost unbroken stretch of superb sandy beaches, as well as historic towns like Harlech on the coast, and Machynlleth – once considered a likely capital of Wales and just outside the National Park. ▸▸ *For Sleeping, Eating and other listings, see pages 158-162.*

Ins and outs

Getting there and around The M4 from the south links with the A470 to Dolgellau and close to Machynlleth, while the northern stretch of the A470, linked to both the A55 and A5, joins the A496 which runs along the coast. Machynlleth and Harlech are both hubs for **trains** and **buses**, and there are good road links throughout. Both train and bus services run along the Cambrian Coast, and to Machynlleth, making travel between main centres relatively easy. The interior is most easily explored by car, although areas like the Rhinogs are not traversed by roads and must be explored on foot or bike. ▸▸ *For further details, see Transport, page 161. See also North Snowdonia National Park, page 186.*

Information Harlech ① *High St, T01766 780658, Easter-Oct daily 0930-1730, www.harlech-i.com, www.harlech-tourism.co.uk.* **Dolgellau** ① *Eldon Square, T01341 422888, tic.dolgellau@eyri-npa.gov.uk, Easter-Oct daily 1000-1800, Nov-Easter Sat- Sun 1000-1700.* **Barmouth** ① *Station Rd, T01341 280787, www.barmouth-wales.co.uk, Apr-Sep daily 1000-1800.* **Machynlleth** ① *Maengwyn St, T01654 702401, summer daily 0930-1730, Sun 0930-1600; winter Mon-Fri 0930-1700, Sat- Sun 0930-1600.* **Snowdonia National Park Authority HQ** ① *Penrhyndeudraeth, Gwynedd, T01766 770274, www.eryri-npa.gov.uk; www.snowdonia-npa.gov.uk.* Also see www.secretsnowdonia.co.uk.

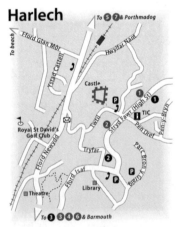

Harlech

To ⑤ ⑦ & Porthmadog

To beach

Ffordd Glan Môr

Hwylfar Nant

Ystad Castell

Castle

Twtil

Stryd Fawr (High St)

TIC

Pen-y-Bryn

Pen Dref

Royal St David's Golf Club

Tryfar

Parc Bron-y-Graig

Ffordd Newydd

Ffordd Isaf

Library

Theatre

To ③ ④ ⑥ & Barmouth

N

Not to scale

Sleeping 🛏
Castle Cottage & Restaurant **1**
Cemlyn & Restaurant **2**
Gwrach Ynys **5**

Hafod Wen & Restaurant **3**
Pensarn Hall **6**
Tremeifion **7**
YHA Hostel **4**

Eating 🍴
Yr Ogaf **1**
Weary Walkers Café **2**
Yr Hen Feudy **3**

Harlech and around

Although it's small, Harlech punches above its weight, due to the presence of its gloriously dramatic castle and unspoiled golden sands. The town was once a fashionable resort attracting figures like Gustav Holst, Sir Henry Wood and George Bernard Shaw – nude bathing even started here in the 1930s. The swish Royal

St David's Golf Course now attracts players from around the world, and there are plans to revive the once flourishing Harlech Festival, and even build a funicular railway from the bottom of the town up to the castle. Whether these go ahead or not, the town still makes a pleasant base for a few days.

Perched photogenically on a rocky outcrop, **Harlech Castle**ⓘ *To1766 780552, Apr-May, Oct daily 0930-1700, Jun-Sep daily 0930-1800, Nov-Mar Mon-Sat 0930-1600, Sun 1100-1600, £3, £2.50 children, £8.50 family, CADW*, was built by Edward I around 1283 after his conquest of Wales. It was once protected by the sea (which has now receded) but, despite its seemingly impregnable position, was captured more than once and had to withstand several long sieges. Owain Glyndŵr took it in 1404, it was recaptured, then was held by the Lancastrians for seven years during the Wars of the Roses – a feat that inspired the famous song '*Men of Harlech*'. The castle's battlements are extremely well preserved, and the short climb (on a clear day) is well worth it for the views across the sea and over to Snowdon.

Harlech's beach is excellent, with soft, clean golden sand – the sort of place where kids still make sandcastles and paddle without missing their computer games. The **Morfa Harlech National Nature Reserve** of sand dunes and estuary protects land where you can see wildlife such as redshank, shelduck and ringed plover.

A couple of miles away, set into the sand dunes at **Llandanwg**, is the fascinating little church of St Tanwg. The church is Early Middle Ages, but gravestones have been found here dating back to the fifth century. The church was used until 1845 but then fell into disrepair. However, it was later restored and candelit services are sometimes held here. Further south is **Llanbedr**ⓘ *www.llanbedr.com*, where there's a good pub and where a narrow road leads down to **Shell Island**ⓘ *To1341 241453, www.shell island.co.uk, daily Mar-Nov, £5 per car*, a peninsula cut off at high tide where you can go boating, birdwatching or fishing. There's also a restaurant and campsite.

There are a number of impressive prehistoric sites in this part of Wales, some of which can be seen south of Llandanwg at **Dyffryn Ardudwy** on the A496. A little path leads behind a school to the Dyffryn Burial Chamber, two Neolithic communal burial chambers sited close together.

Barmouth (Abermaw)

Barmouth was once a busy port and there are reminders of its maritime heritage in the **Tŷ Gwyn Museum**ⓘ *summer, daily, free*, with finds from local shipwrecks. It was here that Henry Tudor's uncle plotted his campaign against Richard III – resulting in Henry becoming Henry VII after the Battle of Bosworth. When the railway came to Barmouth in 1860, maritime trade declined and the town became a fashionable resort for genteel Victorians, attracted by the town's picturesque setting, squeezed beneath the cliffs at the mouth of the Mawddach Estuary. Today the town is more populist than picturesque, a bustling resort with a mishmash of amusements, busy bars and gift shops, in addition to the excellent Blue Flag beach and unspoiled surrounding countryside. It's popular with sailors, particularly each June when the **Three Peaks Yacht Race**ⓘ *To1341 280298, www.threepeaksyachtrace.co.uk*, starts here. This gruelling race goes from Barmouth to Fort William, with contestants scaling the peaks of **Snowdon**, **Scafell Pike** and **Ben Nevis** along the way.

From Barmouth you can get a ferry (£2.50 return) to **Penrhyn Point** where there's a sandy beach. Then you can connect to the narrow gauge **Fairbourne and Barmouth Railway**ⓘ *To1341 25062, www.fairbournerailway.com, single £4.30, £2.50 children, £11.10 family*. This was laid out in 1895 by Arthur McDougall of McDougall's flour fame, transporting the materials used to construct the village of Fairbourne. Originally hauled by horses, the trains are now pulled by steam locomotives.

● *In 1709 a ship, the* Bronze Bell, *sank off the coast of Barmouth with its valuable cargo of*
● *Carrara marble. Around 40 of the two-tonne blocks still lie at the bottom of the seabed.*

Mid Wales South Snowdonia National Park

South of Barmouth

You'll find the resort towns of **Aberdovey** (Aberdyfi) and **Tywyn**, close to the green and scenic Dyfi Valley. Aberdovey is the prettier of the two, while Tywyn is home to the **Talyllyn Railway** ① *T01654 710472, www.talyllyn.co.uk, daily end Mar-early Nov, some days in Feb, Mar and Dec, £10 day rover, £2 children, 8 day runabout fare £28, £14 children*, a narrow gauge railway that steams seven miles through the countryside to the mountain halt of Nant Gwernol, **Abergynolwyn**. It was built to transport slate from the quarries to the coast. You can use the train to get to the starting point of a number of walks in the area, such as the Pendre Station walk (four miles), and the Dolgoch Falls. At Wharf Station there's the **Narrow-Gauge Museum** ① *T01654 710472, www.ngrm.org.uk, free,* which contains various locomotives and wagons from all over Wales.

In Tywyn you can see the **Church of St Cadfan**, said to have been founded in the sixth century. The eighth-century Cadfan Stone in the church has an inscription in Welsh and is said to be the earliest written example of the language.

A mile or so west of Abergynolwyn is **Llanfihangel-y-Pennant**. The hamlet contains the remains of the cottage of Mary Jones who, as a young girl, saved up for six years to buy a copy of a Bible from Thomas Charles, a Methodist preacher who had printed copies of William Morgan's Welsh Bible. She walked barefoot to Bala to get it. As he only had one copy left, he gave Mary his own and subsequently founded the Bible Society. You'll also find the ruins of **Castell-y-Bere** (around eight miles northeast of Tywyn). This is one of the few Welsh (as opposed to Norman) castles and was built in 1221 by Llywelyn the Great, with the aim of securing his southern border against rival princes. It was attacked by Edward I's forces in the 13th century and later abandoned.

Dolgellau

At the head of the Mawddach Estuary, Dolgellau was accurately described in 1932 by HV Morton as 'a hard little mountain town. Its houses are made of the mountains. They look as though they were made to endure forever.' With its stone buildings and narrow streets, this pleasant market town seems to have changed little. It's full of history: Owain Glyndŵr assembled a parliament here in 1404, and in the 19th century it became a Welsh Klondike when the discovery of gold in the local rocks sparked a mini gold rush. The **Quaker Heritage Centre** ① *Eldon Sq, T01341 424442, summer daily 1000-1800, winter Thu-Mon 1000-1700,* has an exhibition on the local Society of Friends, or Quakers. A community was established here in the 17th century and was, like other Quaker groups, persecuted for their non-conformist views. Many Welsh Quakers emigrated to Pennsylvania in the United States, establishing towns with Welsh names, such as Bangor.

Today Dolgellau attracts walkers and outdoor enthusiasts seeking a good base from which to explore nearby **Cadair Idris**, go cycling along the **Mawddach Trail**, fish in the rivers, or go birdwatching in the **Mawddach Valley** ① *RSPB, Dolgellau, T01341 422071.* There are plenty of walks to choose from including the **Torrent Walk** (two miles), along the banks of the Clywedog river, or the **Precipice Walk** (3.5 miles) round Llŷn Cynwch, which starts from the car park just off the road between Dolgellau and Llanfachreth and offers great views of Cadair Idris. North of Dolgellau is **Coed y Brenin**, which offers some of the best mountain bike trails in Wales (see Activities, page 161).

Make time to seek out **Our Lady of Sorrows Church** on Meyrick Street, built by a determined Maltese priest, Francis Scalpell. He came to the town in 1939 when it was mainly Welsh speaking and began celebrating mass in an old stable. He eventually built a makeshift church with the help of Italian POWs but, determined to build something better, wrote 25,000 letters all over the world asking for funding. The money was eventually supplied by an anonymous stranger and the church opened in 1966.

West of town is Bontddu, where the famous **Clogau Gold Mine** is situated (not open to the public). It opened in 1842 as a copper mine and gold was only discovered

⁝ Walks on Cadair Idris

The steepest ascents are from the south, the easier ones from the north. Conditions on the mountain can change rapidly and you should always be well equipped and check weather reports locally before setting off. It's often said that anyone who spends the night on the summit will either wake up either mad or a poet. Dolgellau is a good base for walking on Cadair Idris.

The Minffordd Path (six miles) is the shortest but steepest ascent of the mountain. It starts from the car park at Minffordd, south of Dogellau, goes up through the woods, then wheels round to the summit of Craig Cwm Amarch. The path then continues to the summit where there's a stone-built shelter, then heads east along a ridge to Mynydd Moel, where you make your descent.

The Pony Path (approx nine miles) is the classic ascent, starting from the car park at Ty Nant. You turn right onto the lane, then go left by the telephone box. The main path then leads to the summit. You descend past Gau Craig, down to Meas Coch Farm and back to the start.

The Llanfihangel-y-Pennant Path (10 miles) is the longest route. It starts at the hamlet of Llanfihangel- y-Pennant, takes you over the Afon Cadair then up the valley. Bear right at a col and follow the main path to the summit, then descend southeast.

Further information about these routes is available from: www.walking britain.co.uk.

by accident in 1854. A nugget from this mine was used to provide the gold for the wedding rings of the Queen and Charles and Diana.

A couple of miles north of town are the ruins of **Cymer Abbey** ⓘ *daily 1000-1600, free, CADW*, a once isolated abbey (now sadly next to a caravan site). It was founded in 1198 by the Cistercians, an order that sought remote locations.

Machynlleth

Pronounced *mah-hun-kthleth* and just outside the Snowdonia National Park, this busy market town is a good base for exploring southern Snowdonia. With a reputation for being 'a bit hippy', 'Mac' as it's known to locals is a mix of galleries, pubs, wholefood shops and historic buildings. **Parliament House** ⓘ *Maengwyn St, T01654 702827, Easter-Oct Mon-Sat 1000-1700, other times by arrangement, free*, is a 15th-century building where Owain Glyndŵr assembled a Welsh parliament in 1404. Displays cover Glyndŵr's life and explain his importance in Welsh history.

Plas Machynlleth, on Maengwyn Street, is a 17th-century mansion that now houses **Celtica** ⓘ *T01654 702702, www.celticawales.com, daily 1000-1800, last admission 1620, £5, £4.10 children, £19 family*, which aims to bring to life the history and culture of the Celts. It focuses mainly on the Celts in Wales, but also includes the Cornish, Manx, Bretons, Scots and Irish. Downstairs is a 'trip through time' tour, where you don a headset and walk past figures and scenes from Britain's Celtic past – so you can hear, see and smell life as it was. Upstairs are interesting and educational displays, with exhibits on everything from language (you can hear recordings of six Celtic languages), art and the Celts' place in history. The section on Celtic beliefs explains the importance of water. Offerings were frequently made to it, which explains the importance of the Lady of the Lake in Arthurian legend, and human sacrifice was common; unfortunate victims were often left in bogs, their remains being preserved for centuries by the acidic, oxygen-free environment.

The Museum of Modern Art (MOMA) ⓘ *Penralt St, T01654 703355, www.taber nac.dircon.co.uk, Mon-Sat 1000-1600, free*, is a cultural and performing arts centre with permanent displays of modern Welsh art and regular temporary exhibitions.

Six miles south west of Machynlleth, off the A487 near Eglwys-fach, is **Ynys-hir Nature Reserve** ① *visitor centre, T01654 700222, Mar-Oct daily 1000-1700, Nov-Feb Sat-Sun 1000-1600, £3.50*, a 1,000-acre RSPB reserve set on the estuary with the Cambrian mountains behind. The habitats include salt marshes, woodlands, bogs and reed beds and there are seven hides and several nature trails. In winter you can spot wintering wildfowl like Greenland white-fronted geese, in spring and summer there are woodpeckers, lapwings and redshanks.

Centre for Alternative Technology

① *T01654 705950, www.cat.org.uk, daily 1000-1700 or dusk, Jan-Easter £5.35, £3.20 children, £15.90 family; Easter-end Oct £8, £5.50 children, £22 family.*

Three miles north of Machynlleth on the A487 (and the Sustrans 8 cycle route) the Centre for Alternative Technology deserves its reputation as one of the premiere attractions in Wales – and despite its worthy sounding name, is certainly not just aimed at people who spin their own wool and know 101 ways with tofu. The centre was established in 1974 on an abandoned slate quarry, the idea being to build a self sufficient community, both embracing and promoting 'green' technologies. You reach the centre via an extraordinary water-balanced cliff railway, similar to a cable car, and then watch an introductory video on the centre's establishment and ethos. The rest of the site is taken up with demonstrations of 'alternative' technologies and how they can be applied to modern urban living. There's a prototype low energy house, with displays asking you to think about everything from the distance your food has travelled, to using plants to improve air quality. Working organic plots demonstrate the principles of productive organic gardening, there are working solar panels and wind energy pumps, even a selection of eco toilets. There's also a good value vegetarian café doing hearty soups, cakes and salads – allow a good half day for your visit.

● Sleeping

Harlech and around *p154, map p154*
A-B Castle Cottage, High St, opposite TIC, T01766 780479, www.castlecottage harlech.co.uk. Family-run restaurant with rooms in the centre of Harlech. The modern Welsh cuisine of the restaurant is a feature.
A-B Tremeifion Vegetarian Hotel, Talsarnau, near Harlech, T01766 770491, www.vegetarian-hotel.com. Fabulous views from this exclusively vegetarian hotel. Dinner, bed and breakfast only, good food and a relaxed atmosphere.
B Cemlyn, High St, T01766 780425, www.cemlynrestaurant.co.uk. 2 en suite rooms, Very comfortable and attractively furnished rooms above excellent restaurant. Try and get the room with the wonderful views of the castle.
C Hafod Wen, 1 mile south of Harlech on A496, T01766 780356, www.harlech guesthouse.co.uk. Delightful Edwardian house set in 8 ha of grounds, with private steps leading down to the beach. Some rooms have balconies and glorious views

of the bay. Rooms are individually furnished and the atmosphere is comfortable and welcoming. Meals available.
D Gwrach Ynys, Talsarnau, on A496, 2 miles north of Harlech, T01766 780742, www.gwrachynys.co.uk. Lovely Edwardian house with great views over the mountains, and spacious and tasteful rooms. It's very welcoming and makes a relaxing base for walking and exploring nearby Portmeirion and the beaches of Harlech.
D Pensarn Hall, on A496, near Llanbedr, T01341 241236, www.pensarn-hall.co.uk. Spacious and cosy Victorian house set in lovely gardens, with good views over the Artro Estuary. A good base for walkers as the owners are happy to dry your gear and do you a packed lunch. There's also a self-catering cottage.
F YHA hostel, Plas Newydd, Llanbedr, T01341 241287, open Apr-Oct. Offers dormitory accommodation in the centre of the village.

Barmouth and around p155

A Bae Abermaw, Panorama Hill, T0871 9958204, www.baeabermaw.com. Crisp, clean lines and contemporary decor at this stone-built seaside hotel perched above Barmouth Bay.

A Fronoleu Hall, Llanaber, T01341 280491, www.fronoleu-hall.com. Country house hotel just outside Barmouth with lovely views across Cardigan Bay. Bedrooms are individually decorated and the Victorian house has been renovated to a high standard.

B Ty'r Graig Castle, Llanaber Rd, T01341 280470, www.tyrgraig.castle.btinternet. co.uk. Striking Victorian house built as a summer retreat on a rock overlooking the town. Lovely stained glass windows and wood panelling, and comfortable rooms. 2 have balconies where you can sit and watch the sun go down over the bay.

South of Barmouth p156

A Llety Bodfor, Bodfor Terrace, Aberdovey, T01654 767475, www.lletybodfor.co.uk. Cool contemporary rooms at this new boutique hotel. Rooms are airy with roll top baths, widescreen TVs and great views across Cardigan Bay. Good local food for breakfast and individual touches throughout.

B Penhelig Arms, Terrace Rd, Aberdovey T01654 767215 or T0871 9958256, www.penheligarms.com. Popular local inn with a busy restaurant. Rooms are spacious and some have balconies with lovely views of the estuary.

Dolgellau and around p156

L-A Penmaenuchaf Hall, Penmaenpool, T0871 9958258, www.penhall.co.uk. Grand manor house built for a wealthy cotton trader, now a country house hotel, with plush public rooms, a library and formal grounds.

L-B Plas Dolmelynllyn Hall, Ganllwyd, near Dolgellau, T01341 440273, www.dolly-hotel.co.uk. Victorian house on a lovely National Trust estate. They cater for walkers and mountain bikers and serve good local produce for breakfast.

Machynlleth and around p157

L Ynyshir Hall, Eglwysfach, near Machynlleth, T01654 781209, www.ynyshir. hall.co.uk. 7 suites. For real indulgence you can splash out at this luxurious hotel set in its own tranquil grounds, close to the Ynys-hir Nature Reserve. Only suites are available, all individually decorated with thick carpets, swagged curtains and plump cushions. Special breaks that include dinner are better value than one night's stay.

B Minffordd Hotel, Talyllyn, near Tywyn, T01654 761665, www.minffordd.com. A 17th-century coaching inn that makes a great base for walkers as it's close to Cadair Idris. Log fires and old wooden beams, as well as good food.

D Penrhos Arms Hotel, Cemmaes, near Machynlleth, T/F01650 511243, www.penrhosarms.co.uk. Lovely elegant rooms in this popular pub a few miles from the centre of town. Decor is light and bright, with antiques dotted around: 1 room has a 4-poster bed.

✿ Eating

Harlech and around p154, map p154

♥♥♥ Castle Cottage, High St, opposite TIC, T01766 780479, daily 1900-2100. Restaurant with rooms serving evening meals, specializing in Welsh produce. Dishes might include local lamb or steak.

♥♥♥ Cemlyn, High St, T01766 780425, teas Tue-Sun from 1100, dinners from 1900. Light lunches like Welsh rarebit available during the day, while evening meals might include red sea bream, liver and bacon casserole, or lentil pie. Call before setting off. 2 courses £22, 3 courses £25.

♥♥♥ Hafod Wen, 1 mile south of Harlech on A496, T01766 780356, dinner at 1900. Dine by candlelight in this romantic guesthouse which holds 'dinner party' meals where residents all dine together – along with locals 'in the know'. It's a set 3 course meal and includes home grown vegetables and freshly made bread. Vegetarians happily catered for – reservations essential.

♥ Yr Ogof Bistro, High St, T01766 780888, daily from 1900. Bistro serving range of steaks, chicken dishes and some veggie options.

♥♥-♥ Yr Hen Feudy, Llanbedr, T01341 241555, just off the main road, Mon-Sat 1000-1600. Outdoor seats for summertime tea and cakes, and filling main meals like curries, steaks, and steak and kidney pie.

Mid Wales South Snowdonia National Park Listings

¶¶¶ **Cemlyn**, High St, T01766 780425, teas daily from 1100, dinners from 1900. This tasteful teashop/restaurant serves a wide variety of teas including Rose Congou, Russian Caravan and Formosa Oolong. Team a pot with a rich brownie or freshly baked tiffin and relax on the little terrace.

¶ **Weary Walkers Café**, High St, Mon 1000-1700, Wed closed, rest 0900-1700. Range of snacks and light meals in busy café.

Barmouth p155

¶¶¶ **Bae Abermaw**, Panorama Rd, T01341 280550, daily 1900-2130. Modern British food at this refurbished hotel. There are set menus of 2 or 3 courses and seasonal produce is used.

¶¶ **The Bistro**, Church St, T01341 281009 1800-2030, closed Sun in winter; summer 1800-2100. Rustic bistro decor and good range of dishes, including veggie options.

¶¶¶ **Greeners at Ty'r Graig Castle**, Llanaber Rd, T01341 280470, Mon-Sat 1900-2030 (2100 on Sat), plus Sun lunch. Good selection of modern Welsh dishes, as well as veggie choices, in this quality restaurant. 3 course Sunday lunch available for £12.50. Traditional Welsh dishes on Mon nights.

¶¶ **The Indian Clipper**, Church St, T01341 280252, summer daily 1800-2130, Nov-Apr, Thu-Sat only 1800-2100. This highly rated balti house is worth seeking out.

Cafés

¶ **Wannabe's Coffee Bar**, High St, T01341 280820, Mon-Sat 0930-1700, Sun 1000-1600, closed Wed in winter. Coffee and cake then browse in the adjoining outdoor gear shop.

South of Barmouth p156

¶¶¶-¶¶ **Penhelig Arms**, Terrace Rd, Aberdovey, T01654 767215, daily 1200-1415, 1900-2130. Seafront inn with lots of fish on the menu like lemon sole, swordfish steaks and salmon. Some veggie choices and a good wine list.

Dolgellau and around p156

¶¶¶ **Dylanwad Da**, 2 Ffôs-y-Felin, T01341 422870, Thu-Sat 1900-2100 (Tue-Sat in summer). Chalkboard menu that changes daily and includes the best local produce such as Welsh beef and lamb. There's also plenty of fresh fish. Desserts might include fresh Welsh cheeses.

¶¶¶ **Penmaenuchaf Hall**, Penmaenpool, 1½ miles west of Dolgellau, T01341 422129, daily 1200-1400, 1900-2100. Elegant dining with fresh flowers and plush upholstery. Lots of game and local fish on the menu which features modern British dishes and fresh veg.

¶¶ **Fronolau**, Tabor, on A470 near Dolgellau, T01341 422361, daily 1200-1400, 1800-2130. Farm restaurant with squashy sofas and a relaxed atmosphere. Lots of local game and Welsh beef, as well as several veggie choices.

¶¶ **Y Sospan**, Queen's Sq, T01341 423174. The tea room serves cream teas, while the restaurant upstairs serves main courses like lamb from 1830.

¶ **Lemon Grass**, Finsbury Sq, T01341 421300, Sun-Thu 1200-1400, 1730-2330; Fri-Sat 1200-1400, 1730-2345. Indian restaurant, offers 'eat as much as you like' buffet on Sun.

Cafés

¶ **Yr Hen Efail**, by car park, T01341 422977, Mar-Oct Mon-Sat 1000-1700. Tea rooms with outside seating area serving light meals such as toasties, jacket potatoes and egg and chips.

Machynlleth and around p157

¶¶¶ **Ynyshir Hall**, Eglwysfach, near Machynlleth, T01654 781209, daily 1200-3130, 1900-2030, booking essential. If you can't afford to stay at this swish hotel you can maybe stretch to one of their highly rated meals. Set menus only, lunch 3 courses for £29.50, dinner £55. Tell them in advance if you're veggie.

¶¶ **Penrhos Arms Hotel**, Cenmaes, near Machynlleth, T01650 511243, food Mon-Fri 1830-2100, Sat 1200-1400, 1830-2100, Sun 1200-1400; summer Sun also 1830-2130. The interior of this great pub is modern and simple, with plain wooden tables, stone walls and a fire in winter; beer garden in summer. Bar meals include Welsh black beef and mushroom pie, while mains in the restaurant might include grilled trout.

¶¶-¶ **Victoria Inn**, Llanbedr, T01341 241213, food Mon-Fri 1200-2030. Likeable, busy inn offering a good range of meals. Beer garden is popular in summer.

¶ **Maharani**, 21 Penrallt St, T01654 703088, daily 1730-2330. The pink swathes on the ceiling, chandeliers and plump pink chairs seem slightly out of place among the grey stone that dominates the town, but it's a cheery sight.

¶ **Wholefood Café**, Maengwyn St, Mon-Sat 0930-1700, Sun 1000-1600 (shorter hours in winter). Great for dandelion coffee, a baked potato or a veggie meal.

¶ **Wynnstay Arms**, Maengwyn St, T01654 702941, food Mon-Fri 1830-2100, Sun 1200-1400. Busy pub which also serves decent food.

⊕ Entertainment

Harlech *p154, map p154*
Harlech Dispersed Gallery, T01341 241348, artworks change every 2 months and are displayed throughout Harlech, in galleries, shops and gardens.
Theatr Ardudwy, T01766 780667, ardudwy@ virgin.net, films, plays and musicals.

⊛ Festivals and events

Jul Barmouth Music Festival, T01341 281112. Live country music.
Sesiwn Fawr, Dolgellau, www.sesiwn fawr.demon.co.uk. The 'big session' is a music festival in mid-Jul with live bands performing in venues all over town.
Sep Barmouth Arts Festival, T01341 280392. Established festival that includes music and cabaret. Early Sep.
Barmouth Festival of Walking, week of guided walks in Barmouth area in late-Sep, details from Barmouth TIC.

▲ Activities and tours

General outdoor activities
CMC Pensarn Harbour, Llanbedr, T01341 241646, www.cmcpensarn.org.uk. Outdoor pursuits centre that does residential activities.

Golf
Aberdovey Golf Club, seaside links, T01654 767493, www.aberdoveygolf.co.uk.
Royal St Davids Golf Club, Harlech, T01766 780361, www.royalstdavids.co.uk, championship links, said to be the most difficult par 69 in the world. Weekdays £42, weekend £52 (summer), cheaper rates in winter.

Mountain biking
Coed y Brenin, 5 miles north of Dolgellau off the A470, is a forest area with a range of excellent mountain biking trails. There's a fun trail for novices and several trails for more experienced and adventurous riders.
The **Visitor Centre**, T01341 440666, Easter-Oct daily 1000-1700, rest of year weekends only, has a café and information on the various routes, www.mbwales.com and www.conwyctc.fsnet.co.uk.
Greenstiles, 4 Maengwyn St, Machynlleth, T01654 703543, mountain bike hire, also sells gear and accessories. Information on mountain biking around Machynlleth from www.mach-off-road.org.uk.
Mountain Bike Centre, Bronaber, Trawsfynydd, T01766 540219, www.logcabins -skiwales.co.uk, daily, £20 mountain bike hire.

Pony trekking
Abergwynant Farm and Pony Trekking Centre, Penmaenpool, Dolgellau T01341 422377, £11 for 1 hr trek, £16 for 2 hrs.

Quad biking
Madian Quads, Ty Mawr, Penegoes, Machynlleth, T01654 702746, www.madian quads.co.uk offer 1 and 2 hr treks at £30 and £55, also 1 hr trek for children £20.

Walking
The area offers everything from challenging walks on **Cadair Idris** (see p157) and the **Rhinogs**, to gentle strolls through **Bron Y Graig park**, near Harlech.
Huw Gilbert Mountaineering, 2 Glasfryn, Corris, Machynlleth, T01654 761774, www.climbmountains.co.uk, expert tuition for adventurous walkers wishing to learn more about scrambling, climbing and mountaineering.

⊕ Transport

Harlech *p154, map p154*
Arriva bus No 38 runs to **Barmouth** (10 daily, £2.30, ½ hr), and to **Blaenau Ffestiniog** (4 daily, £2.30, 40 mins).
    The **Cambrian Coaster** train stops here (see under Machynlleth for details).

Barmouth *p155*
Arriva Cymru bus No 94 crosses the country several times daily to **Wrexham** via **Dolgellau** (£2.50, 20 mins), **Bala** (£3, 1 hr) and **Llangollen**. Bus No 38 runs 3 times daily to **Blaenau Ffestiniog** (£2.40, 3 hrs).

The **Cambrian Coaster** train stops here (see under Machynlleth for details).

Dolgellau *p156*
Arriva Cymru run regular daily buses to **Caernarfon** (£5, 1½ hrs), **Aberystwyth** (£4.60, 1 hr 15 mins), **Blaenau Ffestiniog** (£2.30, 45 mins) and **Barmouth** (£2.30, 20 mins). The No 28 runs to **Machynlleth** (£2.85, ½ hr). **Crosville Wales**, T0870 6082608, coaches run to South Wales.

Machynlleth *p157*
Arriva Cymru bus No 28 runs to **Aberystwyth** (6 daily, £4.70, ½ hr) and **Dolgellau** (£2.85, ½ hr). Bus No X32 runs to **Bangor**.

The scenic **Cambrian Coaster** train runs from Machynlleth up the coast to **Pwllheli** (£13.50, 2 hrs) with stops at **Barmouth** (50 mins), **Harlech** (1 hr 15 mins) and **Porthmadog** (1 hr 40 mins). In the other direction trains runs east across the country to **Shrewsbury** (£12.50, 1 hr 15 mins). See www.thecambrianline.co.uk for further information. Trains also run south to **Aberystwyth** (£4.50, ½ hr).

Directory

Internet Free access at: **Barmouth library**, Talbot Sq, Mon 1330-1900, Tue 1000-1230, 1330-1900, Thu-Fri 1000-1230, 1330-1730, Sat 1000-1230; **Harlech library**, Mon 1630-1900, Wed 1000-1300, Fri 1630-1900; **Machynlleth library**, Maengwyn St Mon 1330-1900, Tue 1000-1230, 1330-1900 , Fri-Sat 1000-1230, 1330-1730; and **Twyn library**, Neptune Rd, T01654 710104, closed Wed, Sun, Sat afternoon.

Ceredigion Coast → *Colour map 3*

The area known today as Ceredigion stretches south of the Dyfi Estuary to Cardigan and is a ribbon of coastal communities stretched out along Cardigan (Ceredigion) Bay. This western coast is the haunt of seals, sailors and students, dotted with hidden bays and pretty fishing villages. It's a great place to come for marine wildlife watching and there are some lovely beaches too. The main settlement is the Victorian resort of Aberystwyth, now a lively student town. But if you take your time you'll also discover pretty seaside villages which feel almost Cornish in character, such as Georgian Aberaeron and bustling New Quay – a favourite haunt of the poet Dylan Thomas. ⏩ *For Sleeping, Eating and other listings, see pages 169-172.*

Ins and outs

Getting there and around The A487 trunk road runs between the main towns on this stretch of coastline linking Cardigan to Aberystwyth, and to Fishguard and Haverfordwest. Express **buses** run from Bristol and Cardiff to Aberystwyth. **Trains** from the Midlands run to Machynlleth, where you can then travel on to Aberystwyth. The narrow gauge steam **Vale of Rheidol railway** can take you inland from Aberystwyth to Devil's Bridge, otherwise it is difficult to explore the more remote areas without your own transport. To travel between Aberystwyth and Cardigan you'll have to use buses, which link towns along the coast such as Cardigan, New Quay, Aberaeron and Aberystwyth. There are also links to locations inland such as Tregaron and Llandysul. ⏩ *For further details, see Transport, page 172.*

Information Aberystwyth TIC ⓘ *Terrace Rd, T01970 612125, aberystwythTIC@ceredigion.gov.uk, Jun-Aug daily 1000-1800, rest of year Mon-Sat 1000-1700, may close for lunch.* **New Quay TIC** ⓘ *Church St, T01545 560865, newquayTIC@*

ceredigion.gov.uk, Jul-Aug daily 1000-1800, Apr-Jun, Oct Mon-Sat 1000-1700, closes for lunch. **Aberaeron TIC** ① *The Quay, T01545 570602, aberaeronTIC@ ceredigion.gov.uk, Jul-Aug daily 1000-1800, Apr-Jun, Oct Mon-Sat 1000-1700 , closes for lunch.* **Cardigan TIC** ① *Theatr Mwldan, Bath House Rd, T01239 613230, cardiganTIC@ceredigion.gov.uk, Jul-Aug 0900-1800 daily, closes for lunch, rest of year Mon-Sat 1000-1700.* More information on Ceredigion can be found at www.ceredigion.gov.uk, www.visitcardigan.com, www.pumlumon.org.uk and www.caridganshirecoastandcountry.com. Cardigan Bay also has a conservation website www.cardiganbaysac.org.uk.

Background

For most of its history Ceredigion was largely isolated from the rest of Wales by the Cambrian mountains, and the Welsh language, culture and sense of identity are still strong – though somewhat diluted by English settlers and visitors. The area was once an independent principality and takes its name from Prince Ceredig. Much of this beautiful area is designated Heritage Coast and is one of the best places to come to

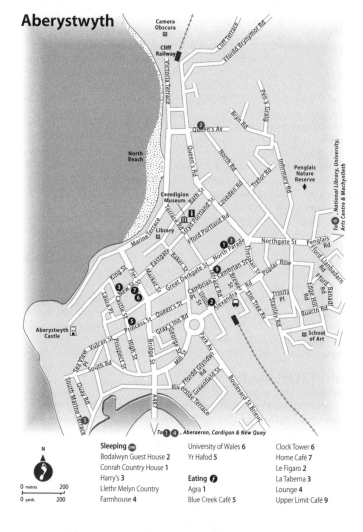

Aberystwyth

Mid Wales Ceredigion Coast

Sleeping 🛏
Bodalwyn Guest House **2**
Conrah Country House **1**
Harry's **3**
Llethr Melyn Country Farmhouse **4**
University of Wales **6**
Yr Hafod **5**

Eating 🍴
Agra **1**
Blue Creek Café **5**
Clock Tower **6**
Home Café **7**
Le Figaro **2**
La Taberna **3**
Lounge **4**
Upper Limit Café **9**

N

0 metres 200
0 yards 200

observe marine wildlife. It shelters some of Britain's rarest birds and is home to a resident population of bottlenose dolphins, as well as harbour porpoises and grey seals. The rivers and estuaries also provide superb wildlife habitats where you have the chance to spot wildfowl, rare plants and otters. Go further inland and you can see red kites which are fed daily.

Aberystwyth and around

Aberystwyth is both a student town and a resort. The university, founded in the 19th century, is now centred on a modern campus above the town, close to the National Library of Wales. The town grew from what is now the suburb of Llanbadarn Fawr, a settlement dating back to the sixth century when St Padarn established a monastic settlement here. It became a popular seaside resort from the early 19th century, the numbers of visitors increasing after the coming of the railway in 1864. Its promenade, seafront Regency terraces and dowager hotels are constant reminders that this was once the 'Brighton of Wales'. Today it's a resort with a radical edge – a Nationalist town, home of the Welsh Language Society with a thriving art and music scene.

The former Coliseum theatre is now the opulent home of **Aberystwyth TIC** and **Ceredigion Museum** ① *Terrace Rd, T01970 633088, Mon-Sat 1000-1700, free*, which provides an unusual setting for a permanent collection on life in Victorian Wales, and changing exhibitions of art and crafts. From here you can walk along Marine Terrace to Constitution Hill, which rises 450 ft and is topped with a Camera Obscura – a cross between a telescope and a CCTV system with a 14-inch lens allowing you to look over the mountains and sea, and watch what's happening in town. It can be reached on foot or by the **Cliff Railway** ① *T01970 617642, Mar-Nov, daily 1000-1700 (1800 Jul and Aug) £2.25 return*, which opened in 1896 and is the longest in Britain. Now powered by electricity, it was originally water balanced when it opened for Victorian pleasure trippers.

At the other end of town are the remains of **Aberystwyth Castle** (*free, CADW*), built by Edward I in the late 13th century. It saw plenty of action, withstanding several sieges including holding out for the king during the Civil War, until 1646 when its forces surrendered to Parliament.

Out of town is **The National Library of Wales** ① *Penglais Hill, T01970 632834, www.llgc.org.uk, Mon-Sat 1000-1700, closed first full week Oct, free*, where extensive collections give a good insight into aspects of Welsh culture. Exhibits include the oldest surviving manuscripts in the Welsh language. Further up the hill is the **Arts Centre** ① *T01970 622882, Mon-Sat 1000-2000 (galleries shut at 1700), summer Sun 1400-1700*, which houses the university's ceramic collection.

Penglais Road leads to the **Penglais Nature Reserve** set in a former quarry. It has a variety of tree and plant life, with a fine display of bluebells in the spring. Not far from the railway station in a fine Edwardian building, is the university's **School of Art**, ① *Buarth, Mon-Fri 1000-1300, 1400-1700, www.aber.ac.uk, free*, where you can see some examples of Welsh art from the university's permanent collection.

North of Aberystwyth

Five miles north of Aberystwyth, the resort of **Borth** comes alive in summer when its extensive sandy beaches become the haunt of windsurfers and kite surfers. On the northern stretch of the sands, on the Dyfi estuary, is the **Ynyslas Nature Reserve** ① *visitor centre, T01970 871640, Easter- Sep, parking £1*, an extensive area of sand dunes that provides a home for wildlife such as lizards, voles, stoats, skylarks, ringed plovers and meadow pipits. There are many wildflowers and butterflies as well. The visitor centre has information on the wildlife and also on the two waymarked paths you can follow. At low tides you might see tree stumps sticking up through the sands, the remains of an ancient forest.

◦ Owain's Uprising

One of the most important figures in Welsh history is Owain Glyndŵr (c1349-c1416), who led a mighty rebellion against English rule. He was an unlikely rebel, a wealthy man descended from the Princes of Powys and Deheubarth, who was well educated, studied law in London and even served in the English army: a pillar of the establishment. His rebellion stemmed from a prosaic dispute with his neighbour in the borders – Lord Grey of Ruthin appropriated a piece of his land and the courts refused to back Glyndŵr, treating him with great lack of respect. Infuriated, in 1400 he attacked the town of Ruthin with hundreds of Welsh supporters. It sparked a national uprising, with Welshmen living in England rushing home to support the cause. He attacked more towns in the north and later that year proclaimed himself Prince of Wales. Henry IV retaliated, not only with force but also by introducing a range of draconian laws forbidding the Welsh from holding public office, taking arms or holding assemblies. Not surprisingly, this fuelled support for the rebellion and Glyndŵr went on to take many castles, including Harlech. In 1404 he held the first Welsh parliament in Machynlleth, made alliances with France and Scotland, and was crowned King of Wales. However, the following year, when he made incursions over the border, he was beaten back by troops led by the king's teenage son – the future Henry V. In 1408, Harlech was taken by the king's forces and Glyndŵr was forced into hiding. He fled into the wilds of Snowdonia, and after that no one knows what happened to him – although he is known to have died by 1417. Only a mound remains of his birthplace Sycharth Castle, near Llangedwyn, north of Welshpool and no one knows where he is buried, but the Welsh will never forget his fight for freedom. See also History, page 226.

Vale of Rheidol

East of Aberystwyth, the Vale of Rheidol is a lush wooded valley most famous as the location of the **Devil's Bridge** and waterfalls – described by George Borrow in *Wild Wales* as 'one of the most remarkable locations in the world' and a long-standing tourist trap. You can reach Devil's Bridge from Aberystwyth on the **Vale of Rheidol Railway** ① *Park Avenue, T01970 625819, www.rheidolrailway.co.uk, Easter-Oct, £12, £3 children*, a narrow gauge steam railway built in 1902 to serve the lead mines and passengers of the valley. The ride through the gorgeous valley takes about an hour.

Devil's Bridge consists of three bridges stacked on top of one another, above the Mynach river. There's the 20th-century road bridge, below which is the Middle Bridge, erected in 1753, and the original Pont-y-gwr-drwg (Bridge of the evil man) which was built in the 11th century by monks from a nearby Cistercian Abbey. Access to the bridges and the Devil's Punchbowl is by a turnstile (£1 coin). On the opposite side of the road is the entrance to a nature trail and path which lets you see the bridges and the stunning **Mynach Falls** ① *Easter-end Oct 0945-1700, £2.50, £1.25 children, paid to attendant, otherwise £2 in coin-operated turnstile*.

The **Bwlch Nant Yr Arian visitor centre** ① *Ponterwyd, T01970 890694, daily 1000-1700 summer, 1000-dusk winter*, gives access to waymarked walks and mountain bike trails, as well as a café. From the visitor centre (daily until 1500, 1400 in winter) you can see red kites swooping in to be fed; in fact if you're on the A44 around that time you'll see the birds flying low over the roadway. You can do more bird watching further north off the A487 at the RSPB's Ynys-hir Reserve (see Activities, page 171).

Just east of Bwlch Nant Yr Arian, the **Llywernog Silver-lead Mines** ① *Ponterwyd, T01970 890620, www.silverminetours.co.uk, mid Mar-end Aug Sun- Fri 1000-1800; Sep-Oct 1100-1700 (only opens Sat in Jul/Aug), last admission 1600, £5.95, £3.75 children, £17.50 family*, drew speculators to the area in 1860. You can join a 45-minute underground tour and try your hand at panning for minerals.

South of Aberystwyth

About 15 miles southeast of Aberystwyth is **Strata Florida Abbey** ① *Mar-Sep Wed-Sun 1000-1700, otherwise open and unstiffen, £2.25, £1.75 children, £6.25 family*, a Cistercian abbey founded in 1164 at a lovely spot in the Teifi Valley. Its name in Welsh 'Ystrad Fflur' means 'Valley of the Flowers' and refers to its original position a couple of miles away. The abbey became an important seat of learning and several Welsh princes are buried here, as well as Dafydd ap Gwilym a 14th-century poet – a yew tree is thought to mark his grave. The vast church (larger than St David's) was damaged by lightning in 1286 and was finally destroyed in the Dissolution. The setting is stunning, though little remains to be seen. The fine West Door survives, and remains of medieval tiled floors bearing symbols including a griffin and a fleur-de-lys. Legend has it that Joseph of Arimathaea took the Holy Grail from Jerusalem to Glastonbury, from where it then found its way to Strata Florida. After the Reformation it came into the hands of the Powells of the Nanteos estate. An olive-wood artefact, known as The Nanteos Cup, became widely known and is thought to have inspired Wagner's opera *Parsifal*, after he saw it when he visited the house. Today the cup is thought to be hidden in a bank vault.

South of the abbey, **Tregaron** is a traditional Welsh market town once used by drovers taking cattle across the mountains to Abergwesyn and Llanwrtyd Wells. There's a small exhibition on red kites and other local birds at the **Tregaron Red Kite Centre** ① *200 yds from Tregaron Sq on the road to Llanddewi Brefi, T01974 298977, Mar-Oct daily 1030-1630, Oct-Mar Sat, Sun 1200-1630*. The centre, an old school, also has a reconstructed Victorian classroom. Feeding of red kites takes place on Tregaron Bog at 1400 in winter. It can be seen from the bridge on the A485 about a mile from Tregaron.

Aberaeron and around

Aberaeron comes as something of a surprise in this most Welsh of areas, as it looks distinctly English. It's a neat, orderly Georgian planned town, built almost from scratch in the 19th century, with wide streets and houses painted in cheery colours, set around a pretty harbour. It was built by the Reverend Alban Gwynne, who spent his wife's considerable inheritance creating the village and was reportedly designed by John Nash. His intention was to create a new port for mid Wales. Unlike other places on this stretch of coast Aberaeron doesn't have a great beach, however the waterfront is pleasant and there are some good pubs.

About two miles away on the A482 is **Llanerchaeron** ① *T01545 570200, Mar- Oct, Wed-Sun, house 1130-1630, farm and garden 1100-1700, £5.20, £2.60 children, £12.60 family, National Trust*, a Welsh 18th-century gentry estate, once common in the area. The house, also designed by John Nash, has been restored and is furnished in Edwardian style, with fascinating servants' quarters and a service courtyard with a dairy, laundry and brewery. The estate operates as a working organic farm.

New Quay (Cei Newydd)

There's a salty tang to New Quay – a little village squeezed, in picturesque Cornish fashion, around a harbour. Dylan Thomas often visited and drank in the pubs, even living here for a time during 1944-1945. It was here that he started work on *Under Milk*

Wood, so the town has a good claim to be the fictional 'Llareggub' in the play. One of the pubs, The Black Lion, witnessed a fight between Thomas and William Killick, a friend who returned from war service to discover that his wife, Vera, had been using his army pay to support Thomas and Caitlin. Killick suspected some sexual shenanigans, and they argued. Killick then got a machine gun and hand grenade, went to Majoda, the house the Thomas family were renting, and fired. He was arrested and tried for attempted murder. He got off and Thomas sensibly left New Quay soon after. You can pick up a good, free Dylan Thomas walking trail of the village in the TIC. The village is very lively in summer, you can go on dolphin watching boat trips to see the bottlenose dolphins that follow shoals of mackerel in the Bay (see Activities, page 171) and there are plenty of pubs and places to eat.

A couple of miles away is **New Quay Honey Farm** ① *T01545 560822 May-Oct daily 1000-1730, £2.95, £1.75 children, £7.60 family*, with a small but informative exhibition on the life of the honey bee. Glass cases allow you to see bees coming and going to a huge honeycomb, and there are panels explaining the different ways they communicate. There's also a great café open all year (see Eating, page 170).

South of New Quay

The coastline here takes on an even more Cornish character, with stunning beaches and hidden coves linked by a maze of narrow, high-banked lanes teeming with wild flowers. **Llangrannog** (parking £2 in peak season) is a charming little village with a tiny beach, bustling old pub, café and shop selling surfing gear and buckets and spades.

Just south of here is **Penbryn beach**, owned by the National Trust, where trails lead to the Corbalani stone burial site of a fifth-century chief. The next beach along is **Tresaith** (parking £1 in field above), another unspoiled cove where a waterfall cascades down from the cliffs; just next door is the busier, more popular beach at **Aberporth**. The most beautiful and unspoiled spot along here is **Mwnt** (parking £1.50), a remote headland owned by the National Trust, with a secluded, sandy beach below, reached by steep steps. Mwnt was a stopping place for the bodies of saints being taken to Bardsey Island, their traditional burial ground and was also on a pilgrims' route to St Davids. There's a lonely little church, **Holy Cross Y Mwnt**, the oldest in Ceredigion. It's a 13th-century building, but built on much older foundations. If you go in you can see that a small window on the north side has been walled up. It's thought that this let lepers, and others forbidden from the building, to observe the service from outside.

Cardigan (Aberteifi) and around

With such a gorgeous coastline to explore you are unlikely to want to linger long in Cardigan, though it's pleasant enough. Of most interest is the **Cardigan Heritage Centre** ① *T01239 614404, Easter-Oct daily 1000-1700, £2, £1 children, £5 family*, in an 18th-century warehouse. It tells the story of the town, once one of the principal ports on Wales' west coast, right back to its pre-Norman days. It was an important embarkation point for emigration to North America and ships such as *The Active* and *The Albion* took many emigrants to New Brunswick, Canada and New York in the 1840s. The family of the architect Frank Lloyd Wright left Wales from here. The **castle**, built in 1093, was the site of the first competitive eisteddfod in 1176, but was later badly damaged in the Civil War. Henry Tudor stayed there on his march to Bosworth. It is not open to the public although there is a campaign to bring it into public ownership.

Outside the town, a short drive on the B4548 to Gwbert, is the **Cardigan Island Coastal Farm Park** ① *T01239 612196, www.cardiganisland.com, mid Mar-Oct £3.20, £2.50 children*, where you can walk (or take a tractor ride) to a viewing point to spot

⁞ Out and about in Cardigan

The area around Cardigan is ideal for walkers and cyclists. For walkers, Cardigan is at the northern end of the **Pembrokeshire Coastal Path** (see page 136), and at the southern tip of the **Ceredigion Coastal Path** (see page 171). There is also a popular annual walking festival in October (see Festivals, page 171).

If you prefer to cycle, you can set off from Cardigan to Llangrannog along the coast (13.4 miles). The route starts at Finch Square in the town centre, goes through Aberporth and Tresaith before arriving in Llangrannog.

seals that breed in the caves below. There are various farmed animals here, such as wallabies, a llama, emus and ponies, some of which children can feed if they wish; special feed is for sale. There's also a café with seats looking out to sea, but no indoor seating so not one for a rainy day.

Cenarth

The A484 from Cardigan leads to pretty, but supremely touristy, Cenarth. This little village is famed for its tumbling rapids and salmon leap (car park £1.50) and first mentioned by a 12th-century traveller Gerald Cambrensis, who passed through the village recruiting for the crusades and wrote of salmon 'leaping as high as the tallest spear'. It was high on the Victorian's 'must see' list. You can also visit the **National Coracle Centre** ① *T01239 710980, www.coraclecentre.co.uk, Easter-Oct Sun-Fri 1030-1730, £3, £2.50 children*, which contains coracles (small round boats dating back to the ice age) from around the world. Cenarth was once a centre for coracle fishing. The centre is housed in a 17th-century flour mill, and you can still see the waterwheel. The village has a craftshop, several pubs and a tea shop.

Cilgerran and around

On a promontory above the Teifi, **Cilgerran Castle** ① *Apr-Oct daily 0930-1830, Nov-Mar daily 0930-dusk, £2.50, £2 children, £7 family, CADW*, is a romantic castle that inspired both JMW Turner and Richard Wilson. Probably built in 1100 the castle was thought to have been the home of Nest, the Welsh 'Helen of Troy'. A beautiful princess of Deheubarth, she was married to Gerald of Windsor but was abducted from the castle in 1108 by her second cousin Prince Owain. Her husband escaped down a privy waste pipe. She later became mistress to others, including Henry I. Today the castle's most striking features are two large towers, each four storeys high.

Just east of Cilgerran, tucked away off the A478, is one of the best places for wildlife watching – the Welsh Wildlife Centre, at **Teifi Marshes Nature Reserve** ① *Cilgerran, T01239 621600, reserve open all year, visitor centre Apr-Oct 1030-1700, free, £3 parking*. The reserve encompasses river, marshland and woods and has walking trails which give you the opportunity to spot (if you're lucky) their resident otters, the rare Cetti's warbler, 18 species of dragonfly and visitors such as sedge warblers and wildfowl. The visitor centre has a very good café (1030-1700) and you can also join guided walks or canoe or kayaking trips (see Activities, page 171).

Further east, off the A484 and past Newcastle Emlyn, is the **National Woollen Museum** ① *Dre-Fach Felindre, Llandysul, T01559 370929, Apr-Sep daily 1000-1700, Oct-Mar Tue-Sat 1000-1700, free*. This area was once the centre of the woollen industry and the museum is housed in the restored Cambrian Mills. You can see the buildings and the old machinery where uniforms for World War One soldiers were made, as well as trying your hand at making woollen cloth.

Aberystwyth *p164, map p163*
A Conrah Country House Hotel, Chancery, Rhydgaled, T01970 617941/624546, www.conrah.co.uk. Aberystwyth's most luxurious hotel, set in its own grounds about 3 miles from town. Fresh flowers from the garden, antiques dotted around and all the comforts you'd expect.
C Bodalwyn Guest House, Queen's Avenue, T01970 612578, hilary.d@lineone.net. Comfortable rooms in this large, Welsh-speaking guesthouse just off the promenade.
C Harry's, 40-46 North Parade, T01970 612647, www.harrysaberystwyth.com. Look for the bright orange awnings outside and that's Harry's, a town centre restaurant with rooms that is gradually being refurbished.
C Llethr Melyn Country Farmhouse, Trawsgoed, near Aberystwyth, T01974 261400, www.welsh-breaks.co.uk. 17th-century farmhouse in the country close to Aberystwyth, set in 20 ha with horses, and other farm animals. Evening meals available.
C Yr Hafod, 1 South Marine Terrace, T01970 617579, johnyrhafod@aol.com. Reliable guesthouse on the seafront, offering good value accommodation.
F University of Wales, Penglais, T01970 621960, www.aber.ac.uk/visitors. Single rooms in university flats (self catering) from mid Jun-mid Sep.

Aberaeron *p166*
A-B The Harbourmaster, Pen Cei, T01545 570755, www.harbour-master.com. Brilliant cool and contemporary rooms with great views of the harbour. There's a fresh seaside feel throughout, with white and aquamarine decor, fine white sheets and CD players.
C Arosfa, Cadwgan Place, T01545 570120, www.arosfaguesthouse.co.uk. 3-star guesthouse by the quay. Serves award-winning breakfasts.

New Quay and around *p166*
C The Grange Country House, Pentregat, near Llangrannog, T01239 654121. Elegance all the way at this pink-painted Georgian house, set down a narrow track in its own grounds. Very clean and comfortable, lovely deep baths and good fresh food.

C Ty Cerrig, 3 Hengell Uchaf, T01545 560850. All rooms are en suite at this clean, comfortable modern house on the outskirts of New Quay. Will take dogs.
D Summat Else, New Rd, T01545 561418. Next door to Ty Cerrig, this modern 4-star guesthouse also has en suite rooms.

Self catering
Neuadd Farm, Llwyndafydd, south of New Quay, T01545 560324, www.neuadd-farm-cottages.co.uk, 5-star self catering cottages with swimming pool in the grounds. Cottages sleep from 2-6 people. From £350 per week for 2, from £480 per week for 6.

Cardigan and around *p167*
C Black Lion Hotel, High St, T01239 612532. Right in the centre of town, clean and comfortable en suite rooms. Restaurant and pub attached.
E Tipi West, Blaenannerch, near Cardigan, T07813 672336, www.tipiwest.co.uk. 3 tipis accommodating up to 25 people all together. Sleep on air beds (bring your own sleeping bag) and sit round the camp fire at night. The tipis are insulated with coconut matting and close enough to Cardigan Bay to hear the waves when you're tucked up in bed.

● Eating

Aberystwyth *p164, map p163*
₩₩₩ Conrah Country House Hotel, Chancery, Rhydgaled, T01970 617941. This is the place to come for a formal meal in lovely surroundings. Food is modern British using local produce, including vegetables from the hotel garden. 2 AA rosettes.
₩₩ Agra Indian Restaurant, 36 North Parade, T01970 636999, daily 1200-1400, 1730-2230. Indian food with veggie options – bring your own wine.
₩₩ Harry's, 40-46 North Parade, T01970 612647, daily 1200-1400, Mon, Thu-Sat 1800-2100. Harry's bills itself as a restaurant with rooms and main courses are a mixture of traditional British dishes like fish and chips, or ham hock with mash, as well as some pasta and veggie dishes.
₩-₩ Le Figaro, Alexandra Rd, T01970 624242, Mon-Sat 1000-1400, 1900-2200.

Mediterranean style dishes at this restaurant near the station. Coffees and light meals served during the day.

La Taberna, 1 New St, T01970 627677, daily 1800-2230. Tapas bar offering tapas or more substantial main courses.

Lounge, 31 Pier St, T01970 626444, winter Tue-Sat 11001500, 1900-2300; summer daily 1100-2300.Freshly cooked food with some veggie choices available.

Cafés

Blue Creek Café, Princess St, T01970 615084, Tue-Sat 1000-1730. Cosy but uncluttered café. Lots of good choices for veggies, with choices like bean burgers. Other dishes include 'posh beans on toast' served with bacon, rocket and parmesan.

Clock Tower, 2 Pier St, T01970 626269, Mon-Wed 1000-1600, Thu-Sat 1000-2100. Café with restaurant upstairs.

Home Café, 13-15 Pier St, T01970 617417, Mon-Fri 0730-2030, Sat-Sun 0800-2100 in summer; shuts as about 1800 in winter. Cheap, cheerful and good value café popular with locals. Serves cakes, toasted sandwiches, BLTs and hot meals.

Upper Limit Café, 27 North Parade, T07814 786863, Mon-Fri 0730-1700, Sat 0800-1600. Good café fare with cooked breakfasts, jacket potatoes and various veggie options.

Aberaeron *p166*

The Harbourmaster, Pen Cei, T01545 570755, food Tue-Sun 1200-1500, Mon-Sat 1800-2300. Great contemporary bar and restaurant offering modern Welsh cuisine. Mains like tuna and plaice with sundried tomato mash or Welsh lamb in smoked bacon. Veggie options available.

The Hive on the Quay, Cadwgan Place, T01545 570445, May-Sep 1030-1700 (Aug 1000-2100). Famed for its delicious honey ice cream, this restaurant overlooking the water also serves fish dishes like haddock chowder.

New Quay *p166*

The Hungry Trout, 2 South John St, T01545 560680, Wed-Sat coffee 1000-1500, lunch 1200-1400, tea 1400-1500, à la carte 1800-2130, also Mon evening, Sun 1030-1400. Good restaurant by the harbour with lots of fish dishes and good veggie choices like black eye bean and squash stew (£10.75).

The Black Lion, Glanmor Terrace, T01545 560209, food winter 1700-2130, summer Mon-Fri 1200-2130. One of Dylan Thomas' many haunts, with a collection of photos and posters inside. Traditional bar meals and priceier restaurant food.

Cafés

Café Connect, Harbourside, www.cafe connect.biz, daily from 1000. Internet café also serving hot drinks and food.

New Quay Honey Farm Tea Room, Cross Inn, outside New Quay, Easter – Christmas daily 1000-1730, but closed Nov-Dec Sun-Mon. Lovely smell of honey and freshly made cakes, soups and sandwiches.

Cardigan and around *p167*

Red Lion Hotel, Pwllhai, T01239 612482 daily 1200-1400, 1830-2100. Serves a decent pint and pub grub in lively surroundings, often backed by live rock.

The Royal Oak, 30 North Rd, T01545 570233, food 1200-2100. Pleasant pub serving pub grub with several seafood options.

Welsh Wildlife Centre, near Cilgerran, T01239 621600, food 1030-1700. Good views over the reserve in this café above the visitor centre. Serves, cakes and hot drinks, as well as hot meals between 1200-1430.

Cenarth *p168*

Three Horse Shoes, T01239 710119, food Easter-Nov daily 1200-1400, 1800-2100; winter 1200-1330 except Tue, and 1800-2030. This pub is the best place to eat in Cenarth. It specializes in fish but also does old favourites like chicken curry as well as veggie options like roast veg and squash filo tart.

● Entertainment

Aberystwyth Arts Centre, Penglais, Aberystwyth, T01970 622882, www.aber.ac.uk, houses a theatre, concert hall and wide range of exhibitions.

The Black Lion, Glanmor Terrace, New Quay has live jazz on Sun nights in winter, and 60/70s music on Fri/Sat in winter.

Male Voice Choir, Tabernacle Chapel, Mill St, Aberystwyth, rehearse Thu at 1930 (not Aug)

Theatr Mwldan, Cardigan, T01239 621200, www.mwldan.co.uk, venue for theatre, music and cinema.

☸ Festivals and events

Jul **MusicFest,** Aberystwyth Arts Centre,
T01442 878654, www.musicfest-
aberystwyth.org, classical music festival.
Oct **Cardigan Walking Festival,** T01239
621200/615554, www.visitcardigan.com,
popular festival of guided walks

▲▲ Activities and tours

Bird watching
Bwlch Nant Yr Arian, Ponterwyd, T01970
890694, www.forestry.gov.uk, red kite
feeding 1400 in winter, summer 1500.
Hafod Lodge, Cwmstwyth, Aberystwyth,
T01970 890281, www.midwalesbird
watching.co.uk. 2-7 day birdwatching trips.
Ynys-hir RSPB reserve on Dyfi Estuary,1.5km
off A487 Machynlleth- Aberystwyth road,
T01654 700222, daily 0900-dusk, £3.50, large
nature reserve. Chance to see pied
flycatchers, redstarts, wood warblers, White
fronted geese, as well as otters, dragonflies
and other species.

Boat trips
Cardigan Boat Charters, T01239 614050.
Trips along the Teifi Estuary and into
Cardigan Bay, as well as self hire boats.
New Quay Boat Company, T07989 175124,
offer fishing trips and ½ hr fast boat rides, £9.
Winston Evans boat trips, T01545 560375,
Apr-Oct. Along the coast, £5 per hr.

Canoeing
Heritage Canoes, Teifi Marshes Nature
Reserve, Cilgerran, T01239 613961,
www.heritagecanoes.co.uk. Canoe trips on
River Teifi and kayaking adventure trips, £20.

Cycling/mountain biking
New Image Bikes, Pwllhai, Cardigan T01239
621275, tom@newimagebicycles.fsnet.co.uk
cycle hire, ½ day £12, full day £18.
Teifi Trails, at Mapstone Newsagents, Pendre,
Cardigan, T01239 614729, mountain bike hire
and route planning advice.
Mountainland Rovers, Tregaron, T01974
821416, www.mountainland-rovers.co.uk.
Deliver bikes in and around the Tregaron
area, £10 per day. Also offer 4x4 safaris of
the countryside.

Dolphin watching
Aberaeron Sea Aquarium, 2 Quay Parade,
Aberaeron, T01545 570142, www.coastal
voyages.co.uk, offer trips in Cardigan Bay
viewing dolphins, seals and birds.
Dolphin Survey Boat Trips, New Quay,
T01545 560032, offers 4- and 8-hr boat trips
from New Quay on scientific survey boats
equipped with hydrophones.

Horse riding
Cwmtydu Riding and Trekking Centre,
Pantrhyn, New Quay, T01545 560494, pony
trekking for all the family, with 1-3 hr treks.

Skiing
Llangrannog Ski Centre, 1 mile out of
village on B4321, T01239 654656,
www.llangrannog.org or www.urdd.org/
llangrannog, Mon-Thu 1630-2100, Sun
1400-1700, dry ski slope and snowboarding,
£7.50 per hour, £6.50 children.

Walking
The **Ceredigion Coastal Path,** is a waymarked walk due for completion in 2006.
It runs for 70 miles from Ynyslas to Poppit
Sands and some sections are already
walkable. For more information ask at
the TIC or see www.ceredigion-coastal-
footpath.com. In October there is a **Cardigan
Walking Festival** (see Festivals, above).
Ceredigion Council have a series of guided
walks during the season taking in everything
from challenging coastal walks to evening
pub strolls. Information leaflet in TICS or
T01545 572142, www.ceredigion.gov.uk.

Watersports
Adventure Beyond, Coed y Bryn, Llandysul,
T01239 858852, www.adventurebeyond.co.uk.
Offer a wide range of courses from coasteering
to mountain boarding, also accommodation.
Cardigan Bay Watersports Centre, The
Sandy Slip, The Harbour, New Quay, T01545
561257, www.cardiganbaywatersports.org.uk,
taster sessions and courses in sailing, wind-
surfing, kayaking and power boat courses.

⊙ Shopping

Crafts
Curlew Weavers Woollen Mill, Rhydlewis,
near Newcastle Emlyn, T01239 851357,

Mon-Fri 0900-1700, family mill producing items like throws, shawls and bedspreads.
Custom House Shop and Gallery, 44-45 St Mary St, Cardigan, T01239 615541, www.customhousecardigan.com, Mon-Sat 1000-1700, has artworks, furniture and gifts.
The Forge Blacksmiths, Gwenlli, near Synod Inn, hand-crafted iron work, T01559 363430, www.fored4u.co.uk.
Rhiannon Celtic Design Centre, Main Sq, Tregaron, T01974 298415, www.rhiannon. co.uk, Mon-Sat 1000-1730, Celtic jewellery.

Transport

Aberystwyth *p164, map p163*
Bus
Local bus company **Richards** (T01239 613756) and **Arriva Cymru** (T01970 617951) use the bus stand on Finch Sq and run regular daily buses to **Dolgellau** (£4.60, 1 hr 15 mins) and **Machynlleth** (£4.70, ½ hr). Bus No 550 runs hourly to **Cardigan** (£4.20, 2 hrs), change at **New Quay**. Bus No X32 runs to **Bangor** (£5, 2 hrs 15 mins). **National Express** has a separate stand, near the train station. Buses run daily to **Welshpool** (£16.40, 1 hr 40 mins), **Shrewsbury** (£22.50, 2 hrs 15

mins), **Birmingham** (£25, 4 hrs) and **London** (£34, 7 hrs); and to **Bristol** (£50, 6 ½ hrs).

Train
The **Cambrian Line** crosses Mid-Wales to **Shrewsbury**, via **Machynlleth** (£4.50, ½ hr) **Newtown** and **Welshpool**. The **Cambrian Coaster** runs up the coast via **Machynlleth** to **Barmouth**, **Harlech**, **Porthmadog** and **Pwllheli** (see Machynlleth, p162).

Cardigan *p167*
Richard Brothers bus No 412 runs hourly to **Haverfordwest** (£3.40, 1 ½ hrs) and **Fishguard** (£2.60, 50 mins). Bus No 550 runs hourly to **Aberystwyth** (£4.20, 2 hrs), change at **New Quay**.

Directory

Health centre Cardigan health centre, T01239 612021. **Police station** T01239 612209. **Internet** Free access at Aberystwyth Library, Constitution St; Cardigan Library, off Pendre; and Aberaeron Library, County Hall. **Café Connect**, Harbourside, New Quay, internet café and gallery.

Central Wales → *Colour map 3*

Squeezed between the bulk of the Cambrian mountains to the west and the rolling English border to the east, Central Wales is wonderfully unspoilt, filled with historic associations and brimming with wildlife. Essentially it consists of the old counties of Montgomeryshire, Radnorshire and Brecknockshire, now lumped together under the unromantic sounding umbrella of Powys. It is probably easier to escape the crowds here than anywhere else in Wales. Much of the area is sparsely populated and it receives far fewer visitors than honeypots like Snowdonia. In the past it was the setting for ferocious fighting between the English and Welsh, notably the battle fought at Pilleth in 1402 when over 1000 English troops were killed by Owain Glyndŵr's men. The landscape is wonderfully varied with mountains, reservoirs, rolling pastures and narrow winding lanes. There are plenty of remote hamlets and little villages to explore, and the towns all have their own distinctive characters, ranging from genteel Victorian spas to bustling market towns. Red kites, rare in other parts of Britain, can be readily spotted and the possibilities for walking, biking and other outdoor activities are endless. ▸▸ *For Sleeping, Eating and other listings, see pages 178-182.*

Ins and outs
Getting there and around The **Cambrian** railway line, www.walesandborders trains.com, serves the northern part of this area, with **trains** running from Shrewsbury to Welshpool and Newtown. The rural **Heart of Wales** line, www.heart-of-wales.com, also

runs between Shrewsbury and Swansea, stopping at towns like Knighton, Llandrindod Wells and Llanwrtyd Wells. To travel between towns and to reach many places, such as the Elan Valley, you must rely on rural **buses** or occasional postbuses, www.postbus.royalmail.com. There is no doubt it is best to have your own transport.
➡ *For further details, see Transport, page 182.*

Information Welshpool TIC ① *Vicarage Gardens Car Park, Church St, T01938 552043, www.welshpool.org, daily Apr-Oct 0930-1730, Nov-Mar 0930-1700.* **Llandrindod Wells** ① *Old Town Hall, Memorial Gardens, Temple St, T01597 822600, llandtic@powys.gov.uk, Easter-Oct Mon-Fri 0930-1700, Sat-Sun 0930-1600; Nov-Easter Mon-Sat 0930-1700.* **Rhayader TIC** ① *Leisure Centre, North St, T01597 810591, www.rhayader.co.uk. Mon-Fri 0930-1700, Sat 0930-1600 (closing 2006).* **Elan Valley Visitor Centre** ① *off B4518 from Rhayader T01597 810898 mid Mar-Nov, daily 1000-1730, www.elanvalley.org.uk.* **Lake Vyrnwy TIC** ① *Vyrnwy Craft Workshops, T01691 870346, laktic@powys.gov.uk, Apr-Oct 1000-1700, Nov-Mar 1000- 1600.*

Welshpool (Y Trallwng) and around

Welshpool has been a market town since the 13th century and with a strategic position on the River Severn, has been one of the main entry points to Wales for centuries. It's only three miles over the border and the architectural influences are more English than Welsh, with half-timbered Tudor buildings rubbing shoulders with Georgian and Victorian styles.

The town's main attraction is the magnificent **Powis Castle** ① *T01938 551944, castle and museum, Easter Thu-Mon 1300-1700, Apr, Sep-Oct closes at 1600, May-Sep 1300-1700; garden Thu-Mon Easter 1100-1800, Apr, Sep-Oct 1100-1800, May-Sep 1100-1800 last admission 30 mins before closing, £8.80, £4.40 children, £22 family; garden only £6.20, £3.10 children, £15.20 family, National Trust,* one mile south of town, accessible by pedestrian path from town centre. This imposing red stoned pile was originally a medieval fortress for Welsh princes, but in 1587 it was bought by an English nobleman Sir Edward Herbert, who started turning it into an extravagant mansion. In 1784, Edward Clive, son of Clive of India, married into the family and today the **Clive Museum** contains a stunning collection of treasures from India, including Mughal armour, ivory playing cards and the tent of the Sultan of Mysore. The state rooms contain carved oak panelling, lavish painted ceilings and fine furniture. Among the many paintings are portraits by Reynolds and Gainsborough, and a landscape of Verona by Bernardo Bellotto, a relative of Canaletto. Allow time to explore the Italianate terraced gardens, virtually unchanged since they were first created in the late 17th century, and now Britain's finest example of a baroque garden. There is topiary so smooth it looks like velvet, lush herbaceous borders, a small fountain garden and wooded walks. The views from the terraces are superb. There's a good tea room and restaurant by the castle.

Close to the town centre is the **Montgomery Canal**, next to which is the little **Powysland Museum** ① *T01938 554656, Mon-Tue, Thu-Fri 1100-1300, 1400-1700; May-Sep also Sat-Sun 1000-1300, 1400-1700; Oct-Apr Sat 1100-1400,* housed in a former warehouse. It focuses on local history from prehistoric times to the 20th century. About half a mile from town is the narrow gauge **Welshpool and Llanfair Railway** ① *Raven Sq station, T01938 810441, www.wllr.org.uk, weekends, daily in Aug, £9 adults, £1 children,* which runs steam trains to the little village of **Llanfair Caereinion**.

North of Welshpool

North of Welshpool is a series of little villages, largely unexplored by visitors. These include the tongue-twisting **Llanfihangel yng Ngwynfa**, birthplace of Welsh hymn writer Ann Griffiths who died aged 29; **Meifod**, an important centre of learning in the Dark Ages and **Llanerfyl**, where the churchyard has an ancient yew tree and the font in the church still bears the marks where Oliver Cromwell's soldiers sharpened their swords against the stone. They are good starting points for walks. **Lake Vyrnwy** ① *T01691 870278, www.stwater.co.uk, 17 miles from Welshpool*, is a reservoir created in 1877 to provide water for Liverpool – flooding the original village of Llanwddyn in the process. Today it's a good spot for birdwatching, walking and cycling and there's also a sculpture trail to follow.

Newtown (Y Drenewydd) and around

Newtown is the largest town in the area and an important centre of the textile industry during the 19th century. The **Textile Museum** ① *Commercial St, T01686 622024, May-Sep Mon-Tue Thu-Sat 1400-1700, £1, children free*, covers the history of the Welsh flannel industry and its importance to the town. The town's most famous son was the industrialist and social reformer Robert Owen, who was born here in 1771 and later founded the model industrial village of New Lanark in Scotland. He greatly improved both living and working conditions for his employees and put great emphasis on education, both for young children and for adults. His birthplace is now a **museum** ① *Broad St, T01686 626345, Mon-Fri 0930-1200, 1400-1530, Sat 0930-1130, free*, which contains letters, a video and portraits of Owen, as well as items from New Lanark, including a Silent Monitor. This was introduced to improve the conduct of workers in the factory and was a coloured marker that was placed beside each worker, publicly reflecting their behaviour. Black was bad, blue was average, while yellow was good and white was excellent. Newtown has a good street market, held since 1279.

Gregynog Hall

About five miles north of Newtown, Gregynog Hall (T01686 650224) is now a residential centre and outpost of the University of Wales. It's a lovely mock-Tudor house which stands on a site that's been occupied since at least the 12th century. In the 1920s the house was bought by Gwendoline and Margaret Davies, whose fine art collection is now in the **National Gallery in Cardiff** (see page 61). The sisters founded a classical music festival, the **Gregynog Festival** (now revived) and also established the *Gregynog Press*, a world famous private printing press. Although you can't visit the house you can stroll in the **gardens** (daily, free). There are 750 acres, with waymarked paths, hides for birdwatching and lots of bulbs in Spring.

Llandiloes and around

Prettier, and a more attractive base than Newtown, Llandiloes is a small market town, once an active centre for Chartism, a movement that campaigned for the rights of the weavers. There's a local **museum** ① *T01686 413777, May-Sep Mon-Tue, Thu-Fri 1100-1300, 1400-1700, Sat 1100-1300, Sun 1400-1700; Oct-Apr Sat 1000-1300*, and several pubs and places to eat. The town's most distinctive building is the **Old Market Hall**, a black and white timber framed building, built around 1612, that's unique in Wales.

From Llandiloes you can go for plenty of walks in wild, unspoilt countryside. It's on the waymarked **Glyndŵr's Way** and is also a good base for exploring the Cambrian Mountains, once proposed as another Welsh National Park. This upland area is divided by the A44: to the north is the Plynlimon massif, the source of the rivers Severn and Wye; to the south are the moorlands of Elenydd, source of the rivers Teifi and Tywi, as well as home to the Elan Valley. About seven miles west of the town is the dense **Hafren Forest**, a pine and spruce plantation that has several walking trails, including a seven-mile route to the source of the Severn that takes you through wild and harsh landscapes. Trails start from Rhyd-y-benwch picnic area. There are also two

⁞ Kite country

Red kites are one of Britain's rarest birds of prey, but due to a stunningly successful protection programme they can be seen in many parts of Wales. The birds, with a wing span of up to 5ft and a distinctive forked tail, were a familiar sight in the Middle Ages and a useful scavenger that kept the streets clean and kept down the numbers of crows; killing a kite attracted a capital punishment. They were known for their habit of stealing washing to line their nests – and are even mentioned by Shakespeare in *The Winter's Tale*. But from the 16th century onwards they began to suffer from persecution, particularly from gamekeepers. Birds were trapped, shot and poisoned, and egg collectors also targeted their nests – by 1900 their numbers had reached crisis point. They were extinct in England and Scotland, and only three or four pairs were left in Wales. In 1903 the first nest protection schemes were established by the Welsh and in 1905 the RSPB got involved. The tiny population just managed to hang on in Wales, but numbers continued to fall. By the 1930s only two breeding pairs were found – and the rarity of their eggs made them an even greater target for egg collectors. Their numbers increased but only gradually: the introduction of myxomotosis in the 1950s poisoned the rabbits on which they fed, and the fact that Welsh kites are living in a marginal habitat means that they don't produce large numbers of chicks. In the 1960s more sophisticated methods of nest protection and monitoring allowed numbers to rise to around 20 pairs, and with support from farmers and other local people they continued to breed. Feeding programmes have played an important part in helping the birds to re-establish and the latest figures say there are 350-400 breeding pairs in Wales. The birds are still vulnerable and poisoning is a particular problem. In Wales this is often accidental but still devastating. Birds can die eating moles that have been killed with strychnine; from taking tainted carcasses left out to kill foxes and badgers; from ingesting lead shot left in dead birds and mammals; and from eating sheep that have died shortly after being dipped.

Red kites have now been re-introduced into England and Scotland, though still suffer from ignorant persecution there. The programme to protect them continues – it is the longest continuous conservation project in the world. See www.gigrin.co.uk for further information.

cycle tracks in the forest. Information on cycle routes in the area can be obtained from www.forestry.gov.uk, T01938 557400, or contact the local TIC.

From Llandiloes there's a superb **scenic drive**: follow the B4518 just past Staylittle then bear left along the unclassified road to Dylife and on to Machynlleth. There's a lovely, eye-stretching viewpoint near Dylife that also serves as memorial to the writer and broadcaster Wynford Vaughan-Thomas (1908-1987).

Rhayader (Rhaeder Gwy) and around

Rhayader is a bustling crossroads in the heart of the countryside and makes a good base for enjoying outdoor activities and visiting two of Central Wales' main attractions: the Elan Valley and the Red Kite Feeding Station. During the 19th century the town was the centre of the famous Rebecca Riots when local men, dressed up as women, went on the rampage smashing the tollgates that encircled the town to protest to those in power about the hardship they were experiencing.

⁝ The vicar of St Harmon

The Reverend Francis Kilvert (1840-1879) became vicar of St Harmon in 1876 and stayed for 15 months. Born in Wiltshire, he went to Oxford, then became a clergyman. After acting as curate for his father, he took up a post at Clyro, then moved to St Harmon. In 1877 he moved to Bredwardine in Herefordshire and in 1879 he married. However, 10 days after the wedding he died of peritonitis aged 38. He kept detailed diaries from 1870-1879, which vividly record the landscape and people of the border communities in Victorian times. His wife destroyed many of his works, but some survived and were eventually published between 1938 and 1940.

Half a mile south of town off the A470 is the **Gigrin Farm Red Kite Feeding Station** ① *T01597 810243, www.gigrin.co.uk, daily feeding 1500 summertime, 1400 winter (GMT) £2.50, £1 children.* Feeding started here in winter 1994 and now there are several hides where you get close up views of red kites, once almost extinct from Wales, swooping down to eat – on some days as many as 150 birds can be seen. Try to arrive about half an hour before feeding so that you get a chance to enjoy the views, watch the films of both kites and badgers feeding, and visit the small exhibition.

There are further opportunities for wildlife watching at **Gilfach Nature Reserve** ① *St Harmon, 3 miles north of Rhayader, T01597 870301, visitor centre Apr-mid Jul Fri-Mon 1000-1700; mid Jul- Sep daily 1000-1630.* It is a Site of Special Scientific Interest and is home to species such as badgers, dippers and pied flycatchers. The visitor centre has cameras linked to nest boxes that show exactly what's happening inside the nests. The centre is run by Radnorshire Wildlife Trust who organize badger watching evenings and wildlife walks.

A few miles north east of Rhayader are the remains of **Cwmhir Abbey** (unrestricted access). This Cistercian abbey was founded in the 12th century, but badly damaged in Owain Glyndŵr's rising of 1401-1402. It was eventually dissolved in 1537. In the ruins you can see a plaque commemorating Llywelyn ap Gruffydd (the Last), the last native Prince Of Wales. He was killed in 1282, and his head taken to London, but his body brought here.

Elan Valley

The enthusiasm with which the English flooded large areas of Wales is in evidence at the Elan Valley (B4518 south west of Rhayader) where a series of four enormous reservoirs were built between 1893 and 1904, to supply the rapidly growing city of Birmingham – and drowning a number of homes in the process. A fifth reservoir was added at Claerwen in 1952. Beneath one of the reservoirs, **Caban Coch**, is the house in which the poet Shelley stayed when he visited the area with his wife. The Victorian dams now make a striking addition to the landscape, and the estate, which covers 70 square miles and habitats varying from moorland to wood, contains nature trails, and paths suitable for walkers and cyclists – including the **Elan Valley Trail**, an eight mile (13 km) path from Rhayader to Craig Goch Dam. Call in to the **Elan Valley Visitor Centre** ① *www.elanvalley.org.uk, daily mid Mar-end Oct, 1000-1730, £1 parking,* first to pick up maps, details of routes and guided walks, and look at the exhibition on the area. Special events are often held such as **birdwatching safaris** and **wildlife walks** ① *contact the Ranger T01597 810880.* Many types of wildlife can be found here, particularly birds, including rare species such as merlin and hawfinch. You'll also find meadow pipits, stonechats, crossbills and red kites.

Knighton (Tref-y-clawdd)

Knighton is as old as Offa's Dyke, and a good starting point for walks along this eighth-century earthwork, which served as both customs' point and a dividing line between Wales and King Offa of Mercia's lands. The Dyke can easily be seen around Knighton and in places was 20-ft high and around 60-ft wide, with a ditch on the western side. It is home to the **Offa's Dyke Centre** ① *West St, T01547 528753, www.offasdyke.demon.co.uk, Easter-Oct daily 0900-1730, Nov-Easter Mon-Fri 0900-1700*. This has information on the **Offa's Dyke Path**, the 177-mile-long National Trail, which runs from Prestatyn in the north to Sedbury near Chepstow in the south, and follows much of the length of Offa's Dyke itself. The path passes through Knighton, the halfway point, and takes you through lovely little hamlets, along river valleys and past castles and hill forts. The town is also on Glyndŵr's Way.

Cyclists can pick up details of the five-day cycle routes around town, available from TICs and on www.radnorforest.com. The town is also on the **Radnor Cycle Ring** ① *information from the TIC or cycling@radnorforest.com*, an 84-mile circular route that takes in Rhayader, Presteigne and Llandrindod Wells too.

Presteigne (Llanandras)

A few miles north of Knighton, Presteigne is a former county town with a good **museum** ① *Broad St, T01544 260650*, in the former Judge's Lodging, the courtroom and residence of visiting judges. The Radnorshire Arms on the High Street is a fine timber framed building which dates back to 1616, built for one of Elizabeth I's courtiers. Later it was owned by the Bradshaw family, one of whom signed the death warrant of Charles I. In 1792 the house became an inn, one of many in Presteigne which was on the coaching route to London.

On the outskirts of town was the estate of Dr John Dee, the Elizabethan alchemist. A ghostly dog was once said to have stalked the surrounding hills, inspiring Sir Arthur Conan Doyle to write *The Hound of the Baskervilles*.

The Wells Towns

This is the collective name given to four Victorian spa towns in the south of the area. The quality and type of water varied in each one, and they attracted different clientele.

Llandrindod Wells

The best preserved of the towns, Llandrindod Wells has a profusion of confident Victorian buildings, wrought iron work and green parkland that leaves you in no doubt of the town's heritage. The magnesium rich waters attracted fashionable types from the English Midlands. You can still taste the waters (not delicious) at the renovated pump room in the town's **Rock Park** ① *T01597 822997*, and there's also a small **museum** ① *Temple St, T01597 824513, closed for refurbishment until Easter 2006*, which has an eclectic mix of exhibits from hospital surgical instruments to a 12th-century log boat. The town's other major attraction is the **National Cycle Museum** ① *Temple St, T01597 825531, www.cyclemuseum.org.uk, Mar-Oct daily 1000-1600, winter Tue, Thu, Sun 1000-1600, £2.50, £1 children*, housed in the Art Nouveau Automobile Palace. The collection has 250 cycles from 1819 to the present day and you'll find everything here from a replica Hobby Horse and a wooden tricycle, to several old boneshakers and pennyfarthings, and various other uncomfortable looking contraptions. Many of the machines are extremely rare.

Builth Wells

Builth Wells was patronized by the working classes, who took the sulphurous waters for their ailments. It is now most famous for being the home of the agricultural extravaganza that is the **Royal Welsh Show** (see page 181). A couple of miles west of the town is the village of **Cilmeri**, where a large monolith commemorates the spot where Llywelyn ap Gruffydd, the last native Welsh prince, was killed while fleeing from the Battle of Builth.

Llangammarch Wells

Sleepy little Llangammarch Wells reached its zenith in the 19th century when the great and the good came to taste its barium rich waters. Both Lloyd George and Kaiser Wilhelm came here.

Llanwrtyd Wells

Llanwrtyd Wells had iron and sulphur springs and attracted Welsh Non-Conformists. Today, it is the best base for activities, visit the **TIC** ① *Ty Barcud, Y Sgwar, T01591 610666, www.llanwrtyd-wells.powys.org.uk, daily 1000-1300, 1330-1700,* for information. The town is set on the Irfon River in stunning countryside and is a good base for walking, pony trekking and mountain biking. There are eight cycle routes around town ranging from the **Victoria Wells route** which is eight miles, to a 12½ mile route in the **Irfon Forest**. Even more demanding is the 38½ mile **Llyne Brianne and Devil's Staircase** route. Walkers are spoiled for choice too, with eight walks in the town and surrounding area. They vary from an easy four mile stroll to a 14-mile hike through the stunning **Abergwesyn Valley**.

The town stages a number of off-the-wall events each year including a man versus horse race in May and the **World Bog Snorkelling Championships** in August. Other events include a Folk and Ale Festival in March, a Morris in the Forest Fest in July and a Saturnalia Roman Festival in January. See Festivals, page 181, for details, or see www.llanwrtyd-wells.powys.org.uk, T01591 610666.

From Llanwrtyd, there's another wonderfully scenic drive, along an old drovers' road the **Abergwesyn Pass**. This covers 14 miles of wild countryside from nearby Abergwesyn over the mountains to Tregaron and is well worth doing, giving you a real sense of the unspoilt nature of the landscape in this part of Wales. Information on this and other scenic drives is available from the TIC.

◉ Sleeping

Welshpool and around *p173*
L-A Lake Vyrnwy Hotel, Llanwddyn, T01691 870692, www.lakevyrnwy.com. Grand hotel where you can spoil yourself with a touch of luxury. Rooms are individually decorated, there are antiques, log fires and a wide range of outdoor activities on offer.
B Buttington Country House, Buttington, near Welshpool, T01938 553351. Georgian rectory set in large garden, offering evening meals by arrangement.
B Cyfie Farm, Llanfihangel-yng-Ngwynfa, near Llanfyllin, T 01691 648451, www.cyfie farm.co.uk. 17th-century farmhouse in a tranquil setting, with lots of period features and comfy rooms.
C Edderton Hall, Forden, near Welshpool, T01938 580339, www.eddertonhall.com. Grand country house with log fires in winter and lots of period features.

C Lower Trelydan, Guilsfield, near Welshpool, T01938 553105, www.lower trelydan.com. High quality B&B on working farm a couple of miles from Welshpool.
D Cwm Llwynog, Llanfair Caereinion, T01938 810791. Working dairy farm set out in the country west of Welshpool. Low beams, an inglenook fireplace and home cooking.
D Trefnant Hall, Berriew, near Welshpool, T01686 640262, jane.trefnant@virgin.net. A couple of miles from Powis Castle this listed farmhouse, on a working farm, offers B&B and also has a self catering unit. Open Mar-Nov.

Newtown and around *p174*
B Milebrook House Hotel, Milebrook, near Knighton, T01547 528632, www.milebrooke house.co.uk. Family-run hotel in its own grounds beside the River Teme. Vegetables

from the garden are served in the restaurant. Good for walking, birdwatching and fishing.

B The Talkhouse, Pontdolgoch, near Caersws, T01686 688919, www.talkhouse. co.uk. Old coaching inn now noted for its modern Welsh cuisine. Make sure you like Laura Ashley fabrics – the rooms are full of them as the original factory is nearby.

C Brynafon Country House, South St, T01597 810735, www.brynafon.co.uk. Just on the edge of Rhayader this former Victorian workhouse is now a 3-star hotel. Comfortable accommodation and is willing to take dogs.

C Elan Valley Hotel, Elan Valley, near Rhayader, T01597 810448, www.elanvalley hotel.co.uk. Family-run hotel offering good food and 2 star accommodation. Special break rates available.

C Lloyd's Hotel and Restaurant, Cambrian Place, Llanidloes, T01686 412284, www.lloydshotel.co.uk. Comfortable rooms at this restaurant with rooms, with friendly touches like hot water bottles on chilly nights.

E Gigrin Farm, Rhayader T01597 810243, www.gigrin.co.uk. 2 rooms, none en suite. If you're keen to watch the red kites, this place is ideal as the kits are fed twice daily. It's a working farm with great views over the surrounding countryside.

Self catering

Glyngynwydd Farm Cottages, Cwm Belan, Llanidloes, T01686 413854, www.glyn gynwydd.co.uk. 5-star cottages converted from traditional stone barn, sleeping 2-12.

Nannerth Fach, Rhayader, T01597 811121, www.nannerth.co.uk. 5-star self catering that sleeps 4. Price from £185-383 per week.

The **Elan Valley Trust** has 2 self-catering properties: **Penglaneinon Farmhouse** that sleeps 6 and **Llannerch y Cawr**, a 15th-century longhouse that is divided in 2 with accommodation for 6 above and 4 below. Both are in the heart of the Elan Valley. Contact **Elan Valley Estate Office**, Elan Village, Rhayader, T01597 810449, www.elanvalley.org.uk

The Wells Towns and around *p177*

L Llangoed Hall, Llyswen, T01874 754525, www.llangoedhall.com. Created by Sir Bernard Ashley, husband of the late Laura Ashley, this mansion gives you a taste of life in a grand country house. Come for a treat.

A-B The Drawing Room, Cwmbach, Newbridge-on-Wye, near Builth Wells, T01982 552493, www.the-drawing-room. co.uk. Restored Georgian house that's now an upmarket restaurant with 3 sleek rooms. Fluffy bathrobes and contemporary design.

B The Metropole, Temple St, Llandrindod Wells, T01597 823700, www.metropole. co.uk, 122 en suite rooms. Grand Victorian building in the heart of town, with comfortable rooms, very much geared to the conference market. There are leisure facilities and friendly and helpful staff. Best town centre hotel.

B-C Lasswade Country Hotel, Station Rd, Llanwrtyd Wells, T01591 610515, www.lasswadehotel.co.uk. Lovely Edwardian house with great views of the surrounding countryside. Organic food and a good base for walking, cycling and wildlife watching.

C Guidfa House, Crossgates, near Llandrindod Wells, T01597 851241, www.guidfa-house.co.uk. Lovely Georgian guesthouse set in its own grounds and serving high quality food.

C Pwll-y-Faedda, Erwood, near Builth Wells, T01982 560202, www.pwllyfaedda.co.uk. Former fishing lodge beside the Wye, set in its own grounds. Period furnishings and a relaxed atmosphere.

C-D Brynhir Farm, Chapel Rd, Howey, near Llandrindod Wells, T01597 822425, www.brynhir.farm.btinternet.co.uk. Friendly working farm just a mile from the town.

D Acorn Court, Chapel Rd, Howey, near Llandrindod Wells, T01597 823543, www.acorncourt.co.uk. Country B&B convenient for wildlife watching and golfing on the outskirts of the town.

D Dolberthog Farm, off Howey Rd, near Llandrindod Wells, T01597 822255, www.uk world.net/dolberthogfarm. Working farm with en suite rooms catering for walkers and cyclists.

D Holly Farm, Howey, near Llandrindod Wells, T01597 822402, www.ukworld.net/ hollyfarm. Restored Tudor farmhouse on a working farm.

🍴 Eating

Welshpool and around *p173*

🍴 **Lake Vyrnwy Hotel**, Llanwddyn, T01691 870692, daily 1900-2100, Sun lunch 1200-1400, afternoon tea 1500-1800. High class hotel restaurant overlooking Lake Vyrnwy. Menu uses local produce including game. Come at least for afternoon tea.

Seeds, Penbryn Cottages, High St, Llanfyllin, T01691 648604, Wed-Sun 1100-1400, Wed-Thu 1900-2030, Fri-Sat 1900-2100. Little country restaurant serving dishes such as rack of lamb or pan-seared tuna. Lots of good vegetable dishes and lovely traditional puddings such as treacle tart.

The Royal Oak, Severn St, T01938 552217, food daily 1200-1400, 1830-2100. Good value food in traditional coaching inn. Other pubs worth trying are *Mermaid* and the *Talbot*, both on the High St.

Stumble Inn, Bwlch-y-Cibau, Llanfyllin, T01691 648860, Wed-Sun 1800-2100, Sun 1200-1400. Country pub serving a variety of pub grub like curries, steaks and Thai dishes.

The Corn Store, 4 Church St, T01938 554614, Mon-Sun 1200-1400, Tue-Sat 1830-2100. Downstairs is a tearoom serving everything from breakfast to quiches, while the wine bar/restaurant upstairs opens in the evening and serves things like crab salad and local beef in whisky and cream.

Newtown and around *p174*

Talkhouse, Pontdolgoch, west of Newtown, T 01686 688919, Tue-Sun 1200-1400, Tue-Sat 1900-2100. Bar and restaurant offering imaginative dishes such as smoked haddock risotto or herb roasted monkfish. Veggie options. Varied wine list.

Lloyds Hotel and Restaurant, Cambrian Place, Llandiloes, T01686 412284. Established restaurant offering a fixed price menu. Booking essential.

Yesterdays Restaurant with Rooms, Severn Sq, Newtown, T01686 622644, from 1830, last food order 1945, closed Sun. Acclaimed restaurant serving Welsh dishes made with fresh local produce, as well as veggie dishes. Accommodation also available.

Elan Valley Hotel, Elan Valley, near Rhayader, T01597 810448, food 1900-2100. Family-run hotel and restaurant which serves bar meals, as well as imaginative restaurant food. Veggies catered for. Real ales.

The Radnorshire Arms, High St, Presteigne, T01544 267406, food 1200-1400, 1900-2100 daily. Attractive pub with black beams. Bar meals and restaurant.

Knighton and around *p177*

Milebrook House, Knighton, T01547 528632, Tue-Sun 1200-1330, 1900-2030. Plenty of homegrown vegetables and fresh local produce at this lovely old house set in its own grounds.

Harp Inn, Old Radnor, near Presteigne, T01544 350655, Sat-Sun 1200-1400, Tue-Sun 1900-2100. Popular pub serving filling meals like lamb steaks or a veggie nut roast. Lovely interior with old beams and open fires.

The Wells Towns *p177*

Carlton House, Dôl-y-coed Rd, Llanwrtyd Wells, T01591 610248, Mon-Sat 1900-2030. Modern British food at this restaurant with rooms. Lots of local meats and fresh vegetables on the menu. Desserts might include homemade ice cream.

Lake, Llangammarch Wells, T01591 620202, daily 1230-1400, 1930-2115. Lovely Edwardian country house hotel offering starters like almond and swede soup and mains such as Gressingham duck with lentils.

Lasswade, Station Rd, Llanwrtyd Wells, T01591 610515, daily 1930-2100. Set menus include dishes like Welsh lamb with garlic. Vegetables are served in imaginative ways. Desserts are traditional and tasty.

Drovers' Rest, The Square, Llanwrtyd Wells, T01591 610264, daily 1230-1500, 1930-2200. Lots of fish and local seasonal vegetables on the menu at this cosy restaurant. Desserts include traditional bread and butter pudding.

The Metropole, Temple St, Llandrindod Wells, T01597 823700. Light bar snacks or main meals in the restaurant of this slightly faded, grand old hotel. Veggie choices.

The Llanerch, off Waterloo Rd, Llandrindod Wells, T01597 822086. Food Mon-Sat 1200-1400, 1800-2100. Good choice of bar meals in this popular 16th-century inn. Light bites such as omelettes served at lunchtime only, while more substantial dishes are always available.

Upstairs Downstairs, Spa Rd, Llandrindod Wells, T01597 824737, daily 1000-1600 winter, Mon-Fri 1000-1700 summer. Pleasant café with a relaxing atmosphere. Wooden floors and old settles inside, as well as some seats outside. Cakes Welsh rarebit, salads or veggie burgers.

🍺 Pubs, bars and clubs

The Wells Towns *p177*
Hundred House Inn, Hundred House, near Builth Wells, T01982 570231, daily 1100-1400, 1800-2130. A former drovers inn, with real fires. Serves good bar food.
Laughing Dog, Howey, near Llandrindod Wells, T01597 822406, food Tue-Sat 1200-1400, 1900-2100. This pub has a games room and offers several real ales.
Red Lion, Llanafan Fawr, near Llandrindod Wells, T01597 860204. This 12th-century pub is possibly the oldest in Wales. It serves real ales and food.

🎭 Entertainment

Oriel 31, Newtown, T01686 625041, Mon-Sat 1000-1700. Gallery with temporary exhibitions and workshops.
Theatr Hafren, Newtown, T01686 625007, www.theatrhafren.co.uk. Stages drama and a wide range of musical events.

🎪 Festivals and events

Jun **Gregynog Festival**, Gregynog Hall, near Newtown, tickets from Theatr Hafren, T01686 625007, www.wales.ac.uk. Classical music festival.
Jul **Royal Welsh Show**, Builth Wells, T01982 553683, www.rwas.co.uk. Agricultural show.
World Bog Snorkelling Championships, Llanwrtyd Wells, T01591 610666. Snorkelling – as the name suggests – in a bog.
Aug **Llandrindod Wells Victorian Festival**, T01597 823441, www.victorianfestival.co.uk. Biggest event in the town with street theatre, drama and music all with a Victorian theme.
Presteigne Festival of Music and the Arts, T01544 267800, www.presteignefestival.com.
Nov **Mid Wales Beer Festival**, Llanwrtyd Wells, T01591 610666, www.llanwrtyd-wells.powys.org.uk. Over 60 real ales, as well as guided walks and evening entertainment.

🧗 Activities and tours

Fishing
Rhayader and Elan Valley Angling Associates, T01597 810383, www.rhayader angling.co.uk. Fly fishing and coarse fishing,

permits required, from Daisy Powell Newsagents, Rhayader, T01597 810451.

General outdoor activities
Elan Valley Lodge, Elan Village, Rhayader, T01597 811143, www.elanvalleylodge.co.uk. Adult outdoor centre offering everything from climbing and canoeing to mountain biking.

Horse riding
Ffos Farm, Ffos Rd, Llanwrtyd Wells, T01591 610371. Offers a variety of treks for all abilities.
The Lion Royal Trekking Centre, Lion Royal Hotel, Rhayader, T01597 810202, www.lion royal.co.uk. Pony trekking May-Sep, booking essential.
Lletty Mawr Trekking Centre, Lletty Mawr, Llangadfan, Welshpool, T01938 820646. Pony trekking from £10 per hr.
The Mill Trekking Centre, Aberhafep, Newtown, T01686 688440, May-Oct. Offer pony trekking and off road karting aimed at children, booking essential, £14 per hr.

Cycling/Mountain biking
Artisans Mountain Bikes, Old Sawmill, Lake Vyrnwy, Llanwddyn, T01691 870317. £2.50 hr.
Brooks Cycles, 9 Severn St, Welshpool, T01938 553582. Cycle shop which also hires out bikes, £8 per day.
Builth Wells Cycles, Smithfield Rd, Builth Wells, T01982 552923. Mountain bike hire and guided rides, £10 ½ day, £12 full day.
Cycles Irfon, Maesydre, Beulah Rd, Llanwrtyd Wells, T01591 610710, www.cycleirfon.co.uk. Mountain bike hire from £10 for ½ day, £15 full day, also do guided tours.
Elan Cyclery, Cwmdauddwr Arms, West St, Rhayader, T01597 811143, www.clivepowell-mtb.co.uk. Bike hire from £3.75 per hr and £15 per day; also do guided weekend breaks.
Freewheeling Wales, circular day routes in Mid Wales, details from T01874 612275.
Red Kite Mountain Centre, Neuadd Arms Hotel, Llanwrtyd Wells, T01591 610236. Mountain bike hire along waymarked routes.

Quad biking
Border Quad Trekking, Bulthy Hill Farm, Middletown, near Welshpool, T01743 884694, www.borderquadtrekking.com. Offer quad biking £25 per hr for adults and grass karting. Also laser clay pigeon shooting £15 per hr, booking required.

Walking
Glyndŵr's Way is a 132-mile-long waymarked trail taking you through some of Wales' least explored countryside. It runs from Knighton on the border with England, through the Cambrian Mountains to Machynlleth, then back to the border near Welshpool. Contact T01654 703376, www.glyndwrsway.org.uk for further information. Other walks include the 6-mile **Anne Griffiths Walk** that runs through the Vyrnwy Valley, www.welshpool.org/activities/walks.

Watersports
Bethania Adventure, the boathouse by the dam, Lake Vyrnwy, T01691 870615. Offers kayaking, canoeing and sailing on the lake.

Wildlife watching
Gilfach Nature Discovery Centre, Gilfach Nature Reserve, St Harman, Rhayader, T01597 870301. Hill farm nature reserve with walks, picnic area and disabled access, on the Wye Valley Walk.

● Transport

Welshpool *p173*
Arriva Cymru bus No 75 runs to **Shrewsbury** (7 daily, 45 mins) and **Newtown** (½ hr). National Express runs to **Shrewsbury** (£7, ½ hr) and **Aberystwyth** (£16.50, 1 hr 40 mins).

The **Cambrian** railway line (www.walesandborderstrains.co.uk) runs trains every 2 hrs east to **Shrewsbury** (£3.90, ½ hr); and west to **Newtown** (£2.90, 15 mins), **Machynlleth** (£9.50, 1 hr) and **Aberystwyth** (£8.50, 1 ½ hrs).

Llandrindod Wells *p177*
Roy Brown bus No T47 runs twice daily to **Builth Wells** (£2.40, 20 mins) and on to **Brecon** (£3.50, 50 mins). Bus No 21 also runs to **Builth Wells** (4 daily, 20 mins). **Crossgates** bus No 19 runs to **Rhayader** (7 daily, £1.50, 25 mins), or the postbus (www.postbus.royalmail.co.uk), runs to **Rhayader** via the **Elan Valley** (Apr-Oct only, 50 mins).

The rural **Heart of Wales** train line (T01597 822053, www.heart-of-wales.co.uk) runs daily to paces like **Knighton** (£2.50, 40 mins), **Llanwrtyd Wells** (£2.40, 25 mins) and **Swansea** (£8.10, 2 ½ hrs).

● Directory

Internet Free access is available from Knighton library, West St, T01547 528778, closed Wed pm; **Rhayader library**, West St, T01597 810548, Mon 1000-1300, 1400-1630, 1700-1900; Wed 1000-1300, 1400-1700, Fri 1000-1300, 1400-1600, Sat 1000-1300; **Presteigne library**, The Old Market Hall, Broad St, T01544 260552; **Newtown library**, Park Lane, T01686 626934; and **Welshpool library**, Brook St, T01938 553001, Mon 0930-1900, Tue, Wed 0930-1700, Fri 0930-1600, Thu and Sat 0930-1300.

Footprint features

Introduction

North Wales is perhaps the most Welsh part of Wales. It was to this area that the ancient Britons retreated following the Roman invasion – the Druids had their last stand in Anglesey – and it still retains a distinctive individualism. It's the part of Wales that feels most culturally different to the rest of Britain. Large numbers of people here speak Welsh as their first language and you will certainly hear it spoken on the streets and in the shops.

North Wales is not noted for its sun, but it does have some striking scenery. Its greatest attraction are the hills and mountains of the Snowdonia National Park, which draw thousands of walkers, climbers and mountain bikers each year. Snowdon, the heart of the area, is the highest peak in Britain outside Scotland. Dotted through the National Park are towns and villages such as busy Betws-y-Coed, which teems with visitors in walking boots and waterproofs, and delightful Beddgelert, one of the most picturesque towns in Wales.

If you're not an outdoor type you can still find things to do here. The north coast is notorious for its raucous 'kiss me quick' strip of caravans and amusement arcades, but it does contain one jewel in Llandudno, a Victorian resort that still has plenty of traditional charm. The eastern corner, closest to the border, is dotted with attractive towns, like historic Ruthin and St Asaph, home to the smallest cathedral in Britain. Go west and you can explore great castles like Caernarfon; neolithic stones on the pastoral isle of Anglesey, and the fantasy village of Portmeirion.

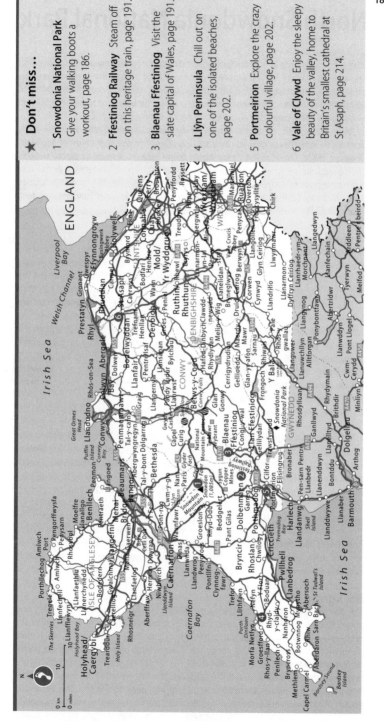

North Wales

★ **Don't miss…**

1 **Snowdonia National Park**
Give your walking boots a
workout, page 186.

2 **Ffestiniog Railway** Steam off
on this heritage train, page 191.

3 **Blaenau Ffestiniog** Visit the
slate capital of Wales, page 191.

4 **Llŷn Peninsula** Chill out on
one of the isolated beaches,
page 202.

5 **Portmeirion** Explore the crazy
colourful village, page 202.

6 **Vale of Clwyd** Enjoy the sleepy
beauty of the valley, home to
Britain's smallest cathedral at
St Asaph, page 214.

North Snowdonia National Park

→ *Colour map 4, grid C3-4*

Wales, for many people, is Snowdonia – particularly the land immediately surrounding Snowdon itself – the highest mountain in England and Wales. The National Park was established in 1951 but Snowdon has attracted walkers, climbers, naturalists, poets and painters from the late 18th century onwards – when the beauty of 'sublime' mountain landscapes, once feared and avoided, first began to be appreciated.

Today Snowdonia , though stunning, can be a busy place and often lacks the 'away from it all' remoteness that you can still experience in the Highlands of Scotland. However, while Snowdon itself may attract many trippers, as well as casual walkers and serious climbers, other challenging peaks such as Tryfan, Glyder Fach and Glyder Fawr are less well trodden. And you don't just have to walk here; the varied landscapes of the National Park make it an excellent place for loads of other outdoor activities, from scrambling to wind surfing. ▸▸ *For Sleeping, Eating and other listings, see pages 192-186.*

Ins and outs

Getting there and around Snowdonia is easily reached by road, with links from the M6 to the M56 and A55 from the north, while the A487 and A470 get you there if coming from the south. The A5 runs through the heart of the area, from Shrewsbury across the border in England, direct to the bustling centre of Betws-y-Coed. **Trains** run from Llandudno Junction to Betws-y-Coed and Blaenau Ffestiniog. Some **buses** run from Betws to Capel Curig. You can take the **Ffestiniog Railway** to Porthmadog, where you can get services along the Cambrian coast. There is no doubt that, even though the roads can get very busy in high season, the **car** is the best way to get around, particularly if you're wanting to explore the area in depth. However the National Park Authority encourage more environmentally friendly ways of travelling and **Snowdon Sherpa** buses run around the main settlements such as Betws-y-Coed and Llanberis. The **Freedom of Wales Flexi Pass** allows unlimited travel on mainline trains and buses.

▸▸ *For further details, see Transport, page 194. See also South Snowdonia National Park, page 154.*

Information Bala ⓘ *Pensarn Rd T01678 521021, Apr-Oct daily 1000-1800, Nov-Mar Fri-Mon 1000-1600, www.bala-snowdonia.com.* **Betws-y-Coed** ⓘ *Royal Oak Stables T01690 710426, Easter-Oct 0930-1730, Oct-Easter 0930-1630, www.betws-y-coed. co.uk.* **Blaenau Ffestiniog** ⓘ *High St, T01766 830360, Apr-Oct daily 0930-1730, may close for lunch, tic.blaenau@eryri-npa.gov.uk.* **Beddgelert** ⓘ *Canolfan Hebog, T01766 890615 daily Easter-Oct 0930-1730; Fri-Sun Nov-Mar 0930-1630, www.beddgelerttourism.com.* **Llanberis** ⓘ *41b High St, T01286-870765, llanberis.tic @gwynedd.gov.uk, daily Easter- Oct 1000-1800, and weekends 1100-1600 in winter.* **Snowdonia National Park Authority HQ** ⓘ *Penrhyndeudraeth, Gwynedd, T01766 770274, www.eryri-npa.gov.uk; www.snowdonia-npa.gov.uk.* More information is available from www.visitsnowdonia.info.

Background

The Snowdonia National Park (Parc Cenedlaethol Eryri) is the largest in Wales and covers 840 square miles (2,175 sq km), embracing areas as diverse as the craggy peaks of the mountains, and the sandy beaches of the Cambrian coast. However, when most people refer to Snowdonia they mean the mountainous area surrounding the park's focal point, **Snowdon** (Eryri), at 3560ft (1085m) the highest peak in England and Wales and a majestic draw for lovers of the outdoors. The first recorded ascent of Snowdon was in 1639, by Thomas Johnson in search of botanical specimens. The summit is known as *Yr Wyddfa* in Welsh, meaning 'the burial place', suggesting that the mountain

Topping Snowdon

There are six major paths to the summit of Snowdon, the routes varying in difficulty. Before you tackle any of them or do any serious walking in Wales, make sure you are properly prepared with boots, warm and waterproof clothing (even in summer), maps (the best for walkers are OS Explorer 1:25,000), compass, food and water. Check weather conditions before setting off (T09068 500449, www.metoffice.com). To give you an idea of how severe conditions can get think about this: Snowdon gets 200 inches (508 cm) of rain each year, the temperature can reach -20°C in winter, and the wind speed can reach 150 mph. A leaflet, *Stay Safe in Snowdonia*, is available from TICs.

The most popular and easiest ascent is the **Llanberis Path**, which follows the Snowdon Mountain Railway and takes about three hours (descent about one to two hours). The other paths are the **Miners' Track**, the **Pyg Track**, the **Rhyd Ddu Path**, the **Snowdon Ranger Path** and the **Watkin Path**. There is also a serious ridgewalk, the **Snowdon Horseshoe**.

Of course you don't have to walk to reach the top of Snowdon (to the disgust of legions of outdoorsy types). Llanberis, starting point for many of the classic ascents of Snowdon, is also the starting point for the **Snowdon Mountain Railway** ① *T0870 4580033, www.snowdonrailway.co.uk, daily mid-Mar-Nov, weather permitting, £20 return, £14 children,* the narrow gauge railway (Britain's only rack and pinion railway) that runs nearly five miles up the mountain and has been operating since 1896. Once on the summit you can have a hot drink at the café (yes, a café, designed by Clough William-Ellis of Portmeirion fame) and in half an hour make the return journey. Book in advance in summer, if possible.

held a fascination for earlier civilizations too. In later years the area has been used as a training ground for serious mountaineers, including those who conquered Everest.

Betws-y-Coed and around

Victorian travellers flocked to Betws-y-Coed (pronounced *betoos-ee-coyd*, often shortened to *betoos*). The village came to prominence following the establishment of an artists' colony in 1844. Waterfalls like Swallow Falls and the Pont-y-Pair bridge were favourite subjects, while the coming of the railway in 1868 made this the premiere tourist centre in Snowdonia. Tourists still fill the little streets today, though once they've had tea, browsed in the outdoor shops and bought some pottery, they've pretty much exhausted the village's possibilities. There's plenty of accommodation though and it's a convenient and pleasant base from which to explore Snowdonia. On the edge of the village you can see Thomas Telford's Waterloo Bridge, built in 1815. Made of cast iron it carries the emblems of the then newly United Kingdom: England's rose; Scotland's thistle; Ireland's clover and Wales' leek.

To get to know the area better you can take a guided walk (see page 193). Other attractions in the village itself include the **Motor Museum** ① *T01690 710760, Easter-Oct, daily 1000-1800, £1.50,* which has a collection of vintage cars and the **Conwy Valley Railway Museum** ① *The Old Goods Yard, T01690 710568, daily 1015-1700, £1.50, 80p child, £4 family,* where kids can ride on a miniature steam railway. The village is really a base for walking and mountain biking. The best biking trails are in the **Gwydir Forest Park** (see Activities, page 193), while all types of walks are accessible, from tough climbs in the surroun- ding mountains to gentle woodland strolls.

A couple of miles west of the village, along the A5, is one of the area's most visited attractions **Swallow Falls**. A draw since Victorian times, this pretty waterfall

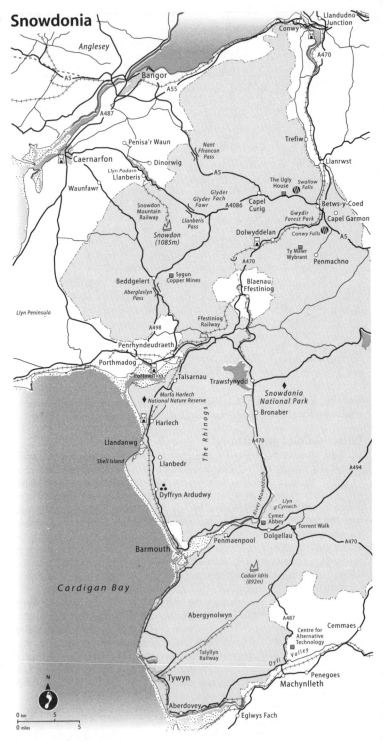

Anglesey

Llandudno
Junction

Conwy

A470

Bangor

A5

A55

A487

A5

Trefiw

Penisa'r Waun

Nant
Ffrancon
Pass

Llanrwst

Caernarfon

Dinorwig

A5

The Ugly
House

Swallow
Falls

Betws-y-Coed

Llyn Padarn

Llanberis

Glyder
Fawr

Glyder
Fach

Capel
Curig

Capel Garmon

A5

Waunfawr

A4086

Gwydir
Forest Park

Snowdon
Mountain
Railway

Llanberis
Pass

Dolwyddelan

Conwy Falls

Snowdon
(1085m)

A470

Ty Mawr
Wybrant

Penmachno

Sygun
Copper Mines

Beddgelert

Blaenau
Ffestiniog

Aberglaslyn
Pass

Llyn Peninsula

Ffestiniog
Railway

A498

Penrhyndeudraeth

Porthmadog

Portmeirion

Talsarnau

Trawsfynydd

Snowdonia
National Park

Morfa Harlech
National Nature Reserve

Bronaber

Harlech

The Rhinogs

A470

Llandanwg

Shell Island

Llanbedr

Dyffryn Ardudwy

River Mawddach

A494

Llyn
Cynwch

Cymer
Abbey

Torrent Walk

Barmouth

Penmaenpool

Dolgellau

A470

Cadair Idris
(892m)

Cardigan Bay

Abergynolwyn

A487

Cemmaes

Centre for
Alternative
Technology

Dyfi
Valley

Talyllyn
Railway

Penegoes

N

Tywyn

Machynlleth

0 km   5

0 miles   5

Aberdovey

Eglwys Fach

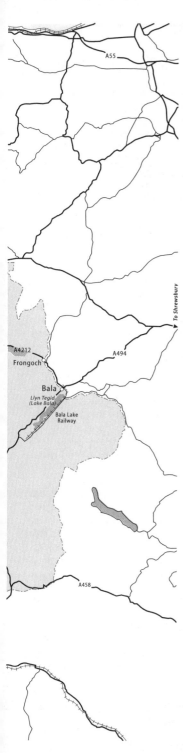

can only be reached through a turnstile (£1 coin, correct money only). Further along the road is **The Ugly House** or **Ty Hyll** ⓘ *T01690 720287, www.snowdonia-society. org.uk, Apr-Oct daily 0930-1700, £1*, a cottage made from a haphazard arrangement of stones – it's said to date from 1475, when 'ty-un-nos' applied. This ancient law stated that a house would be yours if you built it overnight and had smoke coming from the chimney by morning; if you threw an axe from each of the four corners of the cottage the land delineated would be yours too. It's now the headquarters of the Snowdonia Society and has a little garden, woodland walk and nature trail.

From here the road leads to **Capel Curig**, the little village known to all walkers and climbers in Snowdonia. Standing at the gateway to the Llanberis and Nant Francon passes, it is a good base for exploring the surrounding mountains and there are several places to eat and stay, all heavily geared to hearty rucksack wearers. The village is the location of the **National Mountain Centre**, Plas y Brenin (see page 193).

Llanberis

The busy lakeside village of Llanberis (www.llanberis.org) was once a centre of slate production and is the starting point for the **Snowdon Mountain Railway** (see Topping Snowdon, page 187) as well as the most popular walking route up the peak, the Llanberis Path. Now that the slate quarry has shut, the town is a mecca for walkers and climbers, cheerfully rustling in brightly coloured outdoor gear. Attractions include **Electric Mountain** ⓘ *T01286 870636, www.electricmountain.co.uk, Apr-May, Sep-Oct daily 1030-1630, Jun-Aug daily 0930-1730, Feb-Mar, Nov-Dec Wed-Sun 1030-1630; last underground tour 1 hr before closing, £6.50 tour high season, £5 low season*, the lakeside visitor centre for the **Dinorwig Power Station**, a hydro-electric station housed in enormous caverns underground. An exhibition displays the 16th-century Peris Boat, and a 12th century dugout canoe, unearthed during the building of the power station. Entry to the displays and cafés is free; the underground tour takes an hour – best to book in advance.

⁚ A labour of love

Born in Ty Mawr, Penmachno in 1545, William Morgan studied at Cambridge, just a few years after an Act of Parliament was passed in 1563 by Elizabeth I to allow the translation of the Bible into Welsh 'because the English tongue is not understood [by]... her majesty's... obedient subjects inhabiting in Wales.' The first Welsh New Testament was produced in 1567 by Bishop William Salesbury, Richard Davies and Thomas Huet. However, they did not continue their task and the rest of the work passed to Morgan, by now Rector of Llanrhaedr-ym-Mochnant. He did so with enthusiasm, making himself so unpopular locally that he had to have an armed escort to and from the church, and preached his sermons with a pistol in his belt.

In 1588, the first copies of the complete Welsh Bible were printed. This helped to ensure the future of the Welsh language and it became the basis of Welsh services today.

Padarn Country Park

Padarn Country Park (T01286 870892) is an 800 acre park around the shores of Lake Padarn, on land once part of the Dinorwig Slate Quarry, which employed over 3,000 local men until its closure in 1969. The workshops are preserved in the **Welsh Slate Museum** ① T01286 870630, www.nmgw.ac.uk,daily, Easter-Oct 1000-1700, Nov-Easter, Sun-Fri 1000-1600, free, as well as a reconstructed terrace of quarrymen's houses, moved from nearby Tanygrisiau, and a huge waterwheel. You can take a trip on the lake in a pleasure steamer, the **Snowdon Star** ① T07974 716418, £4.50, £3 children, in summer. Trips start from a jetty near the Slate Museum. Also in the park is the **Llanberis Lake Railway** ① T01286 870549, www.lake-railway.co.uk, daily Easter-Oct, £6, £4 children, a steam railway originally built to transport slate from the quarry.

Just south of the railway is the ruined **Dolbadarn Castle**, built in the 13th century by the mighty Llywelyn the Great. The castle predates the English fortresses of Edwardian conquest and provides solid evidence of the extent of Llywelyn's influence. Its simplicity and endurance has inspired artists such as Richard Wilson and JMW Turner.

South of Betws-y-Coed

To visit **Conwy Falls** ① T01690-710696, www.conwy-falls.co.uk, £1, you enter through a turnstile by a pink-painted café, designed by Sir Clough William-Ellis and can then walk down to see the stunning waterfalls and the remains of a Victorian fish ladder.

Northwest of Penmachno village, is **Tŷ Mawr Wybrant** ① A5 south of Betws, then B4406 to Penmachno, 2½ miles from Penmachno, T01690 760213, Easter-Sep, Thu-Sun 1200-1700, Oct 1200-1600, £2.60, £1.30 children, family £6.30, National Trust. This cottage is reached via a single track road that seems to last forever. It is an isolated spot, worth visiting for the delicious sense of remoteness alone. The cottage itself was the home of Bishop William Morgan (1545-1604), the man who first translated the whole of the bible into Welsh (see box, above). The house has been restored to its 16th-century appearance and has a display of Welsh Bibles inside.

Dolwyddelan Castle ① Apr-Sep Mon-Sat 1000-1800, Sun 1100-1600, Oct-31 Mar 1000-1600 Mon-Sat, 1100-1600 Sun, £2, £1.50 children, $5.50 family, was built around 1210-1240 by Llywelyn the Great to guard a mountain pass. The castle was restored in Victorian times and you get great views from the battlements. From Dolwyddelan village you can go for a walk along the river, or hike to the summit of Moel Siabod (2,862ft). In the village is **St Gwyddelan's church**, built early in the 16th century with a seventh-century Celtic bell, Cloch Wyddelan.

Blaenau Ffestiniog

When the Snowdonia National Park was established, the importance of industrial sites was not recognized. So although it's right at its heart, the slate mining town of Blaenau Ffestiniog isn't part of the National Park itself. Yet it's one of the most interesting places to visit. Today, it's essentially a living museum for the world famous slate mining industry that brought the town prosperity in the 19th century, having declined dramatically since the 1960s. Slate still dominates the area, and if you arrive along the A470 from Betws-y-Coed the sudden appearance of this grey, forbidding landscape of shattered slate heaps can be depressing in the extreme. But it also has a harsh, dramatic beauty.

The **Ffestiniog Railway** ① *T01766 516024, www.festrail.co.uk, day rover £16, £12.80 childen*, is a lovely narrow gauge railway built in the 1830s to transport slate from the quarries high up in Blaenau Ffestiniog down to the harbour at Porthmadog. Welsh slate was recognized as some of the finest in the world and in the 19th century was shipped everywhere, particularly for use as a durable roofing material. The trains originally ran downhill – fully loaded – pulled by gravity, and were pulled back up by horses when empty. In 1863 steam locomotives were introduced and passenger trains soon followed. By the 1920s new roofing materials had ousted slate and the industry declined dramatically; the line fell into disrepair and closed in 19460. Enthusiastic volunteers were determined to get it working again and in 1982 the line was re-opened. A ride on the train is a stunning experience, taking you round horseshoe bends, past lakes and waterfalls and through some of Snowdonia's most dramatic countryside. The train calls en route at **Minffordd**, **Penrhyn** and **Tan-y-Bwlch**.

Blaenau Ffestiniog's other main attraction is the **Llechwedd Slate Caverns** ① *T01766 830306, www.llechwedd/slate/caverns.co.uk, Mar-Sep daily 1000-1715, Oct-Feb 1000-1615, free above ground, underground tours £8.75, £6.50 children: buses run from the town, a joint ticket can be purchased with the railway*. This slate mine gives you a real insight into the life of the miners and the importance of the industry to the town. The big pull are the underground tours for which you don hard hats: the Miners' Tramway takes you through slate caverns mined around 1846; the Deep Mine tour takes you underground on Britain's steepest passenger railway. Other attractions include a Victorian mining village with a cottage, inhabited until the 1960s; the working Miners' Arms pub; and a sweet shop, where you can change money into old currency and purchase sweets like gobstoppers.

Beddgelert

Beddgelert, six miles west of Blaenau Ffestiniog, is easily the most attractive settlement in Snowdonia, with picturesque stone houses surrounded by majestic mountains and two gushing rivers running through the village. It is also the end of the beautiful **Aberglaslyn Pass**.

The most famous sight is the **grave of Gelert** (*bedd* means grave in Welsh), the faithful dog who was said to belong to Prince Llewelyn. The story goes that the prince left the dog to guard his child, but when he returned he found the dog covered in blood, while the child was missing. Assuming the dog had killed the child, Llywelyn killed Gelert, then found the child lying safe with a dead wolf (that Gelert had bravely killed) nearby. You can see Gelert's grave under a lone tree, but it's believed the tale was made up in the 18th century by a local publican trying to attract tourists to the area – the place name instead referring to the grave of Celert, an early saint.

A short distance out of the village is the **Sygun Copper Mine** ① *T01766 510101, www.syguncoppermine.co.uk, daily 1030-1600, £7.95, £5.95 children*, where you can take an underground tour through tunnels veined with coloured ores and chambers of stalactites and stalagmites. There's also a small Celtic village, a room containing Bronze Age artefacts and a kids' playground.

Bala is 15 miles southeast of Blaenau Ffestiniog, reached via the A4212, on the edge of the National Park. It sits by the largest freshwater lake in Wales Llŷn Tegid (Lake Bala), a noted spot for all sorts of watersports (see Activities, page 193). Just out of town is the **Bala Lake Railway** ① *T01678-540666, www.bala-lake-railway.co.uk, £7 return, 25 mins*, a narrow gauge, steam railway, which goes from Bala to Llanuwchllyn.

● Sleeping

Betws-y-Coed and around *p187*
C Afon View, Holyhead Rd, T01690 710726, www.afon-view.co.uk. Friendly, clean and comfortable B&B near the river. Non-smoking.
C Bryn Tyrch Hotel, Capel Curig, on A5, T01690 720223, www.bryntyrch-hotel.co.uk. 17 rooms, 10 en suite. Ideally situated for walkers, climbers and cyclists, and with a pleasant, relaxed atmosphere. Evening meals and lunches available too.
C Glyntwrog House, just south of Waterloo Bridge,15 mins walk from the village, T01690 710930, www.glyntwrogsnowdonia.co.uk. Award-winning, with clean and comfortable rooms. Walkers and cyclists welcome.
C Henllys (The Courthouse), Old Church Rd, T01690 710534, www.guesthouse-snowdonia.co.uk. Former courthouse, now B&B, that retains some of its old features – including an old holding cell.
C Pengwern, Allt Dinas, T01690 710480, www.snowdoniaaccommodation.com. Lovely house 1 mile south of Betws-y-Coed, once used by visiting artists. Rooms individually furnished and very comfortable. The Richard Gay Somerset room must boast the best loo-with-a-view in Britain. A former artist's studio is now a self-catering cottage.
C Penmachno Hall, Penmachno, T01690 760410, www.penmachnohall.co.uk. 4-star country house in former rectory. Lovely rural setting by the river.
E Swn-y-Dwr, Pentrefelin, T01690 710648. Pleasant guesthouse, with lovely garden.
F YHA Hostel, Capel Curig, T0870 7705746, www.yha.org.uk. Hostel with family rooms

Llanberis *p189*
C Plas Coch Guest House, High St, T01286 872122, www.plas-coch.co.uk. Comfortable accommodation and good organic breakfasts.
D Marteg B&B, High St, T01286 870207, http://mysite.freeserve.com/martegllanberis. Spacious rooms in 4-star B&B happy to cater for walkers and cyclists.

F Jesse James' Bunkhouse, Buarth y Clytiau, Penisarwaun, T01286 870521. Established bunkhouse a few miles outside Llanberis.

Beddgelert *p191*
B Tanronnen Inn, T01766 890347. Comfortable and cosy inn, with some rooms that overlook the river or the mountains. Meals available and packed lunches can be made up on request.
B-C Sygun Fawr, off A498, near Beddgelert, T01766 890258, www.sygunfawr.co.uk. 10 rooms, all en suite. Lovely old manor house in pretty gardens, close to Beddgelert village. Rooms clean and comfortable, some with views over the mountains. Well worth seeking out. Excellent restaurant (see Eating).
E Plas Colwyn, on A4085, T01766 890458. 6 rooms, 3 en suite. Clean and friendly guest-house set in lovely gardens, with log fires in winter. Walk to Snowdon from the garden.

● Eating

Betws-y-Coed and around *p187*
♛ Bryn Tyrch Hotel, Capel Curig, on A5, T01690 720223. Food 1200-1500, 1800-2100 Wed-Mon in winter, daily in summer. Bustling bar serving wide range of meals, including an excellent choice of veggie/vegan dishes, such as aduki bean cottage pie.
♛ Stable Bar, Royal Oak, Holyhead Rd, T01690 710219, daily 1200-2130. The hub of the village. You can sit outside in summer and there's a wide range of food available. Live jazz on Thu, local male voice choir on Fri.
♛ Ty Gwyn, by Waterloo Bridge on A5, T01690 710383, daily 1200-1400, 1900-2100. Attractive inn serving good bar meals. Very popular with locals and visitors. Best to reserve.
♛ White Horse Inn, Capel Garmon, T01690 710271, Mon-Thu 1830-2100, Fri- Sat 1830-2130, Sun 1900-2100. 1½ miles from Betws-y-Coed, this pub serves highly-rated, home-made food and real ales. Log fires in winter.

Beddgelert p191

Sygun Fawr, off A498, near Beddgelert, T01766 890258, daily except Tue. Popular guesthouse set in its own grounds and using lovely fresh produce. You'll need to book.

Beddgelert Bistro, T01766 890543, daily 0900-1700, 1900-2100. Serves traditional tea and cakes as well as more substantial meals.

Glaslyn Ices, award-winning ice cream shop. Home made sorbets and every flavour of ice cream from good old vanilla to chocolate and ginger or coffee and rum.

Tanronnen Inn, T01766 890347. Food 1230-1400, 1900-2030 daily. Good choice of bar meals. Popular with locals and visitors.

● Pubs, bars and clubs

Betws-y-Coed p187

Stable Bar, Royal Oak, T01690 710219. Bustling pub in the heart of the village. On Fri the male voice choir sing here.

⊙ Shopping

Betws-y-Coed p187

Betws-y-Coed is the main shopping centre for outdoor gear. Outlets include: **Cotswold**, Holyhead Rd, T01690 710710; **Rock Bottom**, T01690 710234 (for end of line stock); **Stewart R Cunningham**, Bryn-Pair villa T01690-710454; and **Snowdon Ranger**, T01690 710888 in a converted church.

▲ Activities and tours

Climbing

Beacon Climbing Centre, Waunfawr, 5-6 miles west of Llanberis, T01286 650045, www.beaconclimbing.com, has an indoor climbing wall and offers short, taster sessions. 1 ½ hrs, £45 for 2 people. Also do outdoor climbing courses in Snowdonia.

General outdoor activities

National Mountain Centre, Plas Y Brenin, Capel Curig, T01690 720214, www.pyb.co.uk, runs residential or 2-hr courses in everything from rock climbing and mountaineering to kayaking, canoeing and skiing. Geared to kids but adults welcome. Indoor climbing wall and ski slope.

Surf Lines Adventure Shop, Unit 2, Y Glyn, Llanberis, T01286 879001, www.surf-lines.

co.uk. Offer activities from coasteering, climbing and guided trips to Snowdon. Also canoe hire.

Horse riding

Ty Coch Farm, Penmachno, near Betws-y-Coed, T01690 760248, www.horse-riding-wales.co.uk, wide range of rides from 1 hr to full day, beginners upwards.

Dolbadarn Pony Trekking Centre, by Dolbadarn Hotel, High St, Llanberis, T01286 870277/871284, www.dolbardenhotel.co.uk. From Easter-Sep, 1hr to full day rides, all levels.

Mountain biking

The **Gwydir Forest**, near Betws-y-Coed, offers biking including the 25 km Marin Trail. Further information is available from *Forest Enterprise*, T01341 422289, www.mbwales.com. Mountain bike companies include:

Beics Beddgelert, 1 mile outside Beddgelert, T01766 890434, www.beics.com, mountain bike hire, full day from £24, 2 hrs £8.

Beics Betws, Betws-y-Coed, T01690 710766, www.bikewales.co.uk, £5 per hr, £18 pre day;

Paragliding

Snowdon Gliders, Mynydd Llandygai, T01248 600330, www.snowdongliders.co.uk. Paragliding for all levels.

Rowing

Padarn Boats, on Llŷn Padarn, Llanberis. Hire out rowing boats in summer, go to the green hut by the playground

Walking

Guided walks round Betws-y-Coed and the surrounding area, start from TIC at 1000, Thu-Sun, and Bank Hol Mon, Apr-Sep, around 6-8 miles, £4, book in advance, T0151 4880052 or T07790 851333.

Watersports

Bala Adventure and Watersports, by TIC at Bala lake, T01678 521059, www.balaadventureandwatersportscentre.co.uk. Windsurfing, kayaking, canoeing and land yachting.

Whitewater rafting

National Whitewater Centre, Frongoch, Bala, 2 hr to full day experiences, T01678 521083, www.ukrafting.co.uk, white water rafting and kayaking.

The Snowdon Sherpa

Snowdon Sherpa buses run throughout the park to encourage people to leave their cars behind. Buses run on fixed schedules every two hours and will let you off at any point; timetables are available from TICs. A **Snowdon Sherpa Day Ticket** costs £3, £1.50 for children, or a **Freedom of Wales Flexi Pass** allow unlimited travel on Snowdon Sherpa buses as well as all mainline rail services and buses.

Contact **Bus Gwynedd**, T01286 679535, www.gwynedd.gov.uk/ bwsgwynedd, for information. Useful routes include:
S1 Llanberis/Nant Peris/Pen-y-Pass
S2 Pen-y-Pass/Capel Curig/ Bethesda/Pen-y-Pass
S3 Bangor/Bethseda/Capel Curig/ Pen-y-Pass
S4 Pen-y-Pass/Beddgelert/Caernarfon

⊖ Transport

Betws-y-Coed and around *p187*
Snowdon Sherpa bus No S2 runs 3 times daily to **Llandudno**, **Llanberis** and **Capel Curig**. Bus No 97 runs to **Capel Curig**, **Beddgelert** and **Porthmadog**.

The Conwy Valley train line runs to several times daily to **Llandudno** (£3.85, ½ hr) and **Blaenau Ffestiniog** (£3, ½ hr). Buses on Sun.

Blaenau Ffestiniog *p191*
Arriva Cymru bus No 35 runs to **Dolgellau**

(4 daily, £2.50, ½ hr); the No 38 runs to **Harlech** (4 daily, £2.30,40 mins) and **Barmouth** (£2.20, 1 hr). **Express Motors** run daily buses to **Caernarfon** (£5, 1 hr 15 mins) and **Porthmadog** (£2.60, ½ hr).

The Ffestiniog Railway (see p191) runs to **Porthmadog** (£14) and links the Conwy Valley and Cambrian Coaster lines. The Conwy Valley line runs several times daily to **Betws-y-Coed** (£3, ½ hr) and **Llandudno** (£5, 1 hr). The Cambrian Coaster runs across to **Pwllheli** and down to **Aberystwyth**.

Conwy

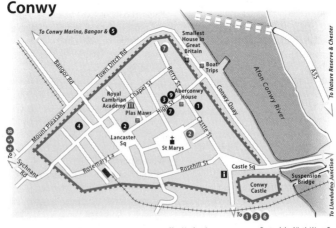

Sleeping	Glan Heulog 6	Beyond the Ninth Wave 3
Bryn Derwen 1	Swan Cottage 7	Bistro Conwy 4
Castle 2	Sychnant Pass House 8	Mulberry 5
Conwy Valley Backpackers		Shakespeare's 7
Bunkbarn 3	**Eating**	Townhouse 9
Conwy Youth Hostel 4	Anna's Tearooms 1	
Crows Nest Hall 5	Alfredo's 2	

N

0 metres 100
0 yards 100

Northwest corner → *Colour map 3*

The northwest corner of Wales feels a world away from the chips and caravans of the north coast resorts. It is the most traditional part of the country, where the language is spoken widely and where the Celtic past never seems far away. You sense a difference as soon as you see the brooding beauty of Conwy Castle and stroll the streets of this neat little walled town – the best base for exploring the area. Further along the coast you come to the busy university town of Bangor and then to the heartland of Welsh nationalism, Caernarfon, famous for its castle. This corner of Wales also includes the two most characterful and isolated parts of the country; the beautiful Llŷn Peninsula and the pastoral island of Anglesey, last refuge of the Celts and rich in prehistoric sites. ▸▸ *For Sleeping, Eating and other listings, see pages 204-209.*

Ins and outs

Getting there and around Conwy is on the main A55 road. To the Conwy Valley, take the A470 or B5106. **Buses** that run along the north Wales coast stop at Conwy. **National Express** coaches run to Bangor, Caernarfon and Holyhead as well as Pwllheli. There are regular **trains** from London and Birmingham to Llandudno Junction, where you can change for Conwy station. The **Conwy Valley Railway**, www.conwy valleyrailway.co.uk, runs between Llandudno on the coast and Blaenau Ffestiniog in Snowdonia. The **North Wales Coast Line** from Chester runs to Bangor and Holyhead on Anglesey. **Cambrian Coaster** trains run to Porthmadog and Pwllheli on the Llŷn. The main towns of Conwy, Bangor and Caernarfon are small enough to be explored on foot. Buses run to the main places in Anglesey, however it is much easier with your own transport. ▸▸ *For further details see Transport, page 208.*

Information Conwy Castle Visitor Centre ⓘ *T01492 592248, conwy@nwtic.com, Apr-Sep daily 0930-1700, Oct-Mar, Mon-Sat 0930-1600, Sun 1100-1600.* **Porthmadog TIC** ⓘ *High St, T01766-512981, Apr-Oct daily 1000-1800, Nov-Mar 1000-1700.* **Holyhead TIC** (Anglesey) ⓘ *Stena Line Terminal, T01407 762622, www.anglesey.gov.uk, daily 0830-1800.* **Caernarfon TIC** ⓘ *Oriel Pendeitsh, Castle St, T01286-672232, daily Apr-Oct 1000-1800, Nov-Mar daily except Wed 1000-1630, www.caernarfon.com.* **Pwllheli TIC** ⓘ *Min y Don, Sgwar Yr Orsaf, T01758 613000, pwllheli.tic@gwnedd.gov.uk.*

Background

The Celts in the northwestern corner of Wales held out longer against the Roman invaders than anywhere else. The Druids, Celtic religious leaders, established a powerful base on the remote isle of Anglesey and it became an important spiritual centre. The Romans were held off until AD 61, when they massacred the Druids. The fall of the Roman Empire left a power vacuum and different parts of Wales were ruled by different leaders, all jostling for position. Those in the northwest, the Princes of Gwynedd, emerged as particularly powerful and extended their influence through much of Wales. But they were eventually defeated by Edward I, who left his stamp on the area when he built castles such as Conwy, Caernarfon and Beaumaris in his ruthless bid to bring the Welsh to heel. The area retains a stronger sense of a Welsh identity than other parts of the country and today Welsh is still the first language of the vast majority of people – particularly on Anglesey.

Conwy

Conwy is a pretty little walled town dominated by a stunningly photogenic castle. With its well-preserved medieval charms, and picturesque setting on the Conwy estuary, it's easy to see why it's a World Heritage Site. The town's history stretches back to Roman times at least, with settlers being attracted to the mussels that are still harvested there today. The castle is certainly the biggest draw but there are enough other attractions, shops and places to eat to occupy you for a day or two.

Constructed between 1283 and 1287, **Conwy Castle** ⓘ *To1492 592358, www.cadw.wales.gov.uk, Easter-end May, Oct daily 0930-1700; Jun-Sep 0930-1800 daily; Nov-Easter Mon-Sat 0930-1600, Sun 1100-1600, £4, £3.50 children, family £11.50*, was one of the key fortresses in the 'iron ring' of castles built by Edward I to contain the Welsh. It took just four years to build at a cost of around £15,000 – about £9 million today – and its exterior, with eight huge round towers, is still largely intact. It's easy to see why it has long been a favourite subject for artists, including JMW Turner who painted it many times. Once inside, make sure you go up to the battlements, from which you'll get striking views of the surrounding mountains and of Conwy's well preserved town walls, which stretch for around three quarters of a mile and are studded with 22 towers.

You can also see Conwy's old **Suspension Bridge** ⓘ *To1492 573282, end Mar-Oct daily 1000-1700, £1.20, children 60p*, built by Thomas Telford and opened in 1826. The bridge today is only used by pedestrians. Your fee gets you into the old Toll House, furnished as it would have been when inhabited around 1891.

From the bridge you can walk along **Conwy Quay**, where **boat trips** ⓘ *To1492 592830, £3.50*, on the *Queen Victoria* leave for Llandudno; wander upriver for views of the Conwy Valley; or visit the **Smallest House in Great Britain** ⓘ *Apr-end Oct 1000-1700, later in summer, 50p, children 30p*. This tiny dwelling has just two rooms yet was inhabited until 1900, the last resident being a 6ft 3in fisherman. You can squeeze inside and see the conditions for yourself.

The oldest house in Conwy is **Aberconwy House** ⓘ *Castle St, To1492 592246, Mar-Oct, daily except Tue, 1100-1700, £2.60, child £1.30, family £6.50*. Built as a merchants' house it dates back to the 14th century and has rooms furnished in various periods of its long history. However, the most interesting property is fabulous **Plas Mawr** ⓘ *High St, To1492 580167, Tue-Sun, Easter-end May, Sep, 0930-1700; Jun-end Aug 0930-1800, Oct 0930-1600, £4.50, £3.50 children, family £12.50, joint tickets with Conwy Castle £6.50, £5.50 children, family £18.50*, a superbly preserved Elizabethan house, built 1576-1585 for Robert Wynn, a prosperous Welsh merchant. Many of the rooms are decorated with elaborate plasterwork, designed to impress visitors in a 'come up and see my ceiling' sort of way. You can get an audio tour of the house, and there's also an exhibition containing horribly fascinating details of the contemporary diet – kids love it.

Art lovers should go to the nearby **Royal Cambrian Academy** ⓘ *off High St, Tue-Sat 1100-1700, Sun 1300-1630, free*. It has changing exhibitions and displays contemporary paintings by artists such as Kyffin Williams, Maurice Cockrill, and Ishbel McWhirter. As you go upstairs you're rewarded with a striking view of the castle.

Just outside town is an **RSPB Nature Reserve** ⓘ *Llandduno Junction, To1492 584091, www.rspb.org.uk, daily 1000-1700, £2.50, £1 children, family £5*, where there are extensive reedbeds, with hides and walks allowing you to spot reed buntings, reed warblers and sedge warblers, as well as many waders.

Vale of Conwy

The lovely Vale of Conwy stretches from Conwy into the Snowdonia National Park to Betws-y-Coed. It's dotted with interesting villages and hamlets and has several good places to eat. Sites to visit are: **Bodnant Garden** ⓘ *near Tal-y-Cafn, To1492 650460, mid Mar-early Nov daily 1000-1700, £5.50*, with lovely terraced gardens covering 80 acres of ground and dating back to the late 1800s – their most celebrated feature is the laburnum arch, on the left as you enter; and **Trefiw Wells** ① *Trefriw, T01492 640057, Mon-Sat Oct-Easter, 1000-dusk, Sun 1200-dusk; Easter-Sep daily 1000-1730, £3 for self-guided tour*, an ancient spa, with iron rich waters, believed to have been discovered by the Romans and later used by Victorian visitors.

Llanrwst and around

South of Conwy along the A470, Llanrwst is a pleasant market town with several good places to eat and drink. The **Pont Fawr**, is an arched bridge attributed to Inigo Jones, the famous London architect who designed Covent Garden. It's often called the Buttermilk Bridge as the central arch, incorrectly fitted by drunken builders, collapsed soon after opening in 1636. The men were restricted to drinking buttermilk until it was safely rebuilt. The lovely ivy clad building by the bridge is **Tu Hwnt I'r Bont**, which dates back to the 17th century and was once the courthouse. Now it's a busy tea room. Take time to pop into **Gwydir Chapel**, beside St Grwst church. Ascribed to Inigo Jones, it's the memorial chapel of the local Wynn family and contains a fascinating jumble of tombs, brasses and marble tablets. Look out for the stone effigy of a knight, and the underpart of the stone coffin of Llewelyn ap Iowerth (the Great), the son in law of King John whose coffin was brought here after the dissolution of Conwy Abbey. No one knows what happened to his body.

Just a short drive over the bridge is the Wynn family's former home, **Gwydir Castle** ① *T01492 641687, Mar-Oct daily except Sat 1000-1700, £3.50, £1.50 children*. A house existed here from the 14th century, though the building you see today dates from around 1500. It's still a family home and its current owners are gradually restoring this extraordinarily atmospheric building. The most striking room is the 1640's Dining Room, attributed to Inigo Jones, and covered with dark woodpanelling and a rare gilded and silvered leather frieze. The interior was sold in 1921 to the American newspaper baron William Randolph Hearst, then passed to the New York Metropolitan Museum in 1956. They kept it locked away in packing cases and eventually, in 1996, it was purchased and returned to Gwydir.

Bangor

If you travel west along the coast from Conwy you reach the university town of Bangor (www.welcomebangor.co.uk), the largest town in Gwynedd and jumping off point for Anglesey. It was a popular destination in Victorian times and is a stop on the Chester-Holyhead railway. The town's Victorian Pier stretches over 1,500 ft into the Menai Strait and offers views of Thomas Telford's Menai Suspension Bridge which links the mainland to Anglesey.

The **Cathedral Church** ① *Deiniol Rd, daily*, was founded by St Deiniol in AD 546, making it the longest continuously used cathedral in Britain. The original structure was destroyed by the Normans, and a later version sacked by the Vikings and rebuilt many times after that; the oldest surviving parts today date from the 12th century. The cathedral is noted for the carved oak figure known as the Mostyn Christ, thought to have been made in the 16th century. The cathedral was the site of the tomb of Owain Gwynedd and became a starting point for pilgrims setting out on the journey to Bardsey Island (see page 204). Outside the cathedral is a **Bible Garden** which contains plants with biblical connotations, such as the cypress variety said to have provided Noah with wood for his Ark.

The town's main museum is the **Gwynedd Museum and Art Gallery** ① *Ffordd Gwynedd, T01248 353368, Tue-Fri 1230-1630, Sat 1030-1630*, which contains a large collection of furniture, including some fine Welsh dressers, as well as other artefacts such as a Roman sword. The gallery has changing exhibitions of Welsh art but you can also see a painting of Caernarfon Castle by Sir Frank Brangwyn.

Two miles east of Bangor is **Penrhyn Castle** ① *T01248 353084, Easter-end Jun, Sep-Oct Wed-Mon 1200-1700, Jul-Aug 1100-1700; grounds open from 1100 (1000 in Jul, Aug), £7, £3.50 children, family £17.50, National Trust.* This extravagant castle is no ancient edifice, but was built in the 19th century in mock-Norman style for Lord Penrhyn, a wealthy Caribbean sugar plantation and slate quarry owner. There are over 300 hundred rooms oozing stained glass, Norman-style furniture and a fine collection of paintings by artists such as Gainsborough and Rembrandt. There's even a massive slate bed that was built for Queen Victoria. The kitchens are laid out in Victorian style and there are extensive grounds and an **Industrial Railway Museum**.

Nearby, the **Hendre Centre**① *Lon Aber, Talybont, around 2 miles from Bangor off A55, T01248 371116, www.hendrecentre.com*, is a 19th-century farmyard that was used as a staging post for cattle on their way to market. There are exhibitions on agriculture and on the wealthy Penrhyn family. There's also a very good tea room where you can fill up with cakes or a Welsh cream tea.

Caernarfon

Further south, along the coast from Bangor, is the town of Caernarfon, a stronghold of Plaid Cymru where a distinct dialect of Welsh is spoken – speaking English can sometimes make you feel unpopular. It is the site of the Roman fort of Segontium and is most famous for its magnificent **castle**① *T01286-677617, daily Easter-end May, Oct 0930-1700; Jun-end Sep 0930-1800; Nov-Easter Mon-Sat 0930-1600, Sun 1100- 1600, £4.75, £3.75 children, £13.25 family*, an enormous structure, almost a town itself, built by Edward I from 1283. It stands at the mouth of the Seiont river overlooking the Menai Strait and was intended to be the focal point for Edward's dominance over the Welsh. It took around 40 years to build and is based around two oval courts divided by a wall, while the massive outer walls are 15ft thick in some places. They're dotted with unique

Caernarfon

Sleeping
Caer Menai 1

Eating
Cofi Roc 1
Macsen 2

Restuarant No 6 3

0 metres 50
0 yards 50

N

polygonal towers, and are made of limestone with strips of inlaid sandstone – features reminiscent of the city of Constantinople on which it was modelled. This was not just a fortress, it was the heart of Edward's imperial dream and it proclaimed him the conquering emperor, a theme continued in the magnificent eagles on the Eagle Tower – probably intended as the residential quarters of Sir Otto de Grandison, the King's representative. The castle also houses the **museum of the Royal Welsh Fusiliers,** Wales' oldest regiment which sticks to the ancient spelling of its name. They fought at Waterloo and have a goat as their mascot, which is ceremoniously given a leek to eat each year. Beside the castle, in the old town, is **St Mary's Church**, which was founded in the early 14th century and is worth seeing for its Jesse Window.

Just east of the centre, 10 minutes' walk along the A4085, is the **Segontium Roman Fort and Museum** ① *To1286 675625, Apr-Easter Tue-Sun 1000-1630; museum daily 1230-1630, free, CADW.* Long before Edward I came to the throne, Wales was occupied by the Romans, who built this fort to subdue the locals and keep control of the area around Anglesey, the last outpost of the Druids. It was occupied from AD 78 until AD 394, longer than any other Roman settlement in Wales and was able to hold around 1000 infantry soldiers.

The **Welsh Highland Railway** ① *St Helen's Rd station, To1766 516000, www.bangor.ac.uk, £16 day rover, under 16s free,* is another of Wales' lovely restored railways, this one runs from Caernarfon into the heart of Snowdonia – to the foot of Snowdon in fact, so you can easily combine a trip on the train with an ascent of the mountain. Restored steam engines haul you uphill to Rhyd Ddu, a journey of 13 miles or so. The aim is to restore the track all the way to Porthmadog by 2009.

Anglesey (Ynys Môn)

Across the Menai Straight is the island of Anglesey. The landscape is pastoral and so fertile that it was known as the 'breadbasket of Wales'. It's a great place to come if you're into prehistoric sites – the island is covered with them. The island's motto is 'Mam Cymru', meaning 'mother of Wales' and its great glory is the coastline, much of which is designated an Area of Outstanding Natural Beauty.

The island is linked to the mainland by Thomas Telford's **Menai Bridge**, which was built in 1826, the first permanent crossing of the Strait. The bridge is 100ft high so as to allow sailing ships with high masts to pass underneath. The second bridge across the Strait was Robert Stephenson's Britannia Tubular Bridge, which carried trains over the water. It was damaged by fire in 1970 and little of the original structure remains as it was rebuilt in conventional style. The Victorian town of Menai Bridge is home to little St Tysilio church, reached via a causeway. It was founded in AD 630.

Beaumaris (Biwmares)

Once the capital of Anglesey, the name is thought to mean 'beautiful marsh' in old French. It was once the chief port and commercial centre in North Wales, and in Victorian times became a popular resort. Moated **Beaumaris Castle** ① *To1248 810361, www.cadw.wales.gov.uk, Easter-end May, Oct daily 0930-1700; Jun-end Sep 0930-1800; Nov-Easter Mon-Sat 0930-1600, Sun 1100-1600, £3, £2.50 children, £8.50 family,* was never completed – the money ran out – but it's a technical triumph, dating back to 1295. Built in concentric style, rather than with a traditional keep and bailey, the castle has inner walls up to 16-ft thick and 43-ft high. Its defences include 14 deadly obstacles, including cunning arrow-slits and 'murder holes' to defend entrances. It was once linked to the sea by its moat, which meant that it could be

● *The old Welsh name for Caernarfon was Caer Cystennin – town of Constantine – recalling*
● *the tradition that Constantine the Great had been born at Segontium.*

readily re-supplied by ships, which travelled along a channel in the surrounding marshes. In the Chapel Tower there's a small exhibition on Welsh castles.

The **Beaumaris Victorian Gaol** ① *Steeple Lane, T01248 810921, Easter-end Sep 1030-1700, £1.50, £1 children, £4.25 family*, comprises Victorian punishment cells, dark secrets and dimly lit corridors. Prisoners were kept busy while confined in their cells, by cranking a handle up to 10,000 times a day – for no purpose other than to earn meals. People could be imprisoned for a month for stealing a quart of milk and public hangings were common. Close by is **Beaumaris Courthouse** ① *Castle St, T01248 811691, £1.50, child £1, family £4.25*, which dates back to 1614 and has seen trials of everyone from murderers to petty thieves. It's the oldest active court in Britain and today most of the proceedings take place in Welsh.

Also on Castle Street and opposite the castle is the **Museum of Childhood Memories** ① *1 Castle St, T01248 712498, Easter-end Oct, Mon-Sat 1030-1730, Sun 1200-1700, £3.50, £2 children*. One for kids of all ages, with over 2,000 items collected by one man over many years. There's everything here from rocking horses to dolls' houses, piggy banks and train sets.

Penmon
Around four miles north east of Beaumaris is **Penmon Priory** (unrestricted access), founded by St Seiriol in the sixth century. Viking raiders destroyed the original church and today you just see the remains of the 12th-century church and part of the cloister. The church contains two early carved crosses. Close by is **St Seiriol's Well**, said to have had healing properties. It has a huge dovecot, dating back to 1600 and able to house about 1,000 birds. Under a mile from the Priory is little **Puffin Island**, once site of one of Anglesey's earliest monastic sites and now home to birds such as puffins and razorbills. You can take a one-hour cruise around the island from Beaumaris Pier with **Puffin Island Cruises** ① *T01248 810746*.

Llanfairpwllgwyngyllgogerychwyrndrobwllllantysilio-gogogoch
The most exciting thing about Llanfairpwllgwyngyllgogerychwyrndrobwllllantysilio-gogogoch, Llanfair PG or simply Llanfair (as it's known to locals) is its name – the longest in Europe. In English it translates as 'The Church of St Mary in the hollow of the white hazel near the rapid whirlpool and the church of St Tysilio near a red cave'. It was contrived as a marketing ploy by a 19th-century tradesman. All there is to see is the name at the railway station; it is still a stop on the Holyhead-Chester line.

Around Llanfair
One and a half miles from Llanfair, on the A4080 is the magnificent building of **Plas Newydd** ① *T01248-714795, mid Mar-end Oct Sat-Wed, house 1200-1700, gardens 1100-1730, £5, £2.50 children, £12 family; gardens only £3, £1.50 children, National Trust*. It was the home of the first Marquess of Anglesey who made a vast fortune from the copper mines at Parys Mountain on the island and was also the principal commander at Waterloo. The house dates back to the 16th century but was re-designed in the 18th century by James Watt, and is now a striking mix of classical and Gothic styles. The house is crammed with oil paintings, the most famous of which is Rex Whistler's enormous *trompe l'oeil* which takes up a whole wall and covers the mountains of Snowdonia, Portmeirion and even some London sights. There is also a **Cavalry Museum** which features the first Marquess's state-of-the-art wooden leg – he lost his leg at Waterloo. The house is surrounded by extravagant gardens and has a good tearoom. You can also take boat trips on the Menai Strait from the property.

Further along the A4080, about a mile northwest of Plas Newydd is **Bryn Celli Ddu** (unrestricted access), one of Anglesey's most important Neolithic sites. It was an important religious site and has been extensively researched by archaeologists.

⁞ Walking on Anglesey

There's a long distance footpath, the **Isle of Anglesey Coastal Path**, which runs for 125 miles around the island and connects over 36 coastal villages, www.angleseycoastal path.com, T01248 752300. There's also the annual walking festival, www.angleseywalkingfestival.com, held in early June, and you can also take **Industrial Heritage Walks**

around Amlwch, home of Parys Mountain, the massive copper mine, T01407 832255.

Other walks you can do include an eight mile stretch from **Cemaes to Amlwch**; a five mile stroll from the hamlet of **Church Bay to Ynys y Fydlyn** and back; and a circular walk from **Aberffraw to Porth Cwyfan**, which is about four miles.

There's a surrounding stone circle and at the centre is a polygonal chamber where bones and arrowheads were found. Unfortunately the original stone was moved to the National Museum in Cardiff (see page 61), so the one you see today is a replica.

If you've got kids in tow you might want to continue heading along the coast to **Anglesey Sea Zoo** ① *Brynsiencyn, T01248 430411, www.angleseyseazoo.co.uk, Mar-Oct daily 1000-1800; £5.95 (£6.95 high season), children £4.95 (£5.95 high season), family £19.80 (£23.80 high season).* This is an absorbing aquarium with over 50 species and a chance to learn about different habitats. Displays include a Shipwreck and a Shark Pool, and there's an underwater camera giving you a fish's view of the world. There's also a chance to learn about seahorse conservation and a lobster breeding area.

Llanddwyn Island (Ynys Llanddwyn)

Llanddwyn Island, a peninsular in the southern corner of Anglesey, derives its name from Saint Dwynwen, the Welsh equivalent of St Valentine who lived during the fifth century and whose memory is commemorated on 25 January. The ruins of Dwynwen's Chapel can still be seen. **Dwynwen's Well** on the island is said to contain a sacred fish whose movements predict the fortunes of relationships. If the water bubbles it's said to be a sign of good luck. The island lies within the **Newborough Nature Reserve**. Canada geese, shelduck and red-breasted merganser are frequent visitors and over 550 different plant species including sea spurge (*euphorbia paralias*) and dune pansy (*viola curtisii*) have been recorded.

The beaches around Malltreath provided the inspiration for the wildlife artist Charles Tunnicliffe (1901-1979) who was famed for his studies of birds. Inland at Oriel Ynys Môn, is his recreated **studio** ① *Rhosmeirch, Llangefni, T01248 724444, Tue-Sun 1030-1700, £2.50,* the island's main gallery which covers the cultural history of the island. It also has a reconstruction of **Barclodiad y Gawres**, the most important Neolithic site in Wales. The original chamber is a 15-minute walk from Cable Bay, a couple of miles north of Aberffraw, off the A4080. Built around 3,000 BC, the stones are decorated with spirals, chevrons and lozenges and the style is similar to stones in the Boyne Valley in Ireland. It is said that excavations have revealed remains of frogs, snakes, hares and mice – as if used to concoct a mysterious magical potion. To visit the site get the key from the Wayside Shop in Trefaelog (£5 deposit) and bring a torch.

Holyhead (Caergybi)

Holyhead, with its busy port, mainly serving Ireland, and bustling market day (Mon 0800-1600) is the largest town on the island. In fact it's on a separate island – **Holy Island** – joined to Anglesey by a bridge. The island got its name as it was once settled by a monk St Cybi in the sixth century. His church is still here, on Stanley Street, built

North Wales Northwest corner

Walking on the Llyn

The **Llŷn Coastal Footpath** has recently opened, a 95-mile-long waymarked path running from Caernarfon to Aberdaron, then east to Porthmadog. Another footpath is the waymarked **Edge of Wales Walk**, which follows the old pilgrims' path and runs 47 miles from Clynnog Fawr to the tip of the Llŷn, and finishes with a boat trip to **Bardsey Island** ① *T01758 760652, www.edgeof wales.co.uk.* For a shorter walk you can go from the National Trust car park by Whistling Sands and walk along the famous sands which squeal as you walk, go up the track to Methlem and back up the road, a circuit of around three miles.

From Clynnog Fawr car park there's an eight mile walk which takes you from the lane behind the Post Office, across the moors to Llanaelhaearn. A bus will take you back to the start. Every December there's a **Llŷn Walking Festival** ① *T01758 712929.*

in the old Roman walls. The building today dates from the 13th century and contains stained glass by Arts and Crafts masters William Morris and Edward Burne-Jones. There's not a huge amount to detain the tourist in the town, save the **Holyhead Maritime Museum** ① *T01407 769745, Tue-Sun 1300-1700, £2.50, 50p children, £5 family,* which has displays on various aspects of seafaring and includes an exhibition of the sinking of the Royal Navy submarine *Thetis* in 1939, and of *HMS Scotia,* a ferry that was lost at Dunkirk.

West of the town is **Holyhead Mountain**, the highest point on Anglesey, which has an Iron Age hillfort on its summit. The Romans used this point as a watchtower and for communication with other beacons along the coast; a signal station was built here in the 19th century. A path leads from South Stack car park to the summit. On the clifftop is the **RSPB Ellin's Tower** ① *T01407 764973, Easter-Sep daily, free,* from where you can watch some of the thousands of birds that nest on the cliffs: puffins, guillemots, razorbills and fulmars can all be spotted. Further west 400 steep steps lead down to a **lighthouse** ① *T01248 724444, £3, children £1, Easter-Sep daily 1030-1730, bus 22 from Holyhead.* This was built in 1809 and visitors can now see the engine room and exhibitions, before climbing to the top for great views of the treacherous seas below.

A couple of miles south of Holyhead is **Trearddur Bay**, which has a Blue Flag beach and is a good spot for surfing.

The Llyn Peninsula

The Llŷn Peninsula (pronounced *'thlinn'*) has a wonderful untamed appeal, particularly along the northern coast and remote tip, yet many visitors never get further than Porthmadog, the nearest town to the famous and gloriously eccentric village of Portmeirion. The area's main beauties are its unspoilt beaches, high banked lanes and sleepy churches – it's the sort of place to explore on foot or by bike.

Porthmadog and around

Porthmadog takes its name from its founder, the MP William Madocks, who created a port linked by rail to the slate quarries at Ffestiniog, allowing vast quantities of slate to be shipped overseas. Rather unprepossessing, it's most notable as the southerly terminus of the delightful **Ffestiniog Railway** (see page 191). It's also a convenient base from which to explore the unique holiday village of **Portmeirion** ① *T01766 770000,*

was the creation of the architect Clough Williams-Ellis, and fulfilled a childhood
ambition to build an idealized village in a coastal setting. Work began in 1926, basing
the village around an Italian style piazza and sprinkling it with a Liquorice Allsorts mix
of buildings, with Gothic, Classical and Italianate styles mixed with arches, fountains
and statues. In 1941 Noel Coward wrote *Blithe Spirit* here as he came north to escape
the bombs of the Blitz. The brightly coloured buildings make an arresting sight, but try
and get here early in summer to avoid the coach parties. Many visitors are 'Prisoner'
groupies, fans of the 60's cult TV series *The Prisoner*, starring Patrick McGoohan,
which was set here. As well as the village, there are 70 acres of woodland to explore.

Criccieth

This is a pretty Victorian holiday resort which snuggles beneath its ruined
castle ① *T01766 522227, daily Easter-end May, Oct 1000-1700; Jun-end Sep 1000-
1800; Nov-Easter Fri-Sat 0930-1600, Sun 1100-1600; £2.50, £2 children, £7 family;
rest of year free access, CADW*. Originally built by Llywelyn the Great around
1230-1240, the castle was later taken over by Edward I, who extended and refortified
it. It was eventually captured and burned by Owain Glyndŵr in 1404. There are
panoramic views from the top and on a hot day it's worth bringing a book and settling
down for a lazy hour or two. In the shadow of the castle is the **Chapel of Art** ① *T01766
523570, www.the-coa.org.uk, Tue-Sat 1300-1700*, which is a restored chapel that
shows contemporary Welsh art.

Llanystumdwy

A mile west of Criccieth is the childhood home of David Lloyd George, the charismatic
Welsh social reformer who became British Prime Minister during the First World War.
His home is now part of the **Lloyd George Museum** ① *T01766 522071, www.gwynedd.
gov.uk/museums, Easter 1030-1700; May Mon-Fri 1030-1700; Jun Mon-Sat 1030-
1700; Jul-Sep daily 1030-1700; Oct Mon-Fri 1100-1600, £3, £2 children, £7 family*,
which has a film about his life, as well as memorabilia ranging from Lloyd George
teapots, to political cartoons – and even the thick yellow pencil with which he wrote
his war memoirs. In the garden is the little cottage in which he was brought up,
furnished much as it would have been during his lifetime.

Pwllheli

The main town on the Llŷn is Pwllheli (pronounced *'Poolth-heh-ly'*) which is most
famous for being the place where the Welsh National Party, Plaid Cymru, was founded
in 1925. It was once a thriving port but declined with the rise of Porthmadog. Three
miles east of the town is **Penarth Fawr** ① *Chwilog off A497, T01766 810880,
Easter-Oct daily 0930-1830, free*, which was built in the 15th century and is the only
surviving hall house of that period left in the area. It was owned by members of the
Welsh gentry and has a large hall with a fine timber roof. The stable block now houses
various crafts and ceramics made by local Welsh craftspeople.

Llanbedrog

Llanbedrog, is a small but pleasant village with a lovely beach. It's notable for **Plas
Glyn-Y-Weddw** ① *T01758-740763, www.oriel.org.uk, daily 1100-1700 Jul, Aug, closed
Tue rest of year, £2.50, £1 children, £5 family*, a Victorian Gothic mansion that is now
an impressive art gallery. With eye-stretching views out to sea, the house provides a
grand setting for its changing exhibition of paintings (you may well find some Polish
works on display as many Poles settled here after the Second World War and there are
strong connections with Poland) and sculpture. In the Andrews Room is the
permanent collection of porcelain, with Swansea and Nantgarw pieces.

Abersoch

The A499 road ends at Abersoch, a yachties haven, leaving the tip of the Llŷn to be explored by a lovely maze of 'B' and unclassified roads. Worth looking out for on the south coast is **Plas-yn-Rhiw** ① *Rhiw, T01758 780219, Easter-end May Thu-Mon 1200-1700; Jun-end Sep Wed-Mon 1200-1700; Oct Sat-Sun 1200-1600, £3.40, £1.70 children, £8.50 family; garden only £2.20, £1.10 children, £5.50 family*. This estate was once home to acclaimed Welsh poet R S Thomas who lived in a cottage on it. The main house is 16th century with some Georgian additions, and was derelict when it was purchased by friends of the poet, the Keating sisters. They restored it with help from Sir Clough William-Ellis and the house today contains many watercolours, painted by one of the sisters. The gardens are particularly fine, filled with wild flowers and run on organic principles. There are lovely views from the house across Cardigan Bay.

Aberdaron and Bardsey Island (Ynys Enlli)

Further along the coast is the little village of Aberdaron, where Thomas was minister. It used to be the last stop on the pilgrim trail to Bardsey Island. This sits off the tip of the Llŷn, and has been an important place of pilgrimage since the sixth century when St Cadfan founded a monastery here. The Welsh name is Ynys Enlli, meaning 'Island of the Currents'– a reference to the treacherous tides that thrash around it. In the days when travel to Rome was difficult, it was said that three pilgrimages to Bardsey were equivalent to a trip to Rome. It was often known as the 'island of 20,000 saints', probably a reference to the large number of pilgrims who came here to die. The island contains the ruins of the abbey, but is most popular today with bird watchers who come to watch the large numbers of nesting sea birds. Trips to the island can be made from Pwllheli and Porth Meudwy with the **Bardsey island Trust** (T08458 112233). There are good views of the island from Mynydd Mawr, the hill at the very tip of the Llŷn.

The north Llyn coast

The northern coast of the Llŷn is less populated than the south, and dotted with quiet beaches and sleepy churches. **Porth Dinllaen** is a little hamlet owned by the National Trust, which was once intended to be the main terminus for ferries to Ireland. One of the loveliest churches is the **Church of St Beuno** ① *Clynnog Fawr, May-Oct 1000-2000*, situated on an old pilgrims' route. Surprisingly large (Dr Johnson praised it as 'very spacious and magnificent for this country' in 1774) given its remote setting, it's a Tudor building but Christians have worshipped here since the seventh century. Inside are informative panels on the church and its history, as well as a parish chest of 1600, and some dog tongs, used to control badly behaved dogs in church, Nearby, at the crossroads at Aberdesach, a little road runs right down to a delightful hidden beach, a mix of golden sand, stones and seaweed. There's nothing but a few beach huts – it's a perfect place to paddle, stroll or just gaze out to sea.

● Sleeping

Conwy and around *p195, map p194*
A-B Castle Hotel, High St, T01492 582800, www.castlewales.co.uk. A former coaching inn in the centre, that has hosted guests such as Wordsworth and Thomas Telford.
B Sychnant Pass House, Sychnant Pass Rd, near Conwy, T01492 596868 or T0871 9958274, www.sychnant-pass-house.co.uk. Wonderful and welcoming, award-winning country house with dogs, cats, books, squashy sofas and individually decorated rooms, all very high standard. Meals on request.
C Crows Nest Hall, Sychnant Pass, near Conwy T01492 572956, www.crowsnesthall. co.uk. Lovely old house in isolated country pass, great location for walking.
D Bryn Derwen, Llanrwst Rd, T01492 596134, www.conwy-wales.com/brynderwen. Reliable B&B, dotted with Grecian style pots and knick-knacks.

D Glan Heulog, Llanrwst Rd, T01492 593845, www.walesbandb.co.uk. Good, clean and friendly B&B just outside the town walls.

D Swan Cottage, 18 Berry St, T01492 596840, www.swancottage.btinternet.co.uk. 3 rooms in basic B&B in town centre. 2 of the rooms have lovely views over the estuary.

F Conwy Valley Backpackers Bunkbarn, Pyllau Gloewen Farm, T01492 660504, www.pyllaufarm.co.uk. About 6 miles out of Conwy this farm offers basic bunk facilities and camp/caravan site.

F Conwy Youth Hostel, Larkhll, Sychnant Pass Rd, near Conwy T01492 593571. 24 rooms, sleeps 80-100. 4-star youth hostel a short walk from the town centre.

Vale of Conwy *p196*

B The Groes Inn, 2 miles from Conwy on B5106, T01492 650545, www.groesinn.com. This old coaching inn claims to be the first licensed house in Wales, dating back to 1573. All rooms are individually furnished. Lots of character with log fires and wooden beams.

B Gwydir Castle, on B5106 just outside Llanrwst, T01492 641687, www.gwydir-castle.co.uk. 2 rooms, extremely atmospheric, haunted medieval manor house with oak panelling, antique furniture and baths so deep you could practically swim in them.

B-C Yr Hafod, Terfiw, Llanrwst, T01492 640029, www.hafodhouse.co.uk. Small hotel in the lovely Conwy Valley. Comfortable rooms and good food.

Caernarfon and around *p198, map p198*

L Seiont Manor, Llanrug, 3 miles east of Caernarfon, T01286 673366, www.hand picked.co.uk/seiontmanor. The swishest hotel in the area with a large indoor pool, a gym and sauna. It's pricey but very comfortable.

A Plas Dinas, Bontnewydd, T0871 9958266, www.plasdinas.co.uk. Elegant hotel with pink washed walls and extensive grounds. Owned by the Armstrong-Jones family, it has lots of pictures and views across the Menai Strait.

C Caer Menai, 15 Church St, T01286 672612, www.caermenai.co.uk. Once a Victorian school this B&B is in the centre of town, close to Caernarfon castle.

C Pengwern Farm, Saron, Llanwnda, 3 miles east of Caernarfon off A487, T01286 831500, www.pengwern.net. Working farm set in 130

ha of ground. Good quality B&B and evening meals available by request.

C-D Plas Tirion Farm, Llanrug, 3 miles east of Caernarfon, T01286 673190, www.plas-tirion.co.uk. Farmhouse B&B in lovely rural location.

Anglesey *p199*

A Tre-Ysgawen Hall Hotel and Spa, Llangefni, T0871 9958280, www.treysgawen-hall.co.uk. Grand old country house with Victorian features, and contemporary spa with pool, jacuzzi and pampering treatments.

B Ye Olde Bull's Head Inn, Castle St, Beaumaris, T0871 9958250, www.bullshead inn.co.uk. Well-established inn that once welcomed Dr Johnson and Charles Dickens. Refurbished rooms, real fires in the bar.

C Llwydiarth Fawr, Llanerchymedd, T01248 470321, llwydiarth@hotmail.com. Georgian farmhouse, with an open fireplace and lots of books. Good country breakfast.

C Parc-yr-Odyn, Pentraeth, T01248 450566, www.parcyrodyn.com. Comfortable farmhouse B&B, with 2 self-catering cottages.

The Llyn Peninsula *p202*

L Portmeirion Hotel, Portmeirion, T01766 770000 or T0871 9958270, www.portmeirion-village.com. Plush rooms, suites and serviced cottages in the main hotel and dotted around the extraordinary village of Portmeirion.

L-A Castell Deudraeth, Portmeirion, T01766 772400 or T0871 9958272, www.portmeirion-village.com. Castle on the edge of town. Cool, sleek rooms and suites, less fussy and flowery than the main hotel and very comfortable.

A Plas Bodegroes, Pwllheli, T0871 9958264, www.bodegroes.co.uk. Lovely Georgian manor house set in its own idyllic grounds. Also has a great reputation for food.

B Plas Tan-yr-allt, Porthmadog, T01766 514545, www.tanyrallt.co.uk. Built in 1800 and once home to the poet Shelley, this country house hotel looks over the Glaslyn Estuary. Stylish base in country location.

C Gosling's at the Carisbrooke, Abersoch, T01758 712526, www.abersoch-carisbrooke hotel.co.uk. Family-run restaurant with rooms overlooking Cardigan Bay. Children welcome.

C Wenallt Guest House, Penrhyndeudraeth, 2 miles from Portmeirion, T01766 770321, www.wenalltguesthouse.co.uk. Clean and comfortable B&B, all rooms en suite.

C **Wern Fawr Manor Farm**, Llanbedrog, T01758 740156, www.wernfawr.co.uk. High quality B&B in this Grade II listed, 16th-century manor house set in over 60 ha of grounds. Freshly laid free range eggs and homemade bread and jams for breakfast, and evening meals available in winter. Also has self-catering cottages from £230 (sleeps 2) to £690 (sleeps 8). Lower rates out of season.

C **Yr Hen Fecws**, 16 Lombard St, Porthmadog, T01766 514625, www.henfecws.com. Once a bakehouse, this central restaurant with rooms has a comfortable, contemporary style.

E **Snowdon Lodge**, Church St, Tremadog, T01766-515354, www.snowdonlodge.co.uk. Lawrence of Arabia's birthplace, now a 4-star hostel, with dormitory and private rooms available. Booking essential.

● Eating

Conwy and around p195, map p194

¶¶¶¶ **Le Gallois**, Pant Yr Afon, Penmaenmawr, 3 miles southwest of Conwy on A55, T01492 623820, Thu-Sun 1900-2200. Well-established eaterie offering French influenced dishes. Look out for Conwy crab or local lamb.

¶¶¶ **Old Rectory**, Llanrwst Rd, Llansanffraid, just south of Conwy, T01492 580611, Tue-Sun 1930 onwards. Booking's essential at this elegant Georgian rectory that offers a fixed menu using fresh local ingredients. Dishes might include brill or roast duck, local cheeses and tasty puddings in a country house setting.

¶¶ **Alfredos**, Lancaster Sq, T01492 592381, Mon-Sat 1800-2200, Sun 1800-2130, lunch Fri-Sun 1200-1400. Popular local Italian joint serving usual range of pizza and pasta dishes.

¶¶ **Bistro Conwy**, Chapel St, T01492 596326, Tue-Thu 1130-1400, Fri-Sat also 1900-2130, closed Sun. Tucked away under the old town walls. Serves tasty lunches like baked herb rolls and contemporary evening meals like liver with red onion and orange sauce.

¶¶ **The Mulberry**, Conwy Marina, T01492 583350, winter Mon-Sat 1200-1500, 1800-2230, Sun 1200-1600, summer daily 1200-2130. Pub serving pricey meals, but with good views over the new marina.

¶¶ **Shakespeare's**, High St, T01492 582800. Award-winning restaurant in the Castle Hotel, serving fresh Welsh food in a formal setting.

¶ **Anna's Tearooms**, 9 Castle St, T01492 580908, daily 1000-1700. Stock up on walking gear in the outdoor shop below, then pop upstairs to this good quality tea room.

¶ **Beyond the Ninth Wave**, 4 High St, T01492 582212, in season Wed-Sat 1030-1630. Light modern café, on the ground floor of a pottery shop. As well as coffees and cakes it serves dishes like feta and olive salad.

¶ **Townhouse Restaurant**, 2 High St, T01492 596436, daily 1100-1500, Wed-Sat from 1830. Light lunches include lamb burgers, evening meals are British with a Welsh flavour, such as lamb with garlic and rosemary.

Vale of Conwy p196

¶¶ **Amser Da**, 32-34 Heol yr Orsaf, Llanrwst, T01492 641188, Wed-Sun 1100-1700, Wed-Sat 1700-2030. Popular brasserie with a coffee bar out the front. Lots of local Welsh ingredients and everything from tasty sandwiches to heartier main dishes.

¶¶ **The Austrian Restaurant**, Capuelo, 2 miles out of Conwy, T01492 622170. Wed-Sat from 1800, Sun lunch from 1200. Authentic Austrian restaurant serving sustaining dishes like wiener schnitzel and apfel strudel.

¶¶ **Eagles Hotel**, Llanrwst, daily 1200-1400, also Sun-Thu 1800-2030, Fri-Sat 1800-2100. This hotel is popular with locals and serves bar meals, Sun lunches and good thick chips.

¶¶ **Groes Inn**, Tyn-y-Groes, on B5106 about 2 miles from Conwy, T01492-650545, daily 1200-1415, 1830-2100. Lovely 16th-century inn serving everything from sandwiches to steak and mushroom pie and rose petal ice cream.

¶¶ **Sychnant Pass House**, Sychnant Pass Rd, T01492 596868. Home cooked food and the freshest ingredients at this comfortable guesthouse. Book in advance as it gets busy.

¶¶ **The Tannery**, Llanrwst, T01492 640172, Tue-Sun 0930-1600, Wed-Sun 1800- 2100, longer hours in summer. Lovely contemporary café/bistro with a wooden deck overlooking the river. Good coffee and cakes, imaginative dishes such as grilled goat's cheese with a strawberry dressing, or broccoli and stilton tart.

¶ **La Barrica**, Ancaster Sq, Llanrwst, Apr-Oct 0930-1600, closed Tue, good Italian style coffee stop also serving Mediterranean snacks, patisserie and hot filled baguettes.

¶ **Tu Hwnt I'r Bont**, by Pont Fawr in Llanrwst, Tue-Sun 1030-1700, Literally 'the house beyond the bridge' this riverside, ivy-covered tearoom has friendly staff, lovely location and great value cream teas.

Caernarfon *p198, map p198*

Restaurant No 6, 6 Castle St, T01286 673238, summer daily 1800-late, winter Mon-Sat 1800-late. The coolest restaurant in the town, only recently opened. The owners promise minimalist interiors and modern British cuisine. Dishes might include roast lamb with leeks and puff pastry.

Cofi Roc, Castle Sq, T01286 673100, daily 0930-1600. Serves traditional Welsh breakfasts all morning, and various lunches like filled baguettes and chip butties.

Macsen, 11 Castle Sq, T01286 676464, Mon-Sat 1000-1700. Popular café serving light lunches and homemade dishes.

Bangor *p197*

Fat Cat, 161 High St, T01248 372233, Mon-Sat 1000-2300, Sun 1000-2230. Popular chain café/bar offering everything from light lunches to filling pasta dishes.

Greek Taverna, 12 Holyhead Rd, T01248 354991, Mon-Sat 1200-2300, Sun from 1700. Greek taverna offering dishes such as moussaka and stuffed vine leaves. Several choices for vegetarians. Live jazz on Sun.

Herbs, 162 High St, T01248 351249. Popular restaurant offering plenty of choice for vegetarians. Lots of soups, salads and bagels as well as more filling dishes such as Thai green chicken curry £8.95.

Anglesey *p199*

Ye Olde Bulls Head Inn, Castle St, Beaumaris, T01248 810329. Traditional pub serving modern British food, with dishes such as roast sea bass and braised lamb. The restaurant serves more unusual dishes.

Lobster Pot, Church Bay, near Holyhead, T01407 730241, Tue-Sat 1200-1330, 1800-2100. Simple restaurant specialising in seafood sourced locally, such as lobster, crab, scallops and sole.

Ship Inn, Red Wharf Bay, off A5025, T01248 852568, daily 1200-1430, 1800-2100. This pub has lots of exposed beams and nautical knick-knacks. Welsh produce features in the menu, and you might find crab, mussels and Welsh rib-eye steak.

Tafarn Y Bont, Menai Bridge, T01248 716888, daily 1200-1400, 1800-2130. Within a stone's throw of Menai Suspension Bridge. Wide range of fish specialities.

The Waterfront Restaurant, Lon Isalt, Treaddur Bay, T01407 860006, daily 1200-1430, 1800-2100, closed Mon-Tue in winter. Lots of fresh Welsh produce on the menu, such as venison, beef and sea bass.

Liverpool Arms Hotel, Menai Bridge, T01248 810362, daily 1200-1400 and 1800-2100. A busy but friendly pub that provides good wholesome food and has a range of fish specialities.

Tafarn Y Rhos, Rhostrehwfa, near Llangefni, at the centre of Anglesey, T01248 724404, 1200-1430 and 1645-2130. A popular meeting place, with delicious bar meals, games room, lounge bar and a friendly smile.

The Llyn Peninsula *p202*

Castell Deudraeth, Portmeirion T01766 772400, 1200-1400, 1800-2130. Brasserie-style food in lovely setting. Welsh twist on meals such as Llŷn crab and Anglesey turbot.

Plas Bodegroes, Nefyn Rd, Pwllheli, T01758 612363, Tue-Sat 1900-2130, Sun 1200-1430. Crisp white tablecloths and high quality food at this Georgian country house. Local produce, imaginative desserts such as cardamon crème brûlée with poached pears.

Portmeirion Hotel, Portmeirion, T01766 770228, 1200-1400, 1830-2100. Upmarket, formal restaurant in the Portmeirion hotel. Modern Welsh cuisine using local, fresh produce. No jeans, best to reserve.

Tir a Mor, Mona Terrace, Criccieth, T01766 523084. Mains might include roast local lamb or leek and potato gratin.

The Galley, by the beach at Llanbedrog, off A499, T01758 740730, daily from 1100, Mar-Oct. Busy bistro overlooking the beach. Serves soups, filled ciabatta, and mains like curries, pizzas and roast beef. It's a restaurant in the evenings, booking essential in summer.

Granvilles, High St, Criccieth, T01766 522506. Coffee shop/bistro, with evening meals. Relaxed and bright decor. Cakes and light meals during the day. Dishes like lamb cutlets or sea bass with herb risotto and veggie choices, in the evening.

Yr Hen Fecws, 16 Lombard St, Porthmadog, T01766 514625, Mon-Sat 1800-2200. Excellent, lively bistro, with wooden beams and slate tablemats. Starters such as Thai fish cakes and mains of fish, meat and imaginative vegetarian choices like herb pancakes with roquefort and sundried tomatoes.

¶¶-¶ **Poachers Restaurant**, 66 High St, Criccieth, T01766 52251, Mon-Sat from 1800. International and British dishes, with lots of fish and some vegetarian choices.

¶ **Caffi Cwrt**, Y Maes, Criccieth. Best choice for traditional teas, scones and cakes in atmospheric old building with wooden beams and a little tea garden.

¶ **The Ship Inn**, Bryn-y-Gro, just outside Llanbedrog, T01758 740270, daily 1200-1430, 1700-2100. Pleasant pub with beer garden and meals like steak, pasta and pizza.

⊙ Pubs, bars and clubs

Vale of Conwy *p196*
The Fairy Glen, Capuelo, 2 miles out of Conwy. Pub serving good food.
The Old Ship, Trefiw, T01492 640013. Traditional pub offering bar meals.
Ty Gwyn, Rowen, 4 miles out of Conwy off B5106. Village pub serving good bar meals.

The Llyn Peninsula *p202*
Brondanw Arms, Garreg, Llanfrothen T01766 770555. Family-friendly, bar meals.
Coach Inn, on A499, Clynnog Fawr, T01286 660212. Pleasant inn offering bar meals, across from St Bueno's church.
The Griffin, Penrhyndeudraeth, at crossroads in village T01766 771706. Friendly local with good pub grub.

⊛ Festivals and events

Jun Criccieth Festival, with jazz, chamber music and art. Abersoch Jazz Festival, www.abersoch.co.uk. Anglesey Walking Festival, www.angleseywalkingfestival.com.
Jul Conwy Bluegrass Festival, T01492 580454.
Aug Bryn Terfel's Faenol Festival, Faenol Estate, Bangor, www.brynfest.com, music fest.

▲▲ Activities and tours

Climbing
Ropeworks, Greenacres, Black Rock Sands, Morfa Bychan, Porthmadog, T01766 515316, www.ropeworks.co.uk.

Cycling/Mountain biking
The **Conwy Valley Cycle Route** loops from Llanrwst to Conwy, 25 miles. There is also a loop from Llanrwst to Penmachno, 21 miles,

see www.conwy.gov.uk/countryside. **Gwydyr Forest** has lots of new single-track links and challenging climbs, see www.forestry.gov.uk. 2 bike paths run from Caernarfon: **Lon Las Menai** from Victoria Dock to Port Dinorwig and on to Bangor, and **Lon Eifion** going 12 miles south to Bryncir and on to Criccieth. **Beics Castell**, High St, Caernarfon, T01286 677400, hire a range of bikes.

Fishing
Sea angling trips can be booked from the Harbour Office in Conwy, T01492 596253.

General outdoor activities
Artro Adventure, T01341 241275, www.porthmadog.co.uk/artroadventure, for canoeing, scrambling, walking.

Sailing
Abersoch Sailing Club, T01758 712290/712338, www.abersochsailingschool.com. Offers sailing tuition for adults and children.
Conwy School of Yachting does RYA practical and shore-based courses, T01492 572999, www.conwy-yachting.com.
Conwy Yacht club, Deganwy, T01492 583690, www.conwyyachtclub.com.
North Wales Cruising Club, Conwy, T01492 593481, www.nwcc.info.
Plas Menai, National Watersports Centre, near Caernarfon, T01248 670964, www.plasmenai.co.uk. Courses in sailing, canoeing and windsurfing.

Walking
Conwy Valley Ramblers, T01978 855148, has information on walking; a pack on walks is also available from T01492 575361.
Edge of Wales Walk, T01758 760652, www.edgeofwaleswalk.co.uk. Excellent walking holidays along the new 95-mile Llŷn Coastal Path (see p202), with accommodation, information and luggage transfer.

⊖ Transport

Conwy *p195, map p194*
Arriva Cymru bus No 5 runs to **Llandudno** (every 20 mins, £1.70, ½ hr) and to **Bangor** (£2.80, 1 hr) and **Caernarfon** (£3.20, 1 ½ hrs).
Local trains stop at Conwy and there are 3 trains hourly to **Llandudno Junction** from there are regular connections to **London**,

Birmingham and Manchester. The Conwy Valley railway runs to **Llandudno** and **Blaenau Ffestiniog**, stopping at places like **Llanrwst** and **Betws-y-Coed**, www.conwy valleyrailway.co.uk.

Bangor *p197*
Arriva Cymru bus No 5 runs every ½ hr to **Caernarfon** (£2, ½ hr), **Conwy** (£3.20, 1 ½ hrs) and **Llandudno** (£3, 1 hr); No 86 runs every ½ hr to **Llanberis** (£1.20, 40 mins); No 4X runs to **Holyhead** (1 hr 15 mins). Express Motors buses run daily to **Caernarfon** (£2.30, 25 mins) and **Porthmadog** (£4.30, 1 hr 15 mins). National Express runs daily via **Llandudno** and **Birmingham** to **London** (£28, 8 ½ hrs).

The North Wales Coast line runs to **Chester** (£13.50, 1 hr 15 mins) and **Holyhead**. There are 4 trains to **London** daily (£32, 4 hrs).

Caernarfon *p198, map p198*
Arriva Cymru bus No 5 runs to **Bangor** (£2, ½ hr) every 20 mins and **Llandudno** (£3, £3.50, 1 ½ hrs). Express Motors run to **Blaenau Ffestiniog** (£4.80, 1 hr 15 mins) and **Bangor** (£2.30, ½ hr). Berwyn buses run to **Pwllheli** every ½ hr (£2, 45 mins) and to **Aberystwyth** (£3.50, 3 hrs) and **Cardiff** (£13, 8 hrs). Caernarfon is also linked to the Snowdon Sherpa bus route (see p194).

Holyhead *p199*
Arriva Cymru bus No 4 runs to **Bangor** every ½ hr (£3, 1 ½ hrs). Trains run to **Llandudno**

Junction (hourly, £9, 1 hr), **Bangor** (£5.50, 40 mins) and on to **Chester**.

Ferries run to **Dublin** and **Dun Laoghaire** in Ireland with **Irish Ferries**, TT0870 5171717, www.irishferries.com and **Stena Line**, TT08704 006798, www.stenaline.ie. See Essentials p26 for further detail.

Porthmadog *p202*
The Snowdon Sherpa (see p194) Bus No 97 runs to **Capel Curig**, **Beddgelert** and **Betws-y-Coed**. Express Motors run hourly buses to **Caernarfon** (£3.50, 50 mins) and **Blaenau Ffestiniog** (£2.60, ½ hr). Arriva Cymru bus Nos ½ runs to **Dolgellau** (5 daily, £5, 50 mins). National Express runs to **Caernarfon**, **Bangor**, **Llandudno**, **Chester** and **London**.

The Ffestiniog Railway (see p191) runs to **Blaenau Ffestiniog** (£14) and links the Conwy Valley and Cambrian Coaster lines. The Cambrian Coaster trains run every 3 hrs to **Machynlleth** (£7.25, 1 ½ hrs) and **Pwllheli** (£2.90, 15 mins).

● Directory

Internet Free at Caernarfon library, Bangor St; Conwy library, Castle St, Mon, Thu-Fri 1000-1730, Tue 1000-1900, Wed, Sat 1000-1300; and Porthmadog library, Chapel St Criccieth Roots, High St, Criccieth, daily in season 1000-1700 (5p per min); **Post office** Porthmadog Post Office, corner of High St and Bank Place. **Police** T01286-673347.

Northeast corner → *Colour map 3*

The northeast corner of Wales covers all shades of the tourist spectrum. It's best known for its sandy coastline which includes the genteel Victorian town of Llandudno, as well as lively and sometimes tacky resorts like Prestatyn and Rhyl – full of caravans, bingo halls and the smell of chips. But venture inland and you'll find little gems that many visitors fail to explore: Britain's smallest cathedral at St Asaph; the pretty market town of Ruthin; the excellent art collection at Bodelwyddan Castle, and gentle walks in the Vale of Clwyd. On the Dee Estuary, is the ancient pilgrimage site of Holywell; and, further south, Llangollen comes to life each July for its International Musical Eisteddfod.
▶▶ *For Sleeping, Eating and other listings, see pages 224-224.*

Ins and outs
Getting there and around The A55 road is the main driving route from England to the northeast coast of Wales, and then on to Anglesey. From the north coast take the A541 to reach towns like Wrexham or the A494 to Ruthin; from here there is a scenic route along the A542 to Llangollen. From the north of England, the M56, then M53 takes you

North Wales Northeast corner

to Chester, from where you take the A55, then A483 to Wrexham, and the A539 to Llangollen. From the south of England, the A5 from Shrewsbury runs straight to Llangollen. The coast area is also well served with **buses** and **trains**. The **North Wales Coast** line runs from Chester to Rhyl and on to Llandudno Junction, making it relatively easy to explore the coast by train, and also to reach Wrexham. Travelling inland is not as easy by public transport. To reach towns like Ruthin and smaller villages you will have to take buses. Timetables are available at TICs and bus stations. ▸▸ *For further details, see Transport, page 224.*

Information **Ruthin TIC** ⓘ *Park Rd, T01824 703992, ruthin@nwtic.com, daily Jun-Sep 1000-1700, Oct-May Mon-Sat 1000-1700, Sun 1200-1700.* **Mold TIC** ⓘ *Earl Rd, T01352 759331, mold@nwtic.com, Mon-Sat 0930-1300, 1330-1700.* **Holywell Town information** ⓘ *T01352-711757, www.holywell-town. gov.uk.* **Denbigh library/TIC** ⓘ *Hall Sq, T01745 816313, www.denbighshire.gov.uk/ libraries, Mon, Wed 0930-1900, Tue, Thu-Fri 0930-1700, Sat 0900-1200.* **St Asaph** ⓘ *www.stasaph.co.uk.* **Prestatyn TIC** and **Offa's Dyke Centre** ⓘ *Central Beach, T01745 889092, www.pres tatyn.org.uk, daily Easter-Sep 1000-1600,* are housed in the same building and have plenty of walking leaflets, books and maps. **Llandudno TIC** ⓘ *1-2 Chapel St, T01492 876413, www.llandudno-tourism.co.uk, Easter-Sep Mon-Sat 0900-1730, Sun 0930-1600 Sun,* ask for a copy of the Town Trail. **Flintshire** ⓘ *www.visit.flintshire.com.*

Llandudno and the north coast

If you're looking for seaside sophistication it's best to steer well clear of the coastal area that stretches from Prestatyn and on through the cheap and cheerful resorts of Rhyl and Colwyn Bay, to Llandudno in the west. Some people have suggested that the

Llandudno

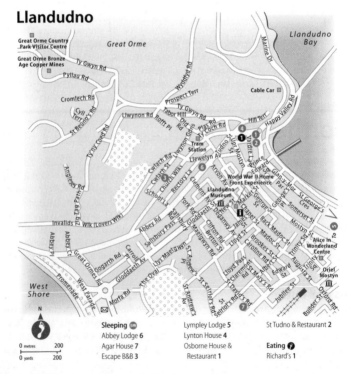

Sleeping 🛏
Abbey Lodge **6**
Agar House **7**
Escape B&B **3**

Lympley Lodge **5**
Lynton House **4**
Osborne House &
Restaurant **1**

St Tudno & Restaurant **2**

Eating 🍴
Richard's **1**

0 metres 200
0 yards 200

reason the A55 was made into a dual carriageway was to allow you to whizz past as 211
fast as possible and unless you've got kids in tow who are desperate to play on the
sand, or spend your money in the garish amusement arcades, that's probably the
best thing to do. Llandudno however, is a lively but still rather decorous seaside town,
with a lingering air of Victorian grandeur; it's the best of the bunch. Just west of the
town is Deganwy, near Conwy, which has some good restaurants.

Llandudno

Llandudno is one of the classier towns on the coast, retaining much of its Victorian
character, when its dramatic setting, beaches, grand hotels and shops attracted the
great and the good. It's lively, but not tacky. The seafront sweeps in a lovely arc
around Llandudno Bay and its sandy and pebbly beaches are overlooked by the
mighty summit of the Great Orme (see below).

Worth seeing is the **Oriel Mostyn** ⓘ *12 Vaughn St, T01492 879201,
www.mostyn.org, Mon-Sat 1030-1700, free,* a contemporary art gallery, which has
changing exhibitions of contemporary artworks, which could include film, installations
and photographs. The **Alice in Wonderland Centre** ⓘ *3-4 Trinity Sq, T01492 860082,
www.wonderland.co.uk, Easter-end Oct daily 1000-1700; Nov- Easter closed Sun £2.95,*
is a low-key attraction which relives the Lewis Carroll story – the connection being that
Alice Liddell, who inspired the books, used to holiday here with her family. The
Llandudno Museum ⓘ *17-19 Gloddaeth St, T01492 876517, Easter-Oct Tue-Sat
1030-1700, Sun 1415-1700; Nov-Easter, Tue-Sat 1330- 1630, £1.50,* has various exhibits
associated with the town, from a footprint on a Roman tile to paintings and sculpture
donated to the town. There's more on the past at the **World War II Home Front
Experience** ⓘ *New St, T01492 871032, www.homefront-enterprises.co.uk, Mar-Nov
Mon-Sat 1000-1630, Sun 1200-1600, £3, £2 children, £7.50 family,* which focuses on
civilian life in Britain during the Second World War. There's an old Anderson bomb
shelter, a recreated wartime street, and plenty to learn about the work of the Home
Guard, as well as rationing and the blackout.

The **Great Orme** itself, a huge limestone outcrop, can be reached on foot, by
tramway ⓘ *T01492 575275, www.greatormetramway.com, Victoria Station, Church
Walks, daily late Mar-late Oct, £4.50 return, £3.20 children,* or by taking the cable car
from near Happy Valley. From here you get stunning views along the coast. It was
settled as far back as Neolithic times and its rich mineral stores were mined as far back
as the Bronze Age. **The Great Orme Bronze Age Copper Mines** ⓘ *T01492 870447,
www.greatorme.freeserve.co.uk, Feb-Oct daily 1000-1700, £5, £3.50 children, £15
family,* can be reached by tram from Victoria tram station or a short walk from the cable
car. You get to don hard hats and go underground to explore these mines that were
worked over 4,000 years ago. There's a visitor centre depicting life in the Bronze Age.

The **Great Orme Country Park Visitor Centre** ⓘ *T01492 874151, www.conwy.gov.uk/
countryside, Easter-end Oct, daily 0930-1730,* has displays and video on the area's
history, geology and rich wildlife – over 400 types of plants grow here, some
extremely rare. There's a live camera link up with a nearby seabird colony and
information on the walks and nature trails on the Great Orme. At the **Summit Complex**
(T01492 860963) there are places to eat and drink. There's also a **Ski and Snowboard
Centre** (see Activities, page 223).

Prestatyn

Not as awful as some of the towns along the north coast, Prestatyn became popular
as a resort in the 19th century, with reports of the clear air and sunshine attracting
people seeking to improve their health. Trains stop here as they go along the north
coast to Prestatyn so it makes a convenient base for people with children, and there
are some decent places to eat. The town has ancient origins: there was once a Roman
fort and a Roman bath house was discovered here in the 1980s. Today it is a market

town and famous for being the start (or end) of the 182-mile **Offa's Dyke walk** (see page 46). There are three good, sandy beaches: Barkby, Central and Ffrith with a four-mile long promenade that is now part of the National Cycle Network. Close to town are the **Gronant Dunes** a Site of Special Scientific Interest.

The Vale of Clywd

The lush Vale of Clwyd lies beneath the Clwydian hills, tucked between the industrial areas of the Dee Estuary, and stretches from the coastal resorts of Prestatyn and Rhyl to the main town of Ruthin. It's not spectacular scenery but it's pretty and pastoral, dotted with little towns and interesting ancient churches – a good area for gentle walks and lazy drives.

Ruthin (Rhuthun)

The small, medieval town of Ruthin was besieged by Owain Glyndŵr in 1400. It has a pretty town centre, some interesting historic sites and several good places to eat and drink. It's the best base for exploring the area.

    Ruthin Gaol ① *Clwyd St, T01824 708250, www.ruthingaol.co.uk, May-Oct 1000-1700 daily except Thu when open till 1900, Nov-Mar as before but closed Mon, last admission 1hr before closing, £3, children £2, family £8* was used from 1654 to 1916, but focuses on conditions for prisoners in Victorian times when a wing was built modelled on Pentonville in London. You can explore the cells, find out how prisoners lived and how they were punished. You also learn about former inmates such as the Welsh 'Houdini', John Jones, who escaped from Ruthin by making a rope from his bedclothes but died of shock after being shot while on the run.

    There are more gory links in **St Peter's Square** where you can see the remains of the town's gibbet just sticking out from the north west wall of the National

Ruthin (Rhuthun)

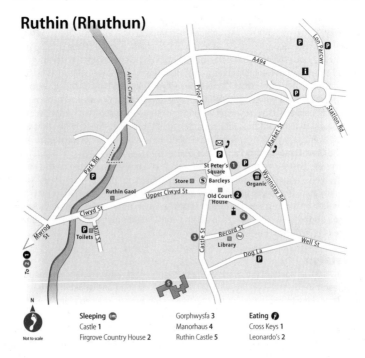

Sleeping	Gorphwysfa 3	Eating
Castle 1	Manorhaus 4	Cross Keys 1
Firgrove Country House 2	Ruthin Castle 5	Leonardo's 2

Not to scale

Westminster bank; this was once the courthouse and was built in 1401. Outside Barclays Bank is a large stone known as **Maen Huail**, where legend has it that King Arthur beheaded Huail, a rival who had beaten him in a skirmish over a woman and had mistakenly bragged about his victory. **St Peter's Church**, just off the square, is famous for its lavish 16th-century carved ceiling, thought to have been commenced shortly after Henry VII came to the throne. There are 408 panels with badges and heraldic devices of noble families who were in favour of his taking the throne.

 Ruthin Castle is now an hotel and the grounds are private. However, you can pop in for tea or coffee to get a peek at this former medieval fortress. Among the animals' heads and ornate carved fireplaces, are photographs of Edward VII at Ruthin, when he was still Prince of Wales. Castle Street contains one of the oldest houses in North Wales, dating back to the 16th century. The house with railings around it was once home to Cynthia Lennon, who was living here when news of John's murder came out.

Llanrhaedr

Llanrhaedr is a tiny hamlet in the Vale and the site of **St Dyfnog's Church**, which is notable for its fine stained glass Jesse Window. The name 'Jesse' is a reference to the subject matter, the family tree of Christ showing his ancestors right back to Jesse, the father of King David, who is shown reclining at the bottom. The window is regarded as the finest in Wales. As you enter the church, on the right hand side, is a huge organ, built in 1899 and famed for being the only surviving example of a 'Hope-Jones' organ – Robert Hope-Jones being the father of the cinema organ.

 If you walk to the far corner of the churchyard, go through a gap in the wall, over a small bridge and turn right to follow the path through the woods, you'll soon come to **St Dyfnog's Well**, a holy well once noted for its healing properties. You can still see the bath, in among the trees. Opposite the church, in the old smithy, is the **Anvil Pottery** ① *T01745 890532, Mon-Sat 0900-1700*, where you can watch pots being made and buy goods to take home.

Denbigh (Dinbych)

Dinbych means 'little fortress' in Welsh, and is a pleasant market town that dates back to the 11th century and retains many of its medieval buildings. It was the birthplace of Henry Morton Stanley (1841-1904), the Victorian explorer of 'Dr Livingstone I presume' fame. The garden of nearby **Gwaenynog Hall** ① *T01745 812066, off A543, 2 miles west of town, Jun-Aug by appointment, £2*, was the inspiration for Beatrix Potter's *The Tale of the Flopsy Bunnies*.

 Denbigh Castle ① *T01745 813385, Apr-Sep Mon-Fri 1000-1730, Sat-Sun 0930-1730, £2.50, children £2, family £7*, is one of the largest in Wales. Denbigh grew up as a centre of Welsh power and was a residence of Welsh princes. Dafydd ap Gruffudd (brother of Llywelyn 'the Last') sparked a revolt against the English Crown, which led to Edward I's final assault on the north. His stronghold here withstood a month's siege before falling to the English in 1282. Dafydd was captured and put to death in the Tower of London in 1283, and the castle erected as part of Edward's anti-Welsh campaign. The medieval town, enclosed by its walls, grew up at the same time. Walking up to the castle you first see a rather lonely tower, all that remains of St Hilary's Chapel, built around 1300 but demolished in 1923. Then you enter the castle through the enormous triple-towered gatehouse, built by Edward's architect Master James of St George, who built all Edward's main castles in the north. The views from here are great. The castle eventually fell into disrepair and in 1563 Elizabeth I gave it to Robert Dudley, Lord Leicester, on a repairing lease – granting him the title Baron Denbigh. You can see the remains of **Lord Leicester's Church**, which he had built to reflect his new importance. He wanted it to replace St Asaph as the local cathedral but it was never completed.

St Asaph seems like a large village yet it is a city, due to the presence of its lovely **cathedral** ① *High St, daily 0800-1830*, the smallest in Britain. The site has been a place of worship since AD 560, when the church was founded by St Kentigern, later succeeded by his pupil Asaph. It survived the Civil War, when Cromwell's soldiers took it over and used the font as a watering trough, and was restored by Gilbert Scott in 1870. The church is notable for the Welsh Bibles on display, to the left of the altar. One is by William Morgan 1588, who made the first complete translation of the Bible into Welsh (see box, page 190). Only 800 of these were produced, and the revised edition by Richard Parry, from 1620, is also on display. They are commemorated outside the cathedral in the 'Translators' Memorial' monument. To the right of the altar, set into the wall in the Lady Chapel, is a tiny Madonna, said to have come from the Spanish Armada. Morgan is buried in an unknown spot in the churchyard, as is the composer William Mathias (1934-1992) who composed an anthem for the wedding of Charles and Diana. Just outside the city centre is the former Victorian workhouse where the explorer H M Stanley was taken after his mother abandoned him. He is said to have run away from the workhouse and eventually went to live with an aunt at nearby Ffynnon Beuono.

East of St Asaph is Tremerchion, close to which is **St Beuno's College** where Jesuit priests were trained, and now a centre for retreats. Poet Gerard Manley Hopkins (1844-1889) trained here and several of his sonnets were written here. He was much inspired by the local landscape.

Bodelwyddan Castle

① *T01745 585060, www.bodelwyddan-castle.co.uk, Jul-Sep daily 1030-1700, Nov-Mar weekends 1030-1600 and Thu 0930-1800; rest of year 1030-1700, closed Fri, 4.50, children £2, family £12.*

One of the area's greatest attractions. A castle has stood on this site since 1640, but the grand structure you see today was built mainly in the 19th century. Once a family home, it now functions as an outpost of the **National Portrait Gallery**, with over 100 pictures from the collection hung throughout the house, in rooms that are decorated in Victorian style and feature furniture from the Victoria and Albert Museum. Upstairs there's a room upstairs with online links to the whole of the National Portrait Gallery's collection. The grounds have a play area, woodland walks and plenty of space for picnics.

Opposite the castle is the stunning **Marble Church**, which contains Florentine marble. In the graveyard are the graves of Canadian soldiers who were billetted here after the Second World War. Some died of illness, but many others were shot during the Kinmel Riot. This took place in 1919 when many soldiers mutinied, angry that they had still not been sent home. Many were wounded and some shot dead, but for years events were hushed up to avoid scandal.

Rhuddlan Castle

Two miles south of Rhyl, Rhuddlan Castle was started in 1277 as one of Edward I's campaigns against the Welsh, like Caernarfon and Conwy. The castle is concentrically designed and is dominated by a distinctive diamond-shaped inner ward. A protected river dock forms one side of the defences.

Mold (Yr Wyddrug) and the Dee Estuary

The industrial area that stretches from Mold to Chester is not the most attractive part of Wales, however at Deeside the estuary gives way to salt marshes, which are home to large numbers of wildfowl and waders. Mold is a good base for exploring the serene Ewloe Castle. While further south the crumbling castle at Flint is worth a look and Holywell continues to draw curious visitors to its site of pilgrimage, St Winefride's Well.

Mold

Despite having origins dating back to Norman times, Mold has many unsympathetic 20th-century developments. It is largely notable as the boyhood home of the artist Richard Wilson, who is buried in the churchyard. Less well known is the writer Daniel Owen (1836-1895), remembered in a statue opposite the Post Office. Owen wrote in Welsh, his subject matter being the lives of ordinary people.

Near Mold is **St Deiniol's Library** ① *To1244 532350, Church Lane, Hawarden, www.btinternet.com/st.deiniols/homepage.htm, Mon-Sat free*, a residential library and the National Memorial to former Prime Minister, William Ewart Gladstone. Gladstone married into the family who owned nearby Hawarden Castle. The church has a memorial window by Burne-Jones.

Six miles northeast of Mold, **Ewloe Castle** (unrestricted access, CADW) is tucked away among peaceful, green woodlands and certainly feels much more off the beaten track than many of the larger castles. Thought to have been built by Owain Gwynedd in the 12th century, it is a good example of a native Welsh castle.

Flint (Y Fflint) and around

North of Mold, on the Dee Estuary, is the former port of Flint, of which Henry Wyndham, travelling in 1781 said disparagingly: "It is scarcely worth the traveller's while to visit the poor town of Flint". Only come to see **Flint Castle** (CADW, free) built by Edward I and now a pleasant ruin down by the shore. Built on 'Y Flynt', an early English term for any hard rock, the castle was largely destroyed in 1647, when taken by Parliamentarians in the Civil War. It is most famous as the place where Richard I was taken after being ambushed and captured by Henry Bolingbroke.

The hills around the town of Flint were once known as the 'Peru of Wales', as they were sources of lead and silver, and were once the richest lead mines in Wales. **Loggerheads Country Park** ① *To1352 810614, www.loggerheads-wales.com, bus B5 from Ruthin and Mold, information To1824 706968*, is a good spot for kids to let off steam, with walks, nature trails, picnic seats and facilities for abseiling. Opposite is the We Three Loggerheads pub (see page 222), whose original sign was said to have been painted by celebrated landscape artist Richard Wilson in the 1770s. The picture recalls a local boundary dispute.

Holywell (Treffynnon) and around

Holywell is the site of an ancient place of pilgrimage and was once known as the 'Lourdes of Wales'. Pilgrims came literally in thousands to be cured, necessitating a branch rail line into the town. The site of the pilgrimage is **St Winefride's Well** ① *To1352 713054, daily Apr-Sep 0900-1730, Oct-Mar 1000-1600, 60p, £1.50 family, bathing times Mon-Sat 0900-1000 Apr-Sep*, which is down a steep hill about half a mile out of town. Legend has it that Winefride, the only child of a nobleman, was killed by a chieftain who was trying to rape her. He cut off her head when she resisted, and a spring appeared where it fell. St Bueno put her head back on, restoring her to life and she became a nun. A chapel was later built around the well, which was said to have curative properties. Hundreds of pilgrims still come each year, particularly around 22 June, which is St Winefride's Day. Pilgrims who wish to may wade through the waters of the well three times, a tradition that probably derives from the Celtic rite of baptism by triple immersion. Dr Johnson came in 1774 and was put out to find that: 'the bath is completely and indecently open: a woman bathed while we all looked on'.

From St Winefride's Well you can follow a walkway along an old railway line, which ① runs through the **Greenfield Valley Heritage Park** ① *Visitor Centre, Farm and Museum, To1352 714172, www.greenfieldvalley.com, Mar-end Oct, daily 1000-1630, £2.75, children £1.65*. This area was the heart of local industry in the 18th century, producing copper for the colonies and spinning cotton. These old works are largely ruined but at the bottom of the valley is an interesting farm and museum, with reconstructed farm buildings from all over North Wales, which have been saved from demolition. Nearby is **Basingwerk Abbey** (*CADW, free*), a picturesque ruin which was founded around 1131 and moved to this location in 1157. It belonged to the Cistercian Order, and around the Middle Ages the area became home to several Welsh poets.

Just a short drive from Basingwerk Abbey, standing in a field between Whitford and Trelogan, is **Maen Achwyfan** ① *1½ miles north of A151, free, CADW*. This 12-ft high Celtic cross is said to be the tallest wheel cross in Britain and has been described as 'the most remarkable stone monument in North Wales'. The cross was probably erected around AD 1000, to commemorate a person or event, or to mark a site of particular importance. The decorations on it include patterns copied from Viking art.

Llangollen and around → *Colour map 3*

Llangollen is best known as the venue for the International Musical Eisteddfod. Close to Wrexham and the border with England, the area is often bypassed by people in a hurry to reach Snowdonia. But it's a likeable place, surrounded by mountains and forests, with the River Dee running through its heart, and is a good base for outdoor activities like canoeing and walking – it's within easy reach of the Offa's Dyke Path for instance. The surrounding countryside is delightful, particularly the Ceiriog Valley which seems like a secret world, dotted with small communities and laced with varied walks. ▸▸ *For Sleeping, Eating and other listings, see pages 224-224.*

Ins and outs

Getting there and around   Road links to Llangollen are good but there's no station here. Nearest transport hub is Wrexham. Llangollen is easily explored on **foot**, but if you want to get out into the lovely Edeyrnion and Ceiriog valleys you will certainly need your own transport. ▸▸ *For further details, see Transport, page 224.*

Information   Llangollen TIC ① *The Chapel, Castle St, Llangollen, T01978 860828, www.llangollen.org.uk, Easter-Oct daily 0930-1730; Nov-Easter, 0930-1700.*

Background

Llangollen is a solid market town and its position on the Dee made it an important crossing point from early times: a 14th-century bridge is still there today. However its greatest expansion came with the building of Thomas Telford's Pontcysyllte Aqueduct, part of the **Llangollen Canal** which runs through the town, and his Historic Highway, now the A5 – both of which opened up the area to visitors. In consequence, Llangollen became one of the earliest tourist towns. George Borrow based himself here in 1854 to write his famous travelogue 'Wild Wales', Turner came to paint the ruins of nearby **Valle Crucis Abbey**, and everyone from the Duke of Wellington to Wordsworth came to visit a legendary lesbian couple known as the 'Ladies of Llangollen'. As well as the gloriously picturesque Cerriog Valley, the town is encircled by some stunning scenery, most notably the Horseshoe Pass, which cleaves the mountains to the north; and the Vale of Edeyrnion to the west.

Llangollen

Llangollen's a lively place, with a good range of pubs, restaurants and cafés. The river and the canal run through the town and are a particularly good place for families with young children to stroll. The area gained celebrity cachet when Harrison Ford and Calista Flockhart chose to spend their holidays exploring the canal on a narrowboat, stopping off for a day in the town and visiting the eisteddfod.

Plas Newydd ① *Hill St, T01978 861314, www.denbighshire.gov.uk, daily 1000-1700 (last admission 1615) Easter-end Oct, £3, £2 children, £8 family*, is a mock-Tudor building famed as the home of the Ladies of Llangollen, a lesbian couple who came here in 1780 and lived together contentedly for 50 years. Sarah Ponsonby and Lady Eleanor Charlotte Butler were a well bred couple who met at boarding school in Ireland and later eloped, dressed in men's clothing, with Sarah carrying a pistol. They were intercepted and returned to their families but ran away again, and were allowed to set up home together. Although they shared a bed they never admitted to having anything other than a loving friendship. Whatever its precise nature, their relationship fascinated fashionable society and they received a remarkable number of well-connected visitors. The Duke of Wellington was a particular favourite and came to the house several times, the ladies describing him as 'a charming young man, handsome, fashioned tall and elegant'. Other visitors included Josiah Wedgwood, Sir Humphrey Davy, Sir Walter Scott and William Wordsworth. The house itself was originally a cottage but the ladies transformed it into an elaborate 'gothic' creation with an overwhelming abundance of ornate dark oak carvings, many of which were presents from visitors. The house is left largely empty today, although the ladies' bedchamber has been refurbished as it was in 1832, a year after Sarah, the last surviving 'lady', died.

The town is also the starting point for the **Llangollen Railway** ① *T01978-860979, www.llangollen-railway.co.uk, daily Apr-Oct, some services out of season, £8 return, £4 children*. This steam railway runs from quaint Llangollen Station (where Queen Victoria arrived when she visited in 1889) for eight miles, stopping at carefully

Llangollen

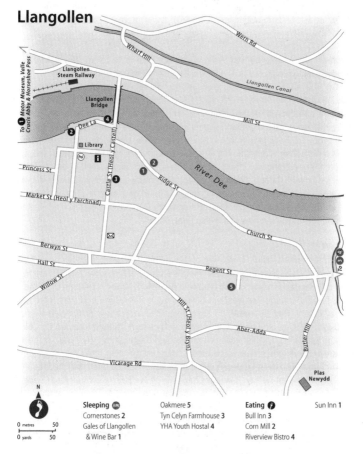

Sleeping 🛏	Oakmere 5	Eating 🍴	Sun Inn 1
Cornerstones 2	Tyn Celyn Farmhouse 3	Bull Inn 3	
Gales of Llangollen	YHA Youth Hostal 4	Corn Mill 2	
& Wine Bar 1		Riverview Bistro 4	

0 metres 50
0 yards 50

N

Llangollen International Musical Eisteddfod

For the last 56 years the pretty little town of Llangollen has hosted the International Musical Eisteddfod.

For six days each July, the normally sedate streets throng with as many as 50,000 visitors, who come to see 5,000 competitors from all corners of the globe partake in a broad spectrum of performing arts. Amateur musicians, singers and dancers from places as diverse as Mongolia compete in 20 very different events. Many are decked out in their national costumes, so the eisteddfod takes on a carnival air.

Although the event has grown in prestige, its essence has remained the same since its inauguration in 1947. The eisteddfod's purpose is as much about creating a glorious visual spectacle and promoting international friendship as it is about competing. For some of today's mega stars, such as Luciano Pavarotti and Placido Domingo, the eisteddfod was the place where they cut their performing teeth.

Amateur events are interspersed with professional concerts given by such luminaries as the above mentioned tenors, Kiri Te Kanawa, Lesley Garrett, Bryn Terfel and Monserrat Caballe.

Diversity is the name of the game, and it's not surprising to find Shirley Bassey, jazz heroes Cleo Laine and John Dankworth, and the Harlem Gospel Choir on the same bill. And for the who fancy something slightly different, there's even a fringe festival.

For further information, visit www.international-eisteddfod.co.uk.

restored stations like Berwyn, from where you can walk to the **Horseshoe Falls**, **Glyndyfrdwy**, where you will find Owain Glyndwr's Mound, and **Carrog**.

On the outskirts of the town is the **Motor Museum** ① *To1978-860324, www.llangollenmotormuseum.co.uk, Mar-Oct daily 1000-1700, £3, £7 family*, which houses a collection of 20th-century cars and motor cycles. From here you continue along the A542 to the romantic ruins of **Valle Crucis Abbey** ① *Easter-Sep daily 1000-1700, £2, £5.50 family, free in winter 1000-1600, CADW*. Although the approach to this once isolated Cistercian Abbey is somewhat ruined by a tacky caravan site, it still has plenty of picturesque charm, with a fine rose window, carved doorway and the monk's original fishpond. Founded in the 13th century, the abbey was deserted after the Dissolution, its crumbling charms later captured on canvas by Turner. The abbey ('the abbey of the cross') was named after a nearby stone cross Eliseg's Pillar, erected in the ninth century in memory of a Welsh prince.

Corwen

It was from Corwen, a little town west of Llangollen, that Owain Glyndŵr set out in his bid to wrest Wales from English rule. There's a statue of him in the town centre, while a few miles east the hump known as **Owain Glyndŵr's Mount** is thought to be the site of his fortified manor. Just west of Corwen are two interesting churches, both in the care of CADW. **Rug Chapel** ① *off the A494, To1490 412025, Easter-Sep Wed-Sun 1000-1700, £2.50, £7 family*, is a private 17th-century chapel, founded by Colonel William Salusbury, royalist governor of Denbigh Castle in the Civil War. In the 19th century a carved rood screen was added, separating the clergy from the congregation. The architect Sir Edwin Lutyens visited the chapel and claimed that he was much influenced by what he saw. **Llangar Chapel** ① *off the B4401, contact Rug Chapel for entry, Easter-Sep Wed-Sun at 1400*, is a medieval building, built on the remains of an earlier structure. It includes some 15th-century wall paintings, box pews and a painting of a large skeleton, representing death. Excavations in the early 1970s were said to have revealed the mysterious remains of 170 bodies beneath the church floor.

Chirk (Y Waun) and the Ceiriog Valley

South of Llangollen, Chirk is notable for its famous **castle** ① *T01691 777701, castle Easter-Sep Wed-Sun 1200-1700 (till 1600 Oct); garden Wed-Sun 1100-1800 (till 1700 Oct) £6.40, £3.20 children, £15.80 family, National Trust.* Built around 1295 on behalf of Edward I, it was the last in the great chain of castles built to subdue Wales. It was never quite completed and in 1595 was bought for £5,000 by Sir Thomas Myddelton, a wealthy merchant whose family still live here. Today it feels more like a stately home than a castle with swish rooms filled with fine furniture, portraits and tapestries. There are also large gardens to explore and some elaborate gates, made by the Davies brothers in the early 18th century. Chirk guards the head of the beautiful **Ceiriog Valley**, a wonderfully pastoral, unspoiled place with great walks and pubs.

Wrexham (Wrecsam)

① *TIC, Lambpit St, T01978 292015.* Wrexham's a busy town close to the English border that became prosperous in the 18th century due to the presence of minerals in the surrounding countryside. Its most famous landmark is **St Giles Church** on Church Street, an ornate structure with a 136-ft Gothic tiered tower; it's considered one of the 'Seven Wonders of Wales'. The church was rebuilt in the 15th and 16th centuries, after a fire destroyed the original building. Inside is a timber roof, traces of a 15th century painting of *The Last Judgement*, and a stained glass window by Burne-Jones. Outside, in the churchyard, is the grave of Elihu Yale, the benefactor of Yale University in America. His family came from the area, and although he was born in Boston he later returned to live in Britain, with homes in Wrexham and London.

The town also has a small **museum** ① *Regent St, T01978 317970, Mon-Fri 1000-1700, summer also Sat 1030-1500,* housed in a former barracks it has exhibitions on the town's history, including Brymbo Man, a Bronze Age skeleton discovered locally.

From the town you can follow the **Clywedog Trail**, a nine-mile waymarked walking route that takes you along the Clywedog Valley in the west. This was the hub of the town's industrial production and the trail takes you past sites such as the **Minera Lead Mines**, which were mined as early as the 13th century, and **Bersham Heritage Centre and Ironworks**, T01978 261529, which date back to the 17th century. There's a visitor centre along the way at **Nant Mill** ① *T01978 752772, open daily.*

Erddig Hall

① *2 miles south of Wrexham, T01978 355314, Sat-Wed, house: Easter-Sep 1200-1700, Oct 1200-1600; garden Easter-end Jun 1100-1800, Jul-Aug 1000-1800, Sep 1100-1800, Oct 1100-1700, Nov-mid Dec Sat-Sun 1100-1600, £7.40, £.70 children, £18.40 family (gardens only £3.80, £3.70, £9.20), National Trust.*

This stately home was owned by the Yorke family from 1733 until the 1970s and remained almost unchanged during their years of occupancy. The 'upstairs' rooms contain some fine 18th-century furniture and paintings, while the 'below stairs' quarters are particularly well preserved with kitchens, servants' hall and, most unusually, portraits of the staff. The walled garden is one of the most important 18th-century gardens in Britain; it contains rare fruit trees and around 150 different types of ivy.

● Sleeping

Llandudno and around *p210, map p210*
L Bodysgallen Hall and Spa, 3 miles inland from Llandudno off the A470, T01492 584466, www.bodysgallen.com. 19 rooms and 16 self-contained cottages set in 200 ha of parkland. The house is 17th-century and

filled with antiques and comfy sofas – the sort of place for a romantic weekend.
L-A Osborne House, 17 North Parade, T01492 860330, www.osbornehouse.co.uk. Wonderfully indulgent, small seafront hotel that has suites with cast iron beds, Egyptian

cotton sheets, Victorian fireplaces, luxurious bathrooms and widescreen TV with DVD.

L-A St Tudno Hotel, North Parade, Promenade, T01492 874411, www.st-tudno. co.uk. Small, swish, luxurious hotel with great location on the seafront. You can ask to stay in the suite used by Alice Lidell (Alice in Wonderland) and her family when they stayed here. Some rooms have sea views.

C Abbey Lodge, 14 Abbey Rd, T01492 878042, www.abbeylodgeuk.com. Comfortable non-smoking B&B with garden.

C Barratt's at Ty'n Rhyl, 167 Vale Rd, Rhyl T01745 344138, e.barratt@aol.com. Lovely old house in its own grounds, with comfortable bedrooms and food from an award-winning chef. All rooms are en suite.

C Escape B&B, 48 Church Walks, T 01492 877776, www.escapebandb.co.uk. Llandudno's newest B&B, very cool and contemporary with individually designed rooms, flat screen TVs and luxurious touches.

C Lynton House Hotel, 80 Church Walks, TT01492 875009. Comfortable, central B&B, among several others on Church Walks.

D Lympley Lodge, Colwyn Rd, Craigside, T01492 549304, www.lympleylodge.co.uk. This 5-star B&B is set in its own grounds and has great views over the sea.

E Agar House, 17 St David's Rd, T01492 875572, www.agarhouse.co.uk. Good value, non-smoking guesthouse close to the centre.

Ruthin p212, map p212

A-B Ruthin Castle, Corwen Rd, T01824 702664, www.ruthincastle.co.uk. 58 en suite rooms in a former castle, now a large hotel. Set in its own grounds near the centre.

C Castle Hotel, St Peters Sq, T01824 702479, enquiries@castlehotel.co.uk. Comfortable, family-run hotel on the main square in Ruthin.

C Firgrove Country House, Llanfwrog, Ruthin, T/F01824 702677, www.firgrove countryhouse.co.uk. 2 en suite rooms and self-catering cottage. Charming Georgian house and lush gardens, 1 mile out of Ruthin. Friendly and welcoming, excellent home cooked meals, with wine, by arrangement.

C Manorhaus, Well St, T01824 704830, www.manorhaus.com. A Georgian town house that is gradually being revamped to offer comfortable, contemporary style

rooms, all with DVD/CD players. A good town centre option.

D Gorphwysfa, Castle St, T01824 707529. 3 rooms, 2 en suite. Town centre B&B with original features like wood panelling and huge fireplaces.

Denbigh p213

C Hafod Elwy Hall, Bylchau, near Denbigh on A543, T01690 770345, www.hafodelwy hall.co.uk. Right out on the Denbigh Moors is this former shooting lodge, now a home on a smallholding. Good 'get away from it all' spot.

D Cayo Guest House, 74 Vale St, T01745 812686, 6 rooms, 4 en suite. Clean, pleasant, central guesthouse. Dogs welcome.

St Asaph p214

C Bach y Graig, Tremerchion, T01745 730627. Farmhouse accommodation and self catering cottage, close to St Asaph.

Mold p214

F Maeshafn Youth Hostel, Maeshafn, T01352 810320. Has 31 beds and no en suite facilities. Easter, Jul-Aug only. Close to Loggerheads Country Park

Holywell p215

C Greenhill Farm, Bryn Celyn, T01352 713270, www.greenhillfarm.co.uk. 16th-century farmhouse and working dairy farm on the outskirts of Holywell. Hearty evening meals on request. Drying room and ironing facilities, good base for walkers and cyclists.

Llangollen p216, map p217

C Gales of Llangollen, Bridge St, T01978 860089, www.galesofllangollen.co.uk. 15 en suite rooms. Centrally situated above Gales wine bar, comfortable rooms.

C Tyn Celyn Farmhouse, Tyndwr, near Llangollen, T01978 861117, www.border lands.co.uk/tyn-celyn. This B&B is surrounded by lovely countryside on the outskirts of the town. 3 rooms, all en suite.

C-D Cornerstones, 15 Bridge St, T01978 861569, www.cornerstones-guesthouse.co.uk. 2 en suite rooms and 1 self-contained. 3-star B&B, good base for walkers and cyclists.

D Oakmere, Regent St, T01978 861126, www.oakmere.llangollen.co.uk. This large house is set in its own grounds a short distance from the town centre. 4 of the 6 rooms are en suite.

F YHA Youth Hostel, Tyndwr Rd, T0870 7705932, llangollen@yha.org.uk. Good standard of hostel in large house about a mile out of town.

Corwen *p218*

A Tyddyn Llan, on B4401 Llandrillo, near Corwen, T01490 440264, www.tyddyn llan.co.uk. There's a lovely, relaxed atmosphere at this Georgian house, set in a secluded valley. Take afternoon tea on the lawn, or curl up on a sofa with a good book.

D Powys Country House, Holyhead Rd, Bonwym, near Corwen, T01490 412367, www.powyscountryhouse.co.uk. Large country house in 3 ha of gardens. Also has 2 self-catering cottages.

Chirk and the Ceiriog Valley *p219*

L-B The West Arms Hotel, Llanarmon Dyffryn Ceiriog, T0871 9958288, www.thewest arms.co.uk. You won't find more character than at this ancient inn, situated in a tranquil valley. Comfortable rooms, all sorts of nooks and crannies in the public rooms downstairs, with settles, huge fireplaces and low beams. Pricey, but a great setting.

A-B The Hand Hotel, Llanarmon Dyffryn Ceiriog, T01691 600666, www.thehand hotel.co.uk. Cheaper but less characterful than the West Arms Hotel, this inn is deep in the Ceiriog Valley. Log fires in winter.

Self catering

Ashgrove, North St, Caerwys, T01352 720095, www.ourworld.compuserve.com/ homepages/dewithomas. Apartments and holiday cottages.

The Olde Granary, Maerdy Mawr, Gwyddelwern, near Corwen, T0771 4186943, www.maerdymawr-cottages.co.uk. Converted granary, with 4 self-catering cottages on sheep farm. Open Apr-Oct.

Treetops, Llanfynydd, near Wrexham, T01352 770648, www.walesselfcatering. co.uk. 4-star Scandinavian style houses.

❷ Eating

Llandudno and the north coast *p210*
🍴🍴🍴 **Bodysgallen Hall**, off A470 near Llandudno, T01492 584466. High quality

British food in posh country house hotel. Dishes might include braised guinea fowl with polenta, or fillet of sea bass. Desserts like Champagne and berry jelly.

🍴🍴🍴 **Osborne's Café and Grill**, 17 North Parade, T01492 860330, Mon-Sat 1000-2200, Sun 1000-2130. Situated in Osborne's hotel, good food and full à la carte menu. Lots of fish and imaginative pasta.

🍴🍴🍴 **Richard's**, 7 Church Walks, Llandudno, T01492 875315, Tue-Sat 1730-2230. Lots of choice for veggies and a variety of mains such as Vietnamese-style fishcakes or Welsh lamb with apricots and rosemary. Coffee house upstairs, with fairtrade coffee and Welsh teas.

🍴🍴🍴 **St Tudno**, North Parade, Llandudno T01492 874411. Highly-rated restaurant offering expensive, sophisticated, French style food. Desserts might include rhubarb cheesecake with ginger ice cream. Also noted for its afternoon teas.

🍴 **Archies Wine Bar and Bistro**, 145 High St, Prestatyn, T01745 855106. Best to book if you want an evening meal at this bistro, away from the hubbub at the seafront.

🍴 **Nant Hall**, Nant Hall Rd, Prestatyn, T01745 856339. Food 1200-2130. Large family-friendly restaurant on Prestatyn outskirts, with garden and play area. Salad and sandwiches at lunchtime, also char-grilled steaks, fish and stir fries, kids' meals.

🍴 **New Inn**, Dyserth, near Prestatyn, T01745-570482. Food daily 1200-1500, 1700-2100. Friendly pub serving wide range of baguettes and sandwiches in addition to soups and meaty main courses.

🍴 **Nikky Ip's**, 57 Station Rd, Deganwy, T01492 596611, Popular Chinese restaurant, with contemporary interior. Dishes such as pan fried pork with ginger for around £7.80.

🍴 **Paysanne**, Station Rd, Deganwy, T01492 582079, open Tue-Fri from 1900, Sat from 1800. A little bit of France in North Wales in this country style French restaurant. Veggie food requires advance notice.

🍴 **Sands**, 59-63 Station Rd, Deganwy, T01492 592659, Tue-Sat 1200-1430, 1800-2130. Attractive bistro with tiled floors and relaxed atmosphere. International influences like squid with Thai noodles.

Ruthin *p212*
🍴🍴🍴 **Ruthin Castle**, Corwen Rd, T01824 703435. If you're keen to try a medieval

banquet with traditional entertainment and dishes like syllabub, you can join in one of the special nights held at this hotel.

Ψ Cross Keys, nearly 1 mile out of Ruthin on B5105, T01824 705281. Good family pub, popular with the locals.

Ψ Manorhaus, Well St, T01824 704830, coffee from 1000, lunch 1200-1400; Wed- Sat 1900-2100. Contemporary, with light wooden floors and retro seating. Also has a small gallery. Good stop for a morning coffee, light lunch or more substantial evening meal.

Ψ Leonardo's, 1 Wells St, T01824 707161, Mon-Sat 0930-1730. Great deli with excellent range of Welsh cheeses, as well as pâtés and meats, which you can get crammed into a baguette or sandwich. Also do salad bowls.

Ψ Market Hall, Market St, every Fri morning there's a WI market with lots of homemade cakes like traditional bara brith, preserves and veg. On Thu there's an organic market.

St Asaph *p214*
ΨΨ Barrow Alms, High St, St Asaph, T01745 582260. 3 courses for £19.95, 2 courses £9.95.

Mold *p214*
ΨΨΨ Glasfryn, Raikes Lane, Sychdyn, T01352 750500, daily 1200-2130. Popular gastropub close to the Theatr Clwyd. Modern food such as Cumberland sausage with mash; good puds like sticky toffee pudding with ice cream.
ΨΨΨ We Three Loggerheads, on A494 west of Mold, opposite Loggerheads Country Park, T01352 810337. Food daily 1200-2100. Good choice of bar meals in this old inn.

Holywell and around *p215*
ΨΨΨ Red Lion Inn and Restaurant, Llanasa, near Whitford, T01745 854291. Bar meals 1200-2200, restaurant 1200-1430, 1830-2200. In the pretty village of Llanasa, this pub serves basics like jacket potatoes and steaks, or veggie options like leek and mushroom crumble.

Llangollen *p216, map p217*
ΨΨ The Corn Mill, Dee Lane, T01978 869555, Mon-Sat 1200-2130, Sun 1200-2100. Lovely riverside setting and outdoor decking area make this converted mill the liveliest place to eat in town. Style is café/bistro, as well as more filling mains like pork and apple sausage with mash, or fried halloumi with roasted vegetable couscous.

ΨΨ Gales Wine Bar, Bridge St, T01978 860089, Mon-Sat 1200-1400, 1800-2200. Great choice of wines at this cosy wine bar that also offers a range of good value meals, such as fillet of sea bream.

Ψ The Bull Inn, Castle St. Popular, youthful pub with a beer garden serving bar meals.

Ψ River View Bistro, Bridge St. Tearoom and bistro beside the river, offering tea, cakes and light meals such as crab and spinach flan.

Ψ Sun Inn, Rhewl, about 3½ miles from Llangollen on B103, T01978 861043, Mon-Sat 1200-1430, 1800-2200, Sun 1200-2200. 14th-century drovers' inn, with low beams and period features. Real ale and good food.

Corwen *p218*
ΨΨΨ Tyddyn Llan, on B4401 Llandrillo, near Corwen, T01490 440264. Dinner only, must book. Crisp white tablecloths, fresh flowers and an air of relaxed elegance. Imaginative 4-course menu with canapés, homemade breads, cheese. Mains might include Welsh black beef or turbot with leek risotto, and delicious desserts vary from blackberry and almond tart to homemade ice cream.

Chirk *p219*
ΨΨΨ-ΨΨ The West Arms Hotel, Llanarmon Dyffryn Ceiriog, T01691 600665. Award-winning fresh food at this lovely old inn. Cosy atmosphere in the bar, with delicious meals such as local pork sausages in Yorkshire pudding, or good veggie options.

---

❻ Entertainment

Male voice choirs
Welsh male voice choirs can be heard at:
St John's Methodist Church, Mostyn St, and at the **English Presbyterian Church**, Chapel, both in Llandudno;
Neuadd Edeyrnion, Corwen every Wed at 2000 (not Aug), T01490 412604;
Neuadd Goffa, Stryd Uchaf, Glyn Ceiriog, Wed 2000, T01691 600242, and at the **Hand Hotel**, Llangollen on Fri (not Aug) at 1930, T01978 860303.

Theatre
North Wales Theatre, Promenade, Llandudno, T01492-872000, www.nwtheatre.co.uk. Theatre staging

everything from musicals and opera to ballet and comedy.

Theatr Colwyn, Colwyn Bay, T01492-872000 or 532668, www.theatrcolwyn.co.uk. Small theatre and cinema.

❀ Festivals and events

Jun Llandudno Festival, www.llandudnofestival.org.uk.
Jul International Musical Eisteddfod, Llangollen, T01978 862001, www.inter nationaleisteddfod.co.uk. World famous festival of music, song and dance in early Jul.
Aug/Sep Balloon Festival, Llangollen, T08700 115007. Hot-air balloon festival.
Sep North Wales International Music Festival, St Asaph Cathedral, T01745 584508, www.northwalesmusicfestival.co.uk. Usually held in the last week of Sep.

○ Shopping

Crafts
The Craft Centre and Gallery, at the TIC, Park Rd, Ruthin, T01824-703992, Jun-Sep daily 1000-1700, Oct- May Mon-Sat 1000-1700, Sun 1200-1700. A great place for gifts. Contemporary work from all over the UK, with glassware, jewellery and silverware. Also independent studios, with units for everything from upholstery and furniture-making to ceramics.

▲ Activities and tours

Boating
Llangollen Wharf, Llangollen Wharf, Wharf Hill, T01978 860702, www.horsedrawn boats.co.uk. Horse-drawn narrowboat trips on the canal (£4.50) and 2-hr cruises across the Pontcysyllte aqueduct (£8.50).
Maestermyn, T01691 662424, www.maester myn.co.uk. If you want to follow Harrison and Calista you can contact this company for a narrowboat holiday on the Llangollen Canal.

Canoeing
JJ Canoeing and Rafting, near Llangollen, T01978 860763, www.jjraftcanoe.com.

Cycling
Snowdonia Cycle Hire, Llandudno, T01492-878771, www.snowdoniacycle hire.co.uk, cycle hire (bikes delivered to you within a 6 mile radius of Llandudno) and guided weekend cycling breaks.
West End Cycles, Conway Rd, Colwyn Bay, T01492-530269, www.westendcycles.com, bike hire.

General adventure
Adventure activity Solutions, PO Box 17, Llangollen, T01978 845009, www.adventure -solutions.co.uk. Range of activities from kiting to climbing. ½ day taster sessions available.

Golf
Prestatyn Championship Golf Course, Marine Road East, T01745 854320, www.prestatyngc.org.uk.
St Melyd Golf Course, Meliden Rd, Prestatyn, T01745 854405, www.stmelyd golf.co.uk, a 9-hole parkland course.

Horse riding
Linden Farm, Rhes-Y-Cae, Holywell T01352-780539. hourly, ½ or full day rides.

Mountain biking
Pro Adventure, Castle St, Llangollen, T01978 861912, www.northwalesbikehire.co.uk. Mountain bike hire for everything from 1 hr to 1 week. Also offer other outdoor activities.

Sailing
Llandudno Sailing Club, T01492 876083 or try the Harbour Master's Office, T01492 596253.

Skiing
Llandudno Ski and Snowboard Centre, Wyddfyd Rd, Great Orme, Llandudno, T01492 874707, www.jnll.co.uk, daily 1000-2200. Dry-slope skiing, snowboarding, snowblading and snowbobbing, 750m toboggan run.

Walking
Offa's Dyke Path Association, T01547 528753, www.offasdyke.demon.co.uk. Has information on the long distance Offa's Dyke Path (see p46). Useful walking leaflets worth picking up include those inspired by Welsh naturalist Thomas Pennant. The **Pennant Group Walks** range from 3-6 miles and can be obtained from the **Greenfield Valley Heritage Park Visitor Centre**, Greenfield, Holywell, T01352 714172.

A useful range of leaflets detailing walks around the Clwydian hills, called *Beyond the*

Offa's Dyke Path, call **Denbighshire Country-side Service**, T01352 810614 or try TICs. There are several walks around Tremerchion. You can walk the nature trail through the forest around Bach-y-graig (small charge), T01745 730627. There are also trails through **Y Graid** Nature Reserve. The **North Wales Path** stretches for 60 miles from Prestatyn to Bangor, through the traditional seaside resorts.

⊖ Transport

Llandudno *p210, map p210*
Bus
Arriva Cymru bus No 19 runs every 20 mins to **Conwy** (£1.70, ½ hr) via **Llandudno Junction**. Bus No 5 runs hourly to **Conwy** (£1.70, ½ hr), **Bangor** (£3, 1 hr) and **Caernarfon** (£3.50, 3 hrs). The **Snowdon Sherpa** bus No S2 runs to **Betws-y-Coed** and **Capel Curig** (see p194). National Express runs twice daily to **Bangor**, **Caernarfon**, **Porthmadog**, **Pwllheli**, and to **London** via **Chester**.

Train
The Conwy Valley Railway runs every 2 hrs to **Conwy** and **Blaenau Ffestiniog**, stopping at **Llanrwst** and **Betws-y-Coed** (£3.75, ½ hr), www.conwyvalleyrailway.co.uk. The **North Wales Coast** line runs to **Rhyl** and on to **Chester**; in the other direction it runs to **Betws-y-Coed**. From **Llandudno Junction** there are daily trains to **Chester**, **Manchester** and **London** (£26, 4 hrs). Trains from here also run to **Holyhead** and **Bangor** (every ½ hr £6.40, 10 mins).

The Vale of Clwyd *p212*
Buses run between the main towns and in summer link **Ruthin** to the **Loggerheads Country Park**. Get hold of the **Clwydian Ranger Leisure Bus** timetable for summer travel details. Bus information from **Traveline** T0870 6082608, The main towns in the Vale of Clwyd can be explored by **Vale Rider** buses (T01824 706968), or if you have your own transport, the A525 and B5429 roads.

Mold and the Dee Estuary *p214*
There is a rail link bus Nos 3/4/X44/X55 to **Chester** and **Buckley**. Coast Rider buses serve the coastline; other buses link Mold with **Ruthin** and **Denbigh**.

Llangollen *p216, map p217*
There is no train station at Llangollen, the nearest is **Ruabon**, south of Wrexham; to get here take bus No 94 or No 555 (every 20 mins, £1.20, 15 mins), www.chester 2shrewsburyrail.net. **Arriva Cymru** bus No 94 runs to **Dolgellau** from where you can get a bus to Snowdonia. **National Express** buses run daily to **Wrexham** (£2, ½ hr) and to **Shrewsbury**, **Birmingham** and **London**.

Llangollen is also linked to **Shropshire** by canal, so it's possible to travel by narrowboat.

Wrexham *p219*
Arriva Cymru bus No 94 runs several times daily to **Llangollen** (£1.50, ½ hr), **Bala** (£3.45, 1½ hrs), **Dolgellau** (£4.25, 2 hrs) and **Barmouth**. Bus No 555 runs every 20 mins to **Llangollen** (£1.20, 15 mins). National Express services run to **Llangollen**, **Shrewsbury** (£4.50, 40 mins), **Birmingham** and **London**.

There are regular train services from Mon-Sat to **Chester** (£3.50, 1 hr) **Shrewsbury** (£4.50, 40 mins) and **Birmingham**.

❶ Directory

Dentist Emergency dentist T01745 887098. **Hospital** Glan Clwyd, Bodelwyddan, near St Asaph, T01745 583910. **Internet** Free at Denbigh Library/TIC, Hall Sq, Mon-Wed 0930-1900, Tue, Thu-Fri 0930-1700, Sat 0900-1200; Ruthin library, Record St; Llangollen Library; Corwen Library and One Stop Shop, Tue 1430-1900, Wed 1000-1200, Thu 1000-1400, Fri 1430-1900. **Library** Holywell library, North Rd, Mon 0930-1700, Tue 0930-1900, Wed 0930-1300, Thu, Fri 0930-1900, Sat 0930-1230.

Background

♟ Footprint features

History

Prehistory

There is evidence of human settlement in Wales as far back as **250,000 BC** when a human tooth was discovered at Pontnewydd in North Wales. It is thought that these ancient Neanderthal inhabitants lived in small groups as hunter-gatherers and made little impact on the area. By **Palaeolithic** times, man appeared to be establishing more significant settlements and the remains of a skeleton, christened the **Red Lady** (actually a man), discovered at Paviland Cave on the Gower, have been dated variously at 24,000 or 16,500 BC. **Mesolithic** peoples left little for archaeologists to find, but the Neolithic settlers who followed them left traces which can still be seen today. The **Neolithic** colonists, short, dark people, sometimes called Iberians, came from the Mediterranean area. They were the first farmers and established settled communities, clearing forests, constructing villages – and building circles of standing stones (henges) and vast burial chambers for their dead. The best known of these is Stonehenge in Wiltshire, made from bluestones hacked from the Preseli Hills in Pembrokeshire, but Wales is littered with such mysterious monuments including Pentre Ifan in Pembrokeshire and Bryn Celli Ddu in Anglesey.

The Neolithic period morphed gradually into the **Bronze Age**, with its use of metals to make implements and pots, and increasingly sophisticated social structures. Hillforts (defended villages) began to appear, then around 600 BC the **Celts** arrived.

The Celts

The Celts originally came from the area around the Rhine in Europe. A tall, fair people with sophisticated social structures, they made a huge impact. They were noted for their love of war and imposed their ways on the existing tribes of Britain very quickly. They used iron, rather than other metals, were artistically skilled and had distinctive religious beliefs – with their religious leaders, the **Druids**, enjoying huge power. Caesar wrote of Celtic society that there were 'only two classes of men who are of any account...the common people are treated almost as slaves ...the two privileged classes are the Druids and the Knights'. They also brought with them a new language which had two distinct strands: **Goidelic** (the basis of the Celtic languages in the Isle of Man, Scotland and Ireland) and **Brythonic** (the basis of Cornish and Welsh).

Celtic tribes established themselves throughout Wales: the Silures in the southeast, Ordovices in the northwest, Demetae in the southwest and Cornovii and Deceangli in the northeast. The Celts flourished until the arrival of the Romans, who first came to Britain in 55 BC, and finally conquered much of it in AD 43.

The Romans

The Celtic/British tribes continued to fight the Romans, notably Boudicca's Iceni in eastern England, who spread throughout the country. Tribal leader Caratacus (Caradog) moved west to organize resistance but it was hard, as the tribes here weren't as socially cohesive as in the south and east. The only uniformity was provided by the powerful Druids, whose stronghold was in Anglesey, described by Roman writer, Tacitus, as the place where young men from all over Europe were trained for the 'priesthood'. However, the rougher landscapes of the west helped keep the Romans at bay and it was not until after AD 75, when the massive fort was built at Caerleon (Isca), that they could be said to have conquered Wales.

The Romans built roads throughout Wales, linking important forts at Caernarfon (Segontium) and Carmarthen (Moriduum), and settled down for a long occupation. Gradually their sophisticated language and ways of living – and later their new Christian religion – started to influence local Celtic culture. Essentially a stable Romano/British culture emerged which ended with the decline of the Roman Empire.

The Dark Ages

As the Roman Empire floundered it became increasingly difficult to defend isolated areas such as the western parts of Wales. The long, exposed coastline meant that Wales was subject to raids from Ireland in the west, with further incursions from the Picts in the north and the Saxons in the south. By the end of the fourth century the Romans no longer ruled Wales. Britain became subject to increasing raids from warring **Teutonic** tribes who established themselves in the south and east of England. **Christianity**, which had only taken a tenuous hold through the Romans, returned to Wales during the fifth and sixth centuries, with the arrival of missionaries from Ireland. **Illtud** introduced the idea of Celtic monasticism and established a religious school at **Llantwit Major** in south Wales; in AD 500 his pupil **St David** founded St David's cathedral in Pembrokeshire.

Around the same time, Irish settlers (who spoke the Goidelic tongue) began moving into western parts of Wales, but were expelled from the north by **Cunedda**, leader of the Brythonic speaking Votadini (Gododdin) tribe. Well organized, they established themselves in north Wales and gradually spread as far south as the Teifi. They set up the royal house of **Gwynedd** and consolidated the Brythonic language in Wales. By the sixth century a distinctive **Welsh language** was evolving. Latin was used for formal affairs like legal matters, but everyday speech was Welsh. The earliest known example of written Welsh is on an eighth-century stone.

The Welsh coast was also subject to raids from **Vikings**, who left their stamp in place names such as Skomer. The tribes in the west, who saw themselves as **Cymry** (compatriots), became isolated. Wales – which had been given an obvious border in the late 700s when **King Offa** built the great earthwork Offa's Dyke, to delineate his Mercian territory – began to develop a distinct identity.

In AD 856 **Rhodri Mawr** (the Great) beat off the Vikings and created a largely unified Wales, although as the practice of primogeniture (first born male inherits) did not apply in Wales, inheritance squabbles meant it was never as stable as England. More Viking raids in the mid-ninth century served only to increase links with England for defensive reasons, but Rhodri's grandson **Hywel Dda** (the Good) became king of most of Wales. He was the first Welsh ruler known to issue his own coins and is also recognized as the codifier of **Welsh Law**. After his death, the country descended into anarchy, only coming together under the rule of **Gruffydd ap Llywelyn** – who even managed to grab some lands off Edward the Confessor – before being killed by his own people at the behest of Harold, Edward's successor.

The Norman Conquest

The first Norman castle in Wales was built in 1067 at **Chepstow** and the Normans gradually encroached on Welsh lands. By the end of the 11th century they had reached Pembroke in the south and other parts of Wales. Norman barons, the **Marcher Lords**, were installed in castles along the border so as to get control of as much land (and income) as possible. Welsh kings paid **homage** to the Normans, securing peace until

Arthur – the Once and Future King

With its ancient standing stones, prehistoric burial chambers, barren peaks and rich history it's not surprising that Wales is full of myths and legends, as well as tales of saints and holy wells, of giants and fairies, of Celtic gods and ghosts. And the best known figure of all is King Arthur.

The story of Arthur and the Knights of the Round Table is extraordinarily enduring and still inspires films and books. But did he exist? His name in Welsh, *Arth Fawr*, meaning the Great Bear, like the constellation Ursa Major, could point to him being a Celtic god. Some think the Arthurian legends date back to the Bronze Age, however, most sources feel he was probably a fifth-century Celtic chieftain who led the Brythonic Celts to victory against the Saxons. Though many places claim to be his birthplace, Tintagel in Cornwall seems the most likely, while Camelot could well be Cadbury Castle in Somerset. He is thought to have died at the battle of Camlan around AD 539 and his burial place is generally agreed to be Glastonbury. Nothing very Welsh there then, yet Arthur has featured in Welsh folklore for centuries.

The first written references to him were made in the ninth century *Historia Brittonum*, written by Nennius a monk from Bangor. Artorius was the 'dux bellorum' the leader who defeated the Saxons at Badon Hill in 518. By the 12th century he was a powerful symbol and was mentioned in the *Black Book of Carmarthen*, the oldest Welsh manuscript; in the *Mabinogion*, the famed collection of Welsh folk tales; and in Geoffrey of Monmouth's mammoth *Historia Regum Britanniae* – a 12-volume history of the kings of Britain. Geoffrey essentially wrote the first Arthurian romance and claimed that Caerleon, near Newport, was the site of his first court; the mound covering the ruined Roman amphitheatre there was known for years as Arthur's Round Table.

Later, writers embellished the myth, gradually turning Arthur from a Celtic leader to an idealized courtly knight. Chrétien de Troyes, a French poet, took the story to France and in the 15th century Sir Thomas Mallory wrote his influential *Morte d'Arthur*.

Welsh versions of his story abound, claiming that he fought his last battle on Snowdon; that Llyn Llydaw, a lake at the foot of Snowdon, was where the dying king was rowed out to the island of Avalon; that Excalibur was thrown by Sir Bedivere into Llyn Ogwen (or Llyn Llydaw or the lily pond at Bosherston…); and that Merlin sank the crown jewels into Llyn Cwmglas, a lake above the Llanberis Pass. Avalon is sometimes thought to be Bardsey Island; and Camlan, the site of his last battle, could be Cadlan on the Llŷn Peninsula. Arthur, the Once and Future King, is still a powerful symbol of the Welsh struggle against oppression – a king who sleeps, waiting to come to the aid of the Celts once again.

William's death. William's son, William Rufus, made some incursions into Wales and the Marcher lords gradually helped to secure much of the country – although the northwest region of Gwynedd remained independent. There was much infighting and under **Owain Gwynedd**, operating from his power base at Aberffraw on Anglesey, Gwynedd began expanding its influence, sucking in weaker Welsh territories. **Llywelyn ap Iorwerth** (known as 'the Great') further extended Gwynedd and even managed to capture some Norman castles, until King John retaliated. Matters were complicated still more when Llywelyn, who wanted to achieve feudal overlordship over all Wales, consolidated his powerful position by marrying King John's daughter. He paid homage to the king and had to accept him as his heir, should his marriage not produce a son. Further struggles ensued, with Llywelyn gaining Welsh support for his demands for land and a degree of autonomy. He united with the barons who made King John sign the Magna Carta and, in essence, ruled most of Wales.

After he died, the infighting started again and the Normans pushed back into Wales until Llywelyn's grandson **Llywelyn ap Gruffyd** ('the Last') took control, managing to regain lost lands. In 1267 Henry III acknowledged his influence with the Treaty of Montgomery, in which Llywelyn recognized the English crown – and in turn was recognized as '**Prince of Wales**'. Llywelyn consolidated his lands, but then Edward I succeeded to the English throne and set out to gain control of the whole of Britain.

The Middle Ages and the last Welsh princes

Llywelyn gradually began to lose Welsh support and his brother Dafydd united against him with the ruler of Powys. Edward I seized his chance and the resulting struggle became known as the **First War of Welsh Independence** (1267-1277). The result was the **Treaty Of Aberconwy** (1277), in which Llywelyn lost most of his lands but was allowed to keep the title Prince of Wales. To keep the troublesome Welsh in order, Edward built castles at Flint, Aberystwyth, Builth Wells and Rhuddlan. A **Second War of Welsh Independence** was fought from 1282-1283, when Llywelyn's brother Dafydd rose against Edward, who brutally crushed the Welsh. Llywelyn was captured and killed at Cilmeri, near Builth Wells in 1282. Edward I strengthened his grip on Wales by starting to build more castles at Conwy, Caernarfon, Harlech and Beaumaris. In 1283 Dafydd was killed and the power of the Welsh princes ended.

In 1284 Edward signed the **Statute of Rhuddlan**, which established how Wales was to be governed; it was to be largely controlled by Norman lords and divided into new administrative units. English law took over for criminal matters, although Welsh law was retained for civil cases. Many of the powerful Welsh worked under this system happily enough and a rebellion in 1294 led by **Madog ap Llywelyn** was quickly crushed. In 1301 Edward revived the title of Prince of Wales, conferring it on his son Edward II, who had been born at Caernarfon.

The 14th century saw Britain plagued by famine and the Black Death, and Welsh anger and discontentment at their subjugation increased. The country was ripe for revolt – all they needed was a leader. In 1400, **Owain Glyndŵr** (1354-c1416) declared himself Prince of Wales and attacked ruling barons. He quickly gathered support and took castles such as Conwy, Harlech and Aberystwyth. Rebellion spread throughout Wales and Glyndŵr briefly established parliaments at Machynlleth and Dolgellau. He established alliances with powerful figures such as the Earl of Northumberland, and planned an independent Welsh state, garnering support from the Scots and the French. However, his support began to wane and after various defeats, with the Crown retaking Harlech and Aberystwyth castles he seemed to fade away. No one is sure how or when he died although it is thought to be 1416.

The Tudors

In 1485 Harri Tewdwr, a Welshman, took the English throne after winning the Battle of Bosworth with the help of a Welsh army. He became **Henry VII**, the first Tudor king, and Welsh hopes in him were high. He rewarded loyal Welsh nobles with high positions at court and sent letters to Welsh gentry in which he said he would restore 'the people... to their erst libertyes, delivering them of such miserable servitudes as they have pyteously longe stand in'. Restoration of 'libertyes' was not necessarily what Welsh nobles wanted – if interpreted in a certain way that could mean a return to the rigid traditional system of equal inheritance and the obstacles presented to the acquisition of land.

Welsh castles

The Welsh landscape is crammed with castles – brooding stone reminders of the country's turbulent history. There are 400 in all. But if you thought one was much like another you'd be wrong. Essentially there are three types of castle in Wales: those built by the Normans, those by the Welsh, and those by Edward I. They all have their own story to tell, and none more so than the handful of native Welsh castles that survive.

The first fortresses in Wales were erected by the Romans, whose imperial forces gradually subdued the ancient Britons who had retreated to this wild, western corner. However, castles, often built close to these Roman sites, did not appear until after the Norman Conquest and were erected by William's conquering forces to ensure that the locals knew just who was in charge. These were originally motte and bailey constructions of earth and timber, but later stone was used to create more robust structures. Most of the Norman castles in Wales are in the south and along the border with England. The first stone built castle in Britain was made by the Normans in Chepstow in 1067. It was the base for their aggressive incursions into Wales. Other Norman castles include Pembroke, Caerleon and Kidwelly.

In the 13th century, Welsh princes began to build their own castles, not just to provide protection against invading forces but also to guard against attacks from rival princes; this was a time when there were fierce internal struggles for control of Wales. These native Welsh castles were built in some of the most dramatic places in the country, utilising craggy outcrops and steep, isolated hills as natural defences. They tended to be smaller than Norman castles and often had a distinctive D-shaped tower. This had an outer, curved edge which gave a wide field of fire, and a flatter inner edge which meant that the rooms inside could be more spacious than in round towers. Only a few of these castles survive and they're often neglected by visitors. They include Castell-y-Bere, near Dolgellau, built to secure the southern border of Gwynedd; Dolbadarn, near Llanberis, and Dolwyddelan, south of Betws y Coed, which both guarded major routes through Snowdonia; and Dinefwr, in Carmarthenshire, which was the principal court of the kingdom of Deheubarth. Welsh castles fell into disrepair after the country was conquered by England, but the ruins are poignant and atmospheric reminders of the past.

The best known castles in Wales are those built by Edward I late in the 13th century. He was determined to complete the conquest of the Welsh, and as most danger came from North Wales, concentrated his building projects there. Some of his early castles were Rhuddlan and Conwy, and later Flint. But after Llywelyn the Last's second uprising he built even more enormous structures to create an iron ring of defence. These later castles of Harlech, Caernarfon, Conwy and finally Beaumaris remain among the most impressive and formidable castles in Europe. More information at www.castlewales.com.

They had seen at close hand the advantages of the English system of primogeniture and greater freedom in the transfer of land. The ruling class rapidly became anglicized.

Under Henry VIII's powerful administrator, Thomas Cromwell, Wales was brought far more under English control with the **Acts of Union** in 1536 and 1542. Although the Welsh were given legal equality, the legal system was unified with English common law taking the place of Welsh. The country was reorganized into shires, primogeniture became the method of inheritance and English became the language of the courts.

Elizabeth I

Under Elizabeth I, who wanted to ensure that Wales became Protestant rather than Catholic, an Act of Parliament was passed which laid down that the Bible be translated into Welsh within four years. This **Welsh Bible** should then be used in parishes where Welsh was the main language. The Welsh New Testament appeared in 1567, followed by the complete Bible in 1588 (see box page 190). It was this that effectively saved the Welsh language. In 1547, the first Welsh book was published and, in 1571, Jesus College, Oxford was founded for Welsh scholars.

Civil War

During the Civil War, Wales was largely on the side of the King. Gradually Parliamentarian forces gained the upper hand but many castles resisted long sieges. **Harlech** was the last Royal castle to fall in 1647.

In 1752, Britain accepted the Gregorian Calendar. However, the Gwaun Valley in Pembrokeshire stayed with the Julian one – they still celebrate Julian New Year now.

Industrial Revolution

Wales was at the heart of the Industrial Revolution. While the north was rich in slate, the south was rich in iron ore, coal, limestone and water and the valleys around Merthyr Tydfil became huge centres for coal and iron production. Huge numbers of people migrated to the Valleys looking for work, and because many of them were not Welsh, local culture and language were weakened. The harsh conditions experienced by the workers gave rise to unrest throughout Britain. In Wales the **Merthyr Riots** of 1831 were particularly violent. The Red Flag was raised for the first time and many people, on both sides, were killed.

Insurrection continued with the **Chartist Riots**, the first of these in Wales took place in 1839 in Newport. The **Rebecca Riots** of 1839-43 were a protest against toll gates on turnpike roads. They started on 13 May 1839 at Efail-wen. Rioters dressed in women's clothes and demolished the toll gates. The name was taken from a verse mentioning Rebecca in the Book of Genesis.

Events such as the Rebecca Riots and the Chartist movement led many in authority to express concern at the increasingly negative attitude of the working classes. The issue of language, which was still being spoken in non-conformist schools, was thought to make the Welsh more prone to rioting. Welsh was also increasingly regarded as a handicap by parents, who saw it was important for their children to speak English so they could get on in industry and the professions. In 1846 a Welshman, representing an English constituency, set up an inquiry into Welsh education, focusing on the 'means afforded to the labouring classes of acquiring a knowledge of English'. English Anglicans were sent round the schools and came back with a report published in 1847. It declared that standards in education were terrible, which in many ways they were, but sadly they put much of this down to the use of Welsh. Their report was branded Brad y Llyfrau Gleision – the '**Treachery of the Blue Books**'. When free primary schools were set up in Wales in 1870, Welsh was largely banned. To dissuade pupils from speaking their language a 'Welsh Not' was introduced. This was a piece of wood on a strap which had to be worn, and was only passed on if someone else was heard speaking Welsh. The child left wearing the device would then be beaten.

In 1872 the system of education was expanded with the opening of the University College of Wales at Aberystwyth. A campaign began to grow for greater autonomy for Wales and there was a revival of interest in Welsh culture. The eisteddfod was reintroduced into Welsh life, the first being the National Eisteddfod of 1858. In 1885 the Welsh Language Society was created, which succeeded in ensuring that Welsh was taught in schools, and a political movement for a separate Wales was formed in 1886 as part of the Liberal party.

The political scene in Wales became increasingly radical and in 1900 Merthyr Tydfil elected a Scot, **Keir Hardie** as their MP – Britain's first Labour MP. World War One saw a Welshman, **David Lloyd George** become Prime Minister. The Labour Party continued to grow in importance in Wales, but there was dissatisfaction at their failure to introduce Home Rule for Wales and the lack of safeguards for the language. In 1925 **Plaid Cymru**, the National Party of Wales was established. One of the founders was Saunder Lewis. He and two other Plaid members – DJ Williams and Lewis Valentine – gained notoriety (and Welsh support) when they set fire to buildings at an RAF station on the Llyn.

After World War Two, Labour came to power and a Welsh MP **Aneurin Bevan** established the National Health Service. Wales was still at the heart of the coal mining industry; the Valleys were tragically brought to the world's attention in October 1966 when a slag heap slid down a hill engulfing a school in the close-knit mining village of **Aberfan**:144 people were killed, 116 of whom were children.

Nationalism and devolution

Over the years, demands for home rule increased again and in 1979 a **referendum** was held. The result was huge disappointment for the nationalists with 80% of people voting against a Welsh assembly. But interest in the Welsh language did increase (the 1967 Welsh Language Act had already allowed the use of Welsh in court) and in 1982 a Welsh language television channel, **S4C**, started up. Nationalist protests began to be directed at English 'incomers' – particularly at those buying second homes in Wales. The Sons of Glyndwr started setting fire to English-owned holiday homes, giving rise to the joke 'Come home to a real fire – buy a Welsh cottage'.

After the Thatcher government was finally defeated and Labour took power again, another referendum was held in 1997. This time there was a tiny majority in favour and elections to the **National Assembly for Wales** took place in May 1999. Unlike the Scottish Parliament it has no tax raising powers. After much wrangling work on a new building to house the assembly finally began in summer 2003 – it is sited in Cardiff Bay and due for completion of Autumn 2005.

Culture

Literature

Myths and legends
The tradition of storytelling in Wales is rich and can be said to have its roots in the country's Celtic past. The Celts' religious system involved worship of gods, associated with natural features like flowers, trees and water. The Druids, the powerful religious and political Celtic leaders, had to undergo 20 years of training to acquire their sacred knowledge. This covered three areas: Druid – focusing on education and philosophy; Ovates – dealing with natural lore, divination and healing; and Bardic – the art of oratory – or powerful public speaking. Nothing was ever written down and everything had to be committed to memory. And with landscapes that inspire myths and legends (moody mountains, isolated islands, dank caves, ancient burial sites) there was plenty of material to inspire the early storytellers. And the battles fought both on and for the land, the arrival of the early Christian saints, and the colourful characters in Welsh history all added to this inspirational cocktail.

Many of the earliest stories survive in the *Mabinogion*, a rich collection of Welsh mythical tales written down around the 13th and 14th centuries but of much earlier origin. The *Mabinogion* were eventually translated into English in the 19th century by Lady Charlotte Guest, who gave them their collective title, which means '*Tales of Youth*'. Characters who feature include Blodeuwedd, a girl who was created from flowers; and Culhwch, who has to perform forty feats to win the hand of Olwen, daughter of a local giant. He pulls it off with the help of King Arthur and his knights.

The Arthurian legends are rich in Wales. Not only do they appear in the Mabinogion but are also mentioned in the ninth century Historia Brittonum, a Latin history of Britain by Nennius who, according to what you read, was either a monk in Wales or a military leader from Scotland. Arthur is considered by many to have been a tribal leader who, much like Boudicca, fought off Saxon invaders. Merlin the magician, of the legends, is also said to be Welsh – probably a sixth-century holy man called Myrddin who was born near Carmarthen. Whether fact or fiction, Arthur certainly featured in an early Welsh poem, *Y Gododdin*; written around the seventh century by the bard Aneurin, it describes a battle against the Saxons.

Travel writing

Travel writers have also been intrigued by Wales' unique combination of ancient language, rich history and stunning scenery. The first was **Giraldus Cambrensis**, or Gerald of Wales, who was born at Manorbier in 1146. Of Norman descent, he travelled widely through Wales trying to drum up recruits to go on the Third Crusade, and wrote detailed accounts of his travels. The books, *The Journey Through Wales* and *The Description of Wales*, give a vivid insight into Welsh life and people in the 12th century. Other travel books include **Thomas Pennant's** *A Tour in Wales* (1773), which ushered in a passion for wild and romantic Welsh landscapes; **HV Morton's** *In Search of Wales*; and **George Borrow's** still widely quoted *Wild Wales* (1854). Borrow was English but had learned Welsh and reported his conversations in detail. He is often seen as typifying English condescending attitudes towards the Welsh – but as this is the man who wrote 'an Englishman of the lower class ....is never savage with you, provided you call him old chap, and he considers you by your dress to be his superior in station' he was obviously happy to patronize anyone, not just the Welsh.

Poetry

Poetry has enormous importance in Wales, with Aneurin and Taliesin – a sixth-century bard associated with the poems that appeared in the 14th-century *Book of Taliesin* – providing the earliest examples of Welsh poetry. Poets were important members of the royal courts and Welsh princes had their own poets to record battles and important events – and praise their bosses, a bit like the Poet Laureate today. The earliest known of these professional bards was a man named Meilyr who lived in the 12th century. An intricate and characteristic form of poetry writing gradually developed at these courts. Known as *cynghanedd* – the use of vivid imagery and elaborate patterns of rhyme and alliteration – its influence can still be seen today.

Poetry was considered so important that competitions were established, with poets competing for privileged positions. The first recorded large scale competition – or eisteddfod – took place in 1176 at Rhys ap Gruffydd's castle in Cardigan. These flourished until the 17th and 18th centuries, when they began to peter out, until they were revived in the 19th century. Poetry had enormous significance for the Welsh, often mourning the loss of great leaders who had fought their English/Norman rulers, and stirring the emotions of a people who desperately wanted to be free.

19th and 20th century literature

After 1870 the speaking of English, rather than Welsh, was enforced in schools and a new Anglo/Welsh literature emerged, with Welsh people writing in English but being influenced by the Welsh writing traditions and patterns of speech. The country itself also acted as inspiration to poets. The Jesuit poet **Gerard Manley Hopkins** (1844-89), writing in the 1870s and 1880s, was inspired and moved by the Welsh countryside as well as the rhythm of the language. And **Edward Thomas** (1878-1917) who was of Welsh extraction, produced fine poems inspired by nature until he was killed at the Front in World War One. **WH Davies** (1871-1940), a friend of Thomas, left Wales for America, where his experiences on the road inspired the once bestselling, but now less widely read, *Autobiography of a Super-Tramp*. However his lines 'What is this life if, full of care/We have no time to stand and stare' have entered the British lexicon.

The 20th century saw the real flowering of Welsh writing – and not only were Welsh people writing in English, Wales itself was inspiring literature. **Caradoc Evans** (1914-45) wrote controversial and satirical works about non-conformist Wales; novelist **Richard Hughes** (1900-76), author of *High Wind in Jamaica*, lived and worked in Laugharne; **Alexander Cordell** (1914-97) settled in Wales and wrote novels inspired by Welsh historical events such as the Rebecca Riots; **Kingsley Amis** (1922-95) lectured at Swansea University – the setting for his novel *Lucky Jim* (1954), and Welshman **Alun Lewis** (1915-44) produced some of the most important poetry of World War Two. The book that really grabbed popular attention was **Richard Llewellyn's** *How Green Was My Valley* (1939), a worldwide bestseller depicting life in the coalfields of south Wales – which later got the Hollywood treatment in a film.

The most acclaimed 20th-century writers were poets, RS Thomas and Dylan Thomas; **RS Thomas** (1913-2000) was a clergyman and prolific writer who was inspired by the landscapes and history of Wales. His work had a bleak quality 'There is no present in Wales/ And no future;/ There is only the past.' He was a fierce nationalist too and spoke out on issues such as the spread of the English language into isolated, mainly Welsh-speaking areas. **Dylan Thomas** (1914-53) is the best known of all Welsh writers, not only because of the high quality of his rich, original and lyrical verse, but also because of his reputation for hard living and hard drinking. Born in Swansea, his first volume of work was *Eighteen Poems* which was received to widespread acclaim. Over the years he moved to London and then back to Wales, producing fine poems with instantly recognisable lines such as: 'Do not go gentle into that good night' and 'The force that through the green fuse'. He also wrote the dense and compelling *Under Milk Wood*, his 'play for voices' which produced characters such as Captain Cat and Polly Garter. When he wasn't writing poetry he was investigating the pubs of southwest Wales. His hard drinking leading to his untimely death in America, where a particularly hard session resulted in 'an insult to the brain'.

Literature today

Literature is flourishing in Wales today and it is worth looking for works by poets such as **Menna Elfyn**, **Owen Sheers** and **Harri Webb**; Welsh romantic novels by the prolific **Iris Gower**, and works by **Kate Roberts** set in the quarries of north Wales. Then there's the Welsh Irvine Welsh, **Niall Griffiths**, whose books like *Grits* and *Sheepshagger* look at the seamy side of contemporary life; **James Hawes**, whose *White Powder, Green Light*, focuses on the Welsh media; and **Malcolm Pryce's** blackly comic *Aberystwyth Mon Amour*.

Music

Wales and Music – a musical tradition

The epithet 'land of song' has been attached to Wales since Adam was a lad. And, true enough, the country has a powerful musical tradition. Its male voice choirs are known throughout the world, and top-flight artists such as Tom Jones and Shirley Bassey are household names. The Welsh National Opera has performed in the world's foremost venues. When virtuoso Bryn Terfel appeared at the Metropolitan Opera in 1998, he made the front page of the *New York Times*, and hot young mezzo soprano Katherine Jenkins already has a huge following. But these are conventional examples of the nation's culture – there's a lot more in the musical melting pot than this. Wales has an eclectic attitude to music, revelling in its many facets. Organizations such as Cultural Concerns bring musicians from around the globe: Burundi, Iran, Zimbabwe, India, Poland, Colombia to name a few, to perform in Wales. Likewise, Welsh artists take the opportunity to explore cultural differences and indeed similarities, in far-flung corners of the globe. And as for rock and pop, Wales produced The Manic Street Preachers, Stereophonics, Catatonia, Feeder, Super Furry Animals and Gorky's Zygotic Mynci, a pretty illustrious track record if ever there was one.

But why Wales and song? Why do the lusty voices of the rugby crowd belt out 'Calon Lan' and 'Sosban Fach' while the match is in full flood? What drives thousands of people to a free concert given by Welsh National Opera in Cardiff Bay? Why do pubs throughout the land reverberate to the sound, not only of the jukebox, but of imbibers boisterously accompanying their favourite number? And this isn't just drunken crooning, it actually sounds melodic!

Music, and song, is, and always has been, a compelling form of self-expression. Furthermore, Celtic societies, be they Breton, Cornish, Irish, Scottish or Welsh, have always cherished music. Music affirms an individual's sense of place and belonging. Traditional Welsh music explores the universal themes of love and desire, but it also explores the condition of *hiraeth*. No single word sums up this emotion, a sense of loss and longing and nostalgia. Expats express a sense of *hiraeth* when they think of home. But *hiraeth* is more than homesickness, it's part of the human condition, an inexpressible yearning. Inexpressible, that is, other than through music and song. Although the Welsh do a fine line in poetry and prose, the voice of the nation is most eloquently and profoundly expressed through the medium of music.

The earliest recorded instrument in Wales is the **crwth**, or lyre. There's evidence to suggest that it was played as far back as Roman times. This rudimentary instrument wasn't peculiar to the Celts though. An illustration on an Egyptian tomb circa 1900 BC shows a musician holding a six-stringed instrument that is, to all intents and purposes, a crwth. Its heyday came in the Middle Ages when players made a good living entertaining the Welsh aristocracy. Its popularity declined with the advent of the fiddle, with its infinitely more dexterous repertoire. Now, originals can be found at the Museum of Welsh Life in St Fagan's near Cardiff and in the National Library of Wales in Aberystwyth. However, the age of the crwth isn't completely over. Enthusiasts, such as widely acclaimed fiddle player Cass Meurig, still perform traditional crwth music and replicas are lovingly fashioned by Cardiff-based craftsman, Guy Flockhart.

Bagpipes may be synonymous with Scotland, but all Celtic nations have their own version. The Welsh manifestation is called the 'piba cwd'. Popular until the latter half of the nineteenth century, it is extraordinary that no examples have survived to the present day. Another popular instrument was the **pibgorn**, literally meaning hornpipe, which was not unique to Wales. This simple instrument is powered by a single reed like the drone reed of a bagpipe.

The **triple harp**, with its sweetly lyrical sound, is another instrument closely aligned with Wales. Unlike the crwth it has a prominent place in today's culture. Prince Charles recently revived an ancient tradition when he appointed 20-year-old Catrin Finch as Royal Harpist. The young Welshwoman's mission is to bring the harp to the masses. With her youth and good looks, she has a better chance of success than most of making the harp hip.

The Welsh **male voice choir** (cor meibion) is something of an institution. Although male choirs are found throughout the nation, they are perhaps most closely associated with the mining communities in South Wales. The demise of the coal industry isn't reflected in the fate of the choirs, joining one might not be a funky move, but the tradition still holds firm.

Classical music enjoys a high profile in Wales. Cardiff hosts the acclaimed *Singer of the World* competition, attended by the great and the good among classical vocalists, on an annual basis. **Welsh National Opera** (WNO) is recognized as one of the UK's finest companies, and was the first ever regional company to appear at Covent Garden. The performing arts are devotedly nurtured at the Welsh College of Music and Drama and within the BBC's National Orchestra of Wales.

The **Manic Street Preachers** paved the way for Wales to become a feature on the rock'n'roll map. Catatonia's **Cerys Matthews**, raunchy and vivid, coined the immortal words 'Everyday I wake up, and thank the lord I'm Welsh.' For a brief and wonderful moment, the South Wales city Newport was hailed as the new Seattle. For those jaded with the 'We'll Keep A Welcome in the Hillsides' image of Wales, this feisty new face represented a freedom from the shackles of tradition. For the first time ever it was cool to be Welsh. The term 'Cool Cymru' or 'Cool Wales' entered the lexicon.

Rhondda, the most famous of all the South Wales mining valleys, struck out into new waters with a musical venture called *The Pop Factory*. This sleek venue and television complex has worked hard to attract big names, with notable success. Names like like Travis, Sophie Ellis-Bextor, Lost Prophets and Victoria Beckham have all graced its stage, while bands like Blue and Mis-Teeq had their first outing here.

Despite the success of Welsh bands, some would say that the contemporary music scene has stalled. At least, in terms of bands big enough to hit the headlines and stay there. However, all is not lost. The Welsh Music Foundation has been set up to nurture modern Welsh music, and maximize its cultural and economic potential. Sadly, to date, the mother country has benefited very little in monetary terms from the success of its high-flying sons and daughters. In future that should change, and Wales can reap financial and emotional rewards from her aeons-long love affair with music.

Welsh language

Welsh origins

Welsh is an Indo-European language presumably descended like many languages in modern Western Europe from languages that were originally spoken on the steppes of Central Asia. It is immediately descended from the Brythonic language, its closest relatives are other Celtic languages – Cornish and Breton. To the present day there remain differences in dialects throughout Wales, the most notable being: Y Wyndodeg (northwest), Y Buwyseg (northeast and mid Wales), Y Ddyfydeg (southwest), Gwenhwyseg (southeast).

During the dark ages, Wales was ruled by a number of different Welsh dynastic principalities who from time to time made alliances with each other and English rulers. It was during this time that the Brythonic language was consolidated and became widespread throughout Wales. It was influenced to a degree by the Roman occupation, and even today, the Welsh language shows Latin influences with words like *pont* (bridge), *ffenestre* (window), *caws* (cheese) and *cwmwl* (cloud).

In the 15th century, Wales was absorbed into the English state under Henry VIII. This was the first reference to the Welsh language. The passing of the 1536 and 1542 Acts of Union brought significant change as it stated that English should be the only language in courts. Use of the Welsh language, in an official capacity, was not lawful again until the passing of the Welsh Courts Act in 1942.

On the request of Elizabeth I, the Bible was translated by William Morgan in 1588, establishing a nationwide standard for the language. Welsh was permitted as the language of religion and church, helping to safeguard it. Had this not been the case the language could have disappeared completely at this stage.

Wales', written by three English commissioners, emphasized the superiority of the English language. The 'Welsh not' or 'Welsh stick' was introduced in some schools – a form of punishment handed out to pupils found speaking Welsh, which could result in a beating. This practice became a symbol of oppression of the language.

The establishment of 'Yr Eisteddfod Genedlaethol' in the 19th century and the importance of the Welsh chapel, frequently the centre of Welsh life, were important in keeping the grass-roots language alive. By 1911, nearly a million people regarded themselves as Welsh speakers. However, social change such as urbanization, industrialization and the secularization of society, led to English becoming the main language (50%) in some areas.

National Eisteddfod

The National Eisteddfod, an annual cultural festival and competition to celebrate Welsh culture, is now a vital part of the Welsh calendar. In 1938, a petition was launched at the Eisteddfod calling for a repeal of the Act of Union, demanding that Welsh be given equal status with English. The petition, signed by more than a quarter of a million people and supported by a number of Welsh MPs, led to the Welsh Courts Act of 1942. The Welsh language became legally acceptable in schools, for academic studies and the media; however, the language clause of the Act of Union remained, which held sway in the courts of law.

Welsh National Party

Plaid Genedlaethol Cymru (The Welsh National Party) was formed in Pwllheli in 1925 by a small group of intellectuals and their leader, Saunders Lewis, focused the party efforts on the defence of the Welsh language. Cymdeithas yr Iaith was established in 1962 as one of the first single issue pressure groups. Using a non-violent means of civil disobedience, it led a campaign towards the Welsh Language Act 1967, which made the existence of Welsh language a more accepted part of life in the principality. It is predominately due to Cymdeithas yr Iaith that you will see bilingual road signs, as this was brought about in the 1960s when they launched a large-scale campaign against monolingual road signs.

The activities of Cymdeithas yr Iaith coincided with the granting to Wales of a significant degree of administrative autonomy by the appointment of a Minister of State for Wales in 1964 and the establishment of the Welsh Office.

Education and media

In 1988 the Education Reform Act ensured that all children aged between 5-16 would be taught Welsh as a core subject in Welsh medium schools. The growth in Welsh-medium education in places such as Cardiff produced considerable numbers of Welsh speakers and helped vary the social base of the language. The growth of Welsh in Anglicized districts was particularly evident in the results of the 1991 census.

Sianel Pedwar Cymru (S4C– Welsh Channel Four) was first broadcast in November 1982. This channel produces Welsh language programmes with English subtitles and a number of S4C's programmes are viewed across Europe. In the early 1980s when other sectors of the Welsh economy were in decline, there was significant rise in employment in Welsh language television. Welsh, in all aspects of life, has been given a higher status, particularly since the launch of the 1993 Welsh Language Act.

Devolution

In 1997 the devolution referendum was seen as an opportunity for greater autonomy for Wales and was supported as a means to reassert the 'Welsh' identity. The economic benefits of the Welsh language are being recognized, leading to the ability to communicate in Welsh and English in the workplace being recognized as a valuable skill and marketable commodity. The 2001 census identified the first increase in number and percentage of Welsh speakers in 20 counties, with the southeast showing the greatest rise. The language is evolving and gradually English phrases are being absorbed into the Welsh language.

Despite the turbulent times the language has experienced, its increased usage in all sectors of Welsh society has ensured a place in the hearts of the growing proportion of the population who chose to learn or pass on knowledge of the language. Welsh, one of the oldest European languages, is now spoken by almost a quarter of the population of Wales and a visitor is sure to see unusual phrases and hear unfamiliar sounds, but this is part of Wales' charm. Try and get your tongue around some basic 'Welsh' and you'll receive a warm welcome wherever you go.

Books

Fiction

Brito, Leonora, *Dat's Love* (1995), Seren Books. Story of the ethnic community in Cardiff Bay.

Cordell, Alexander, *Rape of the Fair Country* (2000), *Song of the Earth* (1999), *Hosts of Rebecca* (1998), Blorenge. This popular trilogy is set in the area around the Blaenavon ironworks during the time leading up to the Rebecca Riots.

Evans, Richard John, *Entertainment (2000)*, *Seren. Lively account of living in the Rhonnda Valley.*

Gower, Iris, *Copper Kingdom* (1984), *Black Gold* (1989), Arrow. Two of a number of books written by one of Wales' best-known romantic novelists.

Griffiths, Niall, *Sheepshagger* (2002), *Grits* (2001), *Kelly & Victor* (2002), *Stump* (2004), Vintage. A sort of Welsh Irvine Welsh, dealing with drugs and the seamy side of life in Wales.

Hawes, James, *White Powder, Green Light* (2003), Jonathan Cape. A sly look at the media industry in Wales.

Jones, Dave and **Rivers, Tony**, *The Soul Crew* (2002), Milo Books. Looking at the sub-culture of football hooligans who follow Cardiff FC.

Llewellyn, Richard, *How Green Was My Valley*. (2001), Penguin. Probably the best known of all books about life in the Valleys.

Pryce, Malcolm, *Aberystwyth Mon Amour*. (2002), Bloomsbury. Black comedy set in contemporary Aberystwyth. Also *Last Tango in Aberystwyth* (2004) **and** *The Unbearable Lightness of Being in Aberystwyth* (2005).

Travel writing

Abley, Mark, *Spoken Here* (2004), Heinemann. Account of the author's travels in countries that have threatened languages – or ones that are fighting back. Includes a chapter on Wales.

Borrow, George, *Wild Wales* (1955), Gomer Press. Classic account of a 19th-century walking tour of Wales by pompous, Welsh-speaking Englishman.

Morris, Jan, *Wales* (2000), Penguin. Rich and informative insight into the country written by Anglo-Welsh travel writer.

Morton, HV, *In Search of Wales* (1986), Methuen. Written when the scholarly author travelled Wales in the 1930s.

Rogers, Byron, *The Bank Manager and the Holy Grail* (Aurum 2003). Travels into the eccentric side of Wales.

Sager, Peter, *Wales* (2002), Pallas. Extremely readable account of the country, its history and its culture.

Poetry

Lycett, Andrew, *Dylan Thomas a New Life* (2004), Weidenfeld and Nicolson. A recent biography of the poet.

Manley Hopkins, Gerard, *Collected Works*, Penguin. The Jesuit poet was much influenced by the landscape of Wales.

Sheers, Owen, *The Blue Book* (Seren 2000). Poetry from Wales' hottest new poet

Thomas, Dylan, *The Dylan Thomas Omnibus* (1999), Phoenix. An accessible collection of the poet's works.

Thomas, RS, *Selected Poems* (2000), Phoenix. Poetry of the fiery, nationalist priest.

Webb, Harri, *Collected Poems* (1995), Gomer Press. More contemporary poetry.

239

Footnotes

Glossary

A
Afon – river
Amgueddfa – museum
Ap (ab) – son of
Ar Agor – open
Ar Gau – closed

B
Bach – small
Bara – bread
Blaen – head of valley
Brenhines – queen
Brenin – king
Bryn – hill
Bwlch – pass
Brecwast – breakfast
Bws – bus

C
Cadair – chair, stronghold
Capel – chapel
Carn – rock, mountain
Carreg – rock, stone
Castell – castle
Cefn – ridge
Clun - meadow
Coch – red
Croeso – welcome
Cwm – valley (or combe)
Cymraeg – Welsh
Cymru – Wales
Cymry – the Welsh people

D
Da – good
Ddu / Du – black
De – south
Dinas – town, fort
Dŵr – water
Dwyrain – east
Dydd – day

E
Eglwys – church

F
Fawr – big
Fferm – farm
Ffordd – road, way
Fforest – forest
Ffynnon – well

G
Glan – river bank
Gardd – garden
Glas – blue
Glyn – vallley, glen
Gogledd – north
Gorllewin –west
Gorsaf – station
Gwely – bed
Gwesty – hotel
Gwyn – white
Gwyrdd – green

H
Hafod – summer dwelling
  for herdsmen
Heddiw – today
Hen – old
Heol – road
Hiraeth – yearning

I
Isaf – lower

L
Llechen – slate
Llety – lodging
Llwybr – path
Llys – court

M
Maen – rock, stone
Maes – field
Mawr – big, great
Melin – mill
Melyn – yellow
Merthyr – martyr
Môr – sea
Morfa – marsh
Mynydd – mountain

N
Nant – stream
Neuadd – hall
Newydd – new
Nos – night

O
Ogof – cave

P
Pant – dip
Parc – park
Pen – head of
Pentre/pentref – village
Plas – hall (large house)
Pont (bont) – bridge
Porth – port or doorway

R
Rhaeadr – waterfall
Rhiw – hill

S
Saesneg – English
  (language)
Sarn – causeway
Sant – saint
Siop – shop
Stryd – street
Swyddfa'r Post – post office

T
Tafarn – pub
Theatr - theatre
Traeth – beach
Tre, tref – town
Twr – tower
Tŷ – house

U
Uchaf – highest

Y
Y, Yr, 'r – the
Yn – in
Ysbyty – hospital
Ysgol – school

Useful words and phrases

Alphabet (Yr Wyddor)
a, b, c, ch, d, dd, e, f, ff, g, ng, h, i, i, l, ll, m, n, o, p, ph, r, rh, s, t, th, u, w, y

Vowels (llafariad)
a, e, i, o, u, w, y

A aah	B bee	C eck	CH ech
D dee	DD edd	E air	F ev
FF eff	G egg	NG eng	H high-tsh
I ee	J jay	L el	LL ell
M em	N en	O oh	P pee
PH phee	R air	RH air-hee	S ess
T tee	TH eth	U ee	W oo
Y uh			

Welsh place names	Meaning	Pronunciation
Abertawe (Swansea)	Estuary	Ab-er-taw-eh
Beddgelert	Grave	Be-the-gel-airt
Betws-y-**Coed**	Wood	Bet-oos uh koyd
Caerdydd (Cardiff)	Fort	K-ie-r-dee-the
Cas**newydd**(Newport)	New	Kas ne with
Dinbych-y-**Pysgod** (Denbigh)	Fish	Din-bich uh pusg-od
Glan **Llyn**	Lake	Glan ll-in
Llandeilo	Church	ll-an-day-lo
Sir Benfro (Pembrokeshire)	County	Seer Ben Vr-aw
Y **Dre**newydd (Newtown)	Town	Uh Drair ne with
Ynys Mon (Anglesey)	Island	Un- is Morn

Llanfairpwllgwyngyllgogerychwyrndrobwllllantysiliogogogoch

Roughly translated as:
The Church of St. Mary by the pool with the white hazel near the rapid whirlpool by St Tysilio's church and the red cave.

Have a go at pronouncing it:
Thlann vyre pooth gwin gith gogger ich chweern drobbooth lann tuss-illyo goggo gauch.

Other useful phrases:

Bore Da	good morning	*Prynhawn da*	good afternoon
Nos da	good night	*Hwyl fawr*	good bye
Diolch	thank you	*Dim diolch*	no thank you
Os gwelwch chi'n dda	please	*Faint?*	how much?
Gwely a brecwast	bed and breakfast	*Lwc dda*	Good luck
Paned o de	cup of tea	*Paned o goffi*	cup of coffee

Index

Map index

Complete title listing

Footprint publishes travel guides to over 150 destinations worldwide. Each guide is packed with practical, concise and colourful information for everybody from first-time travellers to travel aficionados. The list is growing fast and current titles are noted below.
Available from all good bookshops and online at www.footprintbooks.com

(P) denotes pocket guide

Latin America and Caribbean
Argentina
Barbados (P)
Belize, Guatemala &
   Southern Mexico
Bolivia
Brazil
Caribbean Islands
Central America & Mexico
Chile
Colombia
Costa Rica
Cuba
Cusco & the Inca Trail
Dominican Republic
Ecuador & Galápagos
Guatemala
Havana (P)
Mexico
Nicaragua
Patagonia
Peru
Peru, Bolivia & Ecuador
Rio de Janeiro
Rio de Janeiro (P)
South American Handbook
St Lucia (P)
Venezuela

North America
Vancouver (P)
New York (P)
Western Canada

Africa
Cape Town (P)
East Africa
Egypt
Libya
Marrakech (P)
Morocco
Namibia
South Africa
Tunisia
Uganda

Middle East
Dubai (P)
Israel
Jordan
Syria & Lebanon

Footnotes Complete title listing

Credits

Footprint credits
Text editor: Nicola Jones
Map editor: Sarah Sorensen
Picture editor: Robert Lunn
Proofreader: Davina Rungasamy

Publisher: Patrick Dawson
Editorial: Sophie Blacksell, Alan Murphy, Sarah Thorowgood, Claire Boobbyer, Felicity Laughton, Laura Dixon, Angus Dawson,
Cartography: Robert Lunn, Claire Benison, Kevin Feeney, Esther Monzón García, Thom Wickes
Series development: Rachel Fielding
Design: Mytton Williams and Rosemary Dawson (brand)
Advertising: Debbie Wylde
Finance and administration: Sharon Hughes, Elizabeth Taylor

Photography credits
Front cover: Wales on View – Bala Lake, Snowdonia National Park
Back cover: Wales on View – 'People like us' sculpture, Cardiff Bay
Inside colour section: Wales on View

Print
Manufactured in Italy by LegoPrint
Pulp from sustainable forests

Footprint feedback
We try as hard as we can to make each Footprint guide as up to date as possible but, of course, things always change. If you want to let us know about your experiences – good, bad or ugly – then don't delay, go to www.footprintbooks.com and send in your comments.

OS Ordnance Survey® This product includes mapping data licensed from Ordnance Survey® with the permission of the Controller of Her Majesty's Stationery Office. © Crown Copyright. All rights reserved. Licence No. 100027877.

Publishing information
Footprint Wales
1st edition
© Footprint Handbooks Ltd
May 2005

ISBN 1 904 777 37 6
CIP DATA: A catalogue record for this book is available from the British Library

® Footprint Handbooks and the Footprint mark are a registered trademark of Footprint Handbooks Ltd

Published by Footprint
6 Riverside Court
Lower Bristol Road
Bath BA2 3DZ, UK
T +44 (0)1225 469141
F +44 (0)1225 469461
discover@footprintbooks.com
www.footprintbooks.com

Distributed in the USA by
Publishers Group West

Every effort has been made to ensure that the facts in this guidebook are accurate. However, travellers should still obtain advice from consulates, airlines etc about travel and visa requirements before travelling. The authors and publishers cannot accept responsibility for any loss, injury or inconvenience however caused.

Map 1

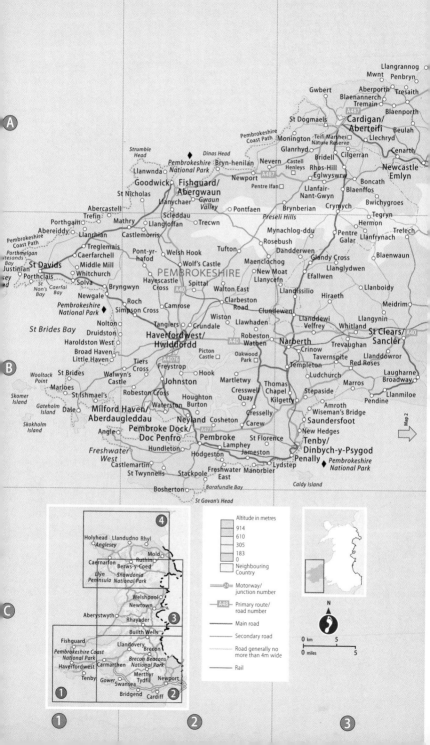

Map 4

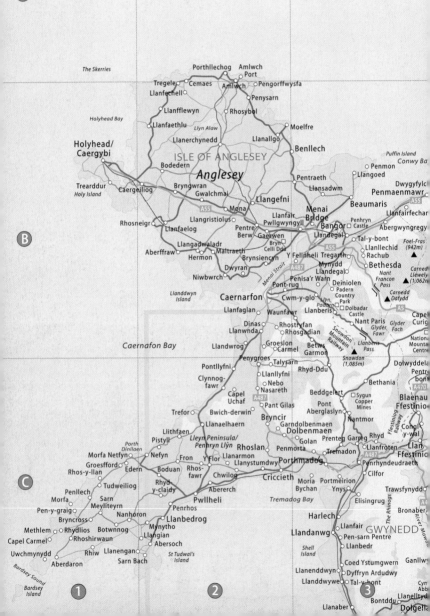

The Skerries

Porthllechog
Amlwch
Port
Tregele
Cemaes
Amlwch
Pengorffwysfa
Llanfechell
Penysarn
Llanfflewyn
Rhosybol
Llanfaethlu
Moelfre
Holyhead Bay
Llanerchynedd
Llyn Alaw
Llanallgo
Benllech
Holyhead/
Caergybi
ISLE OF ANGLESEY
Bodedern
Penmon
Puffin Island
Conwy Ba
Anglesey
Llangoed
Dwygyfylc
Penmaenmawr
Trearddur
Caergeiliog
Bryngwran
Pentraeth
Llansadwrn
Beaumaris
A55
Holy Island
Gwalchmai
Llangefni
Menai
Llanfairfechar
Rhosneigr
A55
Mona
Bridge
Penrhyn
Abergwyngregy
Llanfaelog
Llangristiolus
Llanfair
Pwllgwyngyll
Bangor
Castle
Tal-y-bont
Foel-Fras
Pentre
Gaerwen
Llandegai
(942m)
Aberffraw
Berw
Bryn
Llanllechid
Hermon
Maltraeth
Y Felinheli
Tregarth
Rachub
Carned
Brynsiencyn
Celli Ddu
Bethesda
Llewely
Dwyran
Mynydd
(1,062n
Niwbwrch
Menai Strait
Llandegai
Nant
Penisa'r Waun
Francon
Carnedd
Llanddwyn
Pont-rug
Deiniolen
Pass
Dafydd
Island
Caernarfon
Padarn
Cwm-y-glo
Country
Llanfaglan
Waunfawr
Llanberis
Park
Dolbadar
Cape
Llyn
Curi
Dinas
Rhostryfan
Padarn
Castle
Nant Paris
Glyder
Rhosgadian
Llanwnda
Snowdon
Fawr
Natio
Groeslon
Mounta
Llandwrog
Betws
Mountain
Llanberis
Centre
Carmel
Garmon
Railway
Pass
Penygroes
Talysarn
Snowdon
Caernafon Bay
Pontllyfni
Rhyd-Ddu
(1,085m)
Dolwyddela
Llanllyfni
Clynnog-
Nebo
Bethania
Pentr
fawr
Nasareth
bon
A470
Capel
Pant Gilas
Beddgelert
Uchaf
Sygun
Blaenau
Trefor
Bwlch-derwin
Copper
Ffestinio
Bryncir
Pont
Mines
Llithfaen
Llanaelhaern
Garndolbenmaen
Aberglaslyn
Nantmor
Congl-
Pistyll
Lleyn Peninsula/
Dolbenmaen
y-wal
Morfa Netfyn
Penrhyn Llŷn
Golan
Prenten Garreg Rhyd
Llan
Ffestinio
Nefyn
Rhoslan
Penmorta
Ffestiniog
Groesfford
Boduan
Fron
Tremadon
Railway
Rhos-y-llan
Edern
Y Ffor
Llanarmon
Llanfroten
Penrhyndeudraeth
Rhos-
Llanystumdwy
Porthmadog
A487
Tudweiliog
Rhyd
fawr
Chwilog
Cilfor
Penllech
y-claidy
Criccieth
Moria
Portmeirion
Sarn
Abererch
Bychan
Ynys
Trawsfynydd
Morfa
Meyllteyrn
Pwllheli
Tremadog Bay
The Rhinogs
Pen-y-graig
Penrhos
Elisingrug
Bryncross
Nanhoron
Bronaber
Rhydlios
Botwnnog
Llanbedrog
River Mawr
Methlem
Mynytho
Harlech
GWYNEDD
Capel Carmel
Rhoshirwaun
Llangian
Llanfair
Uwchmynydd
Rhiw
Llanengan
Abersoch
Llandanwg
Pen-sarn Pentre
Aberdaron
Sarn Bach
St Tudwal's
Shell
Llanbedr
Island
Island
Bardsey Sound
Coed Ystumgwern
Ganllw
Bardsey
Llanenddwyn
Dyffryn Ardudwy
A4
Island
Llanddwywe
Tal-y-bont
Abb
Cyn
Bontddu
Llanelltyd
Llanaber
Dolgell

A
B
C

1
2
3

Map symbols

Administration

- ☐ Capital city
- ○ Other city/town
- International border
- Regional border
- Disputed border

Roads and travel

- Motorway
- Main road (National highway)
- Minor road
- Track
- Footpath
- Railway with station
- ✈ Airport
- Bus station
- Ⓜ Metro station
- Cable car
- Funicular
- Ferry

Water features

- River, canal
- Lake, ocean
- Seasonal marshland
- Beach, sandbank
- Waterfall

Topographical features

- Contours (approx)
- Mountain
- Volcano
- Mountain pass
- Escarpment
- Gorge
- Glacier
- Salt flat
- Rocks

Cities and towns

- Main through route
- Main street

- Minor street
- Pedestrianized street
- Tunnel
- One way-street
- Steps
- Bridge
- Fortified wall
- Park, garden, stadium
- Sleeping
- Eating
- Bars & clubs
- Building
- Sight
- Cathedral, church
- Chinese temple
- Hindu temple
- Meru
- Mosque
- Stupa
- Synagogue
- Tourist office
- Museum
- Post office
- Police
- Bank
- Internet
- Telephone
- Market
- Hospital
- Parking
- Petrol
- Golf
- Detail map
- Related map

Other symbols

- Archaeological site
- National park, wildlife reserve
- Viewing point
- Campsite
- Refuge, lodge
- Castle
- Diving
- Deciduous/coniferous/palm trees
- Hide
- Vineyard
- Distillery
- Shipwreck
- Historic battlefield